For the students—past, present,
and future—in my Canadian Drama classes
at the University of Guelph.

Contents

Introduction

The recent publication of three anthologies of Canadian drama—Richard Plant's *The Penguin Book of Modern Canadian Drama* (Penguin, 1984), Richard Perkyns' *Major Plays of the Canadian Theatre 1934-1984* (Irwin, 1984), and Jerry Wasserman's *Modern Canadian Plays* (Talonbooks, 1985)—makes easily accessible to students, teachers, theatre professionals, and the general public thirty-one significant modern Canadian plays. An increase in awareness of, and familiarity with, Canadian drama—in Canada and abroad—might reasonably be expected from the appearance of these anthologies. They are by no means the first anthologies of Canadian plays, but they are likely to have a much wider circulation and impact than their predecessors.

Greater prominence for Canadian plays is to be applauded. As individuals, and as members of a political, geographical, and cultural entity known as Canada, we stand to benefit from the insights and challenges created by our playwrights. That case, I assume, does not need to be argued here. But there is, I think, still a case to be argued that we can best benefit from the creativity of playwrights if we, as readers and audiences, respond with our own creativity, our own *critical* creativity. As passive recipients of what our playwrights give us, we learn little of ourselves, our society, or, indeed, of the plays we see or read. And at the same time we become irrelevant to the artistic development of the playwrights. It is crucial that we respond to plays—as we respond to all else that truly matters in our lives—with a genuine effort to understand, appreciate, and *judge*: to distinguish between the trite and the profound, the fuzzy and the precise, the derivative and the original. That way lies a better drama, a better theatre, and, who knows, a better society.

The art of criticism is at once individual and collaborative. It is individual

7

because, in the end, critical judgement is very much a personal matter. Criticism by consensus necessarily involves compromise, and criticism is too important to be subject to compromise. But criticism is also collaborative in that it nearly always depends on, or is influenced by, what other critics have said and argued. The opinions of other critics can persuade, provoke, clarify. Ultimately, the opinions may be rejected, but any critic's judgement is likely to be enriched by a consideration of the judgement of others.

In an attempt to encourage and facilitate the process of criticism of Canadian drama, I have brought together, in a kind of enforced collaboration, the views of a number of critics on the plays collected in the Plant, Perkyns, and Wasserman anthologies, thereby providing a body of criticism against which readers and audiences can test their own judgements. I have also included criticism on four plays *not* published in the anthologies: James Reaney's *Sticks and Stones*, John Murrell's *Waiting for the Parade*, David French's *Leaving Home*, and Theatre Passe Muraille's *The Farm Show*. Since Parts II and III of Reaney's Donnelly trilogy are in the anthologies, it makes sense, it seems to me, to add criticism of Part I to this collection. The case for bringing in the frequently-performed *Waiting for the Parade* is that Murrell—surely one of Canada's finest playwrights—is otherwise totally neglected, none of Murrell's plays (strangely) having been selected for the anthologies. There may well be a case for adding David French's *Salt-Water Moon* as well as his *Leaving Home* (thereby covering the full "Mercer" trilogy), but I have settled for the older play as a complement to *Of the Fields, Lately*. And the excitement generated by *The Farm Show* in 1972 earns it a place in any critical review of modern Canada drama. Arguments could, of course, be offered for the importance of other plays, but the total of thirty-five constitutes, I think, a reasonably varied and comprehensive survey. Gratien Gélinas is, for the time being, the only francophone Canadian playwright represented in either the anthologies or this volume, though theatregoers familiar with Canadian drama will know of the many achievements of Michel Tremblay and other Quebec playwrights.

The criticism of the plays comes in various shapes and sizes, usually in one of the following categories: the playwright's own thoughts on the play in question; newspaper and periodical reviews of première productions and revivals; reviews of published texts; and scholarly critical analysis. Where appropriate, reviews of British and American productions are included. None of the categories has a monopoly on critical incisiveness or critical banality (much-maligned newspaper critics need not feel ill-at-ease in the company of leisurely scholars). Each kind of critic approaches a play from a different perspective; together they create the incentive for us to make our own informed judgements. The incentive becomes particularly compelling when starkly contrasting opinions confront us: is George Walker's *Zastrozzi* "a work of genuine imagination," as William Lane would have it? Or is it merely a "repackaging of other writers' thoughts," as

Frank Rich argues? Can it be both? What difference does it make—if any—that William Lane directed the original production of the play, and that Frank Rich is an American? Resolving—or at least trying to come to terms with—such real conflicts and potential red herrings is a major challenge in assessing the work of playwrights *and* critics.

I offer no comments here on the quality of criticism in this collection, though I think the opportunity to trace the development of modern Canadian theatre criticism is assisted by the gathering of these reviews and commentaries. It is, for example, instructive to identify and weigh the criteria by which plays have been judged successes or failures by our critics. As one might expect, the script is of major importance for most scholars, but newspaper critics too tend to make the script preeminent. Sheer theatricality—such as the ''circus'' scenes in *Creeps*—sometimes gets short shrift, even when (as is the case in *Creeps)* it deepens the thematic insights of the play. Witness Nathan Cohen's view that the circus scenes ''detract'' from the quality of *Creeps*. (But then it was Cohen who pronounced of the première of *The Ecstasy of Rita Joe* that ''Ryga has written a non-play, and director George Bloomfield has given it a non-production''.) On the other hand, many critics were appreciative of the theatrical inventiveness of the actors in Reaney's Donnelly trilogy, and of Eric Peterson's panache and dexterity in *Billy Bishop Goes to War*. Do critics have *moral* concerns? Or, put another way, do they believe that drama still has a moral function and responsibility? Are critics sensitive to the contribution of designers to production quality? Are foreign critics capable of making *any* sense of Canadian plays (''Miss Pollock is a prize-winning playwright in her native Canada—a fact that may say more about Canadian theatre than the quality of her work,'' was a *New York Times* reaction to *Blood Relations*)? Are critics really as inept as the nincompoop who reviews *The Care and Treatment of Roses* in *Jitters*? A start, at least, can be made on answers to some of these not insignificant questions from material in this book.

The differences in the quantity of criticism provided for each play (plenty for, say, *Creeps*, little for *Drum Song*) are a reflection both of the age of the play and the critical attention it has generated, rather than any editorial priorities on my part. I have attempted to provide a range of critical viewpoints for each play, though the selection has been hampered to some degree by the availability of reviews and essays and, in a few instances, by copyright restrictions. The plays are presented here in order of first production, and the critical commentaries for each play appear chronologically by date of publication.

An earlier edition of this collection was published in the journal *Canadian Drama/L'Art dramatique canadien*, volume 11 (1985). I am most grateful to the journal's editor, Dr. Eugene Benson, for his encouragement and scholarly conviviality on that and many other occasions. In bringing together these critical perspectives, I have also benefited from, and gratefully acknowledge, the help of Denise Dickin, Paula Dancy, Richard Plant, Heather McCallum, Marlene Neal,

Sharon Ballantyne, Susan Morrison, Linda McKenzie-Cordick, Patricia Koenig, Harry Lane, Nancy Sadek, David Warrick, Murray Oliver, Jorgen Peterson, and Elaine Baetz.

Acknowledgements

Permission from the following copyright holders to reprint material is gratefully acknowledged.

Geraldine Anthony; Brian Arnott; Diane Bessai; R.W. Bevis; *Books in Canada*; the *Calgary Herald*; *Canadian Forum*; Neil Carson; the *Citizen* (Ottawa); Michael Cook; Mark Czarnecki; the *Daily Gleaner* (Fredericton); ECW Press; John Elsom; the *Evening Telegram* (St. John's); Marian Fraser; David French; Mira Friedlander; Myron Galloway; the *Gazette* (Montreal); Reid Gilbert; the *Globe and Mail* (Toronto); the *Halifax Herald*; Hounslow Press; Christopher Innes; Christopher Johnson; Urjo Kareda; Martin Knelman; Rota Herzberg Lister; Denyse Lynde; *Maclean's*; Ann Messenger; Patricia Morley; Edward Mullaly; the *New Statesman*; the *NeWest Review*; the *New York Times* Company (© 1967/73/79/80/82/83); James Noonan; Robert C. Nunn; Malcolm Page; John Palmer; Brian Parker; Playwrights Union of Canada; the *Province* (Vancouver); James Reaney; Lawrence Russell; Signal-Star Publishing Ltd.; Simon & Pierre Publishing Co. Ltd.; Mary Elizabeth Smith; Southam News; Susan Stone-Blackburn; the *Sun* (Toronto); the *Sun* (Vancouver); *Time* (©Time Inc., 1973); the *Times Colonist* (Victoria); Times Newspapers Ltd. (©Times Newspapers Ltd., 1975/1981; all rights reserved; reprinted by permission of *The Times*, London, 23.9.75/3.4.81); the *Toronto Star* Syndicate; University of British Columbia Press; University of Toronto Press; Renate Usmiani; Robert Wallace; *Winnipeg Free Press*; Elsie Wood; Max Wyman; Cynthia Zimmerman.

While every effort has been made to identify and contact copyright holders, some errors and omissions may have occurred. Any such oversights are regretted, and the publisher and editor would appreciate having them brought to their attention.

Abbreviations

*	Review of first production
UTQ	*University of Toronto Quarterly*
CD	*Canadian Drama/L'Art dramatique canadien*
NYT	*New York Times*
The Work	*The Work: Conversations with English-Canadian Playwrights*, edited by Robert Wallace and Cynthia Zimmerman (Toronto, 1982)
THC	*Theatre History in Canada/Histoire du théatre au Canada*
CHR	*Canadian Historical Review*
ECW	*Essays on Canadian Writing*
Stage Voices	*Stage Voices: Twelve Canadian Playwrights Talk about their Lives and Work*, edited by Geraldine Anthony (Toronto, 1978)
CTR	*Canadian Theatre Review*

HERMAN VOADEN

Hill-Land

First produced at the Central High School of Commerce, Toronto,
13 December 1934

Directed by Herman Voaden
Lighting Design by William Addison
Stage Design by Duncan MacGregor
Costume Design by Jeanne Lucow

Cast

Nora	Maud Etherington
Jean	Amy Stewart
Rachel	Muriel Death
Paul	Gordon Keeble
The Doctor	Duncan MacGregor
The Commentator	Jameson Field
The Fatalist	Reid McAllister
The Lyric Voice	Thelma Scott
The Voice of Pity	Esther Creighton
The Narrator	Duncan Gillard
The Voice of Hope	Arthur Wilson
The Voice of Ecstasy	Joseph Galbraith
The High Chorus	Margo Allen, Thelma Scott, Esther Creighton
The Low Chorus	Irving Hoffman, Victor Jarvis
The Death Figure	John Cole

"That man is unhappy, indeed, who in all his life has had no glimpse of perfection, who in the ecstasy of love, or in the delight of contemplation, has never been able to say: It is attained. Such moments of inspiration are the source of the arts, which have no higher function than to renew them."—Santayana.

The symphonic theatre should seek to recreate these moments in which perfection is glimpsed—these moments of intuitive illumination. This it can do by intense, slow and lovely picturization—by translating ordinary stage movements into those of ritual and rhythm, by introducing music, dance and choral comment to sustain and lift the moment of complete significance.

The stuff of poetry can be the stuff of the new theatre. Ecstasy is vital in the visual arts, in music and dance. The peculiar power of the symphonic theatre will lie in the capacity for elevated thought and feeling which the introduction of these new orchestral elements will make possible. Poetry will live on the stage because it is enriched with the ecstasy that is acceptable in the other arts.

Such a theatrical language will be capable of supremely exalted statement. It will have music's power of lifting into sudden glory; the lyrical sweep—"The Apollonian glow"—of poetry; and the novel's capacity for reflective comment and varied interpretation. With these it will combine the color and design of painting, the form and mass of sculpture and architecture, the movement and loveliness of dance. It will retain the power of the spoken word and the appeal of great acting, but it will open wide the doors of beauty and imagination.

In *Hill-Land* the author-producer attempts to bring into being this ampler and freer theatre of lyrical intensity, of spiritual release, of uplifting vision: to substitute flashing revelation for prose statement, and to set beside the older theatre of plot alone, this newer theatre of all the arts.

The play and the production represent only the first step in a difficult progress. The method is not an easy one to perfect. But if at times a new theatrical language is heard, however imperfectly, the production will not have been made in vain.

Hill-Land program note, 13 December 1934

• •

The arts approach the central arena which is the theatre. Fusing them we are able as never before to bring to the stage those moments of subtle rapture, of lyrical emotion, of power and triumph—the expression of which constitutes the highest function of the artist.

Hill-Land is in large measure an attempt to make such moments live in the theatre by employing the combined arts in an orchestral stage speech.

Hill-Land bears the impress of the Canadian scene and character. In it there is the excitement and enthusiasm of an author who is discovering a new land—who feels the nation's pulse beating into a more magnificent rhythm—who is thrilled with "the immensity of wide margins"—and who sees in the North the heart of a nobler spirit and a greater land.

The North stirs something in each of us, something of the ideal. This should appear in our music and in our theatre to the same degree that it has shown itself in our painting. It should be the central driving power in our Canadianism. We need a passionate faith in our own future; we need a mystical pride, the profound conviction of our mission and destiny as a people.

This passionate dedication will inspire us in the creation of an art which should be universal because it is the expression of our deepest impulses and desires. It is this faith which sweeps through *Hill-Land*. It culminates in the final moments of the play when Paul and his mother, looking toward the future, hear all about them the voices crying: "Our land! Our land!"

No one can be alive today without a sense of gathering certitude—without seeing the light which appears through the darkness that surrounds us. The time has surely come when man may awake from his dreams believing they can be true—believing that the world of his vision can be realized in the world about him. This faith should animate our art and our religion. We must believe that the time has come, and our belief must be articulate in the theatre.

In *Hill-Land*, Nora, the pioneer, is the seer and prophet of the new life. She and Paul of the third generation are both conceived heroically. They exemplify the greatness and nobility possible in life that is co-ordinated and in harmony with the earth.

When at last the theatre has perfected its new expression it will concern itself with the lasting problems of the human spirit. Its language will be lofty, soaring to sublime themes and conclusions. Like the greatest symphonies, it will voice man's heroic challenge to the forces of evil and darkness that surround him—his prophetic belief in his ultimate triumph and liberation.

Notes from a publicity release for *Hill-Land*,
13 December 1934

• •

Herman Voaden's latest experiment in symphonic expressionism, a play of the Canadian North called *Hill-Land*, turned out to be a profoundly moving and impressive presentation last night at the Central High School of Commerce. The seemingly tragic story is given higher values of faith and courage so that death is swallowed up in victory, and a mood of exaltation is induced which is rare in the modern theatre.

This highly unusual drama was written for "a theatre of many voices," and the skill with which the author-producer has used drum, piano, off-stage singer and chorus, dancers, symbolic commentators, realistic actors, an allegorical death-figure, varied stage settings, and a continually changing investiture of living light with striking color and shadow patterns, is beyond praise. The balanced blending of all these different elements is a remarkable achievement.

The production is Mr. Voaden's most successful effort in his chosen field, which is also a very fascinating and very important field. He very modestly states in his printed program that this is only "the first step in a difficult progress," and no one claims that the production is flawless. It is, however, immensely worthwhile as a whole, with a series of beautiful climaxes which bring tears to the eyes even while they lift up the heart, and his "message" is an ardent and virile Canadianism which should appeal. The large cast and staff deserve individual commendation, but there is no time. Tonight's performance is something which no lover of the theatre should miss.

Lawrence Mason, *Globe*, 14 December 1934*

• •

It is necessary to distinguish very carefully between Mr. Herman Voaden, director of the Play Workshop currently operating at the Central High School of Commerce and producer of a great many interesting performances in which the compostion and lighting of the stage picture have received more than the usual attention, and Mr. Herman Voaden, playwright, and author of *Hill-Land*, a "play for a New Theatre" produced last week at the Workshop. As a producer Mr. Voaden has long been noted for originality of method and for dexterity and inventiveness in the employment of those lighting devices which are the chief contribution of modern science to theatrical art, and his latest undertaking revealed a startling advance in his ability to get pleasing and significant diction and dignified ritual movement out of his performers; one suspects that he now has at his command an unusually able and faithful band of workers, both on and behind stage.

Mr. Voaden the dramatist is another matter, and our own impression is that it is a bad thing for his plays that he and Mr. Voaden the electrician and stage-picture-maker are both inside the same skin, for it lets the stage-picture-maker boss the dramatist around. In a program foreword describing the objectives of "the symphonic theatre" Mr. Voaden tells us that he seeks to enlarge the channels by which the stage makes its appeal to the senses and the spirit by adding "intense, slow and lovely picturization—by translating ordinary stage movements into those of ritual and rhythm, by introducing music, dance and choral comment to sustain and lift the moment to complete significance," and further explains that he aims at the production of "ecstasy." But he says a little further down that he desires "to substitute flashing revelation for prose statement, and to set beside the older theatre of plot alone, this newer theatre of all the arts."

The first of these questions is admirable, but the second will not do at all. It becomes necessary to tell Mr. Voaden that there never was an important theatre "of plot alone"; even the worst atrocities of Sardou were contrived so as to enable clever actors to add to the bare plot something which lifted it at least a little way out of the particular into the universal, and thus permitted the performance to achieve some measure of ecstasy, and all great drama from Shakespeare to Ibsen—to come no further down—has always been characterized by the complete avoidance of "prose statement" and the persistent search for, and achievement of "flashing revelation," by means of language immensely heightened and sharpened from that of the common day. From the time of "Is this the face that launched a thousand ships?" to the time of "Vine leaves in your hair," all great dramatists have striven, and not in vain, to get as far away from the "prose statements" of, let us say, a police court examination, and as near to the "flashing revelation" of high poetic language as they possibly can, and only those lesser dramatists who, like O'Neill, are deficient in verbal power have found it necessary to cover up that deficiency by resorting to other and less inspiring mechanisms.

The mechanisms which Mr. Voaden the dramatist invokes—at the instigation of Mr. Voaden the stage-picture expert—are much too easy. His four main "human" characters say very little indeed and what they do say is in the commonplace language of domestic conversation and does nothing to heighten the significance of the "plot alone." (This is intentional and we make no complaint about it.) The task of raising a particular episode of human suffering to general and emotion-stirring significance is therefore entrusted to a round dozen of commentators, placed on, in front of and at the side of the stage, and representing Voices of Hope, Pity, Ecstasy, Fatality and the like; small spotlights are turned on each commentator during the utterance of his comment, the color varying with the emotional personality which is speaking; some of the commentators are on the stage and take part in the picture, performing ritual movements and attitudes from time to time, and the rest are below the stage level (and were decidedly difficult to follow in a school theatre with a flat floor). The lines ascribed to these commentators were for the most part pleasingly intoned by their performers; but prose statement could not possibly be more prosaic than those lines, and such bald assertions as "She is immortal" are not made more impressive by playing a red spotlight on the speaker's countenance. The simple fact is that if Mr. Voaden's theory *as developed in this particular aspect of his play* were correct, anybody could take a plot and raise it to an ecstasy-producing drama by the use of enough lamps and electrical wiring. It is much too easy.

Furthermore, while it is undoubtedly possible to raise immensely the significance of a given plot by means of either free dance actions or rigid ritual movement, we must remind Mr. Voaden that the first of these is an art requiring long years of apprenticeship and great natural ability, and that the second is a tradition requiring centuries for development. The pantomime of the ballet is one of the most highly finished arts of our age, and has as its aim precisely that lifting of the significance of a momentary and particular action to eternal and universal validity; but its practitioners know its limits, they know that little can be attained without years of practice, and that the eye alone is a feeble percipient of rhythm without the ear. Mr. Voaden seems to be as little concerned about the appeal to the ear by music as by verbal felicity; his performance owed much to a fairly constant and very well executed piano accompaniment, but the program made no mention of the composer or arranger, and the performer, Dorothy Bainger, was listed last among the "artists," coming after the costume manager and the makers of the steps and immediately before the House Manager.

One of Mr. Voaden's claims for his "newer theatre" is that it "will have the novel's capacity for reflective comment and varied interpretation." Well, the theatre has never totally lacked reflective comment, though it has never indulged in it as the novel does; but what it has had it has usually managed to work into the structure of the action and has not left outside of the proscenium arch. Even the Greek chorus were villagers or court servants or people somehow concerned in the action. What has restricted reflective comment in the theatre is not the absence of electric light but the fact that it is a *performance*, not a narrative, that it must do its work in two hours on several hundred or thousand people, that it must produce its ecstasy *then and there*, and that reflective comment *from outside of the action* is a disturbing element which destroys illusion. These objections seem to us to be extremely permanent.

We must not forget to add, for the credit of Mr. Voaden the producer, that some of the lighting effects on the stage proper and incidental to the action were of great beauty and effectiveness.

B.K. Sandwell, *Saturday Night*, 50
(22 December 1934)*

• •

JOHN COULTER

Riel

First produced by the New Play Society at the Royal Ontario Museum Theatre,
17 February 1950

Directed by Donald Harron
Technical Production by Robert Christie

Cast

Louis Riel	Mavor Moore
Mme. Riel	Margot Christie
Priest	John Howe
Marie	Bea Lennard
François	Lionel Ross
Tom	Cal Whitehead
Rabbie	Sandy Webster
Xavier	Barry Nesbitt
Thomas Scott	Donald Harron
Col. Stoughton Dennis	Vernon Chapman
Scots Settler	Don Gollan
O'Donoghue	Ben Gans
André	Jonathan White
Rev. Mr. Young	Cal Whitehead
Donald Smith	John Pritchard
Sir John A. MacDonald	Robert Christie
Archbishop Taché	Leslie Rubie
Sir Georges Cartier	James Scott
Col. Wolseley	Garth Magwood
Sergeant	Barry Nesbitt
Marguerite	Pegi Brown
Woman	Diana Ewing
North West Mounted Policeman	Peter MacFarlane

Clerk of the Court	Cal Whitehead
Mr. Justice Richardson	Vernon Chapman
Crown Council	Murray Westgate
Defence Council	Herbert Gott
General Middleton	Garth Magwood
Father André	Gus Kristjanson
Dr. Roy	Leslie Rubie
Dr. Jukes	Sandy Webster
Foreman of Jury	John Pritchard
Hon. J.A. Chapleau	Doug Haskins
Hangman	Jonathan White
Sheriff	Barry Nesbitt

The Canadian authors dealt with so far by the New Play Society in its current season have all favored the present, in preference to this country's colorful past, as the source material for their plays. Not so John Coulter whose new drama *Riel* was given its initial performance by the N.P.S. in the Museum theatre last night. With the facts of the career of the rebellious Louis before him, Mr. Coulter has fashioned a long, colorful and often-moving biographical play, covering a decade and a half of the Canadian story.

As premiered in the cramped confines of the Museum stage, the play is episodic in form and adopts the technique of the flowing narrative rather than the standard methods of dramatization. Into two segments, divided by the 15 years that elapsed between the two Riel insurrections, he has packed an enormous quantity of detail, all designed to shed light on the baffling and complex character of the leader of the Northwest rebellions. He has painted Riel as a man who believed he heard divine messages, who felt a driving compulsion to fight for the rights of his people and, in the final passages, the author has revealed him as a political football on whose fate may rest the unity of the infant nation. And while he toys around with the subject at various intervals, he never clearly establishes whether he believes Riel was insane or whether he was simply a childlike man, victimized by his own ambitions.

It is a mammoth task to condense these 15 years of strife on the prairies into three hours of theatre, but Mr. Coulter has done it by allowing his episodes to flow together, with some of them providing merely the bridgework between two longer sequences. At times he has been over-talkative and, particularly in the second act, he has allowed his play to become static. On top of that, he seems to have been in doubt as to where to end it and, as a result, has carried it on anti-climactically. Even with [these] few drawbacks, however, it is still an interesting and challenging piece of writing.

The present production is characterized by a remarkably good performance by Mavor Moore in the title role. Mr. Moore has grasped and accented the conflict of the character and has made Riel alternately a pompous martinet and a bewildered, uncertain man, dominated by a possessive mother and haunted by the death of a sweetheart he could have married and didn't.

All the other people involved, with the possible exception of Margot Christie in the role of the mother, are merely fleeting contributors to the Riel story. Of these, there is Don Harron, who also directed the play, as Thomas Scott, the man whom Riel had executed and whose death promptly brought the Queen's troops marching into the west. Robert Christie, as Sir John A. Macdonald, is a trifle more wily and unctuous than many of us like to regard the Father of Confederation, and Bea Lennard and Pegi Brown, the two Indian maidens in Riel's life—the first his sweetheart, the second his wife—are written right out of the drama before their parts ever come to life. The rest of the cast numbers some 40 players and, with one or two fumbling exceptions, all have added substantially to the complicated mosaic of the drama . . .

Jack Karr, *Toronto Star*, 18 February 1950*

• •

Even for Canadians, who are brought up to think of the history of their own country as dry, drear and dull, Louis Riel looms as a figure of some dramatic possibility. John Coulter, being an Irishman and a poet, saw this without difficulty and set about the task of bringing him to the stage.

The result is the fascinating piece of historical drama bearing Riel's name and being presented this week as the fourth of the premieres in the New Play Society's exciting season at the Museum Theatre.

It was an immense task, not only for Mr. Coulter in the writing, but for the New Play Society in the staging of what he has written. The record of Riel's exciting life, his influences, aims, actions and ultimate fate, take 15 scenes and about 35 characters in the telling, for the play encompasses the rebellions of both 1869 and of 1885.

Wasting no time on "the hero as a boy," Mr. Coulter outlines Riel's mission, and much of his character in the very first scene, mixing in just enough of his background temperament and emotional life to stir up a full-grown Oedipus complex.

Then we are away to the riots. It is hard to believe, perhaps, that these warlike scouts stand against the advance of the landgrabbers without recourse to shooting, but it is made plain that they took the execution of Thomas Scott quite seriously.

Riel's position is made clear, not as an upstart firebrand, but as a God-inspired representative of the northwest settlers, who reasonably enough resented the Hudson Bay Company's action in selling their land back to the Crown. The Crown's action in sending in troops who had no respect for Riel as interim governor also comes in for severe criticism.

The soldiers' maltreatment of an Indian girl is used as the fuse which sets off the 1869 rebellion. I do not know whether Mr. Coulter's native romanticism has supplied this feminine fuse or not, but her introduction serves well theatrically, and gives us another intimate glimpse into Riel's personal life.

The first act lacks something of climax. After the long build to the outburst, it is not enough, we feel, to have Riel grab his rifle and whip off the stage. But that build-up has been an exciting one and Mr. Coulter has found much rich humor in setting his various types of early Canadians on the stage. This history of the 1869 rebellion is never dull.

The second half of the play is more pedantic. It is largely devoted to the trial, for the Second Rebellion is over in one brief scene. Courtroom scenes have provided some of the modern theatre's most exciting material, but Mr. Coulter's is not among them.

The individual witnesses are well characterized, but the issues are not bold and the suspense is not overpowering. And Riel's own defense lacked the passion to carry us over a rather literal execution and a concluding service for the dead.

Where the Coulter drama shines out as worthy of the stage is in the sharply explicit characterizations, the unfailing humor, the economy of historical exposition, the swiftness and color of the action, all of which are most marked in the first half of the play.

The two scenes which give the rebellions' perspective, both set in Ottawa, are wonderful examples of the way to make Canadian history on the stage, clear and interesting.

Mr. Coulter has written his drama very sensibly for a partially Elizabethan, partially expressionistic stage, bare of all but the essentials of furniture, with only the aid of lighting, costumes and grouping to supply atmosphere.

Here the New Play Society have done well by Mr. Coulter. Under Donald Harron's direction—as a director he earns the title—the action moves with spirit, and proper advantage is taken of the sparse opportunities of the Museum stage.

The essestial color of each character is well brought out and, save where the actors' occasional unfamiliarity with the lines confused us, the exigencies of production never clouded the emotion.

In a cast of 35 there were surprisingly many performance worthy of special note.

Mavor Moore's was the heaviest load. His portrait of Riel fused many elements into a believable and interesting whole. The scale of the man, the vision of his task and position were made very clear.

The soliloquies put the actor to a harder test, but he met it admirably. Only the trial scene seemed lacking in culminative emotion, and much of this may be attributed to the writing.

Riel defended himself at great length and Mr. Coulter has perhaps had difficulty in compressing his argument to fit dramatic needs, but he must take heart and remember that another Irishman compressed Saint Joan's interminable trial to an exciting 40 minutes.

After Mr. Moore, a handful of good performances crowd for recognition. Taking some of them, for convenience sake, in order of their appearance, we had a grand formidable strength from Margot Christie as Riel's mother, a clearcut priest by John Howe, the lyric Indian maiden of Bea Lennard, Don Gollan's salty Scotsman and Ben Gans' broody Fenian, Robert Christie's superb and witty Sir John A. Macdonald, the wise Archbishop Taché and, later, a simple French doctor, by Leslie Rubie, Garth Magwood's stiff, symbolic British soldier, and a cheerful sergeant by Barry Nesbitt.

The second half of the play, here again, was less rewarding, but there was a pathetic wife by Pegi Brown, a sympathetic Mountie in Peter MacFarlane. There were Murray Westgate and Herbert Gott as Crown and defense counsel, respectively; Gus Kristjanson and Sandy Webster as important witnesses, and, to match Mr. Christie's delightful Sir John, Doug Haskins, excellent as Chapleau.

We haven't forgotten Mr. Harron's own performance as the fated Scott, but felt that he made this important figure too small a rebel and too weak a man for the importance Mr. Coulter and the Orangemen both confer on him.

Despite that sag toward the end, Mr. Coulter's *Riel* is an achievement, both for himself and the New Play Society, especially impressive to Canadians who have seen their history only through clouds of dust.

Herbert Whittaker, Globe and Mail, 20 February 1950*

• •

In a short talk prepared as an introduction to the radio version of his *Riel*, John Coulter discussed the play's origins. For some years, he explained, he had wanted to write a stage play on the theme of Canada emerging as a nation, on some subject "of the very bone and sinew of Canada." The story of Louis Riel's influence on the development of the Northwest occurred to him as one of the greatest opportunities our history offered for such a play. Until recently Riel's name and career have been clouded by legend and prejudice, but Mr. Coulter saw that as a "sort of John Brown of the North" he could, and should, be revealed as much more than a common criminal, a fanatic rebel, an illiterate half-breed, and whatever else his enemies had called him since he had been, in fact, a popular leader of uncommon ability and a personality of extraordinary complexity. Moreover, the principles for which he fought and died could be presented as matters of vital importance and interest to any of us today.

Mr. Coulter's play falls chronologically into two parts. The first tells of the first rebellion in 1870. The second begins fifteen years later, with Riel's return from exile in Montana, and comes to the climax of his trial and execution. The action shifts back and forth from the Northwest to Ottawa and we see the conflicts at several levels: among Riel's own people and among the national leaders (Sir John A. Macdonald appears as Riel's most distinguished antagonist). In order to include the necessary background, Mr. Coulter has built the drama on a pattern recalling the Elizabethan chronicle plays. The scenes are designed to be presented in quick succession against a minimum of scenery, and a large cast is involved. The trappings of pageantry, drums, music, banners, and so forth are used from time to time to highlight the action, link scenes, and sustain the emotional continuity.

But at the centre of the drama is Riel himself; the playwright intends that the focus shall remain on him. *Riel* is neither a pageant nor a historical documentary but rather a dramatic portrait. In its present form, however, though Riel's personality is variously reflected in action, its dramatic impact is not sufficiently sustained. Or, at any rate, in the first production that the play was given, when it was staged under exceptionally disadvantageous circumstances (by the New Play Society of Toronto), Riel emerged only intermittently as a magnetic figure. The developing action lacked tension and suspense so that, consequently, the story of his rise and fall from power was neither as exciting nor as moving as it ought to have been. It is hard to be sure whether the play or the production was at fault, but Mr. Coulter has made the director's and the actor's problems more difficult by adopting a detached and impartial attitude towards the very enigmatic protagonist. The play presents many opinions about Riel and a good deal of evidence concerning him; it records him fully; but it does not interpret him. In the end Mr. Coulter leaves us with the questions that stimulated him, the puzzle of Riel's personality and the problem of placing and evaluating him in history, but without the author's own opinions. Had he been willing to adopt a point of view and set out the story from that perspective, its significance, and the drama inherent in it, might perhaps have been fixed more vividly in our minds.

When next it is produced, if adequate rehearsal time is allowed for the director and the author to tighten and strengthen it wherever this is necessary, *Riel* ought to emerge as an unusually interesting and worthwhile work. It offers a serious challenge to any company and should bring them gratifying rewards.

Vincent Tovell, *UTQ*, 20 (1950-51), 272

• •

John Coulter's discovery of Riel as a significant figure in the life of this country has given us many theatrical occasions since 1950, when his play first appeared. Few can have been so auspiciously supported as the new production of it staged by Jean Gascon for the National Arts Centre.

On a bleached wooden scaffolding designed by Robert Prevost, the Coulter version is given full weight and attention here, by a cast which includes some highly distinguished players from the country's English and French-language theatre.

Gascon has cast cleverly, never more so than in choosing Albert Millaire to play Riel. For Millaire is very capable of giving the central character the impression of a man pushed beyond mere sanity by his spiritual mission to this people.

This figure of the Metis leader, who was the founding father of Manitoba, was accepted by Ottawa at first, then put down by British troops, then forced into exile, is a highly sympathetic one in this production. When he comes back to his country to lead his people in rebellion, we are shown that his obsession has put him above his priests, as it puts him above all other forces of discipline, until the issue of his sanity at the trial seems beyond dispute.

The Coulter version is now a quarter of a century old and shows some signs of an earlier technique of dramatization. In matching it with more modern fashions in documentation (Prevost also provides slides of daguerrotypes) Gascon has perhaps shown up that difference in approach, but neither style dominates by the end of the long evening.

In fact, balancing out the steady verbal confrontations and detailed expositions (it is almost as if we were to be examined on the historical events at the end) with the deeply-felt interpretations of the leading players, tends to extend the play beyond dramatization, beyond documentation or even theatricality, on into a chapter of history seriously viewed through the light of present-day thinking.

Step by step, the elements Coulter stressed are established firmly and boldly. Nothing is thrown away or made of secondary interest. Coulter spends much time on the Irish involvement, with Gary Reineke giving the character of O'Donoghue great thrust, and he also takes time to show how uncompromising and thick are the British militia, attitudes which Gillie Fenwick, as Middleton, and Edward Atienza, as Wolseley, relish for their melodramatic potential.

A portrait of Sir John A. Macdonald in a lighter vein is offered by Sandy Webster, plumply amusing about Ottawa's interpretation of the western uprising which changed the face of Canadian history, while Mervyn Blake presides huffily at Riel's trial as a representative of British justice.

Matching these well-known players from Ontario are equally distinguished ones from Quebec, headed by the intense and emotionally ranging Millaire. The veteran Jacques Auger is the Archbishop Taché, Julien Genay is Father Alexis, Yvette Thout gives a telling glimpse of Riel's mother, Jean-Pierre Cartier is Riel's cousin and Bertrand Gagnon his counsel.

Most of them, as do James Edmond, Donald Ewer, Victor Desy and Daniel Buccos, double in at least two roles, so that the stage is always thronging with new and briefly vivid characters to sweep Louis Riel from his Metis flock into a world of turbulent people and self-seeking strangers.

Gascon, at his element in handling the big assignment, uses the National Arts Centre stage with Stratfordian flourish and is happy conducting this busy surge of history across the bare boards, using a minimum of props or furniture. But he is always sure to make the moments of individual creation count fully, and the Coulter version, amended by Jeremy Gibson to introduce a bilingual element, is full of these.

While there are many characters to be established, each to make his historical point, and so many steps in the sad history of the Metis visionary and rebel, at the end Millaire's performance of that tortured role stands apart.

The actor completes his performance even when the trial threatens to drag on forever, with the opposing positions of the counsels being over-established. For all its breadth of action and its visual scope, Gascon's production will likely be best remembered for bringing us one step closer to an understanding of this rare figure in our darker past.

Herbert Whittaker, Globe and Mail, 17 January 1975

• •

. . . I decided to go back in time and write about some Canadian who had been pivotal in a dangerous revolutionary crisis and turningpoint in Canadian history. I asked around among my friends, inviting them to name such a Canadian, and was surprised to hear from one after another the same name, Louis Riel, of whom I had known only that a western halfbreed of that name had been hanged as a rebel. I was further surprised when, to begin a long and laborious research, I sought assistance from the librarian at Toronto University, Dr. Wallace, and told him I wished to read everything available that had been written about Louis Riel, he did literally blush and exclaim, "What! Louis Riel! You don't seriously mean to tell me you mean to stir up trouble again by writing about that—that infamous scoundrel!" I needed no further incentive than this to go ahead! Everything written about Louis Riel, on which I could lay my hands, I read—often having to brace my knees below the desk to do so, for much of what purported to be history was no more than bitter partisan propaganda and foully written at that. But eventually I had read it all and was ready to write . . . . For two years I continued writing and discarding drafts of scene after scene—so many scenes that I saw no way of staging all except by reverting to the open stage of the Elizabethans, a continuous flow of scenes on a bare stage with the aid of no more than indicative settings and properties and stage lighting . . . .

I had seen Louis Riel as a patriotic, God-obsessed paranoid with a touch of political genius, weak and unstable except in one particular: his passion to fulfill the mission laid upon him, he profoundly believed, by God—to be the prophet of the North-West, the champion of the rights of halfbreed people. I saw in his story the shape of a Canadian myth, yet believed that but for the accident of history, which found him where he was, when he was, he should have lived and died and never again been heard of, an irascible, discontented, religious and political fanatic. Because of this dominant part of religion in his story I felt that my play must, at its tragic conclusion, have a ritual shape and content . . . .

The play opened on Friday, February 17, 1950. For a while before curtain time the opening was uncertain because Mavor Moore, the Louis Riel, while eating perhaps hurriedly and in some anxiety for lines which he had not even then completely mastered, had a bone stick in his throat, I think a fishbone, and, as the audience was coming into the theatre, was in the hospital across the road having the bone removed. But he managed to be on the stage for the curtain, and the performance began and flowed on from scene to scene with, to my relief, surprisingly few uncertain moments, gathering power and momentum to the appalling moment when hangman and scaffold are suddenly revealed awaiting Riel upstage. The harsh realism of this ghastly apparition jarred the audience and jolted them abruptly out of the trance in which they were moving toward the tragic end. I felt this to be a dramatic flaw; and being confirmed in this afterwards by the horrified protest of some in the audience, led by the poet E.J. Pratt, I decided for future performances to have hangman and scaffold off-stage, unseen, but in a lighted place made unmistakeable to the audience as that "place appointed," the place of execution. Part of the audience who were not in the least horrified by the appearance of hangman and scaffold, but on the contrary thought it the best thing in the play, was the little company of bemedaled veterans of the Second Riel rebellion, with whom Mrs. Moore had enterprisingly dressed the front row of the house. One of them said to me afterwards, "Gosh, sir, I was all through that bloody rebellion; but tonight's the first time I ever knew a goddam thing about that bastard!" Amusing too, was the discovery of one of the veterans who had insisted on sitting by himself at the back of the house. I asked him why he had not sat with his brothers-in-arms. Looking slightly pained and straightening himself to attention he tersely explained, "But I was an officer". . . .

John Coulter, *In My Day: Memoirs* (Willowdale, Ont., 1980), 260-264

• •

ROBERTSON DAVIES

At My Heart's Core

First produced at the Peterborough Summer Theatre,
28 August 1950

Directed by Robertson Davies
Designed by Margaret McDonough

Cast

Mrs. Frances Stewart	Brenda Davies
Sally	Marjorie Root
Mrs. Catherine Parr Traill	Kate Reid
Mrs. Susanna Moodie	Clarine Jackman
Honour Brady	Pat Atkinson
Phelim Brady	Frank Perry
Mr. Edmund Cantwell	John Primm
The Hon. Thomas Stewart	Donald Glenn

. . . in many ways, *At My Heart's Core* is a better play than *Fortune, My Foe*. It has as interesting a theme and states it in a simpler, more direct fashion. While its first act is overcrowded, and mostly devoted to developing a sub-plot, its second and third acts restore a most pleasing balance. Furthermore, the play depends largely on its feminine characters, and the playwright has written these roles much more effectively than the female roles in his earlier plays . . . .

But Mr. Davies, in concerning himself with the portrayal of distinguished pioneers, is able to keep them from being as lifeless as is usually the fate of Canadian historical characters depicted on stage. He has done this by establishing not only their sterling pioneer qualities, but by recreating the doubts and fears that troubled even the most stalwart breast . . .

It is a story which allows Mr. Davies plenty of comment on the problems of living in Canada, most of which are easily applicable to present sojourns as well as pioneer ones. His concern with the place of the artist gets a fair hearing, and there is a fine Shavian passage about the intellectual frustrations of women. And there is also time for a tribute to the place of the theatre in a man's life and in a culture when the Hon. Thomas recalls the great clown Joey Grimaldi. A grand moment, this.

There is also, in the often clever plot-laying of the first act, a raucous sub-story about the Irish girl who has a child by her step-father, but won't take it home until he gets the body of his first wife down off the roof. This is amusing, but seems to consume a deal of time that might be better spent on the main plot, one feels, and it does admit to the scene an Irish squatter that is no more convincing than most stage Irishmen.

Having written a play that is undeniably intelligent and witty, and also has emotion, on the unlikely subject of Canadian pioneers, Mr. Davies brought it to the Peterborough Summer Theatre stage himself, making a very nice job of its direction. He has a cast that gives him every support.

Clarine Jackman is most excellent as the positive Mrs. Moodie, forceful without any strain, cheerful and indeed, everything Mrs. Moodie could have wished of her re-creation 100 years later. Brenda Davies, in the more romantic part of Mrs. Stewart, is charming, playing with warmth and humor and grace. Kate Reid fares less well as the lady naturalist, tending to over-play some scenes and failing to make the lady consistent as a character. But her reading of one particular speech and her handling of certain comedy lines can only be accounted admirable.

John Primm is perhaps the best in the cast. In the rewarding role of Edmund Cantwell, he achieved humor, delicacy and a lyric quality, too. Donald Glenn, whose Hon. Thomas serves to give strength and color to the last scene strained toward theatricality at times, but at others was amazingly right. Frank Perry's stage Irishman, like Mr. Primm's Irish devil, had some trouble with his accent, but seemed to be giving what the playwright requires to the role.

There was also a wholly delightful bit as the Irish lass by Pat Atkinson and a wholly unbelievable bit as an Indian maid by Marjorie Root.

Margaret McDonough's setting suggesting the outside and interior of a log cabin was charming in its suggestion. The costumes were good, and the properties must have won the full approval of the Peterborough historians.

At My Heart's Core is certainly one of the most interesting plays written out of Canada's past. This Peterborough centennial production will probably be the first of many.

Herbert Whittaker, Globe and Mail, 30 August 1950*

• •

Robertson Davies' most accomplished play, to date, is as far as we know the only Canadian play to be published during the past year and so constitutes our entire output of dramatic literature for 1950. In spite of a special plea made by the author in the preface, this play has been published to be read by the many who may never see it acted, and must therefore be reviewed as read. It reads very smoothly, amusingly, and entertainingly for the most part, and, except where it is necessary to the plot, is free of the self-conscious Canadianism which mars most reconstructions of the pioneer period.

Mr. Davies has in fact succeeded where others have failed, in bringing the tin-types to life while dissipating the plaster-saint atmosphere. His great success is with his comedians. "Phelim," a backwoods Irishman, is a worthy successor to "Pop" and "Buckety" (two other such memorable characters from earlier plays), and the girl "Honour" of the doubtful relationships is a sheer joy. The first act rises to a height of well-sustained comedy. In the second, in which the serious theme is developed, Mr. Davies has created a woman character, in the person of Frances Stewart, who is really alive and believable. But he is still having trouble with his women, as witness Mrs. Traill and Mrs. Moodie, who in spite of the male heart-balm of the solution to their problem are the play's weakness; both in their relation to Cantwell the tormentor, and in their dialogue, they are repetitious and the reader will have difficulty distinguishing between these two distinguished ladies at times. Obviously, casting will overcome this difficulty in the acting, but the reader can decide whether or not this is what the author refers to as "a truly dramatic fault" (see preface). The three male characters, on the other hand, present a fine range and variety.

At My Heart's Core is a splendid example of what can be done with historical material of this nature when the writer is not inhibited by sanctimonious ancestor worship. Its comedy is of a high order, its serious theme perhaps a little over-worked, its conclusion both graceful and charming.

H.T.K., Canadian Forum, 30 (March 1951), 285-286

• •

. . . *At My Heart's Core* has survived its quarter-century well, its Shavian theatricality and approach to the past being more readily acceptable now than then, when naturalism was more prized. Its situation rides easily on the current interest in Canada's culture, its artists, its past and the rights of women.

But it is also a very shapely work, for Davies is a classicist. To a log home in nearby Douro come the devil of an Irishman to tempt three noble if discontented pioneers. Catherine Parr Traill is tempted by scientific recognition, her sister, Susanna Moodie by literary acclaim, and the hostess, wife to Mr. Justice Thomas Stewart, by the high-born romance in her past.

"New countries mean not only hopes fulfilled but hopes relinquished," observes Mrs. Traill, following Mrs. Stewart out in despair.

Like any effective tempter, this Cantwell sniffs out his victims' vulnerabilities, and makes them recognize their weakness. It is only the return of Justice Stewart to sit in judgment on Cantwell that saves their sanity, and for his reward he wins an expression of true affection from his wife in a beautifully romantic finale.

Davies balanced off this high line with a recurrent low-life, involving an extravagant Irish peasant and his daughter-wife, as well as a grinning Indian woman. This element puts a further strain on inexperienced players, for Davies demands very broad fun to balance his intellectual passages.

Davies also deals in argument highly spiced by irony and this proves difficult for unsophisticated players. The Peterborough actors did not overcome the problem wholly but certainly gave a strong enough showing to the play in their carefully paced production to inspire future revivals.

Ann Stirling, with a charming Irish accent, carried the loving role of Mrs. Stewart from beginning to end, through her duel with Terance Belleville as Cantwell on to her final scene with Lee J. Campbell, as her husband. Una Mellors showed a gentle spirit as Mrs. Traill but Margo Hull lacked the militant spunk with which Davies invested Susanna Moodie.

Belleville made an elegant and persistent devil, and Campbell a strong if not distinguished judge. Louise Guinand was a charmingly casual Irish girl and John Harwood White was noisy enough as her unrepentant pursuer. Eledean Wills brought a presence to the play that was largely silent but still emphatic as an Indian named Sally.

Robert Jordan's setting put fine Upper Canada pine against a dark green curtain of forest, the whole rather cluttering the small Peterborough stage, except when lighting isolated acting areas. Missing entirely, however, were the three significant horn calls to mark each temptation.

What McLeod's direction does bring out is his dramatist's feeling and affection for the Victorian age (the action is set during Mackenzie's Rebellion of 1837) as evidenced by the manners, and such moments as Mrs. Moodie's "You knew

Bryon!'' and the judge's jolly recollection of Joey Grimaldi singing Hot Codins. High moments, both.

Herbert Whittaker, *Globe and Mail*, 8 July 1974

• •

. . . Davies' Preface to the original edition speaks of the play as dealing with a problem which is widespread and continuing. He has chosen to place it in Canada in 1837, which makes the characters early Victorians wrestling with all the hardships of pioneer farms. The play is not intended as a naturalistic reproduction of contemporary life, and the playwright suggests that its successful performance requires ''a judicious dash of exaggeration.''

We are thus alerted to the contemporary nature of one of Davies' major themes. The philistines are ever with us: in Frontenac's Quebec, in Moodie's Upper Canada, and in Davies' native Ontario. Cantwell, the demonic tempter, and Phelim, the drunken Irish bard around whom the sub-plot revolves, are the only two characters in *At My Heart's Core* who really believe in art. Phelim is a self-styled poet and story-teller. Back in Ireland, his stories were needed and loved. In Upper Canada, the busy pioneers have ''the maggot o' respectability in their brains.'' He tells Susanna Moodie that they two are the songbirds that aren't wanted in this bitter land of industry and politics. Cantwell, critic and connoisseur, praises art in more formal terms (art gives form and meaning to life, he tells Mrs. Moodie) and lays bare the materialistic quality of Canadian ambitions. There is a period, Cantwell says, between poverty and affluence during which men feel no need for poetry and stories: ''And there is a sort of education which forgets that the mind needs not only to be polished, but oiled.'' The middle of the twentieth century finds us still in that interregnum. Still short of oil . . . .

Davies has said that he intended to show the terrible sacrifice of abilities required by pioneering conditions and intended to *mock* the concept of the noble pioneer intent in forging a great land. The central irony is that the temptations offered to Traill and Moodie are the truth: ''They were living false lives, lying lives. They have more refinement than sense.'' Cantwell is a genuine aristocrat, Davies added, and his ideas will inevitably seem demonic to bourgeois minds. Cantwell's ''Byronic-Satanic'' manners and appearance play upon the popular misconception of Byron, and Mrs. Moodie is more impressed by the fact that Byron is an aristocrat than by the fact that he is a poet.

There are several problems which come between these intentions and the resulting play. The first is Cantwell's name. If Cantwell is the devil speaking truth, surely a less pejorative name would lessen the confusion. In Act Three of the slightly revised second edition of the play [1966], Davies has deleted a *canting* remark about the poor from Cantwell's part. The result of this deletion is to make Cantwell more sympathetic and sensible at this point. A small matter, but indicative. With such a name, and with the emphasis upon his devilish aspects, the audience is unprepared to accept his advice. The psychological explanation as to why Cantwell has purposely upset the women (they slighted his wife) may be romantic but tends to make us dismiss the validity of his arguments.

Another problem lies in the fact that Davies has made the women's defence of their sacrifice too effective. When Mrs. Traill says that a new country brings hope and demands sacrifice, it seems to ring true. When she says that her life is not pitiful but full of interest, we believe her. Susanna Moodie is a more comic figure, with a hint of the drill-sergeant in her manner and a comic obsession with Methodists. But both Mrs. Traill and Mrs. Stewart evoke our sympathy and admiration.

Mrs. Stewart is the real heroine of the play and the only character with a sense of humour. It is slightly confusing that her temptation is meant to be resisted whereas for the other two women, resistance means self-betrayal. In a hunting incident in Ireland, Cantwell had discovered that Lord Rossmore wears Mrs. Stewart's picture in a locket around his neck. He tempts her to betray her husband with thoughts of Lord Rossmore and his brilliant world of fashion which she has exchanged for the backwoods. Such beauty and charm, Cantwell urges, are wasted here. In a romantic finale by the fireside with her husband, Mrs. Stewart tells him what has happened, and assures him that Cantwell arouses not regret but only discontentment disguised as regret. Her marriage is a happy one, and Cantwell's temptation is powerless against it. The married couple come across as being very much in love, a situation which is likely to confuse a modern director. One questions the term "Women's Lib," since the heroine and the only woman proof against the temptation of regret, is the one whose destiny lies within a traditional sexist role.

The play has an amusing sub-plot which revolves around Phelim Brady, his foster-daughter Honour who is soon to be his bride, their new-born child, and the corpse of his first wife which he has placed on the roof as a precaution against wolves. Various scuffles, physical and verbal, between Phelim, Honour, and Mrs. Stewart's Indian servant Sally provide comic relief. Mrs. Traill and Mrs. Moodie's dispute over the care and handling of babies' heads provides an amusing episode in the first act, and Stewart's imitation of the famous clown Grimaldi enlivens the third with a bawdy song and a jig.

The parallel technique, demonstrated here in having not one but several temptings, is an effective trick, one that Davies uses frequently. Fairy stories and tales of mythic adventures also use parallel incidents, and one is reminded of this sort of literature when Cantwell asks Mrs. Moodie, "Who ever heard a sister praised without wishing to try her own luck?" The Victorian atmosphere is well sustained and allows for satirical jibes such as "not before the servants" and "As we are all females it is not necessary for Susanna to conceal the fact she has an appetite.'' In brief, *At My Heart's Core* is a romantic comedy of great charm, marred by ambiguity as to its central intent . . . .

Patricia Morley, *Robertson Davies* (Toronto, 1977), 22-24

• •

GRATIEN GÉLINAS

Bousille and the Just

First produced in English at La Comédie Canadienne, Montreal,
23 February 1961†

Directed by Gratien Gélinas
Designed by Jacques Pelletier

Cast

Bellboy	Yves Gélinas
Phil Vézina	Paul Berval
Henri Gravel	Yves Létourneau
Aurore Vézina	Beatrice Picard
Bousille	Gratien Gélinas
Mother	Juliette Huot
Noella Gravel	Hélène Loiselle
Lawyer	Paul Hébert
Brother Théophile	Gilles Latulippe
Colette Richard	Ginette Letondal

†(First produced in French at La Comédie Canadienne, 17 August 1959)

Gratien Gélinas' mordant study of a very unpleasant French-Canadian family has now been translated into English and had its official première last night. Although it does not have the drive of the French original—as is only to be expected—it is still a most compelling play. The many touches of humor come across just the same and because the dramatic theme is universal rather than French-Canadian the language makes no difference to the effectiveness of the melodrama. . . .

There are four replacements in the cast held over from the French version and one of them is Paul Berval, who plays the important role of the wise-cracking brother-in-law and plays it very well indeed. It is a livelier, more extrovert and less subtle interpretation than Jean Duceppe's in the French version, but it is just as valid and equally as amusing.

Yves Létourneau, as the brutal elder brother, is just as impressive as he was in French and just as much in character, and the same could be said of Beatrice Picard's Aurore, the sister. Juliette Huot, of course, is perfect as the distraught mother, even though some of her deadpan dryness is lost in the language transition. Paul Hébert's characterization of the lawyer is most satisfactory and he provides the necessary contrast to the vulgarity of the Gravels. The same might be said of Hélène Loiselle's Noella, a well-bred girl who, now realizing what her husband is really like, is regretting her marriage to Henri. Another newcomer to the play who leaves a deep impression (even though she is only a short time on stage) is Ginette Letondal, who contributes a touching but very well-controlled emotional performance.

It would be difficult to imagine anyone replacing Gilles Latulippe in the role of the innocent and well-meaning Brother Theophile. Mr. Latulippe brought the house down at the French première and he is just as successful—though perhaps a shade more restrained—in English.

The play, of course, has undergone many alterations since that French prèmiere. The last act has been rewritten and immeasurably improved and the whole play has been tightened up to run much more smoothly. It is now a first-class and entertaining study of French-Canadian life.

Jacques Pelletier's set is admirable.

Sydney Johnson, *Montreal Star*, 24 February 1961*

• •

Gratien Gélinas' modern morality play *Bousille et les Justes* became one of the great successes of Quebec theatre when it was first performed in the last years of the Duplessis regime.

Although the revival last year in Montreal was also very successful, as I prepared to attend last night's performance in the National Arts Centre, I wondered whether the play was more than a curiosity. However, in the end, I could not help being swept up in the drama of the powerful text . . . .

Bousille is a reminder of the fragility of truth and goodness, a reminder of the ease with which brute force can seemingly overcome simple trust and love.

The play is about failure: the failure of the Grenon family who have lost what little love they might have had one for the other; the failure of justice because the lawyer knows that Bousille has perjured himself yet he does nothing; the failure of Bousille whose only solution is to kill himself when he realizes how weak he is.

Gratien Gélinas is a consummate artist. His many years of experience in the theatre and his ear for the sense of language are evident in this text. The comic becomes tragic yet the tragic never becomes comic.

This present production is also directed by Gélinas. Thus it must be considered the definitive reading of the play.

Bousille, the part made famous by Gélinas himself, has been assumed with skill and understanding by Robert Rivard. Every gesture, every inflection and movement of the eye—yes, this is Bousille.

The other members of the family are played with skill and artistry and a sense of perfection. Pierre Dufresne as Henri Grenon incarnates brute strength, while Jean-Pierre Masson as Phil just wants a good time. Beatrice Picard as Aurore, Henri's sister and Phil's wife, is so worried about her ''good nature'' that nothing else matters.

There is Denise Morelle as the mother—and what a mother. Perhaps she is a slight caricature; however, I have known mothers like her.

If I had to quibble it would be with the way in which Gélinas plays the role of the lawyer. I realize it is a minor one. However, I felt he was simply reciting lines. What a contrast in the marvellous Frère Nolasque of the Christian Brothers played by Ghyslain Tremblay . . . .

John Hare, *Ottawa Citizen*, 18 September 1976

• •

. . . The play originally grew out of a personal experience. Sitting in a Montreal restaurant one evening during the Christmas season of 1947, Gélinas, always observant, noticed at the next table a family group whose gloomy countenance contrasted sharply with the general holiday mood; they were obviously country people who had come to town on some unpleasant business. The situation was enough to trigger the author's imagination; he imagined that the youngest member of the family might be in jail, and the rest had come to the city to attend the trial—hence their gloom. Realizing he had the stuff of a potential drama, Gélinas hastily took down some notes on paper napkins, which he filed away for the time being, as he was then working on *Tit-Coq*. Coming back to this material later, he realized that although he had the makings of a story, dramatic conflict was lacking. He eventually introduced into the story an outsider to the family, an old drunk who happened to hold the key to the testimony, and would therefore be brutalized by a brother of the accused. But he was not satisfied with the dramatic effectiveness of this new character: a worthless old tramp would hardly arouse in the audience the pity and fear at which the author was aiming. Finally, he conceived a different type of key witness: Bousille (*bousiller: to bungle*), a gentle, kind and faithful soul, somewhat simple-minded and deeply religious. Throughout the play, a parallel is drawn between Bousille, the family drudge, and Fido, the family dog: both lack physical attractiveness and intelligence, but make up for these deficiencies by their faithfulness and unending desire to serve. Inflicted on a victim of such childlike innocence, the brutality of Henri seems tragic indeed.

The character of the key witness was thus finalized, but the plot line was not. Gélinas wrote a first version of the play in which Bousille, following his perjury in court, goes on a drunken binge, and, returning to the hotel, dies of a heart attack. This ending, especially the long drawn-out death scene, attracted a good deal of unfavorable critical comment when the play was first performed in the summer of 1959. By the fall of the same year, the author had made some further changes, ending the play with Bousille's offstage suicide as it appears in the published version. With this new ending, Gélinas has made out of *Bousille and the Just* an almost perfect dramatic work. It is an essential improvement both from the point of view of the main character and from the point of view of dramatic structure. Bousille's death as a result of a drunken binge cheapened the character, and made him seem only marginally tragic. Having him kill himself as a result of unbearable feelings of guilt and total despair over his perjury, on the other hand, lifts him out of the ordinary, into the category of a truly tragic hero whose fate leaves us deeply moved. In the same way, the earlier long death scene tended to create an impression of melodrama and anticlimax especially following upon the tension-filled torture scene. In not actually showing the suicide, Gélinas followed the classical tradition, which does not allow violent events on the stage. Just as his use of the classical unities of time and space, this technique of restraint serves to heighten the impact of the event on the audience. It also helps to focus the attention of the public on the irony of the play's ending—''the police want us back for an inquest.''

In structure, the play is more cohesive than *Tit-Coq*. The French version is based on a four-act structure, with three, seven, two and three scenes respectively, in each act. The large number of scenes does remind one of Gélinas' background as a revue artist. But in *Bousille*, these scenes do not break up the action into independent units, as they did in *Tit-Coq*. They are purely formal divisions unnoticeable to the audience. The author also specified that there should be only one intermission, at the end of the second act, so that the dramatic tension remains unbroken.

The English version serves Gélinas' intentions even better than the French: here, the play falls into the natural division of two parallel acts divided into two scenes each, with each act corresponding to the events of one day. Act One covers the morning (expository scenes) and evening (testimony of the two witnesses, Colette and Bousille) of the first day; Act Two, the morning (torture scene) and evening (dénouement) of the second day. The English version has been further streamlined with the omission of some lines and the transposition of others.

Gélinas has been accused of indulging in his love of the picturesque in both dialogue and character and thus getting the play off to an excessively slow start. The real drama, according to some critics, does not begin until the appearance on stage of Colette, which would make the preceding scene dramatically indefensible. It is interesting to note in this context that criticism much to the same effect was levelled at Ibsen for the slow pace of the initial scenes in *Ghosts*! In the case of Gélinas as well as Ibsen, the slow and careful unfolding of character and background is of course essential, since neither writer proposes to present us with a suspense story, but rather with drama of intense social satire, and this requires a great deal of attention to detail. It is no doubt true that the action of the play could proceed just as well if Mother Gravel would not, at one point, waste much of her children's time and ours by refusing to sleep in the hotel without her beads, "like a floozie"; but we would miss the very essence of her personality.

It is through his masterfully drawn characters, rather than through the action, most of which takes place offstage, that the author develops the themes of his play. *Bousille and the Just* is a highly original dramatic work; with it, the playwright has achieved the difficult dramatic feat of running the full gamut from tragedy to burlesque without breaking the basic unity and coherence of the play . . . .

Renate Usmiani, *Profiles in Canadian Drama : Gratien Gélinas*
(Toronto, 1977), 53-55

• •

GEORGE RYGA

Indian

First produced by CBC Radio, 25 November 1962

Directed by George McCowan

Cast

Indian	Len Birman
Watson	Ed McNamara
Agent	John Sullivan

I saw *Indian* . . . on the C.B.C. programme *Quest* in 1962, and it impressed me greatly at that time; now, nine years later, reading the script for the first time, I find myself even more impressed. *Indian* is short; it is a one-act play and is about an identity crisis in a young Cree Indian labourer. The action confines itself to one extended scene (landscape a "flat, grey, stark, non country") in which the Indian is harassed by his bossman, Watson, and later by a nameless Indian Affairs Agent. The Agent does not have the clear-cut malignancy of Watson the bossman; he is simply your average well-meaning white liberal. However, he finds his ethics severely abused when the Indian tells him how, after his brother had been critically injured by a cave-in whilst digging a clay pit, he (the Indian) performed a mercy killing. At the end, the Agent flees the scene, his car driving dust across the stage, and the Indian is left driving his hammer at the head of a post, an indicator of what he would like to do to the white "sementos," the soul traders of the world.

A good play. Beautifully written. The dialogue is dead-on, and the conflict (so necessary to any stage play) is totally credible. There is one excellent monologue (about the clay pit) and, although the plot is minimal, this allows the characters and the theme to emerge as the play's main concern. The coarse texture of the black and white television picture in George McCowan's *Quest* production was particularly suitable for rendering the harshness of the landscape (itself a reflection of the psychic condition of the Indian). The play also reads well, and I hope that this publication will lead to its production by some of our small drama groups across the country. My only criticism concerns the hero: in spite of his fragmented dialogue, I find him extremely sensitive and articulate, and I cannot find this convincing. Ryga has romanticized him in order to make him a sympathetic character (white bourgeois audiences are always responsive to the "noble savage" motif). But what illiterate, Indian or otherwise, would bemoan the loss of his soul? (There is an equally romantic and unconvincing line in *Rita Joe* when Jaimie Paul cries "Gimme back my truth!") However, given that, I think Ryga has scored the essential mystical truth concerning not only the Canadian Indian but Man himself; the *who am I* of the human situation is brought out very clearly . . . .

Lawrence Russell, *Canadian Literature*, 50
(Autumn 1971), 81-82

• •

. . . The musical and ritual aspects of *Rita Joe* diffuse the strength of the language; this does not happen in *Indian*, the first play in the book [*The Ecstasy of Rita Joe and Other Plays* (Toronto : New Press, 1971)] and, in my opinion, the best. A short one-act drama with three characters, it was first performed on the

CBC television programme *Quest* in 1963 [*sic*: 1962]. A simple confrontation between a nameless Indian, a farmer and an Indian agent, it is a classic exploration of the subtle insults and a brilliance of manoeuvre which lie at the root of all relationships between Indians and whites. If anyone ever approaches you to discuss the "Indian problem," give him *Indian*. Ryga's Indian is not passive, dull or feeble; on the contrary, he is a master of physical intimidation and psychological terror, subtle insults and a brilliance of manoeuvring rising from the desperation of a man who has nothing to lose. As in *Rita Joe*, a personal universe is summed up in the lines Indian speaks as the farmer kicks him awake from a drunken sleep:

> *Oy! Ooh! The sun she blind me, goddam! . . . Boss . . . I am sick!*
> *Head, she gonna explode, sure as hell! . . .*

Heather Robertson, *Canadian Forum*, 51
(January/February 1972)

• •

Ryga   . . . [*Indian* is] the only play I can look back on over all these years that I would not write any differently. I was working in a form, in a content—with language and the mythological implications—that was very close to me. And in historical terms this was an actuality. You know I grew up on the outskirts of a Cree reservation. The demoralization and degradation was about as total as any society can experience anywhere in the world. These people had been worked over by the Church; they had been worked over by the Hudson's Bay Co.; there was nothing left. There was no language left any more. Even their heroes they picked up from the dominant culture, like a chocolate-bar wrapper dropped in the street that's picked up as a piece of art and taken home and nailed on the wall.

David Watson   What sort of social relationship did you have with them? *Indian* presents a very objective picture, but there is clearly a great deal of personal involvement.

Ryga   Relationships were pretty basic. One played with a ball, worked together picking up stones. But the degree of intensity in the relationship was exquisitely whole, because we knew there was a 50% chance of not ever seeing each other again. If I caught pneumonia, my chances of survival were about 400% better than theirs, because I would be taken care of by the community, by the family, and taken to hospital, while their reaction to illness was quite fatalistic, and many of the young boys and men did die. As a result there was an openness about relationships, and I think in *Indian* this expressed itself in, not contempt, but the defiance towards death and separation, which means you live much more fully because of the realization that this may never happen to you again, though there is no philosophizing or discussion about it.

D.W. The form of the play was very different from anything else being written in Canada at the time. Would you put this down to the material, or were there any dramatic models you can identify?

Ryga I credit a large part of the fact that *Indian* was written at all, to seeing *The Zoo Story* on television, and watching how that particular play was constructed. It was the freedom that Albee was exercising in departing from the traditions as then practiced, and taking theatre into a kind of arid area, which I found fascinating and which to a great extent I have used ever since. If you remove as much of the framework as possible . . . .

D.W. You mean external trappings, production values?

Ryga That's right. If you remove the flesh and fire that can make style more important than content, social commitment, it should intensify the interest in what is taking place on that screen or stage.

D.W. Although the dramatic situations of your early plays are quite specific, this paring away of externals is really a method of generalization. When you speak of the Cree Indians' lack of authentic language or indigenous cultural heroes, are you really presenting an extreme example of every Canadian's position? The rejection of traditions and the search for new forms seems another aspect of the same thing.

Ryga The play was part of a growing change in the sensibilities of the country. The national question was beginning to arise, and the repercussions from *Indian* were that people became aware that we had to look at ourselves, not as carbon copies of other people, but on our own terms. Recently I've made a study of the Group of Seven, and when you look at what they were doing and what their objectives were, the preliminary work was already in place in the 1930s. The Group of Seven could not paint landscape the way Constable painted it, because that landscape doesn't exist here. You cannot use the same language that describes events that never took place in this country either. You have to modify language. You have to find a new foundation from which to work. That's why the question of mythology is such an urgent priority. We've lost out on almost half a century when we should have formed our own coloration . . . .

An interview with George Ryga, by David Watson.
Edited by Christopher Innes, *CD*, 8 : 2 (1982), 162-163

• •

JOHN HERBERT

Fortune and Men's Eyes

First produced at the Actors Playhouse, New York, 23 February 1967

Directed by Mitchell Nestor
Designed by C. Murawski

Cast

Smitty	Terry Kiser
Rocky	Victor Arnold
Queenie	Bill Moor
Mona	Robert Christian
Guard	Clifford Pellow

Fortune and Men's Eyes, which opened last night at the Actors Playhouse on Sheridan Square, is a distressing play in more ways than one.

It points out, to begin with, several distressing facts of prison life in North America (the play is set in Canada, but would apply to the United States as well) that escaped mention in all those Cagney-Pat O'Brien pictures.

The first fact is that when healthy young men are forbidden normal sexual gratification for a long time, they are tempted to change their working definition of "normal"—a change whose effects can turn out to be permanent.

The second fact, even more disturbing, is that the change is so often forced on a new inmate by those older and stronger than he, that he is forced to choose not between chastity and sex, but between seduction and rape.

These, at least, are the contentions of *Fortune and Men's Eyes*, and since its author, John Herbert, once served six months in a Canadian prison, one assumes he knows what he is talking about.

One also honors Mr. Herbert's attempt to write a serious play on this theme. Obviously, he feels strongly about his subject; obviously, he wants us to feel as enraged, as disgusted at the system that breeds such corruption.

The trouble is that the only live character in Mr. Herbert's play—at least, as it is being done at the Actors Playhouse—is an outrageously funny "queen," played in the style of the immortal Mario Montez by Bill Moor.

Mr. Moor shaves his legs and spits his curls and flips his wrists and says witchy things to his cellmates, and (at least for the first act) it works. He gets the laughs, and he also establishes a character: a tough-minded character who gets precisely what he wants out of "the system" by putting what he wants and what he is right on the line.

By Act 2, however, when Queenie flounces in wearing a pink-chiffon party gown, blond wig and rhinestone earings (for the prison Christmas show, you see), we—perhaps unfairly—begin to wonder: At whom is our play being aimed? The prison-reform crowd, or the Miss Super All America Camp Beauty Contest bunch?

That the question should even come up shows a rather serious imbalance in the casting of the show, if not in the script itself. Terry Kiser, as the young man initiated into "the system," is required to go from utter naiveté to cynical power in two acts but seems too knowing for the first and, basically, too mild for the second.

Robert Christian's part—that of a frail young fellow who "separates" his mind from the things his body is forced to do—is intended to evoke sympathy but is written in such a literary, self-pitying way that sympathy escapes us.

Victor Arnold does a good job as a former Casanova who refuses to admit what he has become: but the character, once we have seen through him, is monotonous and, in fact moronic.

And there is a nasty guard, played by Clifford Pellow; but that role we remember from the Cagney-O'Brien days, and he hasn't changed a bit (still bumming cigarettes and showing his temper).

I don't wish to make light of Mr. Herbert's intention, or those of his director, Mitchell Nestor, but *Fortune and Men's Eyes* should have something more to recommend it than a campy bitpart, lots of dirty words and an entirely commendable indignation about a very real social problem. But that's about all I could find in it.

Dan Sullivan, *NYT*, 24 February 1967*

• •

Penal institutions, used as an image of society, a focus of reformist zeal or merely as a self-contained dramatic framework, make a perfect setting for compulsive entertainment, for me at least. So I was a ready customer for John Herbert's *Fortune and Men's Eyes* that gets Charles Marowitz's Open Space Theatre off to such a promising start in its basement premises at 32 Tottenham Court Road. . . .

Fortune and Men's Eyes is a naturalistic piece set in a Canadian reformatory ("a prep school for the Penitentiary," says the programme). The author apparently knows whereof he writes, and to get the audience into the right spirit we were taken singly down the entrance steps by warders, ogled by inmates behind barred windows, submitted to the indignity of fingerprinting, and led to our seats across the open stage with its four-bed dormitory. Off-stage instructions were barked, red lights flashed on and off along the walls, and we felt as if we were the governor's friends privileged to watch his charges through a one-way mirror. The room is occupied by four inmates: Queenie (Al Mancine), a flamboyant homosexual with dyed hair; Rocky (Peter Marinker), a bullying tough; Mona (Louis Negin), a sad, sensitive queer and Smitty (Robert Howay), a reserved new arrival. They are supervised by Holy Face (George Margo), a not entirely unsympathetic, ulcer-ridden warder on the point of retirement. All are first rate, never putting a regulation boot wrong.

Most of the evening is taken up with a study of group dynamics, showing us Smitty's initiation into the brutal, parallel system that the inmates have themselves created beneath the relatively moderately-run institution. "Names don't mean a goddam thing around here," the warder says, but there's no question of deliberately robbing the characters of their identities. What they have to do is assume roles in an underground order that the authorities deliberately ignore: "Don't go to the guards for help, you got to depend on yourself for your own protection." So Smitty, after first attempting to remain a loner, is drawn into an elaborate power game—the rules of which would justify an elaborate Machiavellian treatise called "The Ponce"—which inevitably has to involve sex, brutality and intimidation. With considerable intelligence and superb dialogue, Herbert charts the ever changing situation that corrupts Smitty as it takes him to the position of king of the block. The process is continually absorbing and lifts the play way above the slice of life it first appears to be. I'm not too happy, however, about the climactic scene where Smitty declares his love for Mona and after being rejected is led into reading aloud Shakespeare's sonnet XXIX (which gives the play its title). I can see that it is essential to reveal that the put-upon Mona is the really strong character, the one who has retained his inner balance and preserved his sensibility and integrity at the expense of physical pain and constant humiliation. Yet excellent and deeply felt though the playing is at this juncture, the scene struck me as sentimental and contrived, which isn't to say that I wasn't moved. Anyway, this is a play to be seen, and an earnest, one hopes, of the theatre of sanity and intelligence that the Open Space will provide in the future.

Philip French, *New Statesman*, 19 July 1968

• •

By setting the climactic scene of his play, *Fortune and Men's Eyes*, at Christmas, John Herbert adds a valuable mythic dimension to what would otherwise be little more than a piece of rather pedestrian dramatic journalism. Everyone who reads newspapers and newsmagazines knows that prisons, in Canada and elsewhere, are in a sad state. Suicide, murder, drug addiction, homosexual rape, brutalities of all sorts blot their records. This play concerns itself with homosexuality, not as a theme valuable for its own sake but as a means of describing the death of a boy's soul. . . .

The pattern of irony that pervades the play rests on three points: Shakespeare's Sonnet 29, from which the play takes its title; Portia's mercy speech from *The Merchant of Venice*, which Mona plans to recite at the Christmas concert; and the Christmas concert itself.

The resonance from the title echoes throughout the play, though the sonnet itself does not appear until quite near the end of Act II when Mona, who had been reading Shakespeare before, reads it aloud to Smitty in the disastrous love scene. Either Grove Press or John Herbert has taken some liberties with the text, but the sense of the poem is not seriously damaged. Outcast from society, the four young men in the play are in grave "disgrace with fortune and men's eyes." Mona, refusing to participate in the power structure run by the "hippos" or "politicians" among the prisoners, is doubly outcast, and pays the price of gang rapes and floggings. The emphasis of the sonnet falls, however, on love as redemption from the despair and self-hatred caused by the casting-out. Thoughts of the Friend, with whom some critics believe Shakespeare had a homosexual relationship, lift the poet's heart to heaven with such joy that "then I scorn to share [*sic*] my state with kings." The notion of love, especially homosexual love, as redemptive is bitterly ironic in this prison world where sex, a primary weapon in the shifting power structure, takes the form of "gang splashes" and "invitations to the crapper." In the immediate context of the love scene, however, the suggestion of redemptive love seems viable, for the moment. Smitty has declared his love for Mona and met with what appears to be a rebuff, although Mona explains that he is rejecting Smitty's body because Smitty belongs to him in the other and better world his divided spirit inhabits, "the world I dream in." Failing to understand, Smitty pounds on the bars of the cell, but Mona punches his shoulder and thrusts the book at him. The division between them is healed as they read the sonnet, giggling in happy embarrassment. For a moment, love and understanding exist. But when the others return from the Christmas concert, they interpret the closeness of Mona and Smitty as a manifestation of the only "love" they know and viciously attack Mona, who, as a known homosexual, is dragged off by the guard to be flogged. Redemptive love cannot survive in this hell.

Portia's mercy speech from *The Merchant of Venice* is the second part of the pattern. Mona, who has been combing the library for a contribution to the dramatic side of the Christmas concert, rehearses the speech for his cellmates, dressed in a red velvet curtain and speaking hesitantly. Only Smitty listens. The others provide a running commentary composed of the usual sexual insults, which one would expect to be especially pointed here as the homosexual boy is playing the part of a girl disguised as a man. But the speech, an unbeatable piece of theatre in any context, maintains its own integrity, introducing into the climate of brutality and hostility the idea of loving mercy, "an attribute of God himself." The irony here is not in the inverted effects of the Shakespeare passage—it has no effects, since Mona is later discouraged by the concert director from delivering the speech. Instead, the irony lies in the juxtaposition of Mona's speech and Queenie's act for the concert in which the sexual impersonation dominates, so much so that some reviewers found the scene distracting and disproportionate. Poured into a spangled gown, complete with wig and glass jewels and a feather fan, Queenie does a spectacular bump-and-grind routine so convincing that even the guard supervising the rehearsal is captivated. Queenie's song, like Mona's speech, is about loving kindness, but this time the kindness being advocated is to be lavished on a satisfactory lover in order to keep him, because "a hard man nowadays is good to find." The contrast with God's mercy is obvious.

The third source of irony is the notion of the Christmas concert itself. It is referred to briefly in Act I, scene i; Mona's quiet study of Shakespeare throughout Act I, scene ii, is said to be in preparation for the concert and is scoffed at; in Act II, Queenie and Mona rehearse their acts, and Smitty declares his love for Mona while the others are absent, attending the concert. Clearly, the motif is significant; its significance is further underlined by the fact that *Christmas Concert* was the original title of the play, according to a preliminary review of the film version in *Maclean's* (December, 1970). The idea of redemptive love, which Christmas implies, reinforces the themes of the sonnet and the mercy speech, and is ironically related to the plights of both Mona and Smitty. Love, in one form or another, is responsible for their being in prison. Mona "reached for the wrong joy stick," according to Rocky, but Mona's own story is quite different: beaten and robbed by a gang of boys, he was accused by them of making passes; the accusation was believed and he was convicted, largely on the basis of his effeminate appearance.

It is John Herbert's own story, as reported in the *Maclean's* review. Smitty is a victim of love for his mother. To help her escape her drunken brute of a husband and run away with "a nice guy," Smitty stole a car, and got caught. Love has damned these boys, rather than redeemed them. Mona attempts to escape by living in two worlds, but Smitty is drawn farther and farther into the depths. He arrives at the prison in mid-October; three weeks later he beats up Rocky, his "old man," and rises accordingly in the power structure; on Christmas Eve he declares his love for Mona and offers to be his "old man," is rejected but requited in another way, and drops from this temporary height to the depths of total damnation as he swears revenge on the whole world. One cannot doubt that Smitty is lost. The statistics of recidivism and the discrimination suffered by the ex-convict are such that his chances of survival in the world are few. Herbert denies even these chances as he makes Smitty symbolically assume Rocky's identity at the end—sitting on Rocky's bed and smoking, for the first time, the cigarettes he has rolled for Rocky—and he has built into his play a threefold denial of salvation. . . .

Ann P. Messenger, "Damnation at Christmas: John Herbert's *Fortune and Men's Eyes*," *Dramatists in Canada: Selected Essays*, ed. William H. New (Vancouver, 1972), 173-178

• •

It's a sure sign that theatres are having problems finding good new plays when the hits of yesteryear start appearing again. That does not mean a revival is bad news, but it is a simple statement of the larger fact. And so the Phoenix Theatre, no doubt banking on its considerable acclaim and prior success has brought back John Herbert's controversial tale of prison life, *Fortune and Men's Eyes*.

This time around, of course, the controversy is no more, and because the Phoenix production directed by Graham Harley contains no shocking embroidery similar to the sexual exclamation marks Sal Mineo contributed to the New York production we have a chance to see *Fortune and Men's Eyes* plain and simple. It stands up very well for the most part.

The cast assembled here to reenact the spiritually corroding and brutalizing effects of Canada's prison system is not the best, it should be pointed out straight off. It's not the worst either, but rather suffers in varying degrees, from a general inexperience. The will was all there, just not the means. Even Bryan Foster as Queenie who did the best work of the evening succumbed to the general failing of the evening—acting in extremis.

Queenie, as his name suggests, is permitted a fairly wide latitude in the histrionics department, but his task is to convince us that all the screaming meemies and mincing mean something important to him. Foster gave it all a good try, but the mechanics of his act of an act were far too obvious.

Nothing reveals flaws and virtues in a play so strikingly as inadequate performers, and if this production has some measure of success it is thanks primarily to the playwright whose lines remain pungent and whose tale is still compelling. If the actors lunge at every high point in the drama with rather frightening gusto, there nevertheless are high points to go after.

This is a special viewpoint of prison after all. Were four such symbolically rich souls ever assembled in one cell at the same time? There's Smitty (Geordie Johnson), the newest inmate, and the character in whom we can most easily observe the dehumanizing processes at work. His logical transformation from natural decency to hardened and vicious cynicism is still a riveting, powerful statement. Rocky (Bruce Bell), with his fragile machismo routine, establishes the futility of those processes. Mona (William Jackson), by far the most putupon and interesting con, brings out the essential tragedy, while good old Queenie can always be counted on for comic relief.

I suppose the homosexual motif that underscores everything was once electrifying. It certainly isn't any more. Perhaps we are more informed now and prepared to accept what happens when you force men to live together for long periods, or maybe it is simply that Herbert's intelligent handling of the problem has become more apparent. We can cavil at the degree Herbert claims it exists, but not the reality or its dramatic effectiveness.

Director Harley deserves credit for instilling the feeling of the play into his actors, even if he couldn't elicit the technique. This is a reasonably well staged affair and anyone who has never seen *Fortune and Men's Eyes* could probably do worse than drop in on this production.

John Fraser, *Globe and Mail*, 20 November 1975

• •

Lister Mr. Herbert, much of your personal experience has gone into the making of your best-known play, *Fortune and Men's Eyes*, has it not?

Herbert It was based on a morals charge and had to do with my sexual nature. Laws were applied which have since been changed, but I was then sent to Guelph Reformatory, charged with homosexuality and convicted, in 1948. I was then

51

twenty-two years of age and came from an old Norman family; my original name was John Herbert Brundage. *Fortune and Men's Eyes* is based on social conscience; I don't see how one can separate his own experience from society's circumstances.

Lister Were you surprised when this play was not only made into a film but produced in the theatres of many countries and translated into fourteen languages?

Herbert When I wrote the play I had no idea of its future. I wrote it about 1964, while I had my own theatre company which I had founded in 1960. At the time we were producing work by Genet and Ghelderode, even Dumas. When we wanted to perform my play in 1965 with my Garret Company, we had just done Genet's *The Maids* and could use some of the props. I was supporting myself as a waiter at the University of Toronto Club; one day, when I was serving Robertson Davies a drink, he asked me about my theatre company. I told him that we were temporarily out of action but that I had a play of my own which I was rather anxious to produce. When he asked me about the play I gave him a summary of it and told him that it was my version of Canadian society as a microcosm. He told me about the Stratford workshop for their young actors, and he advised me to send the play to Douglas Campbell. Campbell liked it very much and turned it over to Bruno Gerussi to direct; Richard Monette played Mona, Ken James was Queenie, and Al Koslik, who did some fine work with the Manitoba Theatre Centre later, played Smitty. It was a fine cast and a beautiful production, but when some of the top Stratford people saw the production they didn't think it was suitable for their audiences. So it played beautifully to a small audience, I was handed fifty dollars and went home.

Lister How did the film emerge out of this very low profile production?

Herbert There would have been no film if it hadn't been for Nathan Cohen, who heard about the production and asked to read the play. He then sent it on to a New York producer, David Rotenberg, who wanted to stage the play. Lee Strasberg of the Actors Studio of New York also liked it very much. It was the first time in my life that dedicated professional people had taken an interest in something I was doing. The New York production was very successful, and the film interest began almost immediately after the reviews came out. It went to several film companies, including Cinemax International and the Canadian Film Development Corporation, even to M.G.M.

Lister But the film was made on location in Canada, with Canadian actors. Wasn't it set in an abandoned reformatory in Quebec?

Herbert   It was the oldest jail in Canada, the Quebec City jail, and it had only been vacated for two weeks when we moved in. It was a terrifying building. In one of the cells, in which Rocky commits suicide in the film, an eighteen-year-old prisoner had hanged himself a couple of months earlier. This prison was like something from the Middle Ages, it had a dungeon-like atmosphere.

Lister   In recent years there has been much concern with guard brutality in prisons and suicides among juvenile inmates. Do you think that the play and, especially, the film have served as consciousness-raisers for the Canadian public?

Herbert   I don't know how much influence it had in Canada. But in the United States, while the production was running, prisoners were invited to the Tuesday night panel discussions during the year's run of the play. The Fortune Society was formed and it has become the most influential organization for prison reform in the United States; it has found much support, especially from the entertainment profession. The play has been performed in more than a hundred countries around the world now. When the film was entered in the Venice Film Festival in 1971 it received a great deal of praise from the Italian critics; the only negative word came from the Vatican press, which said that the poor lost souls should have been left to suffer in peace without this kind of exploitation.

Lister   Did other countries translate the play into social action the way the United States did?

Herbert   Australia formed a prison reform society on account of the play. Here in Canada the John Howard society saw the Fortune Society as an intrusion on their territory. I feel that they have not done much for prisoners here in Canada, we have one of the highest rates of recidivism in the world. . . .

Lister   It is surely astonishing that *Fortune and Men's Eyes* was translated into fourteen or more languages and played in a hundred countries. How does this relate to your concern with humanity and civilization?

Herbert   The consensus of opinion seems to be that I struck a universal chord; the audiences everywhere realize that people behave pretty much the same way everywhere. Instead of saying, this is about homosexuality or about prison life, they said, this is about imprisonment, about envy, destruction, masochism and sadism. All the great forces of life, as the Greeks saw them. Audiences seemed to feel that I had come to grips with some of the basic realities of life; they liked not so much the humour and wit of the play as the balance of elements and the fact that it is structured almost traditionally within the shape of the original Greek design which developed into the well-made play and influenced writers like Chekhov and Ibsen. They, too, wanted to take the ordinary, natural behaviour of people and expose the buried elements. My play's appeal has not been, as many of my detractors would have it, to a predominantly homosexual audience. If I'd had to depend on that for survival the play wouldn't have made its way to the extent that it did, in New York and elsewhere. It has lasted because it deals with perennial problems; that is also the reason why it has been translated into so many languages. . . .

Interview with John Herbert, by Rota Lister,
CD, 4:2 (February 1978), 173-176

• •

GEORGE RYGA

The Ecstasy of Rita Joe

First produced at the Vancouver Playhouse, 23 November 1967

Directed by George Bloomfield
Set and Lighting Design by Charles Evans
Costume Design by Margaret Ryan

Cast

Rita Joe	Frances Hyland
Jaimie Paul	August Schellenberg
Father, David Joe	Chief Dan George
Magistrate	Henry Ramer
Mr. Homer	Walter Marsh
Priest, Father Andrew	Robert Clothier
Eileen Joe	Patricia Gage
Old Indian Woman	Rae Brown
Teacher, Miss Donohue	Claudine Melgrave
Policeman	Bill Clarkson
Witness; Murderer	Merv Campone
Witness; Murderer	Alex Bruhanski
Witness	Jack Leaf
Murderer	Jack Buttrey
Young Indian Men	Leonard George, Robert Hall
	Frank Lewis, Paul Stanley
Guitarist	Willy Dunn
Singer	Ann Mortifee

Playwright George Ryga Thursday night peeled a cicatrice off Canadian society and showed the raw, bleeding flesh beneath.

The world première of his play, *The Ecstasy of Rita Joe*, to a capacity audience at the Queen Elizabeth Playhouse, was a thing of sorrow and anger deeper than mere tears.

It was not a smooth play. It was jerky and fragmented. It had the awkward embarrassment of a society which has had tossed in its face the body of an Indian girl beaten to death in a skid row hovel.

Ryga does not preach. He does not paint either side with the colors of martyrs or saints. He says only that there are two worlds in our society and neither understands nor accepts the other.

He offers no plan for a bridge across the chasm that exists between native Indians and white society. He simply insists that we do not keep our eyes on the horizon of a bright future without noticing this ugly chasm at our feet, a chasm he feels we are too prone to forget at the slightest excuse.

Ryga has a magnificent messenger in Frances Hyland, the Toronto actress in the title role. This superb actress created a Rita Joe off the police blotter, off the small, sordid story buried in the newspaper far behind the headlines of world events and the pictures of international society.

Every movement, every gesture, every word sketched a vivid and all-too-familiar picture of the Indian girl from a reservation in the country, bewildered and degraded in the urban society of the whites.

But the play is not only about that. It is more than Rita's bewildered failure to find a decent life.

It is about Jaimie, strongly played by August Schellenberg, equally bewildered but striking back in bitter anger. And about Rita's father, movingly portrayed by Chief Dan George, hoping against hope for the best.

And it is about misunderstanding or, rather, the absence of understanding.

The older Indians do not understand the young, they just sorrow for them. The young Indian does not understand the white man—his laws, his institutions, his social structures, his mores. And the white man certainly does not understand the Indian—not the priest, or the social worker, or the magistrate.

In that, the play reaches the proportions of Greek tragedy in its inevitability. Everyone in the play could see the disaster that approached. But no one could do anything about it.

It is a play of frustration because it ends really nowhere. Everyone in that first night audience knew it was not an isolated tragedy but an ugly pattern that will be repeated.

Wally Marsh as Mr. Homer, the man who ran the Indian centre; Robert Clothier as Father Andrew, and especially Henry Ramer as the magistrate, the embodiment of the white man's laws and morals, all contributed greatly to the strength of the piece.

The strident, intrusive voice of folk singer Ann Mortifee, with her recurring refrain which ended, "God wanted to laugh so he got me a job in the city," was still another flick on the raw conscience of society.

There was no scenery. Designer Charles Evans simply painted the stage floor to represent the butt of a cut tree, an excellent piece of symbolism.

There was a single backdrop and the glorious Miss Hyland in front of it all, making it difficult for anyone in the audience to slip neatly back into their niche in the world unknowing and uncaring about those among us who have been bypassed in the race to outer space.

I don't know if it is a great play. But if the role of the stage is to communicate, and I believe it is, Ryga and director George Bloomfield have accomplished their purpose.

Jack Richards, *Vancouver Sun*, 24 November 1967*

● ●

"And because I am happy,
    and dance and sing,
They think they have done
    me no injury
And are gone to praise
    God, and His Priest,
    and His King.
Who make up a Heaven
    of our misery."

Blake's chimney sweeper, and George Ryga's Rita Joe have much in common. At the climax of the Playhouse premiere of *The Ecstasy of Rita Joe*, there was a very still, very hushed, and very beaten audience as Rita Joe's raped and abused body was laid to its restless ecstasy on the torture of our minds.

As an emotional experience it is exhausting, as theatre it is an exercise in stark simplicity, and as a documentary of the Indian problem it is singularly one-sided.

But I do not think it intended to be any one, or even any combination of these things. It is a documentary of a bewildered and confused people, a misunderstood people with strange gods caught up in the irreconcilable conflict that arises from imposing the urban and organized values of society on simple, rural children.

Rather than produce a bridge between the treed and blue-skied river, and the sidewalk jungles, George Ryga has painted a simple, disturbing picture of life without dignity, and without hope.

When Frances Hyland laughs her memories at her father's knee, and her childhood friends play their games, her smile makes much magic of the words. She is smiling anxiously into the sky, smiling herself out of the city, and the words then make magic of her smile—black magic, for she is destroyed by her own innocence.

The play is a combination of contemporary multi-screen cinema and television techniques, a careful, planned dream-like confusion of time, truth, imagination and reality.

Rita Joe is in court—her mind is far away in her youth. The magistrate behind his desk is desperately denying today in a romantic vision of yesterday.

These are the conflicts, and they interplay fast on each other's heels till, like the nursery rhyme, "we all fall down."

And this, too, is where the production falls down, or at least stumbles. George Bloomfield has his cast weaving their words in as complicated and effective a pattern as Norbert Vesak has choreographed for their movements, but somehow their emotions lack the tight, slick, split-second timing that the technique demands.

I would like to see the play in a week's time, when the cast has had time to accustome itself to the undeniably electric atmosphere of the production and the mystery of little, naked emotions running around the Playhouse.

James Barber, *Vancouver Province*, 25 November 1967*

• •

It takes energy and effort of a sort to domesticate and render entirely uninteresting the Indian's mistreatment by white men in this country. But this is the dubious achievement of *The Ecstasy of Rita Joe*, which opened Thursday night at the Playhouse. . . .

George Ryga has written a non-play, and director George Bloomfield has given it a non-production.

What the story is supposed to be about is transparent. It is about a girl who comes to a big city from the reservation, is turned into a vagrant, a prostitute, and a thief, and finally is raped and killed. Her fate exemplifies the fate of the other Indians who pass in and out of the narrative, and of the Indians generally.

Counterpointing their misfortune is the obtuseness and inhumanity of the white man, represented by a magistrate who babbles about the law and suggests that Indians are drunk and lazy all the time, an ineffectual priest, a social worker who complains about do-gooders and a teacher who is furious with the heroine, Rita Joe, because she refuses to study Wordsworth and Omar Khayam (Fitzgerald version).

But since none of the events are dramatized, and since the characters lack color and texture even as stereotypes, nothing that happens on stage elicits any sense of credibility, even as reportage, let alone as genuine emotional experience.

The only thing real in the entire performance is the author's sense of outrage. Clearly he feels that Indians are harshly treated, and society is insensitive to its crime or to its need to make expiation. But beyond that genuine feeling of indignation, he contributes nothing of solid weight or revelation.

The one time when it seems he might—when Rita Joe's boy friend protests against the condescension of the social worker and with his friends begins to wreck the shelter—the action (for want of something else to call it) quickly shifts to something less specific.

Perhaps *The Ecstasy of Rita Joe* might have some dramatic merit as a social document told in the conventional sense, beginning with the girl's departure from home, and then following her as, step by step, she winds up in shantytown, a cruel caricature of what she was. In that event, at least, her personal story might constitute a worthwhile experience.

Certainly, considering how little she has to work with in the way of motivation, Frances Hyland draws the outline of a believable human being as she shuffles around the stage in sweater, jeans and sneakers, wrinkles her nose, and hopes against hope that she will be released from jail, that she will get a decent meal and a warm room for the night.

But Ryga tells her story instead in terms of a ponderously allegorical scheme, which requires her to be facing a trial during the first act and fighting for survival in the second act, all this on an empty multi-level stage, while a musician and a folk singer on the audience's right side dolefully go on about "sleepless hours, heavy nights" and dreams that are not so pretty.

The weaknesses of the writing are hammered home by the pedantic staging. In both acts there is an endless amount of circular movement and cinematic style lighting. The actors are encouraged to adopt poses which emphasize that they are types rather than people. In the second act, when Ryga tosses in one or two situations that might just possibly stand on their own as naturalistic drama, the actors suddenly have to switch from types to people, a reversal that only accentuates the utter formlessness of the whole approach.

As indicated earlier, Miss Hyland makes an effort to transcend the author's limitations and make Rita Joe at least true in her own right. She does not succeed because she is toiling in a void, but at least her approach is interesting. August Schellenberg has been handed an even more baffling role, as Jaimie, who announces that the Indian must fight for his dignity and status, but, except for one rather pointless outburst in the shelter, epitomizes the racist's image of the shiftless, lazy, drunken Indian.

Although Henry Ramer is given nothing but the most pedestrian lines to speak as the magistrate, at least the bafflement he registers is in character. Chief Dan George as Rita Joe's father, Pat Gage as her sister, Wally Marsh as Mr. Homer, and Rae Brown as the priest are figures. Any relation their characterizations or performances bear to literal or imaginative truth is purely coincidental.

The rationale with misfortunes of this kind is to suggest that, although the play is a calamity and the production is a scandal, those connected with it meant well and the problem is real.

But if good intentions are not good enough excuse for social mistreatment and discrimination in actual life, why should they be considered extenuable on stage?

The Ecstasy of Rita Joe only adds to the red man's sack of burdens and woes. Indefensible as art, it is unpardonable as a tract. It fails to influence the ignorant and the indifferent, and it weakens the faith of the converted. However heavily the dilemma of the Indian weighs upon him, author Ryga hasn't the foggiest idea of how to assimilate and present it in terms which are dramatically meaningful. . . .

Nathan Cohen, *Toronto Star*, 25 November 1967*

• •

Ecstasy explores this Indian despair more fully [than in *Indian*], in a more experimental form which aims to present the whole complexity of Rita Joe's destruction simultaneously, as a *gestalt* or overview which makes impossible any attempt to dismiss it as a particular tragedy avoidable by particular means. Rita Joe's destruction is a commonplace (in Vancouver alone an average of twenty such girls die each year), but, as Ryga points out, it is also

> . . . a story of people in conflict struggling at a disadvantage . . . This issue is the burning crisis of our time. It is what the Congo, Bolivia, Vietnam, are about. People who are forgotten are not forgetting. To overlook them is a dangerous delusion.
>
> *Ecstasy* makes no distinction between the rights and wrongs of a question. The conscience of each person seeing it may hopefully do this. But essentially it is a play—drama—picking up where life too often leaves off or becomes obscured by the protective shutters of civilization.

Again we may trace Ryga's main themes. The theme of the four-year-old Indian girl lost in the Cariboo, a vignette with rich implications. At a literal level, it may perhaps be Rita Joe's own child, as the magistrate suspects; it is also the desire for a family with Jaimie Paul, which is denied her; and, more profoundly, it is Rita Joe herself lost in the white man's world and, beyond her, the childlike Indians in general. It relates to the incident when Rita Joe and her sister were lost in the bush as children and Rita Joe had to act prematurely like a grownup, and also to her favourite story of how, when she herself was four years old, her father David Joe refused to sell her—unlike Clara Hill who gives her children away to welfare agencies, as the magistrate advises Rita Joe to do too.

For David Joe children are life itself (''You never forget you are alive with children''); but he is inadequate to the contemporary need for Indians to change, ''scared'' before the demand to adapt so completely. The surrogate ''parents'' with whom white society replaces him do not care personally enough: the worker priest; the unimaginative schoolmarm; and the settlement worker, Mr. ''Homer,'' who, like all Ryga's welfare agents, is contemptuous of the people he assists, wanting, as Jaimie Paul objects, to keep them as subservient children. Finally, there is the benevolent magistrate who, with all ''the rambling confidence of the detached authority,'' forgets his vision of the lost child in superficial concern for Rita Joe's health, until his questions about venereal disease become merely an excuse for isolating her further, like the ''leper'' image in *Indian*. Similarly, his assurance that ''no one is a prisoner here'' not only contradicts *Indian*'s ''We been in jail a long time now, sementos,'' but is contradicted by his own later comment that ''The obstacles to your life are here, in your thoughts . . . possibly even in your culture.'' With such complacency behind it, his warning of Rita Joe's probable fate has all the effect of a death sentence at the end.

The ''parent'' theme connects with a theme of integrity. All the false guardians are more concerned with rules than persons (''You got rules here that was made before I was born,'' says Rita Joe), and their advice is always to conform (''There is no peace in being extraordinary,'' ''There is nothing special here,'' ''We are a melting pot''). Both Eileen Joe and Clara Hill, with whom Rita Joe is implicitly compared, conform in their different ways; but Rita Joe will not, though integrity is fatal. Rather than surrender her ''child,'' she tells the magistrate, she will kill it; and towards the end she deliberately gets herself caught for stealing. It is this state of mind that explains the play's title. As for the heroes of Genet, integrity for Rita Joe entails self-destruction, so that in a perverted way her rape and death are the ''ecstasy'' of a martyr.

The theme of nature mysticism versus social reform comes in the conflict between David Joe and Jaimie Paul, the one standing for the ''old stories'' of family love and sympathy with nature which he knows no longer assure survival, the other, with his schemes for an Indian berry industry denied, wasting his energy on brawls and gestures of defiance, the farcical nature of which Ryga carefully emphasizes. The defeat of Jaimie on a social level, therefore, complements that of Rita Joe on a sexual level (though there is some danger of their association sentimentalizing the racial tragedy by making the crisis depend on Rita Joe's decision to stay in the city merely because of her love for Jaimie Paul—unless we assume that this is also her choice of Jaimie's protest over David Joe's passivity).

Ryga's distrust of self-indulgent artists appears in his use of the ballad singer. She is described by the stage directions as Rita Joe's ''alter ego,'' ''a white liberal folklorist with a limited concern and understanding of the ethnic dilemma.'' Accordingly, her songs are meant to contrast with, as much as to complement, the emotions of the heroine, and are often too romantic or too knowingly cynical. This is seen most importantly in their conflict over the fate of Jaimie Paul, where Rita Joe's stubborn optimism is countered by the singer's uncritical ballad assumption that he is doomed. This perhaps explains the rather arbitrary nature of Jaimie's death by train, which though heralded from the beginning, lacks the inevitability and appropriateness of Rita Joe's death by rape. The opposition between reality and ballad concludes the play in the contrast between the singer's description of Rita Joe's death as the flight of a bird that has found its wings and Eileen Joe's down to earth comment "When Rita Joe first come to the city—she told me . . . The cement made her feet hurt."

This Brechtian use of the singer as (partly) an alienation device, is connected with the "workmanlike and untheatrical" entrance and exit of the cast while the house lights are still on, and with two occasions when the audience is blamed directly for the Indians' plight. The object is, of course, to make them remember their real identity, so they may accept their real responsibility. However, this aim is contradicted by a much more thorough attempt to draw the audience right into Rita Joe's thought processes, to make them share in the confusion of a mind where the past is more "real" than the present and the present has the unreality of a night-mare because of hunger and exhaustion. The stage directions refer constantly to "memory," "reverie," "dream," and "mood" as keys to the sequence of events, and it is also several times emphasized that such thinking is typical of the intuitive Indian mind, which communicates by fragments of reminiscence not by abstract concepts—as in David Joe's stories of the geese and dragonfly.

Another effect of this technique is to universalize the situation, as in *Indian*. The several trials of Rita Joe are intermingled until they all seem the same trial, recurrent throughout Act I and recapitulated, with an almost musical effect, in the penultimate scene of Act II. Similarly, the climactic rape and deaths are her-alded from the first, and this circularity is emphasized by the circular ramps of the playing area (and further by the blocking of the original production). Linearly, events are linked by Rita Joe's memory and emotional associations; their casual relations become clear only by dint of repetition, like the development of a theme in music. Often the normal sequence of cause-and-effect is reversed to make this delayed understanding possible; thus, to give two examples, we learn that Rita Joe let herself get caught for stealing a sweater before we see the scene where Jaimie advocates this and forbids her to accept a charity sweater from Mr. Homer; or, more subtly, Rita Joe conveys her lost happiness by a dream of children chas-ing blown chocolate paper, and only later do we see Jaimie give her chocolate in a scene where she realizes they cannot afford to start the family she longs for. In the play as a whole there is a similar movement, from the closely intercut memories, premonitions and clues of Act I (originally called "Evidence") to the relatively simpler selection of subsequent events in Act II (originally called "Sur-vival"); so the effect is of a slowly clarifying *gestalt*, where the gradual falling of pieces into place creates a sense of inevitability.

Ecstasy is not without its faults, of course. It is perhaps overwritten, too densely interwoven for the theatre—certainly some of the detail seems unnecessary; its counterpoint of developing hints is very hard to follow, especially at first (the initial appearance of the schoolmarm, for instance); and the use of the singer is arguably too subtle. It is a play that certainly makes great demands on its audiences; yet, as the enthusiasm at Vancouver and Ottawa attests, well done it is perhaps the most moving play that Canada has produced.

Brian Parker, introduction to *The Ecstasy of Rita Joe and Other Plays*, by George Ryga (Toronto, 1971), xiii-xvii

• •

. . . *The Ecstasy of Rita Joe*, the title play in this collection of three plays . . . [*The Ecstasy of Rita Joe and Other Plays* (Toronto: New Press, 1971)], has gained Ryga his first popular recognition outside of Vancouver. *Rita Joe* was first performed in the Vancouver Playhouse in 1967 and later in the National Arts Centre in Ottawa. A good deal of its vogue comes from the fact that it is a play about Indians; this edition contains a little note by Chief Dan George about Rita Joe's ''message''.

To the majority of us who have not seen *Rita Joe*, this emphasis on the play's social significance is pretty chilling. An evening spent watching a tract about a skid row Indian girl who is convicted of prostitution, raped and killed could be appalling. It came as a surprise and revelation to me to find that *Rita Joe* is marvellously written, compelling and exciting theatre.

As the title suggests, *The Ecstasy of Rita Joe* is written as a mediaeval morality play, a salvation drama which at times is almost dance or pageant . . . The story is simple. We all know how it is going to end; the thrill is in the unfolding. The characters are symbolic, divided into good and evil as clearly as their skins are brown and white. Rita is a martyr and the play is a series of visions. A chorus of other Indians—her boyfriend, Jaimie Paul, an aged father, her sister Eileen—confronts a group of nameless white people, the Magistrate, the Teacher, the Priest, in a way which opens up profound insights. Rita Joe's trial and death take place outside time, in a state of suspended animation; the characters talk not so much to one another as at one another.

This alienated style ideally matches Ryga's theme—racial, class and personal isolation. It is a style which can easily degenerate into bombast and tedium; Ryga keeps the play moving with short scenes, music, intense lighting and bursts of violent activity. He writes concisely, economically, with a sense of character so truthful that his people are far more than stereotypes, and Ryga is, thank God, devoid of sentimentality. Yet the endless and very touching subtleties of personality are conveyed primarily in one way—through Ryga's extraordinary language.

It is so strong, so visceral and honest that it doesn't really need an actor's voice; in fact I felt while reading the play that most actors would screw it up. It is the language of Canada's Main St.—tough, blunt, profane, graphic. I hadn't really been conscious of how Canadians talk until I read *Rita Joe* and the first play in the book, *Indian*. A feeling of identity, of recognition came over me with a rush—yes, this is right, this is how we are. Ryga captures the bureaucratic pomposities, the embarrassed inarticulateness of the do-gooder, the narrow and sterile speech of the Canadian middle class. To this he opposes the wonderful speech of the Indians, full of cadence, rich images, powerful words and the reality of experience . . .

Ryga conveys the Indians' universe with the magic sense of dialect of Pinter's Cockneys and Brecht's street people. . . .

Heather Robertson, *Canadian Forum*,
51 (January/February 1972), 79-80

• •

George Ryga is a Canadian writer of Ukrainian descent, which may partly account for the pogrom-like atmosphere which distorts this study of the Canadian Indians.

It tells the story of an Indian girl, Rita Joe, who leaves her family on the reserve and follows her lover to the city where she is hauled up on a series of petty charges and finally killed in a gang rape. Starting with her appearance before a magistrate, the piece develops through a fluid series of brief scenes mingling past, present, and fantasy, and which may or may not be happening in Rita's head.

The effect is as if author and heroine are squabbling over who is to tell the story. On one side we get a level-headed view of the situation, giving due credit to the forces of white law and order for their good intentions, and acknowledging that Indians make a lot of trouble for themselves. On the other side, the plight of Rita Joe and her lover is presented as a straight cause of martyrdom at the hands of bent policemen and brutal employers.

There is no necessary contradiction here. If Indians have difficulty in adapting to white society, that merely puts their martyrdom into historical perspective and raises the question of whether white society is worth the price of adaptation. But no such resolution is attempted by Mr. Ryga, who slaps down the argument and the melodramatics side by side with the inevitable theatrical result that the melodrama comes out on top and the Canadian situation dissolves into the whole international myth of victimized minorities.

Nicholas Renton's production [Hampstead Theatre, London] knits the tiny scenes into fluent sequence, rising effortlessly into instant brawls and quite elaborate tribal ceremonies. He might have cut down on the lurid atmospherics, which detract considerably from the gritty immediacy and bleak lyricism of the writing. Whatever his structural handicaps, Mr. Ryga can certainly write dialogue. Toby Robins, alternately glowering dejectedly in the city and radiating joy in the reserve, slams Rita across with forceful simplicity. Bernard Lloyd makes something more interesting of the lover, as a man with no suitable target for his black fury: an alienated performance in both senses of that term.

Irving Wardle, *The Times*, 23 September 1975

• •

It will soon be nine years since George Ryga's *The Ecstasy of Rita Joe* had its première in Vancouver and altered the course of Canadian theatre. In Ryga, we discovered a new and formidable dramatic presence—a presence determined to sear both the social and cultural conscience of the nation.

This bitter, wounding but magnificently human play about the failure of an Indian girl to survive in a white man's world gave Canadian drama credibility it had never achieved previously.

Rita Joe acquired a reputation and a significance that extended far beyond the confines of the Canadian theatrical community. Its emergence and the reception accorded it constituted an event of national importance.

The chemistry was right. Rita Joe happened during Centennial year when Canadians were anxious to look at themselves. But the look that this play provided was an unsettling one. It punctured the euphoria and the smug complacence of Canada's birthday celebrations and declared unequivocally that all was not well with this country and its institutions.

The first Vancouver production has acquired something of the status of legend as did the performances of Frances Hyland as Rita Joe and Chief Dan George as her father. Both were to recreate the roles in subsequent productions in Ottawa and Toronto.

But it was also *The Ecstasy of Rita Joe* that—more than any other play—touched off a Canadian cultural ferment that still continues today. This was an indigenous Canadian drama that surfaced and succeeded at a time when indigenous Canadian drama was generally considered to be an aberration. It was a play of merit, worthy of production in any Canadian theatre. It prompted an awareness of the existence of other plays potentially worthy of production. It provided resounding evidence that it was not necessary for any Canadian theatres to rely solely on imported fare.

With the arrival of *The Ecstasy of Rita Joe*, Canadian plays ceased to be a rarity in English-speaking Canada. Companies dedicated to the production of new Canadian drama sprang up, and in so doing nurtured the further growth of playwriting activity. Canada's regional theatres—some of them grudgingly—found themselves forced to take the Canadian playwright seriously for the first time.

There were negative aspects to the revolution, the most regrettable being the campaign mounted by several playwrights, including Ryga himself, to force Canadian-content quota regulations on to Canadian theatres benefiting from government subsidies.

Nevertheless, the importance of *The Ecstasy of Rita Joe* cannot be over-estimated. Its appearance nine years ago was a watershed event.

It's difficult to view and judge a production of the play today outside of this historical context. Is *The Ecstasy of Rita Joe* really that good? Or was it merely significant for its time? John Osborne's *Look Back in Anger* was a breakthrough in the English theatre 20 years ago, and its historical importance cannot be denied—yet, as a play, it seems increasingly dated and contrived.

Is the *The Ecstasy of Rita Joe* similarly vulnerable? The answer is no. A new production of Ryga's play recently opened in Calgary under the banner of Alberta Theatre Projects, an organization that has done remarkable work in fostering Canadian drama.

Despite an uneven production, the play's impact remains. It's like a fist through a window, this story of an Indian girl who comes to the big city from a reservation in the Cariboo and who eventually dies horribly because she cannot cope. In explaining to us why she can't cope, playwright Ryga indicts some of our most cherished trappings of civilization. He indicts Canadian justice, education, the church—the lexicon of a Rita Joe, even God is a white man's agency—and the condescending do-gooders who profess themselves liberal by reason of fashion rather than commitment.

The conditions that prevailed a decade ago still exist today. What the play has to say about the plight of Canada's native people is as unpleasantly valid now as it was in the 1960s.

It's a play that scourges Canadian society—or, if you like, the Canadian system—for the appalling crimes, both social and spiritual, that are committed against the Rita Joes of this world.

It is Ryga's comprehension of the nature of spiritual anguish as well as social misery that makes Rita Joe more than a transitory sociological tract.

It's a brutal play, but not a brutalizing one. There are times when it throws out an urgent compelling beauty. It is a play distinctive in form and language—Ryga has used the term "ballad play" or "orchestrated composition" to describe his work—and there is a fugue-like quality in the way past mingles with present, the one commenting on the other.

The tragedy, therefore, extends beyond the sociological in this play. It presents us with a free spirit, splendidly equipped to experience and celebrate the wondrousness of life, and it shows how this spirit can be crushed by forces she cannot comprehend.

It would have helped to have had more of these qualities in Karen Austin's performance in the title role—a performance too obviously calculated in approach and too cultivated in accent to be credible. Miss Austin reminded me of a finishing-school product self-consciously indulging in a bit of uneasy slumming. Her Rita Joe would stand out like a sore thumb on East Hastings in Vancouver or Eighth Avenue East in Calgary.

On the other hand, the character presented by Dean Hawes in the role of Rita Joe's occasional lover, Jaimie Paul, would be totally credible. Hawes' brilliant performance revealed all the raw, self-destructive arrogance and frustration, the inarticulate raging at the confines of a System, the sheer despair. It was by far the best performance in the production, although Alan Robertson came a close second with his patriarchal work in the Dan George role of old David Joe.

Other performances worked intermittently—hampered in their effectiveness by the heavy-handed direction of Brian Rintoul who had an unfortunate necessity to belabour too many of his points.

Yet, in the final analysis, the play still worked. Rita Joe was a landmark in more ways than one. It was—and remains—a play for all seasons and for all peoples.

Jamie Portman, *Vancouver Province*, 12 April 1976

• •

. . . After its initial production at the Vancouver Playhouse, *Rita Joe* became one of the most widely produced English Canadian plays of the late sixties. It was chosen to open the Studio Theatre at the National Arts Centre (1968); it was broadcast on CBC television (1969), and made into a ballet (1971). It was also produced abroad in Washington, Edinburgh, and London.

Rita Joe was a seminal work in modern English Canadian drama. To begin with, it showed that there was an audience for Canadian plays which attempted to deal seriously with important social issues. The original Vancouver production provoked editorials in the local press and was the subject of an extended open-line radio programme. Secondly, it demonstrated the effectiveness of Canadian (as opposed to mid-Atlantic) speech in Canadian drama. Although there were exceptions such as the doughty Nathan Cohen, most critics felt that Ryga had succeeded in transforming the speech of uneducated Indians into a moving, even poetic, dramatic language. Finally, *Rita Joe* was a triumphant vindication of the close collaboration between writer and actors. Ryga, who had written for radio and television, had practically no experience of the stage. During the creation of the play he worked closely with director Malcolm Black and the actors. The result was a fertile interaction in which Ryga's rather amorphous poetic vision was given exciting theatrical form and reinforced by moments of psychological truth contributed by performers such as Dan George. More than any other single work, perhaps, *Rita Joe* combined the new dramatic and theatrical ideas current in the mid-sixties into a relatively accessible dramatic experience. The seventies were to see a rapid proliferation of dramatic activity in English Canada in which the happy balance of *Rita Joe* was rarely recaptured. . . .

Neil Carson, ''Towards a Popular Theatre in English Canada''
Canadian Literature, 85 (Summer 1980), 64-65

• •

DAVID FREEMAN

Creeps

First produced at the Factory Theatre Lab, Toronto, 5 February 1971

Directed by Bill Glassco
Designed by Peter Kolinsky

Cast

Pete	Victor Sutton
Jim	Robert Coltri
Sam	Steven Whistance-Smith
Tom	Frank Moore
Michael	Len Sedun
Saunders	Kay Griffin
Carson	Bert Adkins
Girl	Christina Zorro
Shriners	Bernard Bomers, Mark Freeborn

A ferociously funny play, *Creeps*, by David Freeman, has just opened at the Factory Theatre Lab at 374 Dupont St.

Directed with fine control for the most part by Bill Glassco, and given a realistic set by Peter Kolinsky, *Creeps* deals with four male spastics employed in a "sheltered workshop." Freeman's argument is that these shops are places where disabled people work without pressure from the competitive world outside.

The aim is not to provide them with useful work and decent wages, but just to keep them occupied. Freeman's further argument is that such organizations as Kiwanis and the Shriners turn charity into a circus. To show off their own philanthropy, they simply exploit the people whom they claim to be helping.

Freeman is a novice playwright, and it shows, especially in a tacked-on ending involving an official of the workshop. It's not clear whether he or Glassco contrived some very brief interludes underlining the carnival motif—perhaps they did it together—but this too detracts from the thematic propulsion. All the same, his principals are credibly delineated. The flow of conversation among them, as one argues his case for going into the cold, achieves at its best a lacerating intensity of emotional anguish.

Among the players, Victor Sutton in particular and Steven Whistance-Smith take the most perceptive and unsentimental approach to their parts. At the start, watching them and the others, observing them simulate victims of cerebral palsy who make out by themselves, you wonder how such a situation can be made endurable. Fortunately, Freeman treats his people as people, showing how in their world too there is humor in abundance, and things can be hugely comic.

The action takes place in the men's washroom, the only place where they can have some privacy from a prying woman supervisor. Director Bill Glassco works in certain bits of business that are obviously in bad taste, but never the wrong artistic taste. The language is studded with obscenities. Yet they do not damage their speakers' dignity. Better than anything else, that tells you the solid measure of Freeman's play, the serious quality of Glassco's staging.

Nathan Cohen, *Toronto Star*, 6 February 1971*

• •

New theatres traditionally begin their lives with a resounding flop and their only consolation usually is that there's no place to go but up.

But magic seems to have struck Bill Glassco's new Tarragon Theatre which opened at 30 Bridgman Ave. last night. The first play, *Creeps*, by David Freeman, is unique and absorbing, a nervy work of stature, glorious and defiant.

Like all drama that comes to mean anything for us, *Creeps* is alive with an urgent, witty, raging voice which insists on being heard and understood.

It can evoke no neutral responses. The tightness of the writing, the corrosive humor and the compassionate characterization all impose a fervor which demands an utterly committed response from the spectator as well. *Creeps* allows no escape.

To say that *Creeps* is a powerful play is to say very little. There is such enormous power implicit in the subject matter—an encounter with five victims of cerebral palsy—that one's interest shifts to the skill with which the author moves beyond the shock tactics of the premise.

David Freeman, himself a victim of cerebral palsy, probes his characters with ruthless precision, making them profoundly moving by rejecting any possibility of sentimentality.

The remarkable thing about *Creeps* is its humor—rough, vicious, crude, desperate. This isn't even the humor which skims the edge of anguish, but instead, the humor which has plunged itself absolutely into and beyond anguish, the humor which must seem its own victory when hope is so remote.

This humor makes the play both easier and more difficult for the audience.

Creeps gives us a very shrewd, hard time. Anyone who has ever flinched at the sight of a cerebral palsy victim must meet his anxieties head on. But Freeman's humor, just by meeting the crippling illness itself head on, helps us to see his characters through their own comic objectivity.

Creeps is set in the men's washroom of a workshop for cerebral palsy victims, a location where the disabled are put to work weaving rugs, folding boxes or carving wooden blocks.

Freeman provides a subtle spectrum of the disabled. Pete has a serious speech impediment as well as severely crippled hands. Sam is in a wheelchair. Tom is able to speak clearly but is severely crippled in movement, Jim is spastic, and Michael seems both physically and mentally handicapped.

Whenever they can, they meet in the washroom to share gossip, to smoke, to joke with one another, and to escape the degradation of their jobs and an insensitive female supervisor. From outside, we hear again and again the tortured screams of a female patient begging for a priest. This is the unseen Thelma, their link with ultimate mortality.

One rapidly acquires an understanding of their bitterness, their sense of helplessness and isolation.

Charity organizations can offer them free dinners and organized treats, but it comes with condescension.

They are equally critical in self-analysis. They have an instinct for their own fear, a revulsion against their own compromises. Knowing the tricks of charity, they use them to ease their comfortless lives. Dreams—carpentry, writing—have been abandoned, and yet the question persists whether survival at any cost is any survival at all.

David Freeman handles his material triumphantly. The dialogue is alert, alive, trenchant, the intense comic insight always in control, and the moments of despair and fear subtly judged.

The 75-minute play (performed without intermission) presents a flow of conversation broken only by three hallucinatory interruptions. Three times we are presented with a nightmare vision of organized charity, all rowdy, romping do-gooders and an obscenely grinning Miss Cerebral Palsy.

The performance itself it quite beyond praise. This is some of the most coherent, courageous and generous ensemble acting that Toronto has seen in years.

All the actors are remarkable, but it will be impossible to forget Victor Sutton's heartbreakingly funny Pete, Steve Whistance-Smith's edgy, moving Sam, and Frank Moore's tormented Tom.

It is hard to gauge the extent of Bill Glassco's contribution, but one suspects that it must be huge. He first directed the play at the Factory Theatre last winter. He helped David Freeman re-work it extensively, and he has put it on as the show-case to open his new theatre.

His direction is unfailingly sensitive and astonishingly tactful. His production, like the play itself, is the work of an artist.

Urjo Kareda, *Toronto Star*, 6 October 1971

• •

. . .What Freeman is writing about, from inside, is the world of cerebral palsy victims. He initiates us to it without undue compassion or pity. In the men's room of a sheltered workshop, in language always appropriate to that surrounding, he lets the frustrations, conflicts and antagonisms spill out relentlessly.

But he also tackles this world with a keen sense of absurdity, for Freeman's gift of humor is such that he can make his audience split into raucous laughter while attempting not to crumple into tears. We side with the inmates against the do-gooders who gain satisfaction from helping them and we understand, perhaps for the first time, just how much of that help is painful to the spastics.

"They don't want any creeps messing up their world, " explains one of them. "They don't want us." That point is over-emphasized in the only part of the production which doesn't work, and perhaps can't work on stage, though it might on film. Several outbursts of circus jollity from service club members splatter over the scene, perhaps for comic relief, although they reach their point in a speech of what seems gratuitous horror.

But the inmates, who are interrupted by these outbursts, have already made it perfectly clear how clown-like and inadequate are these charities to them. The outsider's role is far better expressed by the late arrival of the voluntary worker on whom most of the men depend.

He arrives after a long bull-session of bickering, bathroom jokes, and barracks-room camaraderie to try to get the men out of the washroom and back to work.

He interferes with the escape of two of the younger inmates, the two who best stand a chance at making a place for themselves outside. He is therefore the piece's villain and is strongly played for that value by Richard Davidson.

But the acting soars much higher than helpful firmness. As Pete, Victor Sutton does an uncanny job of setting up the terrible stage handicap of spastic speech then pounding through it to reveal a man of rare humor, good sense and fine spirit, capable of great hurt but not destroyed by it.

Almost matching him is Steve Whistance-Smith, the soured cynical Sam, "a horny cripple in a wheel chair." The play's attitude to sex is never sugared over, which helps give it such notable strength. Frank Moore completes a remarkable trio as the rebellious artist, too young to recognize the bonds fastened by charity.

The Tarragon is obviously no place to go for the mindless laugh but it deserves full support for the impact of its opening gun. May all its playwrights be as talented as David Freeman.

Herbert Whittaker, *Globe and Mail*, 6 October 1971

• •

There is a steady enough ring of truth to David E. Freeman's *Creeps*, not simply because the author has himself spent time in a workshop for cerebral palsy victims but because he has been able to stand back and extract from the experience the little bits of self-knowledge that hurt most.

All of the play's principal characters are bound in varying degrees, by fists locked into claws, feet that splay, torsos that heave unpredictably, lips that form words only with great deliberation. Almost all have desires—only one is hopelessly lost in an eddying private world, taking his delight in flushing toilets and munching secreted cookies—but desires they are forbidden to pursue: sex apart, they are passionate about carpentry, painting, writing.

Instead they are condemned to folding boxes and weaving rugs, though the weaving of rugs is not the worst of it. The worst of it—and here we are one and all stabbed—is in listening to the ecstatic praise of visitors exclaiming over rugs that they know, and the weaver knows, to be pure botches. Actor Steven Gilborn is affectingly honest as he thumps not for a kind word but for an ounce of candor in a world already sufficiently distorted.

Richard DeFabees summons up just as much ordinary and inevitable pain as he looks straight at the probabilities if he and a friend should bolt the institution that employs them more or less therapeutically and take an apartment for themselves, where they might write and paint for an unlikely living. Suppose they could make it, eke out a workable existence. Do they really want the neighborhood children following them down the block and calling them drunks?

The play doesn't cheat, either in the direction of sentimentality or rage. When Mark Metcalf, who would like to be an abstract painter even if one of his companions sneers at his "chicken-tracks," receives a letter of encouragement from an art critic, we are expecting a conventional "keep at it" letter routinely dictated. But when Mr. DeFabees reads the letter for him—Mr. Metcalf's hands won't stay still enough to let him do the job—it's not a casual cheering up at all. It is thoughtful, balanced, startlingly hopeful precisely because its hope is qualified. The man and his painting have both been taken seriously; the silence that suddenly falls among the rusted urinals in the men's room where friends gather for cigarettes and stolen conversation is a silence that reaches us, too. Expectations need not be great to be real.

The performances of the principals are sensitively modulated, blunt rather than begging, straightforward about the occasional treats that come along ("If the Kiwanis want to give me a free meal just to look good, it's okay with me") and about the commonplace but necessary tricks the disabled learn in the process of living together (only one of the group knows the hand-hold that will help Mr. Metcalf from the floor when he falls). If there is a serious drawback to the evening, it comes with its need to go beyond carefully distilled documentation.

Because we are watching actors, rather than genuine invalids (in *The Concept*, of a few years ago, actual or former drug addicts worked out and played out their own problems as therapy) we begin to ask for those things actors normally bring us: a dramatic line, a theatrical shaping. Author Freeman himself senses the drive and makes attempts to satisfy it.

These, unhappily, don't work out very well. The washroom bull-session is interrupted now and again with an invasion from vaudeville: clowns, brash M.C.'s, painted chanteuses and peppery football stars come on to a blare of music, offering us ironic comment (a telethon is in process to help "these poor blunders of God") and obvious contrast. But the irony is both minimal and heavy; after its first appearance it is also irrelevant, a mere act of unwanted relief for the rest of us.

And the try for tension by setting the friends against one another, sometimes violently, is inexplicable—or at least logically unexplained here. Tempers flare, mutual ridicule heats the filthy room. But the men's histories aren't developed enough to help us grasp these quick animosities and we come to feel that the outbursts are rigged simply to meet the requirements of a "show." The evening is split between a kind of gut accuracy that is immediately involving and a stab at theatrical intensification that brings the accuracy into question. Interesting, then, but not quite resolved as either document or drama.

Walter Kerr, *NYT*, 16 December 1973

• •

The four principal characters in *Creeps* are victims of cerebral palsy, as is David E. Freeman, the playwright. The dramatic setting is a men's room outfitted with the shabbiest imaginable toilet facilities, including two mottled urinals. The inmates, for that is how they view themselves, use this room to hide out from the larger premises of what they call "the spastic club."

Its official name is "the Workshop," and it is run by a rather smarmy doctor and a highly officious nurse. The atmosphere is somewhat reminiscent of the mental asylum in *One Flew Over the Cuckoo's Nest*. The men do the simplest kind of make-work. While their presence is voluntary, they are psychically crippled by a desperate need for safety and a deep fear of being objects of ridicule, scorn or pity in the outside world. One man, who wants to be an artist, makes the big break for dignity and freedom. Another, who wants to write, cannot summon up that last demanding ounce of courage. That is about all there is to the plot, and it is not really enough.

However, as a documentary slice of life about a condition and a place that physically handicapped people dread even to think about, the play is powerful, harrowing, grimly humorous and altogether absorbing. The cast, in its superbly graphic work, leaves nothing to be imagined or desired. One cannot guess from a work as distinctly personal as *Creeps* what David Freeman's precise future as a dramatist will be. But in this stubbornly resilient play, he holds up a mirror to the grievously wounded lot of some of our fellow humans and asks us to have the moral courage to face them as they are.

T.E. Kalem, *Time*, 17 December 1973

• •

. . . *Creeps*, by David Freeman, is about [a] kind of sickness, the crippling of the psyche caused by emotional dependence on a Big Mama. The plot and structure are similar to Sidney Howard's *The Silver Cord* (1926) in which two sons struggle to break away from a domineering mother; one succeeds and one fails, forever. In *Creeps*, Tom, a painter, manages to break his chains, but Jim, who wants to be a writer and whose spirit is weaker, stays home. However, Big Mama here is not a person but a kind of home, a "sheltered workshop" for the victims of cerebral palsy. Except for the two social workers, all the characters in the play are spastics. They gather in the men's lavatory at the workshop to relieve themselves literally and metaphorically: to talk, and to escape for an hour their demeaning tasks of folding boxes, sanding blocks, and weaving rugs, tasks at which they earn seventy-five cents a week. Their talk is the heart of the play; its steady beat is the life force of the story of Jim and Tom.

All the men speak of their alienation from the world outside, the physical, social, and emotional barriers that drive them together into their own community. Each man reacts differently to his condition. Pete, for example, who wanted to be a carpenter, soon found the going rough and came to the workshop with a "why not?" attitude, willing to pay for ease with humiliation. Sam, in a wheelchair, but sexually active, is bitter and destructive; he fights with every weapon he has—his urine, his vomit, his sexuality—to pay the world back for pitying him. Here I have one small quibble with the play. Sam has been in bed with Thelma, an apparently spastic girl who attends the workshop. Her parents' discovery of their act and reaction to it drove Thelma into madness. Thelma is still at the workshop, but her attendance now is somewhat improbable: she is the only female spastic there, and a mad one at that. She serves a useful purpose, always off-stage and calling out regularly, "I need a priest!", which underscores the theme of spiritual death. But she is part of the realistic level of the play—the men speak of her and shout back at her—so her presence needs to be justified more clearly.

The play has an unrealistic level as well. Three times the remembered outside world breaks into the men's lavatory with circus clowns, hot dogs, Shriners, and pretty girls. They treat the men like children and like freaks (or creeps) in their circus show, but it is really they, with their silly costumes and phony benevolence, who are the creeps. These unrealistic intrusions are good theatre, flashing colour and action across the stage; they also make a point about the inversion of reality with which these men must live.

Creeps invites comparison with John Hebert's *Fortune and Men's Eyes*, another recent Canadian play written out of its author's particularly painful experience. Yet despite the time that Herbert spent in prison, his play lacks the ring of authenticity, the genuineness of language and feeling that Freeman's play has. For Freeman himself is spastic, but *Creeps* does not tell us so. It is the artist's skill, not simply his experience, that makes the play good . . . .

Ann Messenger, *Canadian Literature*, 59
(Winter 1974), 102-103

• •

. . . The set of *Creeps* is naturalistic. When the play opens, Pete is occupying a stall in the washroom. Michael enters and begins flushing toilets, chuckling to himself, enjoying a trick he is playing on Pete as he refuses to answer to "Who is it?" Michael is mentally retarded, about 18, and obsessed with flushing toilets. Almost immediately, the entrance of Tom rescues Pete. Tom, a painter of abstract art, has come to discuss the workshop with Pete; he can't "hack it much longer," and is considering quitting. Sam, a diaplegic whose body is dead from the waist down, apart from his genitals, and is thus confined to a wheelchair, has now joined the others. Sam's intense cynicism and rage are straightway apparent; he is derogatory about Tom's art—"Chickentracks. That's what you paint, Tom. Chickentracks"—and bitter towards the whole world—"The only way you're going to get to use that talent of yours, Tom, is to give someone's ass an extra big juicy kiss." Jim's appearance completes the group and makes present all necessary elements for the conflict.

The writing in *Creeps* is tight, controlled, as is its structure, so the tension is always maintained. The divisions in the structure are clearly marked; they are divisions which describe stages in the discussion, rather than in the action, though in each case an action propels one division into the next. There are three divisions or movements, the first ending with Saunders' knock on the door, and punctuated internally with the entrance of Saunders in the washroom, and the third ending with the arrival of Carson. Each of the movements proceeds on an increasing plane of tension. Though there is little forward movement in the action (in fact the play is static, with almost no action at all), the dialogue is anticipatory of the key actions. From [early in the play], when Pete says, referring to Saunders' earlier washroom experience with Rick and Stanley, "No, Saunders won't come in here now. Not after a shock like that," the audience knows with certainty that Saunders will appear; equally certain is the actualization of Saunders' flat assertion: "Right! Mr. Carson will be here any minute." Thus a framework of certainty surrounds the discussions of the spastics, though the outcome of the conversations is not equally certain—we do not know for sure that Jim will stay or that Tom will leave, but the enormous pressure exerted by the external certainties forces the discussion to increasing intensity, especially after the climactic shocking of Saunders; time is at a premium.

Freeman strictly observes all three of the unities in *Creeps*. The play, both visually and orally, is heavily naturalistic, a slice of life intimately observed and vicariously shared by the audience. Its length is exactly the same as that actually required for the events described; its washroom setting is totally realistic, its fixtures functional; the acting style it requires is imitative of actual spastic behaviour; its language is raw gutter talk, savage though at times beautiful. Only the three non-realistic sequels, the two circus-party mimes and the penetrating advertisement for the spastic brain by the freak-show barker, save the play from complete naturalism, and these both sharpen the focus of the play's satire and provide the needed relief from the sordidness of the washroom. Freeman demonstrates in this play a gift for knowing when and how to offer relief while simultaneously intensifying the thrust of his argument. *Creeps* is at times hilariously funny, not so much in what actually transpires on the stage as in description of what has transpired elsewhere. Equally memorable as vivid verbal pictures are Sam's description of himself in bed with Thelma and his reading of the "banana" passage from Tom's pornographic book; tragedy and comedy constantly spill over into one another.

No characterization is subtle or complex. Each is representative of a type, his function being to contribute to the statement Freeman is making in the play. Pete, Jim, Sam, Tom and Michael present sort of a composite image of paraplegic victims; Saunders and Carson are symbolic of "the system," of conservatism, and especially of "authority." Considerable liveliness and vitality emerge from the spastic portraits, whereas the authoritarian figures are predictably noted for their lack of these characteristics. None of the characters develops during the course of the play, but each is clearly delineated.

Pete, 37, is the unofficial leader of the spastic group, keeping order, calming tensions. Pete is no fighter. Once he had dreams of becoming a carpenter, but the experience of having doors shut in his face encouraged him to choose the easier way. Now, reconciled to life in the workshop, he gladly accepts offerings from the Shriners, believing this the only practical course:

> I ask myself what am I supposed to be fighting? What do these jokers want me to do? The answer is they want to make life easier for me. Is that so bad? . . . . They just want me to enjoy life, and the government even pays me just for doing that. If I got a job, I'd lose my pension. So why have I been breaking my ass all this time looking for a job? And I got no answers to that . . . . The only price I gotta pay is listening to old lady Saunders giving me hell for not weaving her goddam rug.

By deciding to accept what the system offers while refusing to co-operate with it, Pete has got rid of his frustration while retaining some of his self-respect and is therefore in a position to referee the conflicts which arise among the others (Michael, as a retardee, is of course exempt from the psychological conflict).

Sam has accepted nothing; he simply seethes with hatred towards the system (an all-embracing label, in his thinking); his revolt, understood only in terms of revenge, is total, expressing itself repeatedly in verbal and physical shock tactics. The roots of his anger lie deep in parental attitudes towards him in childhood, his mother assuming an air of martyrdom and his father a "where have I failed?" attitude towards an embarrassment of their own breeding. The logical revenge now is to compound the embarrassment—thus Sam deliberately vomits over his parents' dinner table when the "boss" is being entertained. By extension, society as a whole is guilty and must be punished, so Sam, having urinated into a dixie cup in a theatre restroom, leaves the cup on a sink instead of disposing of it immediately, thereby offending the nose and sensibility of the next patron.

Underlying much of Sam's rage is a basic sexual frustration; he is as obsessed with the sexual as Michael is with flushing toilets. A "freudian slip" brings forth from him "physical [for physio] therapist"; after all, he adds, perhaps ironically, "They're all after my body." Most of his verbal taunts are sexual in nature, e.g., to Tom: "Hey, I bet he's gonna get laid and he doesn't know what to do"; to

Saunders: "Hey, be careful, he's [i.e. Carson] got one too"—and he derives immense delight from teasing the matron with the possibility that the "Rick and Stanley" episode may be repeating itself in the washroom. Too, the escapades which have earned him most notoriety among his fellows are the "feeling up" of a Rotarian's daughter at a picnic and the deflowering of Thelma, whose nerve-wracking, wearing wail, "I need a priest," punctuates the play at intervals.

Jim is the outsider in the group; Sam calls him "Mommy's boy" and "white nigger." The trouble is that Jim licks stamps in the office *on salary* and is president of the Spastic Club—in other words, he co-operates with the system. Unlike the others, Jim has been to university, earned a degree, and had aspirations to become a writer. He has employed his talents on behalf of the disabled when he "wrote all that crap for the paper about how shitty it was to be handicapped in this country," but now he has given up the struggle and is, according to Sam, eager to "kiss the first ass you see," apparently satisfied to write articles for "The Sunshine Friend" and to plan trips to the Science Centre and the African Lion Safari as well as finger painting contests and parties for the Spastic Club. Like the others, he has found the excuse to justify himself: "But you can't change things until you're in a position to call the shots." His philosophy places him in direct opposition to Sam who, because he cannot bear to wait "99 years" until the Jims manoeuver themselves into positions of power, must wreak what vengeance he can now (the essential activisit-passivist controversy present in all movements for change). Since Jim has not been to a bull session since his "promotion," his unexpected visit to the gang is cause for suspicion. Is "Cinderella" spying for Saunders? Apparently yes, as Saunders' knock on the door in search of Jim indicates. Jim is thus forced to make a choice, either to join the rebels or to obey authority. "Yes, Miss Saunders, I hear you, but I'm on the toilet at the moment," casts the die temporarily in favour of rebellion and smooths the way for the conversation to develop through discussion of the opposing attitudes of Jim and the others; if Pete is the referee, Jim is the pivot-point off which Sam and Tom bounce.

Tom is the only one of the group who has not yet found his niche, who has so far been unable (or unwilling) to find a mode of self-justification which would enable him to cope with the workshop. He is at a different point in the cycle of struggle-compromise which the others have undergone; he has yet to discover how hard it is to survive on the outside. Tom, besides his penchant for pornographic literature, reads Edgar Allan Poe, whose stories have served to crystallize his dissatisfaction into a haunting fear of being buried alive. He is determined to try to succeed as an artist—we have no idea how good he is, though he has had one complimentary letter from an art critic. Except for Pete, no help is available from his peers; Sam says Tom should stick to his regular diet of reading material, Jim that he has "illusions of grandeur" and must come down to earth sooner or later." Nevertheless, Tom is strong enough to maintain his determination in the face of all opposition, and we admire him and wish him well as he leaves to enter a new phase of his life outside the protective atmosphere of the workshop.

Miss Saunders, the matron, and Mr. Carson, the manager of the workshop, are the only other characters who appear on stage, and little can be said of them since their appearances are so brief. Saunders is easily shockable, a cold, rigid, domineering character, the sort who, lacking inner strength, compensates through threats and bossiness, consequently becoming a target for mischief. Carson is simply the stereotype establishment authoritarian figure of the late sixties, his one brief appearance vindicating Pete's belief that his chief motive is to keep the ''niggers'' in their places. The narrowness of these two portraits seriously limits the play's visions, but more could not be handled within its structural pattern. Freeman can see from only one point of view, that of the disabled; he cannot yet distance himself sufficiently to be sensitive to the motivation on both sides. The social problem is more complex than the play implies.

On the one level, *Creeps* could be read as part of the literature of the anti-establishment movement of the late 60's, mostly because the portrait of Carson is dangerously close to being a cliché; the work then becomes another expression of youthful discontent with ''the System'' as system. It would not be difficult to sum up the play as a sort of manifesto of sexual frustration, an early expression of part of the problem of *Battering Ram*, because so much of the conversation is sexual in nature, or to deposit it among the literature of lust and excrement because of its vocabulary. *Creeps* has been compared with *Waiting for Godot*, in that both supposedly involve an existential waiting for someone or something, but *Creeps* is in a way even more pessimistic than *Godot* in that all except Tom have resigned themselves to an acceptance of the status quo and are thus no longer actively waiting. In no other way can the two plays be compared, because where *Creeps* is exclusively one-dimensional, *Godot* is multi-dimensional. Freeman is savagely satirizing those service clubs who seek to ''help'' the spastic without recognizing him as a thinking, feeling human being within a deformed shell. Relentlessly, unremittingly, he portrays the effects of society's inhumane treatment on the spastic. Depressingly, the result is that the little society within the workshop is but a microcosm of the larger one outside it, yet another ''dog eat dog'' environment. The members of the workshop community are totally insensitive to one another's feeling; there is no refuge from the harsh realities of the outside world, no comfort to be had. Jim is maligned for being different; the artist is neither appreciated nor encouraged. Most find it easier to find fault with the system than to look for a way to mend it, so there is no banding together to achieve a goal, nor is there a goal. Though they object to parties and folding boxes, Pete reads comics and the whole group enjoys childish pranks. There is no such thing as dignity acquired through adversity; if it were not for Tom's determination to try and the possibility that he might succeed, Freeman's vision would be totally pessimistic; as it is, the door is left slightly ajar for redemption, as the lights fade to the sound of Thelma's sobbing and Sam's laughter . . . .

Mary Elizabeth Smith, "Freeman's *Creeps* and *Battering Ram*: Variations on a Theme," *CD*, 4 (Spring 1978), 25-33.

• •

WILLIAM FRUET

Wedding in White

First produced at the Poor Alex Theatre, Toronto, 2 February 1972

Directed by Doug McGrath
Set Design by Lillian Sarafinchan
Costume Design by Carol Carrington
Lighting Design by Tom Schweitzer

Cast

Jim	Antony Parr
Mary	Nan Stewart
Jeanie	Sam Langevin
Sandy	Leo Phillips
Jimmie	Paul Bradley
Billy	Doug McGrath
Dollie	Bonnie Carol Case
Sarah	Doris Petrie
Hattie	Linda Houston
Barnie	Colin Shaw
Scotty	Charles Hayter

It doesn't often happen that a play with as much competent and even excellent acting—or with as many graceful lines of dialogue or apt observations as has *Wedding in White*, the play by Bill Fruet that opened last night at the Poor Alex— leaves you feeling so disappointed, cheated and even used.

Nor does it often happen that a play whose rudimentary plot is telegraphed early in the first act fails as much as did Fruet's to provide a complication or turn which might unsettle the viewer's self-confident reading of the writer's intent.

Yet for all these perversities it is hard to find a play that would continue to entertain as consistently as did *Wedding in White*. Screenwriter Fruet's smooth first essay in writing for the stage is excellent in its brief, film-like scenes, a bit shaky in its three separate acts, and gelatinous and much like a soap opera by the time the entire work is done.

As a collection of vignettes from the life of a Prairie family in wartime, *Wedding in White* is deft and acute, even it if does sacrifice the integrity of the father, Jim (Antony Parr) and mother Mary (Nan Stewart), in favor of quick and easy laughs that are provided by standing any situation on its head the moment it's been mooted.

And much as it's tempting to suggest that the play, directed by Doug McGrath, is long on substance though lacking in form, it would seem more reasonable at the disappointing end to conclude that Fruet chose to write not so much a play as a work in which he could make the asides, the smart lines, without being responsible for the fate of his own characters.

Jim and Mary are concerned with the fate of their daughter, Jeanie, who seems to them of little use to any serious-minded young man after her one and only night of indiscretion with her brother's army buddy.

Jim and his Legion Hall friends provide Fruet with a large target as they invent the wedding in white as the means of saving the family honor, but the picayune darts that can be tossed at the concepts of honor, virginity, or the hypocrisy of righteous fathers who are actually male chauvinist pigs, are not matter enough on which to hang a three-act play.

The production proceeded at a headlong pace that left one gasping for breath. One hoped for a slower expository scene which wouldn't need stage business for actors raring to go, but with nowhere—not in plot or their own characters—to escape from situations so familiar that we can taste them.

And that's the frustration *Wedding in White* creates. That dialogue should be so apt, or Sam Langevin could be so young and innocent as Jeanie, or Leo Phillips so masterful and hilarious as the buffoon, Sandy, and that their efforts should yield so little besides facile, fashionble laughs, seems a travesty when so many plays are begging for half as much.

Had McGrath managed to keep a better rein on some of the exuberant scenes, which were over-acted to within an inch of ham, Jeanie's predicament might have stood out with more vigor. But he couldn't plug the play's gaps, and keep one from begging for a quick divorce from this hasty *Wedding in White*.

Kaspars Dzeguze, *Globe and Mail*, 3 February 1972*

• •

William Fruet's play *Wedding in White* opened at the Poor Alex Theatre last night under Doug McGrath's direction, and a fascinating production it turned out to be. . . .

Fruet's play is pure, clean, gutsy drama centering about an ignorant, lower-middle class family in Western Canada near the end of World War II.

The 16-year-old unmarried daughter becomes pregnant, pretty hot stuff for the mid-40s. It's still hot stuff in 1972, through Fruet's poignant characterization not only of a rather lost, simple bunch of people, but of the period which condemns them all to an ugly emptiness.

In setting this ugly, cluttered mood, Lillian Sarafinchan's ghastly set and Carol Carrington's horrendous costumes (not even Stratford can touch her) are perfectly marvellous.

The cast is excellent in its superbly unmannered acting. The stage is not "electrified" by technique or solemnly held pauses. The people on it are real, and it is rare moment indeed in our theatre when we are confronted not by actors doing their bit, but by human beings going about their lives. . . .

It's really unfair to single out any of the cast in *Wedding in White* since ensemble playing is the key to its ultimate theatrical success.

But Nan Stewart as the mother is so terrific that one just wanted to tip-toe onto the stage to tell her not to cry.

Doug McGrath's direction is smooth and efficient. He doesn't allow himself to get in the way of the production, and this earns him full marks for realism.

The scenes build very well, although more attention might have been given to building the acts towards their climaxes. But this is partly a flaw in the construction of the play itself. If Fruet could find a way to fewer, more lengthy scenes, he might ultimately have a more satisfying play. Some of the scenes are so short that we are cut off just as we are getting heavily involved.

But the writing in its simplicity and honesty attains a kind of poetry that rivets our attention because we are put under the illusion that we are watching real people.

It is smashing theatre, and it should also make a smashing film.

John Palmer, *Toronto Star*, 3 February 1972*

• •

Wedding in White, as written by William Fruet, is a superb piece of theatre. *Wedding in White*, as presented by the Manitoba Theatre Centre in the Warehouse Theatre, is an outstanding production.

Wedding in White deals with a particular brand of male chauvinism which was really a way of life in the early '40s in Canada. It centres around one family and their daughter. As the plot slowly unfolds, it reveals the horrible and disgusting side of people who on the outside are "ordinary folk." It shows them in all their drab and filthy pettiness; thinking only of themselves and not how their selfish actions will affect the people around them.

Jeanie Dougal, the daughter, was played by Nancy Beatty. Miss Beatty was slow to warm to the intimate audience Wednesday evening, but came into her own in the second and third acts. In the first act, she seemed unreal, possibly because of her difficulties with the characterization. She was shy, yes, but when she was approached by a young man, she showed no surprise or emotional response. In the last two acts, however, Miss Beatty had complete control of her emotions and developed a successful characterization from the printed word.

Jim Dougal, the father, was played by Richard Farrell. Mr. Farrell was cast beautifully as the domineering male figure in the household. His stature and his mannerisms were in tune with the character. One felt he might just react the same way the character did. It is to Mr. Farrell's credit that he was able to create such realism on stage. He was believable and instilled a real sense of horror and disgust as his role unfolded.

Mary Dougal, the mother, was played by Doris L. Petrie. Miss Petrie won the best supporting actress award in Canadian films recently for her portrayal of the mother in the film version of this play. Wednesday evening, Miss Petrie was realistic in her emotional responses and her reactions. She carried the role well with the proper amount of sad-eyed dreaminess and faraway dreams of grandeur required of the character. It is easy to see why critics felt she merited the award. Wednesday evening, she was superb.

Leo Phillips, as Sandy, was a delightful but strong characterization. Mr. Phillips was in character at all times and added a great deal of dimension to the production.

Sue Helen Petrie as Dollie was superb. She has a good control of her emotions and handled the role with great aplomb . . .

Mr. [Alan] Dobie [director and designer] has rehearsed his actors and set crew to perfection. It is said an amateur rehearses until he gets it right; a professional rehearses until he can't get it wrong. Wednesday evening it was professionalism all down the line. The characterizations were sharp and clearly defined. The sets were well handled and dressed with just the proper Spartan effects. The set changes were beautifully handled and a real work of art in themselves. . . .

The lighting by Ken McKay was subtle and well handled. The slide presentations were excellent for setting the stage and creating a link from scene to scene. . . .

Peter Crossley, *Winnipeg Free Press*, 10 May 1973

• •

Wedding in White properly was begun in 1943, when William Fruet was ten years old. In his own words, ". . . this young girl was wheeling a baby buggy down the street, and this very old man was with her. I knew it was not her father or grandfather. I knew it was her husband just by the way he walked with her, and I knew there was a tremendous imbalance. Years later I brought it up to my mother and she revealed the whole story to me." The story, in fact, was that the girl had been raped by a soldier and forced, for the sake of her family's reputation, into a marriage with a "respectable" substitute—an old and sloppy grotesque. . . .

[Rolf Kalman], Preface to William Fruet, *Wedding in White,*
A Collection of Canadian Plays, vol. 2 (Toronto: Simon & Pierre, 1973)

• •

DAVID FRENCH

Leaving Home

First produced at the Tarragon Theatre, Toronto, 16 May 1972

Directed by Bill Glassco
Set Design by Dan Yarhi and Stephen Katz
Costume Design by Vicky Manthorpe

Cast

Mary Mercer	Maureen Fitzgerald
Ben Mercer	Frank Moore
Billy Mercer	Mel Tuck
Jacob Mercer	Sean Sullivan
Kathy Jackson	Lyn Griffin
Minnie Jackson	Liza Creighton
Harold	Les Carlson

. . . *Leaving Home* . . . is set in the fifties and smacks of autobiography. Its young man, Ben, sounds very like the author as a young victim of an impossible father. Such public accusation is too often more satisfactory to the writer than the viewer, but not so in *Leaving Home*. For all of its characters have the quality of theatrical life. Each one pulls its weight as two Toronto families clash before a wedding rehearsal. Being Irish Protestant and Catholic, they don't spare each other.

French has the skill to make this mundane upheaval interesting. It is so because the characters are so well matched. While we sympathize with the son as victim, we also cherish the father's destructive passion. The noble mother, scared kid groom-brother, tragic little bride and her brassy mother, even her silent stud, all prove worthy of our attention, understanding and laughter.

A forced marriage brings Minnie Jackson into the house of an old flame, Jacob Mercer, because it is their teenagers who must be wed. Mercer is a man who combats his own sense of failure by lashing out at others. His greatest success at this has been with his son, Ben. Shielding Ben from Jacob's comic rage, Mary Mercer has furthered the split.

When the marriage is no longer necessary, the two mothers take opposite sides on whether it should take place. Then comes the second bombshell: Ben is planning to flee the home, too.

The wedding rehearsal eventually does take place, but Jacob stays away, destroyed by the final attack on him by first Ben, then Mary. . . .

Sean Sullivan drives the play to its heights as the furious Jacob, whipping him from a jig and a song to the high old anguish of self-destruction. Frank Moore bides his time as Ben with sensitivity until the outcry of a lifetime. Maureen Fitzgerald is ready when that time comes to be the goddess of the household, after a somewhat coy start as Mary. Mel Tuck mirrors the groom's every reluctance.

Formidable opposition came from Liza Creighton, the splendidly vulgar Minnie, supported by Les Carlson, who makes himself the audience favorite without a word spoken. And as the bride, Lyn Griffin brings true pathos to this most welcome domestic brawl.

Herbert Whittaker, *Globe and Mail*, 17 May 1972*

• •

On the Tarragon Theatre's beautiful poster for David French's play *Leaving Home*, there is an image which will be difficult to forget. In a poignant photograph by John de Visser, two small children stand on top of a hill with a small Newfoundland village behind them and the sea itself beyond. They stare out at us as if into a profound unknown, their faces expressing an apprehension modified with hope.

That photo has almost nothing to do with the play itself—which opened last night and proved so memorable—but the image of that watchful, waiting stare echoes through it. It rhymes with the generating impulses of the Mercer family which David French presents so vividly and fearfully in this exceptional work.

That slight fear, plus an intuition for survival, brought Jacob and Mary Mercer, with two sons, from Newfoundland to Toronto, in 1945, with hopes of recharging aspirations which had eluded them in the east. But in spite of hard work and rigorous self-improvement, the Mercers find, in the mid-'50s events of the play, those hopes deflected. It is at the very moving conclusion of the play that the poster image returns most hauntingly, as Jacob and Mary sit speechless, staring at an unknowable future, now mature, even aging, versions of the children on the hill.

David French selects the crux of the dream's collapse the evening before Billy, the youngest son (Mel Tuck), at 17, is to marry his pregnant, Catholic girlfriend Kathy. Ben, the only slightly older brother (Frank Moore), confesses to his mother, almost parenthetically, that he too is anxious to leave home.

The girl's abrupt miscarriage removes the immediate need for a wedding; Mary is quick to collect back her son, but the girl's sluttish cheap mother—herself once Jacob's girlfriend—insists that the marriage take place to save her own pride. In the ugly, bigoted, vehement quarrel, Jacob learns that he isn't losing only one son, but both.

The final sequences begin with father, mother and the older son each sitting in emotionally solitary confinement in the cramped living room. Their words shift harrowingly from laughter to anger to brutality, and in the final isolation from crushing defeat to a tiny, important sliver of affirmation.

By the end the point of view has shifted from the two sons' departure to the parents who have been abandoned, perhaps justifiably. Jacob (Sean Sullivan) remains proud, bull-headed, dangerous, infuriating, fiercely supported by Mary (Maureen Fitzgerald), possessive, fractionally condescending, defiantly visionary. The whole process of their lives has been a departure from one uncertain home after another, to others, even more tenuous.

Leaving Home springs from a traditional form, and one could quickly enumerate any number of models for it. But a genre play cannot be dismissed when the writing is as mature, intelligent and compassionate as here.

This is a play of remarkable dynamic life. The lacerating quality of inter-family warfare carries both superb comedy and powerful emotional force, for the very reason that only family members are so acutely aware of one another's spheres of vulnerability. About the Mercers, David French never lies.

We feel our knowledge of the Mercers so strongly that it is slightly disappointing that the outsiders aren't drawn in similar depth. The sketchy quality of Kathy and her awful mother seems to have caused Lyn Griffin, as the girl, to play attitudes rather than to examine the subtext, and Liza Creighton, as her mother, to shove her scenes very hard. There is also the mother's friend, a morose undertaker, who, in Les Carlson's brilliantly comic performance, throws the play quite off balance. I think the notion of keeping him speechless is too improbably gimmicky; perhaps French, Carlson and director Bill Glassco could collaborate to make him less riotously intrusive.

Those reservations apart, there is nothing but awe for Bill Glassco's glorious, heartbreaking production. He subtly evokes a low-key, realistic symbolism out of the most ordinary facets of everyday life, and enriches the play with amazing detail. Watch the lovely way that Jacob, in mid-tirade, slips in a "Thanks" for having his shoes polished, or the way that Billy, unexpectedly freed from the threat of marriage, develops a huge appetite, or the way that Mary, at the end, finds a tiny physical gesture of wary contentment.

The four main performances are incomparable. Frank Moore's Ben has an agonizingly unspoken awareness of his own pain, and Mel Tuck's Billy—a definitive vision of mid-'50s youth—is wrenchingly accurate. Maureen Fitzgerald beautifully takes us along through all Mary's thoughts and confusion.

And Sean Sullivan, as Jacob, gives a performance which simply could not be equalled anywhere. Brawling, tormented, self-defeating, the anger always a beat ahead of the thinking, Sullivan's contribution is extraordinary. Like the actors who play his family, like the Mercers themselves, like David French's marvellous honesty, this has the difficult, urgent complexity of truth.

Urjo Kareda, *Toronto Star*, 17 May 1972*

• •

David French's *Leaving Home* was, along with David Freeman's *Creeps*, one of the successes of the 1971-72 season at the Tarragon Theatre in Toronto. Both are naturalistic dramas that stage better than they read. The stronger of the two, *Creeps*, manages both sympathy and humour towards the spastics who are its subject; they are three-dimensional human beings whose problems, though special, are recognizably related to *la condition humaine*, and this is a considerable achievement. The play's principal weakness is its unsympathetic portrayal of Carson, the director of the "sheltered workshop," who appears late (better never?) and is surprisingly flat—almost a caricature. Here the author's (and the play's) point of view about the authoritarian Carson is too egregiously that of the spastics, and whereas their reaction to him is understandable, it is too limited to serve us as a *total* perspective on such a character.

Leaving Home has an analogous problem. Both Freeman and French are young playwrights who seem to have difficulty treating father-figures with understanding. In *Creeps* it is only a minor problem, for Carson is a minor character—though he symbolizes the home that needs leaving. But *Leaving Home* is much more seriously marred by a failure of authorial sympathy for the *pater familias*, Jacob Mercer. It is his home that Ben (18) and Bill (17) are trying to leave throughout the play, as Tom and Jim are trying to escape Carson's in *Creeps*. In outline, at least, Jacob is not an unattractive character: a kind of Newfie hardhat—Archie Bunker with a dash of Zorba the Greek. At fifty, after a hard day's work, he can sing, dance, and court his wife with the Song of Solomon. Even his bigotry has a comical innocence:

> How many drunks you suppose is wearing Roman collars? More than the Pope would dare admit. And all those thousands of babies they keep digging up in the basements of convents. It's shocking.

But the play is so "loaded" against Jacob that it becomes impossible to take his side, difficult even to take him seriously. Now this is a problem, for a drama requires tension, which needs a rough balance of opposing forces for a while, at least. But here the scales are constantly weighted in favour of one side, and hence the drama suffers. French's identification with Ben is flagrant. Setting the action "in the late fifties," when *he* was about 18, he makes Ben articulate, reasonable, intelligent, liberal, and generally *right*; the heaviest father would be hard put to find fault with this:

> Dad, will you listen to me for once? It's not because home's bad, or because I hate you…I just want to be independent, that's all. Can't you understand that?

Of course we can— only Jacob cannot. But then Jacob is inarticulate, unreasonable, narrow, and wrong, as a rule. First he lies to the family, saying there is no whisky in the house and pulling out the screech to test his sons' "virility". Later, when he realizes Ben really means to leave, Jacob "charges into Ben's bedroom" and begins impetuously hurling personal effects onto the living room floor. After three such trips French pulls the rug, as Ben coolly comments: "I don't want to spoil your fun, Dad, but so far all that stuff belongs to Billy." While Jacob is reeling from the blow, he absorbs two more. First French hits him with a scene direction: "Jacob stares at the scattered records and shirts, alarmed." Then Mary, his attractive wife, lets fly:

> Now you've done it, boy. Will you sit down now? You're just making
> a bigger fool of yourself the longer you stand.

Jacob's only halfway successful relationship has been with Mary, but throughout the second half of the play they round on each other. Mary is the play's most sympathetic character, and when she criticizes or refutes or gives the lie to Jacob, we listen: "I have no sympathy for you. You brought this all on yourself." Agreed, and what the play needs is a sympathetic father, who can counterpoise Ben as Pierre Gravel balances André in Gratien Gélinas's *Yesterday the Children Were Dancing*. Near the end Mary tells the "slightly incredulous" Jacob that Ben supported the family with his own money during the previous year while Jacob was in the hospital. Jacob is suitably flabbergasted, but the whole *deus ex machina* misses the point. The problem is not to make Jacob appreciate the likeable Ben, but to make us like Jacob.

Leaving Home would be a good effort by a bright undergraduate. Though late-adolescent in tone and perspective, it does give shape to a story that is common and important, several of the characters are genuine creations, and much of the dialogue is workable. But French is 34; he has been writing television plays for ten years. Perhaps that's the trouble: working in the different and, I think, less demanding medium of TV may have retarded his development as a legitimate playwright. Certainly he should be further on. When we hear from him again, as we certainly shall, we have a right to expect work of broader sympathies and firmer balance.

R.W. Bevis, *Canadian Literature*, 59 (Winter 1974), 106-108

• •

The lack of the tragic hero in modern drama has become an accepted fact. One no longer seeks, or expects, the noble character whom Aristotle described, whose fall from great heights is balanced by his spiritual strength and growth, whose suffering is in excess of his deserts, but whose fall is due, in part, to his own character. The tragic hero, victim of fate and of himself, carrying within him the seeds of his own doom and of his spiritual triumph, the Prometheus of Aeschylus, the Oedipus of Sophocles, the Hamlet of Shakespeare, has been replaced in modern drama by a series of victims of accident, society or heredity, a series of little men whose fall (if there is one) is not far, whose dignity is questionable, and whose insights—introspective or otherwise—are negligible.

David French, no less than many another modern playwright, such as Miller, Osborne, Williams, or Pinter, presents us with the little man, with the victim rather than the victim/victor of heroic stature. It would be wrong, however, to assume that French is merely following the path developed by these other writers, for he utilizes the "hero as victim" in his own unique way. Although *Leaving Home* is David French's first [stage] play, it reveals striking control and a powerful sense of the dramatic. In fact, one could easily argue that *Leaving Home* has become such a successful and popular play because French has proved himself capable of revitalizing the now old and weary theme of man as "victim."

Jacob Mercer, the central character of interest in *Leaving Home*, is not merely the victim of accident, society or heredity, but a weak man who not only courts, but virtually indulges (even wallows) in victimization. "I'll give you a revelation!" he declares angrily to his wife, "I'm just a piece of shit around here!" Jacob continually spits, curses, taunts, cajoles and argues until he gets his own way, until he forces others to alienate him from themselves, until, finally, even his wife in frustrated outrage can only scream at him, "You don't know when to stop, do you? You just don't know when to call a halt....You'd go on until you brought your whole house tumbling down."

Leaving Home is a drama of a man who cannot allow his children to leave, who must, unwittingly, force them out of the home by compelling them to reject him as a father and even as a man. Jacob Mercer, like most modern protagonists, lacks a redeeming sense of self, of order, and of harmony. At best, he responds with inner feelings and emotions which, although they are honest and direct, often betray him because he cannot control them, or understand them. Confounded by life and its often ambiguous demands upon him, Jacob finds that even such natural inner urges as love and the desire for children somehow trap him, somehow reduce him, and he can only demand of his wife that she admit "I don't count, I've never counted. Not since the day [his sons] were born."

Sensing that he has somehow been victimized by life, realizing that he doesn't "count", Jacob, in a desperate and pathetic attempt to gain some shred of dignity and self-importance, courts victimization, demands victimization, and, finally, destroys everything which might save him from it. Jacob, to a large degree, appears in the first act of the play as the very personification of "a caricature of discomfort"—he simply doesn't seem to fit into social clothing—and he is so insecure of his own worth that anything and everything can ruffle his mind and manner, bringing him to irrational outbursts of anger and frustration. Finally, incapable of confronting himself directly, he unwittingly elects victimization, even self-victimization, in a desperate and confused attempt to retain at least some measure of dignity.

In order to outline both the movement and the significance of Jacob Mercer's deliberate self-victimization, it is best to consider the nature and roots of the kind of drama presented in *Leaving Home*. One may initially classify it as a descendant of the modern domestic tragedy, such as *Death of a Salesman, Cat on a Hot Tin Roof,* or *A Streetcar Named Desire*. In each play, the central focus is upon the home, the family, and the parental and filial relationships which have become warped, twisted and destructive. Although the family plays a dominant role in *high mimetic* tragedy, as *Hamlet* or *King Lear*, the domestic tragedy can be differentiated from this kind of drama because it lacks the larger universal framework which suggests that familial bonds are akin to the bonds which unite man and his universe. When a Lear is shocked and dismayed at a daughter's seeming disobedience, the whole world quakes, shatters and collapses. In fact, Shakespeare often likes to parallel familial disorder and cosmic disorder, and, in his work, the collapse of the family usually precedes the collapse of the kingdom and universal order. In the modern domestic tragedy, however, the central character and his family are separated from "the real world" that exists somewhere outside the home and the actions of the central characters are not reflected in the large order of things. The modern dramatist confines his view directly to the disjoint family life and refrains from characterizing it against the larger background of life which exists outside the family door.

One could, furthermore, assert that the ever-increasing interest in the collapsing family in modern drama is a counterpart to traditional tragedy's dependence upon a larger universal framework. In Shakespearean drama, for example, the author could rely upon the chain-of-being as a constant referent to give his play not only greater dramatic effect, but also universal import. Because this notion of a universe harmoniously linked into a single whole, from God to the most insignificant pebble, was already questionable in Shakespeare's day, he could create dramatic tension between the world view which was beginning to collapse, and the new view which was beginning to crystallize. Today, man believes less and less in such grand universal schemes, and the dramatist is compelled to look for smaller and smaller units of order to bring coherence to his work. The family, as a natural and universal ordering of human relationships, had taken an ever-increasing hold upon the modern literary imagination. And, now that even this institution is beginning to crumble, now that no single member of the family can, with any certainty, understand his role and function within this order, the dramatist can reveal how man again is caught in a dilemma of almost tragic proportions.

The import of a father as the head of a household, confronted by the decline and collapse of his family, however, can never really gain truly tragic proportions— at least in modern drama. Man has already been too diminished in the world to create that kind of awesome effect. Yet, a play such as *Leaving Home* can still achieve a powerful and dramatic effect by centering upon a structure of human relationships which is both common and significant in most men's lives. . . .

Ed Jewinski, "Jacob Mercer's Lust for Victimization,"
CD, 2 (Spring 1976), 58-60

• •

. . . For years I'd tried to write about my family in one form or another: two chapters in my unpublished novel, an unproduced short film script, two or three unpublished short stories. But always as a disguised Ontario family. And the reason for that was because I didn't think I could capture the Newfoundland dialogue. I couldn't, for instance, even tell a verbal story with an accent. And because I hadn't made a concentrated effort to do it, I didn't know that I heard it inside my head.

This time out I decided to be true to my family background. As a simple exercise I typed a few fragments of remembered conversations and was surprised to hear my father's voice on paper. I wrote a few more scraps and they got better. I then started the play. It had one set and three characters: father, mother and son, Ben. The working title was *The Keepers of the House*, from a passage in Ecclesiastes [xii,1], I believe. Eventually it became the play *Leaving Home*.

As usual, I never mapped anything out. How could I when I didn't know what was going to happen? Oh, I knew that Ben would leave home at the end of the play, but that's all. That was the point of light to aim towards at the end of the dark tunnel. But what would happen in between I hadn't the slightest idea. If a writer does map his play out beforehand, that presupposes he knows his characters well eough to determine what they will do, ten, twenty pages down the road, what fork they will take. I didn't know that yet. I had to become acquainted with them. Sure, I intended to write about my family, but I knew from past experience that the characters would end up just being *based* on real people, not carbon copies. There would be other character traits I would invent or discover in the writing, and those parts I couldn't anticipate. The way I often create a character is to use a real-life model, but also to make the characters composites of more than one person, project a lot of myself into each one, plus whatever I know about people from my experience and observation. So I preferred to feel my way along, letting the objectives or wants of each character determine the dramatic action and conflict. It seemed to me the only organic way to work.

I typed the title page and began. By the bottom of page one, Ben told his mother he wanted to leave home, and that stopped me. It was too sudden, almost coming out of left field, and too arbitrary for dramatic action. And once again I ran up against the same old obstacle that had stymied me in the past, the lack of a strong catalyst. I cursed and walked away from the typewriter—and ran right back because the simple idea had suddenly occurred to me crossing from the table to the coffee pot on the stove that if there was another son and he was also leaving home for some reason—*a shotgun wedding?*—that might be the central event to set off the powder keg. The marriage would also give Ben the excuse he needed to escape the father who was devouring him. He could pretend to be moving in with the two kids to help them out financially.

So far, so good. I began the play again with the two kids coming home from school and the mother, Mary, preparing supper for her husband, who would soon be home from work. I established the fact that the wedding rehearsal was that night, the wedding the next day. Then the father came in and I had a problem. I wanted Jacob to be on the offensive as soon as he stepped in the door, to establish the conflict with his older son, Ben. Otherwise it would again be too arbitrary. So I began the play a third time, with this additional fact: the night before had been Ben's graduation from high school. My own graduation had been in November, so I decided that's when I'd set the play. Ben was now going to university, Billy was still in high school, and Ben had neglected to invite his father to the graduation, a deliberate omission that sorely hurt the man. That gave Jacob a grudge right from his first entrance and he was not a man to forgive or forget easily. . . .

When I sat down to the play again, I realized it made little sense, and certainly not good dramatic sense, to be marrying Billy off without the bride-to-be showing up. After all, it was *her* wedding too. Mary would naturally have invited her to supper before they all trooped off to the wedding rehearsal. The introduction of Kathy would undoubtedly add more conflict and thus more density to the play, and I was not against that. I now had to give some thought to her character and background, and one of the ideas contained the source of more conflict: What if Kathy were Catholic and Billy Protestant and Billy had turned Catholic to marry her? That would surely upset Jacob, who came from a background where the Knights of Columbus and Orangemen often murdered one another.

I started over for the fourth time, making all the necessary adjustments—i.e., slipping Kathy into the play long before she appeared, planting the fact that she was coming to supper. But I hadn't thought much about her yet, which is why as soon as she stepped inside the front door I was stumped.

At this point in the play I sensed the need for a complication. If the forthcoming wedding was the catalyst, something now had to happen that would lead sooner or later to a blowup in the family. It was also apparent to me that the meat of the play dealt with the relationship between Ben and his father, and if Ben was using his younger brother's marriage as an excuse to slip out from under his father's shadow, then it followed that an obstacle had to at least threaten the possibility of escape. That pointed logically to the wedding being called off. Not likely, I thought. The young girl was pregnant and Billy hadn't much choice but to marry her. If she wasn't pregnant, of course—right. If she wasn't pregnant...What if she had a miscarriage? That was believable. I'd known several girls that had happened to and I knew the circumstances.

I wrote the scene between the two kids, which proved to be the most difficult scene in the play to write. I kept writing it, worrying it like a dog with a bone. There was no problem from Billy's point of view. I knew what he wanted, which was to get out of marriage and stay in school. Unlike Ben, he was quite content to live at home.

But what about Kathy? For the life of me I didn't know how she felt about the wedding. I kept trying to write the scene in the hope the character herself would suddenly tell me. She had to want the wedding to happen or there was no scene and probably no play. But why would a seventeen-year-old girl want to get married? I didn't know and the reason I didn't know was simple, though I should have known better. I just hadn't gone into her background enough to look for a possible answer. When it struck me that I could draw a parallel between her and Ben, I knew I had the answer. She wanted to leave home as much as Ben did and for the same reason: to escape one of her parents. In her case the mother. Father dead.

Now that I knew what Kathy wanted and why, the scene was written without too much difficulty. Then I moved on to the long supper scene. No one, except the two kids involved, knew about the miscarriage yet, so that lent dramatic irony to the scene.

Suddenly the front door burst open and in marched Kathy's mother, Minnie, a character who simply invited herself into the house and into the play. I was quite grateful she showed up. I could now show the audience why her daughter wanted to escape her clutches, instead of telling them.

But I still had to create her. I still couldn't see her clearly in my mind. How did she feel about the wedding, for instance? I could sense that Minnie would be a formidable opponent if she, too, wanted the wedding to happen. Sooner or later it would come out that there was no reason now for the wedding to take place, but if both she and Kathy, and Ben, for his own selfish reason, wanted it to happen, the sides might be evenly matched in a battle of wills.

But why would Minnie want her daughter married off? Especially if she was a widow and Kathy an only child? You might think she'd at least want the girl at home for company, if for nothing else. Well, I thought, she might want her daughter out from underfoot if she had a new boyfriend and wanted to be alone with him. That made sense. Finally I decided to make her a bawdy, middle-aged woman, recently widowed, with a new lease on life. The idea of making her boyfriend the undertaker at her husband's funeral seemed to strike the right note of outrageousness for Minnie's character. But where was that new boyfriend? Why wouldn't she bring him along? She wasn't the type to let the poor guy out of her sight. So Minnie went back out the door and came in the second time followed by Harold, her silent stud, whose silence only set Minnie's character into sharper relief.

And so it went, my solving each problem as I ran up against it. Each time a problem was solved, the solution in turn would create a host of other problems that had to be solved. It is a slow and stumbling way to work, but it does offer at least one consolation and a rather important one: each character in the play will be there for a definite dramatic purpose.

The first draft took me three weeks, logging fifteen to eighteen hours a day. There were two more drafts over the winter and spring, and I don't remember a day when I wasn't eager for the typewriter and not a night I didn't resent the necessity of sleep. My characters chose to go their own way, and I just followed. If I thought I knew what a character would do a page or two ahead, which was rare, he would surprise me and do something else.

It was the most cathartic experience of my life. The more I began to understand the relationships in the family the more moved I became. There were times I couldn't see the keys of the typewriter for tears, and times I would almost topple my chair howling with laughter at the funny things those people said and did.

For the first time I managed to find the balance between comedy and tragedy that I had always wanted, and for the first time, too, I found the kind of satisfaction from the writing of plays that had eluded me for ten years.

Since then I have written two other full-length plays for the stage: *Of the Fields, Lately*, which is a continuation of my projected trilogy about the Mercer family, and *One Crack Out*, a play dealing with characters from the Toronto underworld. Each of these plays was written with the same stumbling difficulty and the same sense of discovery.

Nothing is more exhausting and exciting than looking for ways to put my own interior life on the stage. And of course, never being satisfied. Ever.

David French, *Stage Voices*, pp. 241-247

• •

CAROL BOLT

Buffalo Jump

First produced at Theatre Passe Muraille, Toronto, 18 May 1972†

Directed by Paul Thompson
Set Design by John Boyle
Costume Design by Gale Barnett

Cast
(Multiple roles for each performer)

Anne Anglin
Larry Benedict
Michael Bennett
Peter Boretski
Brenda Darling
Howie Cooper
Richard Farrell
Alan Jones
Gordon May
Miles Potter
John Smith

†(An earlier version of *Buffalo Jump*, called *Next Year Country*, was produced at the Globe Theatre, Regina, in 1971)

Riding in on the Spring upsurge of strong local creativity in the theatre, Theatre Passe Muraille has now brought Carol Bolt's *Buffalo Jump* to life. In Paul Thompson's ingenious production, it offers a comic strip version of a famous Depression upheaval—the march on Ottawa.

This work, created in the West by Mrs. Bolt, was earlier scheduled by Toronto Workshop Productions, but contractual differences blocked the undertaking, and Theatre Passe Muraille inherited it. This means that we see Mrs. Bolt's scenario for a documentary presented as a company creation instead of as the work of a single stylist in the theatre.

What difference this makes to *Buffalo Jump* is impossible to estimate, but one can recall that Canadian history has been seen through different eyes before this, and interpreted variously.

What concerns us is what the actors assembled by Thompson at Passe Muraille have set forth on its wide platform stage. The production they have evolved—much of it through intelligent improvisation—has been given automatic visual distinction by the St. Catharines' artist, John Boyle.

Boyle's pop art sketches of objects and people relevant to the march on Ottawa have been blown up into life-size cut-outs and are incorporated into the show in a most effective way. Members of Parliament, trains, crowds, Mounties and even Parliament Hill are all given visual representation that brightens the whole stage creation.

In front of Boyle's helpful contributions, the figures which move are taken from the headlines of the day, from Prime Minister R.B. Bennett to Red Evans. The latter headed the marchers from the Farm Relief Labor Camps in their hegira from the Midwest to the West Coast and back to Ottawa.

That historic journey, which was a matter of stark reality and starvation situations, has been remembered here as a piece of Canada's folk history. This telling is notable for the thumbnail characterizations developed to carry the action and the Passe Muraille actors' accuracy in re-capturing the songs and sound of the day.

Occasionally, and once for a long stretch of recitative, the script employs song to help the workers on the way. Perhaps John Smith's evocation of Wilf Carter may not pass muster with the devotees, but other songs offer welcome variations, especially those carried by Anne Anglin, who also doubles as most of the good Canadian housewives who offer food and hospitality to the footsore marchers.

Brenda Darling, the other actress in the cast, spurs the men on with quotations from Sabatini to Tennyson, and from one girl's father. Highlight scenes involving strong company creation include a tag-day sequence, a train mime and Calgary Stampede scenes.

Other solo efforts of equal note include Peter Boretski's work as Red Evans (and particularly his account of a riot in a Hudson's Bay store) and Richard Farrell's imposing impersonation of Prime Minister Bennett. The latter occurs in the final scene in which the workers each state their demands, only to be shot down by gunman Bennett, after which the audience is cleared out and the documentary ends.

Both Boretski and Farrell contribute other amusing vignettes, but then so do all 11 members of the cast, covering between them a generous sampling of Canada's Depression years population. Among those identified, Larry Benedict and a new small clown named Howie Cooper were particularly outstanding.

Perhaps historians of the trade union contribution to Canada's development may find *Buffalo Jump* a somewhat frivolous and simplistic interpretation, but one can only say that in time even the most serious upheavals can be faced with some kind of humor and perspective. Perhaps if Theatre Passe Muraille is still around and still as irreverent in another three decades or so, today's union situations may be cause for amusement to the young theatre folk.

In the meantime, Mrs. Bolt's documentary treatment is allowing us to look back on a most serious moment in national history with some degree of enjoyment. How much this stems from her own particular vision of the events she describes is a matter of guesswork, but whatever it is it contributes to a welcome divertissement, as well as to recollections of worthy struggles in our past.

Herbert Whittaker, Globe and Mail, 19 May 1972*

• •

Social conscience in the theatre is one thing, and social history in the theatre is another. The first cannot stand as a substitute for the second.

The Theatre Passe Muraille's production of *Buffalo Jump*, which opened last night, clutches at a huge patch of Canadian social history. But the fact that it seems so proud that its heart is in the right place politically—though given this theatre's audience, whose heart is elsewhere?—can't keep the production from being amorphous, shallow and wearying.

From the history of the Canadian Depression, playwright Carol Bolt has isolated the on-to-Ottawa March of 1935 in which some 1,500 men, many from the relief camps, travelled across the country to protest personally to their government. And though this production is very much a lesser effort, it is distinctly in the Theatre Passe Muraille's style of historical documentary.

Historical data alternates with vignettes of individual response. Mime, songs, dramatic cartoons, satire, monologues, surrealism and a sheer weight of information compete for our attention. When it works, as it did last year, for instance, in the production of *Doukhobors*, the result is exhilarating. But when it crashes to the ground as *Buffalo Jump* does, the effect is arch and strained.

Many of the scenes were developed from inprovisations among the actors, shaped by director Paul Thompson and articulated by the playwright. When the final results are so banal and embarrassing, it is difficult to find precise sources. Perhaps the actors simply weren't good enough to improvise material of substance. Or perhaps Mrs. Bolt could find no way to give the incidents a dramatic form. Or perhaps Thompson tried to stretch the stylistic elasticity too far.

It isn't difficult to lose the focus of the narrative. Oddly enough for a show about a cross-country journey, *Buffalo Jump* contains absolutely no momentum. Mrs. Bolt hasn't begun to give the results of her research any dramatic shape; not nearly enough has been discarded for clarity, accent and atmosphere. Only the easiest ironies are encouraged.

This on-to-Ottawa trek is willing to stop for anything at all. Here, Paul Thompson's eagerness for stylistic variety often slows the production to a standstill. *Buffalo Jump* halts for three rodeo sequences (one of which would have been blatant enough), the hackneyed carnival midway metaphor, some very irrelevant music, nostalgia trips (Wilf Carter), mawkish social encounters, and a dreadful, extended comic opera sequence. When, after two and a half hours, the production again came to a halt, this time for a polka contest, one was ready to scream.

The flaccid slackness of the production's social history leads you to wonder about its purposes. Is *Buffalo Jump* a serious attempt to understand what happened to a group of people in the not-too-distant past? Or is it merely a springboard for an unhealthy nostalgic romp for those people who'd like to believe that the '30s were some sort of lovely bittersweet age, and that even an economic depression was was exquisite?

In the play's second half, there is a brief appearance by a bespectacled girl whose response to the march is to gush forth into poetry. The production plays this chapter for laughs, but are its own intentions so much better, even really any different? Isn't it too responding to history in a slick, stylish, self-consciously sensitive way?

One knows that actors adore playing poverty and despair. But there is something patronizing in these performers' radiant glee in enacting economic misery. The dewy sentimentality of poverty and hardship in *Buffalo Jump* seems awfully easy and maybe even a little cheap.

Urjo Kareda, *Toronto Star*, 19 May 1972*

• •

Buffalo Jump, a political and social indictment of Canadian society of the thirties, manages to be a less serious work than either [Carol Bolt's] *Gabe* or *Red Emma*. The play borrows from the mythology of the old west for its central metaphor, equating the workers' protest march to Ottawa with a herd of buffalo about to be stampeded off a cliff. It has tentative links with the romantic epic mythology of a reform quest headed by a virtuous leader who is prepared to do battle with the demons of the land. But any such association must be seen as overt, satirical and comic rather than subliminal, reverential and grave.

With its explicit breakdown between villains and heroes, the play might have become a modern melodrama were it not for its cut-up, cartoon style which turns it into a pastiche of thirties' films, theatre, social conventions and language. The governing mood of the play is the evocation of nostalgia; a nostalgia that is not only concerned with a general picture of the depression but with such specifically Canadian events as the Estevan riot, the On-to-Ottawa trek and the Regina riot. Just as nostalgia for two heroic men structures the mythology of *Gabe*, so nostalgia for heroic events (or at least potentially heroic events) gives rise in *Buffalo Jump* to a myth rooted in popular idealism—the story of what might have been.

The final version of the play is imprinted with the "collective creation" approach of director Paul Thompson and the actors of Toronto's Theatre Passe Muraille, working in conjunction with Carol Bolt. Theatre Passe Muraille uses social history or social actuality as a foundation for communal folk tales of its own devising. The technique of having each actor research and develop individual vignettes, drawn from a central shared experience, results in play with an amoeba-like fluidity and growth process. The outcome of such an informal arrangement is that the plays tend to remain an appealing collection of parts rather than to become a unified dramatic whole.

Buffalo Jump has a strong line of action represented by the decision, process and result of going to Ottawa but it is also a colourful montage of theatrical pieces. The tone and texture of the play become progressively darker as it becomes clear that the oppressive establishment forces will win. At first R.B. Bennett is depicted as a political cartoon figure spouting speeches which accumulate a dense and glorious assortment of mixed metaphors. In the concluding meeting with the worker delegation his lines are clipped and coldly real.

Before she is through Carol Bolt has utilized most of the agit-prop techniques common to the social issue plays of the thirties, transformed them in the end into a carbon-copy of living guerrilla theatre and stopped off along the way for the mock opera sequence of the Golden episode, where the hungry strikers are fed by townspeople singing arias. One special innovation, however, results directly from the Bolt/Passe Muraille process of making plays—the use of concrete image wherein one short sequence capsulizes the larger, on-going conflict. Implementing the rodeo idea used again in *Gabe*, Bolt constructs a fanciful Calgary Stampede scene in which Red Evans rides a bull called R.B. Bennett, to the accompaniment of typical announcer verbiage.

> *There goes the horn. They're out of the chute. Red is holding on but this Bennett is a lot of bull. He's a tough one, ladies and gentlemen, but Red's a fighter. Oh no, he's thrown. Bennett's turning back at him, ladies and gentlemen. Get out of there, Red. Get moving . . .*

This conversion of political antagonism into a bull wrestling contest conjures up the wider more deadly associations of the 'buffalo jump'; a focus shifting from the individual battle between Evans and Bennett to the mass of workers bucking an entire system.

Throughout the play, each actor assumes several parts, emphasizing caricature or surface mannerism instead of character development. This is a practical method of suggesting greater numbers, manipulating reactions and limiting emotional engagement with a character so that political postures can dominate. Role exchange is supplemented with the comic, anti-naturalistic device of having the strikers carry painted cut-out marchers to give a sense of mass. The real and unreal, caricature and character, stylized theatricality and sombre realism nudge constantly against each other until finally the boundaries of the stage are obliterated and the audience is incorporated into the body of strikers and forced to disperse along with them.

Sandra Souchotte, introduction to Carol Bolt,
Playwrights in Profile: Buffalo Jump, Gabe, Red Emma
(Toronto, 1976), 8-10

• •

. . . In its loosely constructed projection of the events of the On-to-Ottawa Trek of 1935, [*Buffalo Jump*] explores the basic antagonisms between the forces of social protest of the period, represented by the depression work camp strikers, and the forces of reactionary conservatism as represented by the government and personality of R.B. Bennett. Actually the text here printed [in *Playwrights in Profile: Buffalo Jump, Gabe, Red Emma*] does not live up to expectation as a fully developed play, but rather as a series of fluid guidelines for performers. *Buffalo Jump* was brought to its present form through Bolt's close working association with specific companies; first under the title of *Next Year Country* with the Globe Theatre, Regina, 1971, and in the following year to its much revised version with Theatre Passe Muraille as here published. . . . Perhaps because it is essentially a collaborative effort developed with performers who have a purely theatrical effect in mind, *Buffalo Jump* lacks the full coherence of an explicitly authorial point of view in its handling of characterization and social-political themes. The *Next Year Country* version was more explicitly documentary with a closer examination of the facts and opinion surrounding the event, particularly as focused on the Saskatchewan milieu of the period; it included the Estevan strike and riots as well as a very detailed examination of the Regina riot of July 1, 1935 by which the easterly movements of the strikers' on-to-Ottawa protest was brought to an end. The Passe Muraille version offers a less specific analysis of the documentary material but a livelier awareness of the styles of political revue with its variety of agitprop techniques.

Consequently *Buffalo Jump* in performance gives a dramatic identity to a major Canadian left-right confrontation in the manner of its own time, although it also works convincingly as an incitement to specific forms of national awareness in our own. However, on the page it is less effective; as a text it cries out for a more thoughtful dramatic craftsmanship than its present theatricality provides. The significance of the title is relegated to a stage direction. There are any number of episodes which need a more coherent dramatic justification, for example in the Wilf Carter and Calgary Stampede sequences, the farcical banana-skin episode in the Vancouver tag-day scene, or in the operatic version of the Golden sequence. From a reader's point of view these scenes suggest simply gratuitous trickery, even though on stage they may evoke shifts of mood, ironic contrast, or sheer physical exuberance appropriate to naive proletariat intentions. But without a proper commentary to give a fuller indication of performance techniques and intentions, the text too frequently collapses into amateurish *non sequiturs*.

Nevertheless, in principle the publication of the text is valuable. What this play achieves in performance is more than an energetic romp into the past (although it is that too). It is also a direct evocation of the *folk-lore* of a significant social-political event of the Canadian past. *Buffalo Jump* is, therefore, remarkable in at least two ways. It flatters the national consciousness of its audience through its cheeky assumption that document can now be eschewed in favour of spirited lore. More important, it refocuses our view of ourselves in that dirty decade from the self-pitying victim pattern of *As For Me and My House* and *Ten Lost Years*: even if the trekkers failed in their mission to R.B. Bennett, the spirit of their attempt reminds us of something positive in those grey years. For a few weeks the trekkers literally reclaimed the land of their pioneer prototypes; since their easterly quest on the rails in search of social justice was an ironic reversal of the fabled westward thrust, both myths must survive in our so-called national dream. . . .

Diane Bessai, *CD*, 4 (Spring 1978), 64-65

• •

Zimmerman You began working collectively with George Luscombe at Toronto Workshop Productions and then you revised *Buffalo Jump* with Paul Thompson at Passe Muraille. . . . Are there advantages with the collective approach?

Bolt If everyone is committed to the project in the same way, I mean, if there is a real collective, then there's a wonderful energy that comes out of that. In a straight play you can have the same kind of energy but not at exactly the same level. I've never been involved in any kind of collective situation where everybody wasn't giving and caring about the project. Obviously what happens in, say,

Buffalo Jump is that the characters reflect the actors who originally played them and the input of those actors. *Buffalo Jump* was a bit different from the usual collective in that it had already been a script although, finally, I think there was only one line of the original left in the version that we opened at Passe Muraille. But that was a decision that I made, just to see if I could do it, really.

Zimmerman   To let it keep evolving and not tie actors to the script?

Bolt   Yeah, because Paul believed that would be an interesting experience and really fun to try and, of course, it was.

Zimmerman   Were you concerned about the accuracy in *Buffalo Jump* of, say, R.B. Bennett's speeches? Did you use Liversedge's *Recollections of the On To Ottawa Trek*?

Bolt   I did use Liversedge and I did go to Ottawa and go through the Bennett papers. We had a lot of different things that the play came out of. I also had done research for *Next Year Country*, the revue that it evolved from. I did some research in the Saskatchewan archives too. Obviously Bennett never said any of my lines. But some of the images like the ship of state and things like that were typical of the time and typical of him. Unfortunately, he wasn't profound or interesting; he wasn't an interesting speaker at all. So we extended those images to make him into a cartoon of himself, really. That's the way the speeches were created. The structure of the play developed to keep him as a larger-than-life-figure while the guys were going toward Ottawa to find him. He just stayed there and talked about betrayal and things.

Zimmerman   The Liversedge book had a Marxist ending, the we-haven't-won-yet-approach. It stressed the communist connection and concluded fairly optimistically. I felt the play's conclusion was very depressing.

Bolt   The play has been ended differently. In the Ottawa production [1977] we ended by using Annie Bowler who had been around Ottawa after the trek fell apart, and had had people marching up and down the streets. They didn't really get anywhere but they were trying at least, and they were making a statement. The Great Canadian Theatre Co. built the play around that; it seemed to reflect what they wanted to say. I think that for a play like *Buffalo Jump* that's the way it should be. . . .

Interview with Carol Bolt, by Cynthia Zimmerman,
The Work, pp. 266-268

• •

THEATRE PASSE MURAILLE

The Farm Show

First produced by Theatre Passe Muraille in Clinton, Ontario,
13 August 1972

Directed by Paul Thompson
Designed by Ed Fisher

Cast
(Multiple roles for each performer)

Janet Amos
Anne Anglin
David Fox
Alan Jones
Fina MacDonell
Miles Potter

Clinton area residents are agog and are still talking about the recent play produced at the old Bird Farm by the Passe Muraille theatre group. Last Sunday afternoon the gravel road outside the farm and the long driveway leading up to the house and barn were lined with cars representing a crowd estimated at nearly 200 people. Old and young, farmers and "hippies" alike, gathered with blankets to sit on and lunches to nibble.

Many of the people in the audience came to see the play because the company had come to them asking questions about farm life. Since the subject of the play was rural Canadian life on a farm, and the group had come to Southwestern Ontario in order to research that kind of life and experience some of it first-hand, they had gotten to know many of the inhabitants of the Maitland and 16th lines.

Paul Thompson, the director of the group, looked around the crowd and judged that he recognized about a quarter of the people to be from the area, and a quarter more to be from Stratford and Toronto. The other half were strangers to him. Everyone there, however, seemed extremely interested in what they saw on the makeshift stage, and the director and actors were thrilled with the tremendous reception they were shown.

The play was held in the big old barn which the company had been using for rehearsals in the past weeks. Bales of hay were stacked nearly to the ceiling in steps and were used as seats, although some more daring souls climbed up onto the rafters for a better view. The audience was generously sprinkled with children, who had as much fun as their parents, laughing and clapping.

With songs, poems, skits, interpretive exercises, and monologues, the three actors and three actresses from Toronto bewitched their audience. When Miles Potter depicted what happened when he offered to help his neighbor with the haying, he nearly brought the barn down. The audience fell apart in glee to recognize the arduous job many of them perform twice a year.

Janet Amos, as she stepped into an old-fashioned wringer-washer, became a frazzled housewife whose family's demands nearly turned her into a washing machine in the agitating cycle.

Anne Anglin and David Fox crawled under two crates and did a delightful skit of a family in winter. Anne's voice was amazingly varied as she switched back and forth from mother to children.

Fina MacDonell's hands turned into swans and ducks as she nibbled imaginary grass from Les Jervis' animal sanctuary. And everyone who knows Les Jervis recognized the character sketch done by David Fox. As a matter of fact, those in the audience who were from the area recognized most of their neighbors in the scenes. Howls of laughter and groans of embarrassment burst continually from the straw bleachers.

And somehow the actors managed, while laying open the characters of the community for all to see, not to offend anybody (they hope) and not to bear false witness to the personalities of any of their new-found friends.

The program ended with the magnificent skit set to rhyme, of the Saga of Big John Deere and the coming of the tractor to farm-life. Alan Jones as John Deere led the pantomine through to its conclusion, where machinery triumphs and John Deere is drowned.

When all the actors had disappeared off stage through a trap-door, the show was over, and Paul Thompson invited the audience to have some refreshment and stay to chat with the actors. This chance for discussion among actors and audience was as appreciated by one group as by the other, for the six actors wanted to hear whether their interpretations had been successful in the opinions of those from whom they had gotten their information.

Evidently they had, for compliments flew, even from members of the "Lobb Dynasty".

The show is over now in Clinton, but it will live on in Toronto. Paul Thompson explained that the material gathered during the summer will be turned into a production for a city audience as well. Great changes will have to be made in the show as it was presented in Clinton, including more explanatory content for those who are not at all familiar with farm life, and who, of course, don't know Clinton residents. . . .

Liza Williams, Goderich Signal, 17 August 1972*

• •

The Farm Show, which is opening the season at Theatre Passe Muraille, gives a lot of pleasure for a lot of reasons.

As a dramatic work, it is vigorous, informative, stylish and often insanely funny. . . .

The Farm Show is a Paul Thompson-organized collective creation, a form which has been uniquely perfected at the Theatre Passe Muraille and which, because this talented man has chosen to work in Toronto, is now ours as well.

This particular collective creation seems an advance on the past because the performers have had a much more direct relationship to the material. As a result, there is a richness in the performances which adds depth and colour to the whole experience.

For six weeks this summer, Thompson took his actors to live on a farm near Clinton, Ontario, with the object of creating a production about, and for, the farmers of that region.

Working through both a subjective and objective response to the environment, joining farmers at their tasks, meeting local residents and listening, always listening, the company developed the dramatic material which was first presented in a barn to the farmers themselves and has now been transported to Toronto.

The performance in Clinton must have been electrifying in its immediacy. In Toronto, we receive the data not with a shock of recognition but with a glow of familiarization.

The Farm Show is performed on a raked acting area, the floor of which is a large map of the rural area involved, with the names of the individual farms boldly labelled. Some very nice entertainers from the area—Russ and Dorothy from Teeswater—provide preliminary music, and though the fire marshall has vetoed bales of hay, the atmosphere is unbelievably evocative.

The authenticity is the triumph of the performers, who also, of course, created the material. This is by no means a conventional documentary, but it is certainly realism of a magic intensity. Through mime, song, narrative, sound poetry, monologues—the whole range of possible communication—we come very close to the heart of their experience.

There is a succession of inspired ideas. A farmwife (Janet Amos), prattling happily about her cleaning chores, sits in her wringer-washer, and eventually becomes the machine itself.

There is a stirring heroic drama (in verse) about the mythology of tractors. We have a hilarious plowing match and with extreme ingenuity we are given the fearfulness of a rural winter, with its dual responses of cages and escapes.

The fear that the actors might sentimentalize farming is dispatched in Miles Potter's memorable monologue about a day's hayloading. Cool looks are given to such furors as Orange parades and Jesus revivals. Miss Amos has a wonderful sequence about weddings, rising to the great line, ''We laughed until we died at the stupidity of it all.''

Darker regions are probed as well. There are moving insights into farm tragedies and a sharp vignette about people drifing to the cities. Very fine, too, is the section devoted to the strange recluse Charlie Wilson (David Fox), with his religion, his encyclopedic knowledge of plants and his cruel, self-inhibiting facial tic.

It is difficult to account for the excitement which this production brings. Partly there is the lucid beauty and ease of Paul Thompson's methodology, and the vividness of six actors—Anne Anglin, Janet Amos, Fina MacDonell, David Fox, Miles Potter and Thompson himself—performing with such versatility, tact and palpable compassion.

The evening is filled with subtle cross-references so that we come to discover a whole contained world. In *The Farm Show*, Thompson and his actors have helped us to know, understand and love a community of people beyond our sphere of familiarity. As artists they can have no higher ambitions.

Urjo Kareda, *Toronto Star*, 22 September 1972

• •

The Farm Show, playing at Theatre Passe Muraille, renews one's faith in the theatre as a positive force in the community. It presents a balanced view of a way of life that despite all its problems—and farmers have many—is intrinsically decent, dignified and downright healthy.

The members of the cast garnered their material from real life during a summer's stay in the Clinton area of southwestern Ontario. Paul Thompson, the author, admits that *The Farm Show* is not really a play; rather, it's a collection of skits, monologues and narrative poems. He calls it a Sunday School concert and it resembles one in its apparently thrown-together structure.

But there is purpose beneath the seeming aimlessness. All the snippets add up to a complete picture of life in rural southern Ontario from Saturday at the market to Sunday at the prayer meeting, from the Orange Day parade to the township council meeting, and from working in the kitchen to dying in farm accidents. And all the characters are there too: the district eccentric who lived in a shanty but read Dante's *Inferno*, the old man who keeps a wildlife sanctuary and the young go-getter, "second best farmer in the township."

All these characters—and anything else that moves like animals and tractors— are played to perfection by the cast. There are six members, three of each sex, and not a bad apple in the barrel. Each one specializes in a range of characters rather than representing only one. Fina MacDonell takes the children's and teenagers' roles, while Janet Amos and Anne Anglin share duties playing mature and old women. Among the men, David Fox takes the older roles, Miles Potter the younger and Paul Thompson more than fills the gaps.

Each one had at least one beautiful moment, usually a monologue in which a character was fully developed. But the strength of the company lies as much in its ability to mime as in its gift for mimicry. MacDonell, a blonde whose features are more than chiseled, was lovely doing ducks in a pond. Paul Thompson did a terrific tractor and Miles Potter throbbed as a broken down automatic washer.

The set consisted of a simple and very effective map of the Clinton region painted on raked risers. There was also a screen overhead that showed some rather unnecessary slides of fields and tractors. The words of the actors, who were quoting real people of the area, invariably did a better job of establishing an atmosphere.

The Farm Show was a risky undertaking in the sense that it could have been a superficial snapshot of country life depicting the people as cute and folksy hayseeds. Playwright Thompson (perhaps editor is a better word) seems to have been aware of that danger. He included a sequence on the dreariness and enforced insularity of the people in winter that balanced the bacchanal of the Orange Day parade. The troupe mimed a farm accident in which a man lost half his face to a binder and eventually died.

One scene that could have been a travesty was the prayer meeting. The group conveyed the optimism of the faithful that every disastrous trip has its good side;

and their painful honesty in witnessing was delivered straight out front. There was no cheap attempt at parody.

The audience stopped laughing as it realized the genuine feeling that was represented and the one person who applauded at the end of the scene stopped, perhaps ashamed, after three claps. The rest of the audience sat silent—cowed, maybe, by the farmers' faith?

Robert Martin, *Globe and Mail*, 22 September 1972

• •

A modern farming community is the subject of *The Farm Show* . . . a collective creation of Theatre Passe Muraille, who sent a group of actors to study farm life; the result was a play performed for both rural and city audiences. Ted Johns has prepared the script, based on the actors' improvisations; it is a tribute to his work that the play reads with freshness and spontaneity, evoking an actual performance. And it is a tribute to all concerned that the play takes us so close to its subject. In the photographs that accompany this edition [Coach House Press, 1976] we can see a fascinating but slightly unnerving contrast between the soft faces of the young actors from Toronto and the tough, weather-beaten countenances of the men and women who were their first subjects and their first audiences. But the actors have shown a proper respect for their material, avoiding condescension on the one hand and naive admiration on the other. They begin, in fact, with a little healthy self-mockery as a young actor coos joyfully about "organic vegetables from your own garden and all, far out!" and then, a scene or two later, experiences the agony of loading bales on a hot day. Best of all, he avoids the easy claim that he learned something from the experience: "Why would any human being *choose*, for the better part of his life, *twice* a year, to put himself through that total and utter hell? I didn't understand it then . . . and I don't understand it now." Then (apart from a brief return towards the end) the actors as actors fade out of the play and the locals take over. There are local characters—Charlie Wilson, an eccentric loner, self-educated in bits and pieces, suffering a painful tic; and Les Jervis, who was abroad in the war and keeps a menagerie as a hobby (carefully avoiding *Canadian* deer so that he doesn't have to cope with government regulations). We hear the circling and backtracking of ordinary speech, with the occasional pungent turn of phrase: "people 'ud steal the Lord's supper nowadays." There is an Orange Parade (we get everything from the slightly nervous speeches at the centre to a little casual drunkenness on the sidelines), a wedding, and a marvellously evocative winter scene in which the voices of children quarrelling over hockey cards at breakfast are juxtaposed with the weather report warning of "a cold front moving in a northeasterly direction over Moosonee."

112

For the most part the dominant attitude is a matter-of-fact acceptance. As one speaker says, describing an eccentric wedding, "Oh well, I guess some people just do things differently than others." But gradually we become aware of an artistic shaping and selection. The farmer's dependence on machinery becomes an increasingly dominant theme, and the actors have fun impersonating various farm machines, including two rival tractors. The significance of machinery is extended beyond the farmers themselves: the preaching of an evangelist group is slyly juxtaposed with the mechanical difficulties afflicting the "Jesus bus." A farmer's wife, describing a harassing day, stands symbolically *inside* her washing machine. And towards the end another theme surfaces, as we begin to see the farmer as a threatened species. References to young people leaving the land, and to the auctioning of farm property, accumulate. The second-to-last scene is a long speech, full of grim statistics, on the economic absurdity of farming. But the last scene, the comic tall-tale ballad of John Deere (which among other things celebrates a tractor of supernatural power), tilts the balance away from morose documentary. Throughout the play there is a shaping tension between the tough reality of farming and the fun that goes with it, and this final juxtaposition brings the tension to a head. The play, which began as a documentary, becomes in the end both a warning and a celebration.

Alexander Leggatt, "Letters in Canada: Drama",
UTQ, 46 (Summer 1977), 385-386.

• •

. . . In the tradition within which Passe Muraille works, performance is a means of achieving aesthetic unity rather than a means of transmitting a unity already present. Their "concerts" resist translation into print: the reader is not able to predict the development of the concert's shape, and he experiences no delight in theatrical surprise to compensate for his confusion, problems which do not arise in the reading of a play whose conventions both guide the reader's expectations and supply consistent illusions to project in the theatre of the mind. *The Farm Show* not only avoids plot, but also abjures the conventions of illusion to which, still, most of us are accustomed. Passe Muraille's work resembles Brecht's in its dissociation of actor and mask, Peter Cheeseman's in its juxtaposition of the authentic documentary detail and the flamboyantly theatrical gesture, and Megan Terry's and Joan Littlewood's in its efforts to break the one-to-one relationship between actor and role, assigning each actor many roles and using the movement between roles as well as the movement between theatrical and depicted realities as a vehicle for theatrical statement. None of these innovations are as effective on the page as they are on the stage: the actors merge into their characters, the jazz-like flow from role to role is broken into blocks of dialogue lacking the cohesion provided by the single player, and the interplay between real stage object and mime is lost, for the onstage bale of hay and the elaborately mimed hay-baler are equally feats of the imagination to the reader.

While elements of performance assume structural and image-making tasks more often assigned to language in the conventional drama, language is not without its function and value in Passe Muraille works such as *The Farm Show*. In large part, language in this set of conventions is documentary data, lifted out of its everyday context by a highly theatrical performance style and heightened by artful editing and calculated juxtaposition of speeches or of speech and stage image. The approach produces powerful moments when the presentational technique records and transmits a subject's discussion of something which means a good deal to him; the spare declarations have been honed further still in the rehearsal process, leaving and thereby highlighting the stronger features of Clinton's speech in the reading of a hermit's letters, an account of a farm accident, a man's description of the thoughts he thinks while he works in the fields, Bruce Pallett's analysis of the economics of Canadian farming. Through the accumulation of such heightened moments, the audience receives an impression of Clinton's opinions, values, and, most effectively, Clinton's fears; in this way, *The Farm Show* succeeds in reaching beyond the boundaries of the Canadian farming community.

Field thoughts and memories of accidents show us that in Clinton, death frequently takes the form of a tractor. When we know what a tractor engine's stopping may mean, silence between carefully chosen words acquires new depths of meaning. Later, the effect of the preceding silences adds a new dimensoin to the essentially comic treatment of the tractor tug at a local fall fair. Indeed, one is struck by the relationship between men and machinery, both by the frequency with which it is a factor in the lives of the characters and by the presence which the perception of the farmers and the clarity of Passe Muraille's reporting give the relationship. There are references to the old, natural antagonists, drought, crop failure, flood, fire, and storm, so familiar to readers of earlier Canadian plays with farm settings, but in *The Farm Show*, the ambivalent machine is a much stronger theatrical presence. An audience of city-dwellers not only gains a new perspective on a universal fear, but finds in death's twentieth-century shape on the farm further comment on their own way of life. . . .

Thompson has described work on shows like *The Farm Show* or *Under the Greywacke* as attempts to produce "a living community portrait or photograph." In this respect, *The Farm Show* resembles the sort of older Canadian concert or pageant described by W.H. New in his introduction to *Dramatists in Canada* [1972]; there is little continuing sense of individual characters and hence no character development, for these are forgone in favour of the collective character, Clinton. Passe Muraille's presentational techniques thus conform to the preference for collective heroes over individual heroes which several critics have informed us is typically

Canadian, but which is also typical of the left-wing perspectives of the European companies which first used many of the conventions Passe Muraille employs, and which is, probably most significantly, characteristic of the work of Roger Planchon, the French director under whom Thompson served a two year apprenticeship. While there is little dramatic movement toward conflict in a conventional sense, dramatic conflict does occur at the level of the collective, as the audience becomes aware, through an accumulation of individual scenes pointing in the same direction, that the way of life Clinton represents is in danger of dying. This menace achieves a stage presence chiefly in the second act, and makes *The Farm Show* more than the mere celebration of a community which many of the pageants and concerts of earlier Canadian drama were. Chamber of commerce optimism is not allowed to gloss over what Thompson calls the "texture" of small town reality.

Additional tensions, serving to replace dramatic conflict between individuals, arise from the separation of performer and depicted reality, a separation which is frequently clearly revealed: recited stage directions establish setting with the precision of imagist poems, the audience is called upon to applaud the sheer virtuosity of almost acrobatic acting (the council meeting sequence seems to serve little other purpose), and in story-telling sequences, we are aware that the act of story-telling occurs on two levels. The Canadian playwright frequently has his characters tell stories; in older plays, the stories too often interrupt the play, as the playwrights seem incapable of resisting rhetorical temptations, stopping their plays in order to allow characters to tell stories. In more recent plays, the story still makes frequent appearances, but the act of story-telling itself has been made dramatically functional; in Cook, Tremblay, Ryga, story-telling is a dramatic action which the character employs to achieve a dramatic objective. In the exploitation of this device, Passe Muraille excels. Les Jervis's story about his deer, the Jesus bus story, and others are not included for their own sake only, nor is their primary purpose merely to add local colour. They are actions, means by which Clinton expresses its values in opposition to those forces which the community sees as threats, and in so doing resists the threat. Because the theatrical reality is clearly before us, the story-telling is also the means by which Passe Muraille can establish dramatic conflict between stage and auditorium: while an urban performance of *The Farm Show* loses the communal celebration present in an auction barn performance, the city production compensates through dramatic strengths created by the company's casting the audience, from time to time, in the role of the antagonist, a collective antagonist balancing the collective protagonist. The intention is certainly political, but because their style provides a model of the political conflict, incorporating that conflict within working dramatic actions, Passe Muraille usually succeeds in avoiding the animated pamphlet, so often the bane of overtly political theatre.

Often, adverse criticism of Passe Muraille's work fails to take into consideration those conventions within which the company works: the result is a consideration of what a Passe Muraille show is not rather than of what it is. All this is not to say that the conventions of the collectively created show do not admit of failure. One of the primary requirements of the form is honesty, an honesty which Passe Muraille often proclaims, frequently with a bit too much self-congratulation. In the company's community portraits there is, accompanying the stylization, some idealization; this idealization is usually excused by the romanticism of Passe Muraille's perspective, for the romanticism is usually a vital one which attempts to inject the dramatic into the reality of Canadian life, deliberately choosing this approach over an ordering of that life and a bringing of its elements into formal harmony. Nonetheless, the temptation to show Clinton what it wants rather than what it needs must be enormous. (The distinction is difficult to make and even more difficult to heed within Passe Muraille's theoretically egalitarian philosophy.) The consequence of yielding to the temptation to flatter is dishonesty, and precisely because Passe Muraille's conventions are what they are, such slips from grace are jarring, and damaging to the tone of the show as a whole. Such a stumble is "Miles Meets Mr. Merrill," the second scene in the show. A Passe Muraille actor represents himself meeting for the first time one of the Clinton farmers whose lives he wants to observe and interpret. Since this scene purports to show the audience the beginning of the process which led to *The Farm Show* (the proverbial box containing the sound of its own making), we expect some clues as to the validity of what we are seeing. Passe Muraille is at great pains to be honest about the subject, but in this scene especially, the showmakers do not take such care to be honest about themselves. Miles' city yokel self-parody is too crude a picture of naiveté: "Boy, it sure must be great being a farmer. . . . I mean you get up in the morning and get your hands down into that good honest dirt." Sometimes the Passe Muraille actors' eagerness to depreciate themselves becomes a form of condescension: the farmers are implicitly flattered and patronized by the false contrast. These tactics, fortunately rare in *The Farm Show*, clearly diminish the credibility of the Clinton portrait, working directly against the show's central objective.

The faults of the second scene are particularly clear in contrast to the success of the justly celebrated bale scene. Again, a Passe Muraille actor is playing himself, helping with the haying in the mow in the heat and the dust, scrambling and heaving and scrambling some more to keep up with the loader. Here, the self-mockery is not at all obsequious, and can, therefore, achieve some satiric bite; comparisons are not forced, and the qualities of the farmers emerge as a matter of course. The juxtaposition of reflective anecdote and the immediate conflicts between man and hay, man and machinery, city man and country life, give substance to the concluding rhetorical question about farming as a way of life. This time, the "sound of the making" is truly part of the portrait. . . .

Chris Johnson, *Canadian Literature*, 85
(Summer 1980), 133-136

• •

MICHAEL COOK

The Head, Guts and Soundbone Dance

First produced at the Arts and Culture Centre, St. John's
4 March 1973

Directed by Tony Chadwick
Lighting Design by Tony Duarte
Set Design by John Roddis
Sound Design by Sharon Buehler

Cast

Skipper	Clyde Rose
Uncle John	Pat Byrne
Rachel	Flo Edwards
Absalom	Dick Buehler
Children	Kelly Buehler, Paul Kelly
	Perry Fowler
Lew	Geoff Seymour
Aiden	Leslie Mulholland

Michael Cook is a comparative newcomer to the Newfoundland scene, and, like many of us who are not native, feels that he has something to say about Newfoundland that Newfoundlanders have not said for themselves.

Some will say that this is impertinence. This, of course, is probably quite true.

However, his play, the title of which is deceptively repellent, is one of the most perceptive things I have ever seen. It's rather like peeping through a window. A church window.

Skipper Pete is an old man—old, knowledgable, Master of his community, obsessed by his own power. Skipper. What a powerful word that is in Newfoundland.

The entire play is set on a stage-head and it is all about power—a Newfoundland obsession. Who is master, who is not? Particularly, the remembrance of things past. Things like great catches of cod. King Cod they used to call it, like mastery over all the beasts of the earth, cold protestant style, where pigs can be dropped from the mast and splatter all over the deck for fun and everybody laughs, if they are not Master, that is.

The play was well staged. The set was too small for the stage, or seemed to be for about two minutes, after which nobody cared for the surroundings—the focus was central, and interest was concentrated on the action.

Skipper Pete (Clyde Rose), an old man, remembers his past glory, which consists entirely of shoals of fish and his ability to appear an iron master of lesser men. That they were men in their own right is not relevant—he was Master. How many, who have lived under these circumstances, can deny this? But the Skipper makes the supreme mistake—he believes his own fantasy, and goes mad.

Not observantly mad, of course. His adopted son loves him. He loves all the primitive strength Skipper Pete possesses, his quality of mastery over boats, fish and women. His blind, idiot courage and the ignorant assumption that such courage existed nowhere else. . . .

The stage-head becomes the Skipper's life, and his adopted son Uncle John, brilliantly played by Pat Byrne, joins the fantasy. What else can he do? Saved from drowning by the old man, kicked in the backside whenever he stepped out of line, married to the old man's daughter, dedicated to the Skipper's concept of what is true—"the old way is the only way." He must do what is expected of him.

He hates it all—the word of God, as interpreted by the Skipper, the lies he must swallow in the name of tribal memory, the whole sorry ritual so well described by T.S. Eliot in *Murder in the Cathedral*.

> "This is the last temptation, the final Treason.
> To do the right thing for the wrong
> reason . . ."

I have been told, by those much wiser than I, that reviewing plays calls for a description of the action, rather than analysis of the author's meaning.

All right then. Here's what I think of the action. First, Tony Chadwick directed the play with a unique understanding, back and forth, and [Pat Byrne as Uncle John?] emerged as genuinely human and genuinely baffled by pressures over which he had no control. (I am told, too, that he had a genuine Placentia Bay accent, but this was by a man who came from that "far greater Bay"). Whatever the facts may be, this was a noteworthy performance.

Clyde Rose, as that terrible old man, scared the hell out of me. He wasn't just a Newfoundlander, he was everything that John Knox dreamed about, and, thank God, failed to realize. A brilliant performance, by an actor who believes in Banquo but understands Skipper Pete.

Dick Buehler played Absalom, the Skipper's son, and he told me more about mis-breeding than Sigmund Freud ever dreamed about.

There was one big problem. At the beginning of the play everybody looked at least as old as the Skipper. There is a make-up problem here which should be attended to.

Flo Edwards (the Wife) was beautiful. She gave the feeling that she came from "a Newfoundland outport," and I for one hated the things she hated because they were and are so clearly wrong.

The function of a playwright is to observe, to understand and finally present his conclusions, with sympathy and tolerance. Mr. Cook does almost all of these things, but perhaps because his dedication gets in the way, his tolerance tends to slip sometimes.

At times last night he reminded me of J.M. Synge, with only this difference. Synge only recounted, he never consciously commented. Mr. Cook has not yet mastered this art, but he is near enough to the thing to becoming an important person in the theatre.

In short, I have never sat on a stage-head and watched a people die, but I think I did last night.

Patrick Treacher, *St. John's Evening Telegram*, 5 April 1973*

• •

In spite of a reasonably commendable production by the Saidye Bronfman Centre Theatre [Montreal] where it opened on Saturday night, Michael Cook's new play *The Head, Guts and Soundbone Dance* is more than a little disappointing.

More than a little, because being an original Canadian work one would like it to compare favorably with the imported plays from England and the United States which most of our theatres are still obliged to produce each season to remain in operation. Such however is far from the case. I shudder to think of the reception it would receive either on Broadway or London's West End. To feign enthusiasm here on the basis of it being a home-grown product and therefore in need of

119

chauvinistic praise would be to do Canadian theatre a grave disservice.

To begin with it is not even a full-length work. Its playing time is little more than an hour and even within such a short span it is shamelessly padded with stage business in a desperate attempt to give it a semblance of reality and substance.

Cook has obviously absorbed a good deal of the atmosphere of Newfoundland (though still not nearly enough) and observed the external characteristics of some of the more rugged of its individualists. What he has failed to do however is get beneath the surface idiosyncrasies of these people and invest them with a degree of dimension. Unable to illuminate their personalities with a single saving grace his characters remain cold, hard, unyielding and ultimately unsympathetic.

The result is we watch them from a great distance as peculiar oddities we are unable to identify with, or feel for them. Newfoundlanders are hardly like to feel flattered.

The central character is Skipper Pete, an elderly fisherman who is lost in the past dreaming of outmoded methods of bringing in a good catch which no longer work. Rendered to the sound bone, this is all the play is really about.

In the course of the hour we learn that he rules with an iron fist a middle-aged son-in-law and a mentally retarded son and succeeds in casting a mindless spell over both. At the same time he treats his daughter, who recognizes the futility of his reactionary attitude to progress, with bitter contempt. Long before the play opens he has come between daughter and husband until they now all but despise each other. On the other hand the daughter has little to offer her husband as an alternative to her father's empty dreams apart from a cosy chair in front of the television and an electric blanket on his bed at night.

Having established this much, Cook then concocts a feeble and totally unconvincing piece of business concerning the drowning of a neighbor's child which both men might have prevented had they been less preoccupied with the past. It is as a result of this thin device that the husband becomes aware that he should pay more attention to what is going on around him, escapes the old man's spell of a lifetime and joins his wife in front of the telly, to watch the CBC, no doubt.

To sustain our interest, the playwright tosses in a number of visual gimmicks, such as the gutting of fish (the stench which permeates the theatre is sickening), the mending of a net, the sloshing of water about the stage and several scenes in which both men urinate, none of which can, in all honesty, be considered adequate compensation for the play's complete lack of any real drama.

The rudimentary direction by Roy Higgins is heavily overburdened with the undramatic pause, though Gerard Parks creates such a convincing portrait of the Skipper that once he has established it we find ourselves wishing the playwright had given him something to do with it, and Joy Coghill is splendid in a brief, etched-in-acid vignette as the daughter.

As the son-in-law, however, Len Doncheff founders badly, unsure of the accent and amateurish in his body movements and gestures. R.D. Reid, as the son, has little more to do than stand around looking suitably simple-minded.

Michael Eagan has designed an elaborate set which is a little too stagey and antiseptic looking to be much more than superficially acceptable.

The play is a folksy exercise which no experienced theatregoer is likely to confuse with legitimate drama. What it is in need of are the master strokes of a Eugene O'Neill or a J.M. Synge, whose sea plays it somewhat absent-mindedly recalls.

Myron Galloway, *Montreal Star*, 29 April 1974

• •

Before I went to The Playhouse [Fredericton] last evening, I felt in my bones that Theatre New Brunswick's new production would be worthwhile, and I found that it is. TNB's artistic director, Walter Learning, has done a great deal to produce honestly a Canadian play, even one written in and set in our part of the world, Newfoundland. He has gone so far as to place in the theatre halls an exhibition of prints by Newfoundland artists. He has employed good performers. His total gesture says here all of you who complain that TNB caters too much to pedestrian tastes: accept this gift, which carries with it confirmation of a sincere interest in quality material. (He may prove our words about the need for upgrading to be no more than the screech of gulls. Where were the fault-finders last evening, for example?)

Michael Cook's *The Head, Guts and Soundbone Dance* is a queer play. It upsets one, knocks one off-keel. I don't like it because it's pessimistic and contains some unpleasant things, yet I like it because it doesn't prostitute itself to any tradition, and just because it does unbalance me and make me think.

What is a good tragedy supposed to be, we ask. Must we be Aristotelian and conclude that the good guy must be considerably noble, one way or another, that after seeing the hero's downfall we must feel purged, experience a quiet after a storm? Can't a good tragedy have a hero who's pretty lousy? And can't the play be good even if we do leave the theatre feeling as low as all Hades?

I've always held with Aristotle, myself, but *The Head, Guts and Soundbone Dance* causes me to reconsider the basis for my criticism. And anything jolting our ensconced notions, even if only to assist in their settling in with securer hold, is surely worth a lot in that regard alone.

Once I have accepted the pessimism in the play and the lack of moral uplift, I find the main fault to be a structural weakness. Near the end of Act I, the main character in the play, Skipper Peter (age 90), and his son-in-law and sidekick, Uncle John (age 60), are looking out the back door of a stage-head (structure built over the sea) talking about a little boy they once knew who fell overboard into a school of dogfish and was devoured. (The play is full of this sort of disagreeableness.)

Just then a child appears, crying that a little Jimmy Fogarty has fallen into the water. The men continue their reverie, paying no attention to the child. In the play as it was written, the child tugs the men's clothing. In TNB's production, the child hardly comes onstage. In the written version, with the child making himself quite obvious, the lack of response by the men is extremely difficult to accept as realistic action. In the produced version, at the expense of heightened drama, Skipper Peter and Uncle John are made more natural and likeable. The play is weak here. Rewriting doesn't help.

About three old Newfoundland fishermen who find themselves out of water, with fish no longer abundant, as they once were, the play contains enough to set pens of letters-to-the-editor writers wriggling. There are swearing, urinating (but not quite on stage), and the throwing of fish guts to the four corners. (Those six huge fish caught by Skipper Pete's son Absalom smell to low Hell. One's nostrils are assailed, and there's the fear of getting splattered with an innard. In places the play turns into something nigh like an Aldous Huxley feelie.)

Like or dislike the material worked with, surely one must admire what's done with it by TNB. Walter Learning has directed it with dedication and forcefulness, trying hard to keep a realistic play interesting. Michael Eagan has designed a set that is most effective, looking in some light as skeletal as fish bones, or as allied to the bareness of death as the characters using it. The performers, the lead ones especially, Doris Petrie, Sean Sullivan, Stuart Kent and Henry Beckman, all act competently.

Doris Petrie as Rachel (wife of Uncle John, daughter of Skipper Pete) doesn't have many lines, but the ones she does have are delivered with appropriate fierceness and even hatred. She indicates well that Rachel has a grip on reality that the men have lost.

In his portrayal of Uncle John, Sean Sullivan finds the correct balance between reliance and defiance. The Uncle John here becomes more and more intoxicated as the action progresses, but he is always believable, Mr. Sullivan never permitting him to indulge in unacceptable farce. Uncle John is quite funny at times, but a pathetic figure.

Stuart Kent's Absalom, in a last analysis as much a disappointment to his father as King David's son was to him, looks really stupid, as he's supposed to. He's so happy to have caught six fish, and all by himself, and thoughts of going to St. John's to sell the large catch mightily please him. When he fishes from the water the body of the drowned Jimmy Fogarty, he says pridefully, but to chill the audience, that he never caught a boy before. As only a mentally retarded person might, he asks his father if he can keep the child. This character might have slipped out of control through exaggeration, but it never does.

Henry Beckman, whom we all liked, even loved, in *Death of a Salesman*, excels again in this play as Skipper Pete. Mr. Beckman enters looking like a powerful old man of 90. His voice, speaking and singing, is right for the old "foghorn".

(This voice causes that of the other actors to seem especially weak. They need to be louder.) His body has the sturdy build that's necessary. He is able to create a character who at an ancient age is still able to control people, except his daughter. He has developed a man in whom there are contradictions, a man who might have looked to the heavens upon occasion but whose feet are very much made of clay. Mr. Beckman's fisherman is as noble as adherence to the text would allow.

There's sure to be much talk about this play. It will anger some, shock some. People will disagree about Michael Cook's abilities as a playwright (which I'll argue are of consequence), but I can't imagine anyone's forgetting the admirable effort of Walter Learning, in selecting this relevant play, directing it, and even playing a small role in it, or forgetting the fine performances by Henry Beckman and the others. . . .

Marion Owen-Fekete, *Fredericton Daily Gleaner*, 22 October 1974

• •

. . . Our attitude to the Skipper is contradictory. He is admirable in his intransigent insistence on natural truths that lie beneath the surface of contemporary society; but, at the same time, he is a monomaniac like Melville's Ahab, who refuses to recognize change or alternative styles of life and is prepared to sacrifice everyone to his own stark vision. Though in the past he was famous for never losing a man, Uncle John accuses him of tyrannizing over his crews for self-aggrandizement:

> You saved 'em alright. But not to stand up. Not to walk the world. Crawl!
> Ye made 'em crawl. Ye made me crawl . . . We escaped the rule of others.
> And exchanged it for the rule of our own kind . . .

and he reminds the Skipper that . . . he never showed humanity except to disarm men on the brink of mutiny. This same brutal imposition of personality continues into the present with the Skipper's vendetta against seagulls; his sneer that, if John had gone to war, "You'd never have survived. Unless I was with you"; and, more comically, with his insistence that his son-in-law must urinate decently, as though he were still on board his ship. Most strikingly, it is shown in the elaborate work rituals—preparing equipment, cleaning, salting, and cooking the fish, and careful cleaning up afterwards—that he enforces before he will allow his companions to celebrate, also ritualistically, his son Absalom's "end of voyage" and miserably small catch.

The Skipper sees these rigid codes as necessary to impose order upon chaos:

I 'low the sea's a big place. Now a man's a small place. You've got to
have order. Decency. There 'as to be a way of doing things. A man's
way. That's why we're here, isn't it? They's only we left.

And according to the opening stage direction, this tension should be reflected in
the play's set. The "splitting room" is crammed with

an immense variety of gear representing man, and fish and sea in a totter-
ing, near derelict place, and yet also [revealing], as we become accustomed
to it, an almost fanatical sense of order.

The egotism of the Skipper's need to impose order is qualified, however, by
a strain of mysticism in him. He holds that it is useless to demand meaning, as
Uncle John does at one point; life can only be accepted: "It doesn't matter what
it means. It's enough that it's there." Fishermen in the past knew their proper
place in nature: "We understood each other—the sea, the cold, and the dogfish,
and the sculpin and the shark and the whale. They knew us and we knew they. . . ."
And in spite of the fish's disappearance, Skipper Peter believes—or wishes to
believe—that this state of things will return, ousting the modern world of relief,
welfare, and education, for which he has total contempt: "We waits. . . . And
one day, they'll come back in their t'ousands. . . . They's waiting for the old days
like we is."
These two sides to his attitude—the "Satanic" compulsion to an order based
on egotism and his mystique of man's relation to nature—are given religious overtones. . . . On the surface, the Skipper is an intolerantly conservative Catholic
who will not attend his sister-in-law's funeral because it is to be held in a Pen-
tecostal church, nor welcome the visiting bishop because he has come by car instead
of boat and the traditional floral arches have not been built to welcome him. The
Skipper's orthodoxy is wholly superficial, however. He warns Uncle John that
"God is not merciful. Don't ye ever forget that," and seems to substitute his own
authority for the bishop's when he defends the sternness of his regime by claiming
"I made an arch for ye." When the Skipper boasts of never changing a habit or
opinion, Uncle John replies with irony: "You and the Pope 'as got something in
common after all then, Skipper . . . ," and John's wife pushes the implications
of this a stage further when she says her father is "Only one breath away from
God or the Devil himself." On the other hand, the Skipper's reaction to the news
of young Jimmy Fogarty's death is wholly pagan and fatalistic, deifying not himself but the sea: "The sea wanted him. Old Molly. She took him in her good
time. . . ."
The set reflects this pantheism. The left wall of the "splitting room" has "a
ragged window—once a church window, saved from an abandoned church somewhere and put to use by a crude insertion into the room . . . ," and it is through

this window that the Skipper gazes as he rhapsodizes about the past and envisions its return. At the end, when he is left alone, the setting sun dies through it to conclude the play.

For a while, with memories, work rituals, drink, and snatches of song, the Skipper and his two companions manage to create their own reality within the shack, culminating in the drunken dance of triumph that gives the play its title. A stage direction tells us that during this dance "For a moment they are all one. All free"; and one implication of the title is, of course, the celebration of a sense of life in the raw, a dance of fundamentals. But as the title also implies it is a dance of discarded remnants as well, the pieces of the fish that are thrown away: the dance is ultimately a dance of death. All along, the emphasis on heroic individualism has been balanced by a recognition of the sterility of the Skipper's way of life. His is a world with no place for women or children. Though his sister-in-law, we hear, was good to the family, Skipper Pete has no intention of attending her funeral; and he despises his daughter, Uncle John's wife, partly because he wanted to father only sons, but also because he realizes she is a bitter rival for John's loyalty, without which he cannot keep his vision alive: "Memories ain't no good unless you can see someone else working out the same ones" . . . .

Except for the rather forced situation where the child's plea is ignored, *Dance* is remarkably economical and successful in fusing realism and symbolism. Cook admits that the Skipper's disregard of the child's request is "unrealistic," but says "The scene was intended to drive home the Skipper's character"; and the advertisement for a CBC production of the play expands this by explaining that in the Skipper "fatalism reflects an acceptance of tragedy that seems like inhumanity." Yet it is less the situation itself that is at fault than the fact that so little of its significance gets into the dialogue. The Skipper's remarks about "Old Molly" emphasize his fatalism retroactively, but his deliberate *willing* of the disaster at the time of the child's plea is left wholly to the actor; the closest the dialogue comes to it is that, at that time, the Skipper and John are discussing the drowning of a young man whose father was restrained from trying to rescue him. Similarly, the Skipper's *anagnorisis*, when the tragedy of Jimmy Fogarty's death at last strikes home to him, is all in dumbshow; Pete does not speak again after he has seen the body in Absalom's arms.

Apart from this particular incident the ingredients of the play are admirably coherent. The characterization of the four main personages—Skipper Pete, Uncle John, Absalom, and John's wife—is sharply individualized; the set, while realistic, has rich symbolic suggestiveness; sounds-off—the sea itself, the mocking cry of seagulls, the bells of Aunt Alice's funeral, and the encroaching noise of the searchers for Jimmy Fogarty's body—all acquire thematic significance; and the elaborate rituals of preparing equipment, feeding the stove, making tea, cleaning and cooking fish, and preparing a celebratory drink, do not substitute for action, mere visual filler, but reflect the old men's attempt to use routines to recreate the past. This culminates in the grotesque dance, which, like the shanties sung by Pete, absorbs "presentational" techniques into the play's realism yet also carries a level of symbolism. The use of a modified Newfoundland dialect which is sparse, proverbial, coarsely comic, and repetitive, gives a sense of authenticity which can rise effortlessly to poetry—as, to give one brief example, Uncle John's comment that Absalom dreams "Of the mackerel thicker'n on the water than moonlight, whispering together." And the result is a powerful, credible picture of the end of an heroic tradition. . . .

Brian Parker, "On the Edge: Michael Cook's Newfoundland Trilogy," *Canadian Literature*, 85 (Summer 1980), 30-34

• •

Wallace I'd like to talk about Skipper Pete in *Head, Guts and Soundbone Dance* because the ambivalent response he evokes in me I find central to all your work. On one hand I admire Skipper Pete's adherence to the old ways, the so-called natural truths that he is able to affirm against change; yet I abhor the way this leads to his self-absorption which contributes to the boy's death. What is your opinion of the Skipper inasmuch as you've made him so complex?

Cook That ambivalence exists in the Newfoundland character and Newfoundlanders don't like me to say it. In fact, many Newfoundlanders were appalled by that play because they recognized so much of themselves in it. But I am not dealing with docu-drama there; I'm dealing with an imaginative creation about parts of the Newfoundland psyche. Historically, there are precedents for the boy's death in that way. One of them is the Newfoundland ice disaster of 1918 which has been documented by Cassie Brown in her book *Death on the Ice*. One of the old skippers, confronted with the facts of a falling glass and a possible storm would not let people from another boat onto his boat, a result of which was a lot of men died. The erosion of traditional human values is written into Newfoundland history. The boy's death is an appalling image because it is so individual, so human, and because the child runs in and forces Skipper Pete to become aware of it. But he, of course, is trapped in his dream of the past. I think that's the pain of it, that's what people don't want to face. Increasingly in Newfoundland people want to turn away from the past; but the only way you learn to go into the future is to recognize everything that existed before.

Wallace It seems to me that your plays are not just about survival, as has been suggested, but that they are about the price of survival—what, in this case, Skipper Pete pays to hang on to the old ways. Are you suggesting that by adhering to the past, Newfoundlanders are forfeiting their future?

Cook What I am trying to do in *Head, Guts and Soundbone Dance* and in *Jacob's Wake*, to some extent, is write a classic tragedy as much as one can in the twentieth century. Skipper Pete and Elijah in *Jacob's Wake* sacrifice an elemental, social part of themselves in order to maintain their stance in the world. The cost is enormous. I am more sorry for Pete in the play than I am for the boy because he loses everything. When he shuts the door at the end of that play, he shuts out the world, and he shuts himself in forever. That defiant song that rises from his mouth is meant to be tragic. He has failed to adapt and he is dead as a dodo.

Wallace Also, in the process of that failure he has allowed his progeny to die; he not only is finishing his own life, he's killing others as well. That seems to me a devastating vision. Are we to interpret Skipper Peter as the representative of a dying culture?

Cook There are certain ambiguities in that play which will never be resolved. The Skipper Petes of this world are unable to change. But Uncle John, at least, leaves. He makes a moral decision which is very profound for him—he abandons ship knowing damn well the values no longer apply. John is the future. And, you know, although Pete is that incredibly rigid, authoritarian person, he has heroic qualities in terms of the way he has weathered the environment. There's a heroic quality there, even though it's been achieved at the expense of the spirit.

Wallace He achieves order at the sake of his own humanity. In that sense he reminds me of Black Jack Musgrave in Arden's *Sergeant Musgrave's Dance*, the hero who in his adherence to altruistic values destroys not only himself but others around him.

Cook I fell in love with *Sergeant Musgrave's Dance* at a very early age. I still think it's an amazing play precisely because Black Jack Musgrave, in pursuit of an idea, destroys everything. I thought it was the closest creation of a genuine tragic figure that we'd seen in the twentieth century. Despite what Arthur Miller says about *Death of a Salesman*, I don't see Willy Loman as a tragic figure; the play is a profoundly moving human drama but it's not a tragedy. I was trying to do the same thing with Skipper Pete that Arden attempts with Musgrave . . .

Interview with Michael Cook, by Robert Wallace, *The Work*, pp. 162-164

• •

DAVID FRENCH

Of the Fields, Lately

First produced at Tarragon Theatre, Toronto
29 September 1973

Directed by Bill Glassco
Set and Costume Design by Tiina Lipp
Lighting Design by Bill Williams

Cast

Ben Mercer	Tim Henry
Jacob Mercer	Sean Sullivan
Mary Mercer	Florence Paterson
Wiff Roach	Sandy Webster

Of the Fields, Lately, David French's new play which opened at the Tarragon Theatre Saturday night, provides the sort of theatre that makes you think Toronto must be the only place in the world worth living in. It's that good and it's here among us and it makes all the muck and junk that gets on the stage seem somehow less gruesome. And, surprisingly, it's Canadian.

Surprisingly, because its Canadianism isn't worn in a lapel button-hole or flashed about with deep significance: it's just unflamboyantly, obviously there, as comfortable and undeniable as Hockey Night in Canada. There's this Newfoundland family living in Toronto, you see, and there are problems.

The family is familiar. David French gave it to us with his last play, *Leaving Home*, which had a highly successful run at the Tarragon last year. Then the family was struggling, during the late fifties, to overcome domestic brawls and a certain autobiographical obsession French himself had. This time around, it's two years later, and the family is seeking to come to terms with life, not just its periphery, making *Of the Fields, Lately* vastly superior fare and very good theatre.

Ben (Tim Henry) has returned home for the first time since he ran off following the melodramatic outcry of a lifetime, ostensibly to attend the funeral of a favorite aunt, but really to check out his own immediate past. He is suprised to learn that his parents have turned affectionately to each other after he and his brother skipped out—the egotism of youth is constantly assaulted by such discoveries.

His father, Jacob Mercer (Sean Sullivan, who played the same role in *Leaving Home*) remains, on the surface, the old man ready to do battle at the merest hint of conflict. But that's only on the surface and only at the beginning. Very quickly, French lets us into a more complex—and satisfying—Jacob than the one in *Leaving Home*. A heart attack and its reminders of mortality, nothing more complicated than that, is what unravels Jacob, who no longer rails away because he feels like a failure, but because he is confronting death. "The flowers don't smell of the fields, lately," Jacob's friend Wiff Roach (Sandy Webster) tells us, "only of funerals."

Out of the conflicts that arise because of this very common human situation, French has fashioned his play, fleshing it out with warmly humorous dialogue that is often taken to the brink of sentimentality and then soundly rescued. French makes his points directly and simply and they are all the more effective because of that.

As Jacob, Sean Sullivan turned in a masterful performance. Whether he's snatching his wife's glasses to read because he won't admit he's near-sighted, or peering into a scrapbook that has enshrined his youth in the ranks of Newfoundland's Church Lads' Brigade, or quietly listening to Abide With Me on the radio, he has his character down cold. You could sniff Sullivan's Jacob a mile away.

Sandy Webster's Wiff took longer to convince, but with a fine secondary role providing many honest laughs, he did grow into it nicely as the evening went on. Henry's Ben was the only role that was a strain to accept, partly because of some discomfort on Henry's part, and partly because French has concentrated on the parents so much it was hard to accept him as a worthy catalyst to the dialogue.

To Florence Paterson as Jacob's wife, Mary Mercer, belongs the highest accolade. If the lady is not a Newfoundlander by birth, she should be made an honorary citizen—she practically wears Bay Roberts and Conception Bay around her neck. She alone had the accent down pat (the lack of it with Jacob and Wiff, though, was not disconcerting) and this coupled with the humanity and genial charm of her acting made her performance a stunning thing to behold.

Bill Glassco has taken the playwright's offering and the two leading actors' consummate professionalism and directed a production that is as smartly finished off as one suspects Jacob's carpentry assignments must be. The pacing, the flow of dialogue and the deliberately low-keyed tempo testified to a great theatrical imagination. He was aided by Tiina Lipp's good set, accurate to the period (1961) without being too obsessive.

If there is one flaw in the play, it is that the first act is too long—and would benefit from some extremely judicious editing. There is some needless repetition of themes, preserved, one suspects, for the sake of a few good lines. The play would survive without these lines—there are so many others—and would be that much better with the tidier look. But that is quibbling from the cheap seats. *Of the Fields, Lately* is very fine.

John Fraser, *Globe and Mail*, 1 October 1973*

• •

David French's Mercers—the family thrust into life through his first play *Leaving Home*—have found so resonant a tone in the national consciousness that it seems inevitable that he has returned to them for a second work, *Of the Fields, Lately*.

The new play, which had its premiere at the Tarragon Theatre on Saturday, is not merely an attempt to extend the trans-Canada success of its predecessor; it is French's perceptive response to our uncompleted need, as well as his, to examine ourselves through the experiences of this acutely specific, yet hauntingly familiar family.

Three Mercers recur: Jacob, the battling, difficult father; Mary, the anxious, watchful mother; and the older son, Ben, whose troubled departure wrenched apart the family structure in the earlier work. They are reunited, two years later, pulled apart by crucial incidents which went unshared, drawn together by the same unbroken ties of nervous feeling.

The effect of their re-appearance, and the relationship between the two plays, is like the use of a constant group of instruments in two separate pieces of chamber music. That means that the essential timbre of the characters remains unchanged while the themes and harmonies are different.

The playwright's theme in *Of the Fields, Lately* is death, but viewed from an interestingly oblique perspective. No death occurs within the play's action, but one initiates the events, and another is glimpsed in the fading moments. The work hovers between these two terminations and the discoveries are made not through the actuality of death, but within its shadow.

An old man who had lost his love for a wife re-discovers it after her death; a young man finds that he can express his love for a father only by allowing him to move toward death.

Ben Mercer has returned home from Regina to Toronto on the occasion of the death and funeral of his aunt Dot. He finds a father intent on making their relationship as emotionally violent as before, though the man himself has aged abruptly through illness.

The mother is caught in a confusion of grief for her lost sister, anger at Dot's boozing, philandering husband Wiff, and apprehension about the future of her own Jacob. The centrality of work is as critical to French's characters as it is to Chekhov's.

Like the first play, *Of the Fields, Lately* enfolds a simplicity of action which is both natural and deceptive. Through the uncommon honesty of his observation, the unfailing truth of his feeling, David French brings us to an understanding of the interrelation of death and pride, love and fury.

A loss of pride is the beginning of death, and a grasp on one's own mortality is the last and perhaps most important manifestation of pride. The potential for rage is a balm.

In a subtle complement to *Leaving Home*, French argues the necessity of children setting their parents free. In the first play, Ben left home to save himself; in this play, he leaves to save his father.

The texture of the new play is quite different. It does not turn upon a single traumatic incident, nor is it structured toward a series of raw, raging encounters. *Of the Fields, Lately* is more layered, elusive, reposed, possibly even deeper in its quiet impact. French's extraordinary inner ear responds once again to heartbeat shifts in emotion and perception, and his lovely sense of comedy controls the contradictions of human nature. Bill Glassco, working with his best-balanced cast yet, responds to the new play with a breathtaking synchronization of purpose. His production unwinds the tangles of motives and sensations with extraordinary lucidity without for a moment jarring the sense of the unexpectedness, the unaccountability, of much of universal behavior. Tiina Lipp's designs, too, have their eyes open and their wits sharp.

The performances are, quite literally, incomparable. Sean Sullivan is again the Jacob, and the very first instant that the light hit him, I realized how much I'd missed him, missed his fierce sense of life, his tenacity. His son is now played by Tim Henry, shifted into the role of outside observer; Henry manages beautifully, as sharply watchful as his mother, as explosive as his father.

Florence Paterson, with her fantastic sharp eyes and her rejection at every point of sentiment, is magnificent as Mary. And I have never seen Sandy Webster do anything finer than his funny, touching, utterly individual Uncle Wiff.

Of the Fields, Lately concludes with a brief, transfixing coda. In its poignant valedictory, a gnawing regret is transformed, in a microscopic visual detail which is the last thing we see, into love and reconciliation. It is a blinding moment, growing richly from a play and a production which are so profoundly moving that though we may be forced to bid the Mercers farewell, we will not, cannot let them go.

Urjo Kareda, *Toronto Star*, 1 October 1973*

• •

. . . Hopefully, *Of the Fields, Lately* will not only allow French to free himself from his father, but also from Arthur Miller. Ben Mercer and Bill Loman have as much in common here as had their fathers in *Leaving Home* and *Death of a Salesman*. Both left home in reaction to their fathers. Neither has really found himself, although each is looking. Both are unintentional in their disruption of home life. Both decide, momentarily, to try to make a go of it at home—in each case a decision pleasing to the father. Both are followed as they come to some degree of understanding which comes shortly before the fathers' deaths. And in each case, ultimately, the discovery by the son is of less importance than the humanity shown by the father.

No doubt it seems like a typical academic ploy to discuss one play by comparing it with another. From the aesthetic viewpoint, the experience of each play is personal in terms of the effect of that production on the individual. But both scripts are part of the collective theatrical consciousness of the "modern" stage. And the fact that Miller was there first has got to be recognized. Moreover, this looking backward extends not only to the play's structure, but also to its theme. Eugene O'Neill, in his dedication of *Long Day's Journey into Night*, speaks of facing "my dead at last," and writing " with deep pity and understanding and forgiveness" toward his mother and father and brother. Pity, understanding and, to a lesser extent, forgiveness are French's themes. And while he is not writing an O'Neill play, it is also obvious that his themes dwell not among untrodden ways.

As long as we're throwing in quotations: "In my end is my beginning." Man is constantly moving from the known to the unknown. And this is what the play is all about. Jacob Mercer contains a depth and stature that *Leaving Home* didn't have room to build. He defines himself in the existential terms of his own past and the possibilities that lie ahead. Despite his three heart attacks he is not willing to go gently into that good night. And it is this fight against the impossible odds which gives Jacob the large dimension he gradually comes to contain. Arthur

Miller could talk of Willy's flaw. It would be much more difficult to talk in such terms about Jacob Mercer. He is neither heroic in his actions, nor tragic. But he exists with a humanity to which attention must be paid. And this, more than any understanding of his father to which Ben comes, is the strength of the play. Theatre widens our comprehension of what it means to be human. And French's second play has widened this comprehension much more than *Leaving Home*. In the process, hopefully, French has been able to face his own ghosts, to realize that the butterfly dream eventually does give way to a more faceless reality. The experience must have been one of personal growth for the playwright. And it will be interesting to see just where he goes from here . . .

Edward Mullaly, *The Fiddlehead*, 100 (Winter 1974), 65-66

• •

The biggest problem with sequels is that one inevitably starts making comparisons with the original source work.

Understandable as that may be, it is hardly relevant because a piece must be judged strictly on its own merits.

Just over a year ago, the Playhouse Theatre Centre enjoyed tremendous success with its production of David French's *Leaving Home*. It was the sequel's turn Monday night as the Playhouse opened French's award-winning *Of the Fields, Lately.*

Comparisons will undoubtedly be made between the two because three characters are carried over into the new play. Although the story is still centred around the Mercer family, the situation and concept is quite different. Like *Leaving Home*, the style is highly naturalistic, and deals with a traumatic family situation, but there is much more to it than that.

Two years have passed and Jacob Mercer, the virile, delightful and totally-aggravating father of *Leaving Home* has suffered a heart attack that has kept him from working. His wife, Mary, is now the bread winner. Ben, the sensitive younger son who left home in dispute with Jacob has suddenly returned for the funeral of Aunt Dot, Mary's sister.

Predictably, attention is spent on the attempts to establish communication between father and son, but those externals provide little more than skillful soap opera. What raises *Of the Fields* above that is a perceptive look at people facing death and, thereby, coming to grips with life. The point is made that fighting death is futile. It is an unavoidable physical fact. The death to be fought is the one of the soul and that is done by living with purpose. That includes understanding that death doesn't resolve things.

Uncle Wiff, dead Dot's husband, faces that as does young Ben. The barrier between father and son doesn't end with Jacob's death. It is a thing Ben must resolve for himself. *Of the Fields, Lately* has its faults—it rambles somewhat and seems a little contrived—but it still has strong emotional power.

The Playhouse production, under Jace van der Veen's sensitive direction, brings it off well, Jacob is beautifully played by Powys Thomas, and Kenneth Ferrell provides a good counterpoint as the young Ben. Florence Paterson provides fine support as Mary, and Barney O'Sullivan in equally effective as Uncle Wiff . . . .

Bob Allen, *Vancouver Province*, 15 January 1975

• •

SHARON POLLOCK

Walsh

First produced at Theatre Calgary, 7 November 1973

Directed by Harold Baldridge
Set and Lighting Design by Richard Roberts
Costume Design by Jane Grose

Cast

Harry	Frank J. Adamson
Clarence	Hardee T. Lineham
Louis	Jean Archambault
Walsh	Michael Fletcher
Mrs. Anderson	Margaret Barton
Crow Eagle	Stephen Russell
McCutcheon	Ron Chudley
Gall	Denis Lacroix
Sitting Bull	August Schellenberg
White Dog	Nolan Jennings
Crowfoot	Frank Turningrobe Jr.
Colonel MacLeod	Hutchinson Shandro

Conflict is the stuff of which good theatre is made, and it is conflict which is at the core of *Walsh*, the new Theatre Calgary play which received its world première Wednesday night in the Arts Centre Theatre.

A few members of the audience left after the first act, and that was a mistake. Had they stayed, they would have seen the central concerns of Sharon Pollock's fascinating play take urgent vital shape.

The genesis of the play is a historical event—the fact that after the Custer massacre Chief Sitting Bull and his followers took refuge in Canada, remained there peaceably for four years before eventually being forced back to the United States.

All of us learned of this event at school—but that is about all that we learned. We knew nothing of the emotional drama which surrounded the Canadian government's decision to deny Sitting Bull his exile under the protection of the Great White Mother, Queen Victoria. We have cared little about the cynical expediency which governed the Macdonald regime's policy in this regard or of the anguish which resulted from its implementation.

Miss Pollock's play takes unrepentant, dramatic licence on occasion, but it also puts living flesh on the bare and dusty bones of history.

The protagonist is Major Walsh, superintendent of the North West Mounted Police at Fort Walsh, and the man ultimately saddled with an assignment he detests.

The assignment requires him to turn his back on Sitting Bull, a man he has befriended and whom he respects, and to force him back across the border into the vengeful embrace of the American authorities.

It is an assignment at which he balks, jeopardizing his friendship with Colonel MacLeod as well as his future usefulness with the force. His duty is to obey orders, to uphold the law of the land. "That is the law," he explodes in frustration, "but where the hell is the justice?"

To that question, of course, the play supplies no answer, but it does leave the implicit suggestion that in sending Sitting Bull and his fellow Hunkpapa Sioux back across the border, the Canadian government was condoning genocide.

Yet, all this is essentially background to the personal conflict which is the main reason for the play's existence. And the conflict is two-fold—the conflict between Major Walsh and his superiors over the best way of dealing with Sitting Bull, and the conflict within his own heart and mind between duty and his conscience and sense of justice.

It was Act Two of Wednesday night's performance that this moral crisis sprang to agonizing life.

It happened in a lacerating confrontation scene between Walsh, played by Michael Fletcher, and Col. MacLeod, played by Hutchinson Shandro, in which a solid and longstanding friendship between the two officers disintegrated in a few moments because of Walsh's stubborn defence of Sitting Bull.

It happened again later in the act when Walsh, defeated and bitter, turned savagely against Sitting Bull, portrayed by August Schellenberg, the instrument of his current misfortune, and subjected him to humiliation similar to that endured at the hands of MacLeod.

Both scenes are written with great skill and dramatic awareness, and they fulfil their potential, thanks to the excellent efforts of the three principals and the taut staging of Theatre Calgary artistic director, Harold Baldridge.

There is no denying Miss Pollock's sharp sense of the theatrical, her ear for the tiny characteristics of speech which distinguish one piece of dialogue from another, and her ability to telescope events without for the most part resorting to a comic-book narrative approach.

The play's strengths, then, are substantial. Although a key traumatic event—the death of Sitting Bull—occurs off stage in the third act, Miss Pollock ensures that we hear about it in a way which is theatrically effective in the quality of poignancy and irredeemable loss which it evokes. And this loss involves not only the passing of a great leader but, for Walsh, the death of honor and self-respect.

The play is episodic, the various scenes linked together by voice-over readings of actual government documents of the day pertaining to the Sitting Bull problem and U.S.-Canadian relationships.

It is also, in many respects, an old-fashioned well-made play, with deft bits of humor and a set of supporting characters which, thanks to Mr. Baldridge's clever casting, are reminiscent of a John Ford movie stock company of living, breathing types. The approach is great for audience identification, and there was some fine work last night from Jean Archambault, cheerfully resourceful as a Metis scout, Frank Adamson, very good indeed as a boozing, rough-spoken wagon master, Margaret Barton, flapping frenziedly about as a settler's wife, Hardee T. Lineham injecting humor and humanity into the role of a gauche new recruit, Ron Chudley, stalwart as an oak as an NWMP constable, and Hutchinson Shandro, gruff and convincing as MacLeod. There was good cameo work from Stephen Russell, Denis Lacroix, Nolan Jennings and Frank Turningrobe Jr.

August Schellenberg's Sitting Bull was the dominant performance of the evening—a dignified, heroic and very, very human characterization. His final scene with Walsh was wrenching in its depiction of a nobility sustained in the face of humiliation and degradation.

Michael Fletcher's Walsh began frenetically and rather bombastically, almost as though he was feeling intimidated by the first act of the play, as well he might. Act One was uneven last night—beginning on a strong comic note and then subsequently floundering. It's an act which sets the scene for what follows. Much of it is expository in nature, and perhaps the exposition has been telescoped too much by its author with a resulting slackness in narrative drive. Walsh's first appearance lacked dramatic impact Wednesday. So, although not quite to the same degree, did Sitting Bull's. It was as though pace and tempo had dissolved, and it wasn't until the second act that Mr. Fletcher's characterization gathered its necessary strength and conviction to see it through to a most powerful climactic scene.

Despite the first act problems, *Walsh* is an undeniable red-letter event for Theatre Calgary and its author. It offers, at its best, vibrant and exciting theatre. It raises valid moral issues. And it provides solid mass-audience entertainment. It's the most substantial new Canadian play TC has so far given us, and before I forget, it also features a superb set design by Richard Roberts.

Jamie Portman, *Calgary Herald*, 8 November 1973*

• •

The color of the red coats in *Walsh*, which opened Wednesday night at the Third Stage here [Stratford, Ontario], is not the color of Rose Marie, or of the Union Jack, for that matter. It is a faded, dusty, unspectacular red, and it is the true color of one of the saddest episodes in the history of the Canadian West.

For Sharon Pollock has set down the aftermath of the famous massacre of the United States' General Custer at Little Big Horn, as it concerned this country. It is an account of international relationships transcending human ones and though it is told laconically, it is a very distressing one.

It was that episode at Little Big Horn which drove the Sioux back to Canada to take refuge under the Great White Mother, Victoria, as once promised. Having been in this land before the Europeans divided it up for themselves, the Sioux recognized no boundary. They learned to.

Rather than have any embarrassment with the United States, Sir John A. Macdonald eventually returned the Sioux to the slave camp of the U.S. reservation. Their chief, the redoubtable Sitting Bull, was murdered in revenge for Custer, and his little son, Crowfoot, died too.

We are prepared for this fatality through the efforts of Major James Walsh, of the North-West Mounted Police, to offer Sitting Bull both a haven and the kind of treatment he deserved as a man of great character and wisdom. Bureaucracy stifles Walsh's effort and his spirit.

As Miss Pollock's play showed here Wednesday night, this is a play about that man and that destruction. Sitting Bull is in it enough to impress us that Walsh's esteem was justified. But Walsh is the central figure in this drama of a man trying to fight the system and failing.

To this end, Miss Pollock now starts off her story in the Yukon, with Walsh's destruction already accomplished. She doesn't dwell on it for there is a lot of history to set before us. Although she has refined her script for this production, there is still a lot of our history that we have to be told.

For this reason, we worry that the drama of Walsh will not get started, only to discover it already has, and that we are now becoming aware of the dreadful inevitability of it. We are offered no false hope, only solemn steps toward a kind of doom. It is not Sitting Bull's doom, we can recognize, though he was the obvious victim. It is Walsh's doom, and our share in it as Canadians.

The remarkable thing is that Miss Pollock has been able to tell us this wide, sweeping tragedy with only 14 actors, only three of whom play different parts. This is not the theatre game of doffing personalities with hats. Donna Farron's characterizations of all the women in the play—dance hall girl, Indian squaw, settler woman and Mrs. Walsh—are completely different and believable in character and appearance.

And handsome John Bayliss is acceptable, even admirable, as a noble savage and as a stuffy commanding officer, with Terry Judd playing two other Indians, Cree and Assiniboine, differently and well. John Wood's direction is without affectation. His is a very well organized production, dedicated to a straight narrative technique.

The variable space of the Third Stage finds the audience aloft on banks of grandstands to observe this trudge-past. Below, a long irregular bridge of a stage has been thrown by John Ferguson, the designer, to carry us back into the last century, out on to the prairies, into tepees and barracks. Having no character save roughness, it suits all the settings of this rough tale.

But the contribution of Alan Laing must also be reckoned with, for in addition to the haunting little songs, he has provided the wide echoing sound of a great empty land, a place of distances removed. And Michael Whitfield has enhanced this space with his lighting, while directing our attention where it must go profitably.

Into this long space step the half dozen characters. Backing Walsh are a trio of men who stand for the whole body of Canada's early law enforcers. Two of them wear uniforms, young Clarence and old McCutcheon, with a Metis scout as counsel for the inhabitants. At Sitting Bull's side stand a few impermanent supporters and his son, Crowfoot.

As Sitting Bull, Derek Ralston is a totemic figure, the bronze effigy of a legendary hero. His speech is measured, as we expect, but there is never an "ugh" to shame us. Here is, most impressively, a wise man and a symbol. As his son, Kim Jones shares a fine scene of tribal instruction with him.

John Stewart is the young recruit, avoiding the sentimentality of the role with laconic speech and stoic bearing, but supplying the full punch when he brings the news of Sitting Bull's death as Walsh is moving toy soldiers into place. In contrast, David Hemblen is positively rock-faced as the old sergeant, but his presence, questioning, supporting, and despairing, is strong in the play.

Other important support comes from J. Kenneth Campbell, the wagonmaster who is also chorus to the play, and as such stands apart from Walsh's retinue. Miss Pollock has entrusted different tasks to each secondary figure.

In the title role, Michael Ball grows in stature. The first glimpse tells us nothing, the next that here is a man of the military. No, more. Young and erect of figure, Ball has a way of aging in expression. We are made aware of the deterioration which ensues as the man-to-man bond with the Indian conflicts with his duty, and that duty with his belief in his life. But for all of Ball's development as a character, he never takes the stage away from history. Wood has seen to that. His first duty is to the dramatist's intention. His staging here is as impressive as was that he contributed last year to Michael Ondaatje's *The Collected Works of Billy the Kid*.

The important difference is that *Walsh* deals with our own legendary figures and the truth behind them. Calgary has sent Stratford a piece of Canada's history to enrich the classic festival season.

Herbert Whittaker, *Globe and Mail*, 25 July 1974

• •

. . . Pollock in *Walsh* wants both to challenge the idea, still prevalent among students, that Canada's history is a dull one, of laws, reports, constitutions and boring and indistinguishable politicians, and to direct attention to neglected aspects of that history. (Many other contemporaries have shared this concern, among them Michael Cook in *Colour the Flesh the Colour of Dust*, Herschel Hardin in *The Great Wave of Civilization*, Rick Salutin and Passe Muraille in *1837*, Arthur Murphy in *The First Falls on Monday*, and Ann Henry in *Lulu Street*.) In *Walsh* Pollock looks at the greatest of Canadian myths, the Mounties, those glamorous red-coated heroes. She is disturbed most specifically by the treatment of Indians, which is part of her message for the present. Harold Baldridge, director of the Calgary production, commented, "I believe we have made our audience *think* about our responsibility for the modern-day problems of the Plains and Woods Indians. I think that not one of us will ever be able to regard a drunken Indian on the street corner in quite the same way" [*Canadian Theatre Review*, 3 (1974), 120].

Pollock has much information to give, so frequently depends on messengers, for accounts of Custer's last stand, the flight of Chief Joseph and the Nez Perce, the death of Crazy Horse, the entry of Chief Sitting Bull and his Sioux into Canada, the decline of the buffalo herds, and finally, the killing of Sitting Bull. She paints a broad panorama of the Prairies in the 1870s, in short scenes on a multiple set, for the police fort, Walsh's office, a store room, Indian tents and the open prairie. Representatives of the various groups appear: Mrs. Anderson, the pioneer settler; Crow Eagle and White Dog, the Canadian Indians; Louis, the Metis; Clarence, the new Mountie recruit. The first version of the play has speeches through the loudspeaker preceding each of the twelve scenes, "taken," notes Pollock, "from documents of the day." These are not so much Pollock determinedly educating her audience, as adequately informing them. The later version, however, discards this awkward device. (It also adds Walsh's wife and a Prologue, set much later, in the Klondike in 1898, where we learn how corrupt Walsh had become, and of course wonder why he had changed.)

Pollock's task as dramatist is to cover Sitting Bull's four years in Canada, including the Indians' way of life, the central situation of the conflict between Sitting Bull and Walsh, and the conflicts within Walsh. Further, much of the real power, of decision-making, is held in Ottawa, London and Washington, while settlers, traders, and other Indian tribes have also to be taken into account. Indian instinctive perception of the world contrasts with white scientific knowledge, when Sitting Bull instructs his son Crowfoot, watched by Clarence. Louis sums this up: "Take all da books, da news dat da white man prints, take all dat bible book, take all dose things you learn from—lay dem on da prairie—and da sun . . . da rain . . . da snow . . . pouff! You wanna learn, you study inside here (taps head) . . . and here (taps chest) . . . and how it is wit' you and me (indicates) . . . and how it is wit' you and all (indicates surroundings). Travel 'round da Medicine Wheel. Den you know somethin'." At the end the Mounties *play* at being Indians and ambush a train, behaving like Indians in movies: the Indians we have seen in the play have done nothing like this.

Sitting Bull remains a remote figure. Urjo Kareda wrote of the first version: "The characterization of Sitting Bull himself is a catastrophe, a portrait of the noble savage so noble and pious and dignified that he has no reality" [*Toronto Star*, 13 November 1973]. Kareda's view ignores both Sitting Bull as mystic and shaman, and as the victim of circumstances over which he has no control. Walsh is an appealing figure for much of the play: full of humanitarian feelings, while loyal and dutiful (and a workaholic willing to remain apart from the wife he loves). Clarence is third in importance, full at first of boyish relish for the fighting of which he knows little: "An Indjun War! . . . I could get to kill the man who killed Custer!" He changes, giving his coat to a freezing Indian child, then accepting "*our* Indians" and protesting "You don't let people starve! You can't do things like that!", finally sharing a pipe with Sitting Bull, so that Walsh concludes of him, "That young man should never make the Force his life." Clarence's moral ascent parallels Walsh's decline. *Walsh* is one of the finest Canadian historical plays—and the dilemma of the liberal torn between his duty and his principles can be found as easily in the present. . . .

Malcolm Page, "Sharon Pollock: Committed Playwright,"
CD, 5 (Fall 1979), 104-106

• •

In 1876, after the battle known as Custer's Last Stand, the Sioux chief Sitting Bull fled with a group of followers to Canada, where he remained until 1881, at which point the U.S. government offered him amnesty. The man who granted him temporary refuge from the Great White Father, a.k.a. the U.S. president, was Major James M. Walsh, superintendent of the Northwest Mounted Police and a servant of Queen Victoria, a.k.a. the Great White Mother. Walsh allowed Sitting Bull to camp outside Fort Walsh, in what is now southern Saskatchewan, but Great White Mom did everything she could to drive the Sioux back into the hands of Great White Dad.

Walsh, argues Sharon Pollock in her play by that name, which opened Tuesday night at the National Arts Centre, was trapped inside the great white colonial clutches of the United States and England, a situation which could only spell tragedy. The play begins with an epilogue set in a Dawson City saloon in 1898, eight years after Sitting Bull was finally killed. A white-haired alcoholic Walsh is asked for a handout for an Indian youth and responds by overturning the table and roaring, "I can give you nothing. I can give you nothing." The rest of the play attempts to trace the origins of Walsh's utterance and sad condition—his friendship with Sitting Bull and the despair it caused a worthy soldier from Brockville who had mistakenly made the army his life.

Not to make the army your life is one of the big lessons of *Walsh*, a play as stocked with Big Lessons as the prairies once were with buffalo. Sitting Bull's stay in Canada lasted for just over four years, but the play is so given to pedagogy and platitudes it seems like 40. Most of the action takes place off-stage in the manner of loud noises and wailing. Very little occurs on stage that's sufficiently intense to balance the drama the audience never sees.

In the first act, for example, Walsh's men recount at length the history of Custer's attempts to decimate the Sioux while making up their cots and patting their blankets. They seem unable to fill the large, slightly tilted, largely empty circular stage designer Sue LePage has seen fit to provide them with.

As the action—or near action—progresses, it becomes as obvious as a bugle call that partitions of some kind were needed, particularly in the scenes between Sitting Bull and Walsh that are supposed to be intimate. The big bare disc is presumably meant to evoke the Indian philosophy of the circle—which Sitting Bull explains, again at great length and with no apparent reason—and the vastness of the prairies. The dimensions of the Saskatchewan landscape, however, were probably one reason for the existence of rooms and walls.

To make matters worse, director John Wood often has the characters deliver their lines while sitting on the big bare disc, as though taking his cue from the name Sitting Bull. Long speeches delivered in this posture are deadly and provoke yawns. It comes as a relief whenever the characters in *Walsh* stand up and stretch their legs, but even so, they're likely to spout long lines verging on the educational.

Bull, played with quiet dignity by Ray Jewers, is one offender, but poor Walsh (Benedict Campbell) must bear the full brunt of Walsh's [sic: Pollock's] tomahawkish pen. Like a pendulum, he is made to swing between preachiness and poetry.

"They'd be a credit to any community," he blusters, when it becomes clear the Sioux will have to go. "Suspended in amber, will I grow old in the west," he concludes.

Walsh is one of Pollock's early plays, and it shows. It's a mystery why the NAC decided to mount it in the first place, unless it was to capitalize on the issue of native rights raised by the Constitution, which would be in keeping with the earnest intentions of the play. Among the few signs of life in this long-winded production are the performances by the RCMP staff, especially Paul Gross as Clarence Underhill, and that of Louis, the Metis scout, played by Gordon Clapp. Ron Hastings, in the roles of General Terry and Col. MacLeod, occasionally thunders onto the stage and makes a few waves. Martha Burns, in the roles of Sitting Bull's daughter and Walsh's wife, succeeds in the first but can't make much of the second because it is so silly. F. Mitchell Dana is responsible for the lighting design; music and sound by Alan Laing.

Adele Freedman, *Globe and Mail*, 12 May 1983

• •

. . . *Walsh* first brought Sharon Pollock national attention. It was produced in Calgary in 1973 and the following year at Stratford. It has been in print for ten years now, and has worn well, although more as a play to read than as a play to perform. What keeps it fresh is its passion and sincerity and its ability to arouse troubling thoughts about Canada's treatment of aboriginal people and about its relations with the United States.

The impressive heart of the play is the encounter of Sitting Bull, chief of the Hunkpapa Sioux, and James A. Walsh, superintendent of the NWMP, two men of great racial and cultural divide. It chronicles how these men join the thousands of victims on the romantic myth of The Opening of the West, which casts the Indians as villains, the whites as heroes, and is utterly impervious to the truth. Walsh is forced, indeed, to become part of the ugly real-life destruction of aboriginal people which the myth rationalizes. The legend of General Custer, "flower of the American Army", proves to be stronger than the reality of his exterminatory raids, the retribution which caught up with him at Little Big Horn, the Sioux' exemplary behaviour during the four years they stay in Canada, and Walsh's struggle to acquaint his government with the facts. Walsh, haunted through the play by Custer's marching song, "Garryowen", is pressed into the service of a fantasy cynically subscribed to by the Canadian government in order to maintain good relations with its mad neighbour to the south.

Walsh, imagining that he serves a government that bases its Indian policy on recommendations from the field, is brought face to face with the truth that he is a puppet and the Sioux are pawns, and that there is no justice or even sense to the policy he is obliged to carry out. When he breaks, he does so in the only way possible for a man of his integrity, by brutally, physically, acting out the cruelty hidden in the Prime Minister's directives. At the cost of both his and Sitting Bull's self-respect he strikes him and sends him sprawling. The moment is of a sort that seems to fascinate Sharon Pollock, for variations on it occur in most of her plays. After slamming the door so finally, or finding it slammed shut, on the way you have lived up to that moment, even on the very principles you have lived by, how do you go on from there?

The answer in *Walsh* is the powerful anti-climax which concludes the play. Walsh returns to his post after an extended leave (the audience having been kept in suspense in the meantime), quite willing to substitute the myth of the savage Indian for the reality he knew first-hand, to substitute "style", "show" and "image" for substance; he illustrates his plan to stage a mock-attack, Indian style, on Eastern dignitaries arriving to open the new railway, with toy soldiers mounted on a model: a precise metaphor for the state he has been reduced to. The plan is derailed by the news of the abject end of Sitting Bull at the hands of the United States Army. Walsh's helpless rage and grief at the news intensify the pathos of his surrender.

The play resorts to some awkward tactics to set this action up so that it will be viewed from the proper angle. The prologue, a flash-forward to the end of Walsh's career, is necessary so that we will understand from the start that his spirit will suffer destruction; the cynical Harry's long account of Custer's raids and his death at Little Big Horn is necessary to utterly demolish the legend of Custer, so that the audience will possess the ironic awareness of its persistence regardless of the facts; scene after scene in the first act are required to establish Walsh as a man of integrity sympathetic to the native people; a long scene in Sitting Bull's teepee is necessary to introduce the audience to the Way of the Medicine Wheel. . . .But the result of all this is that the first half of the play sinks under the weight of exposition.

Pollock's interest in montage as a principle of composition first appears in *Walsh*, not completely successfully. The juxtaposition of scenes in different styles seems partly due to a need to get certain things into the play, at least in the first act. Act II is much more successful at making montage contribute to the total effect, mainly because there is a much stronger through-line to carry us forward from scene to scene. For example, two scenes in very different styles—prosaic with Walsh, poetic with Sitting Bull—place the exhaustion of the two leaders in piquant contrast, and prepare for the climactic scene in which they confront each other for the last time.

Finally, in contrast to Pollock's later writing, the dialogue is such that every character means only what he says. There is no unverbalized subtext enriching, contradicting or counterpointing the text, as there is in her later work. Hence characterization is emphatically two-dimensional. What we see is what we get. . . .

Robert C. Nunn, "Sharon Pollock's Plays: A Review Article," *THC*, 5 (Spring 1984), 73-75

• •

JAMES REANEY

Sticks and Stones:
The Donnellys, Part One

First produced at the Tarragon Theatre,
Toronto, 24 November 1973

Directed by Keith Turnbull
Lighting Design by John Stammers

Cast
(Multiple roles for each performer)

Bob Aarron
Richard Carson
David Ferry
Jerry Franken
Rick Gorrie
Miriam Greene
Ian Lange
Carol Lazare
Patricia Ludwick
Don MacQuarrie
Fletcher T. Williamson

There was a great sense of beginning to the Tarragon Theatre's first showing of *Sticks and Stones*, Part One of James Reaney's trilogy, *The Donnellys*, on Saturday night. Here started the poet-dramatist's celebration and conclusions on the province's most-favored folk-legend.

As we have grown more conscious of our heritage, it is interesting that we light on a pack of Irish settlers from outside the throngs of the law-abiding to characterize Ontario's view of itself. Perhaps we are asserting our North Americanism when we reach back to old disorders for heroes, just as, nationally, Louis Riel was elected to similar status a decade ago.

Reaney has been assimilating the legends surrounding the Donnelly family of Biddulph, massacred by neighbors in 1880, for more than half that time, as poet as well as historian, and obviously found the material compelling. He has shaped it and reshaped it into his own form of well-documented fantasy, relying heavily on Keith Turnbull to match his verbal images and to crystallize the Reaney vision.

The result of their collaboration is a thoroughly involving theatrical experience. The bloodshed which first drew the attention to the Donnellys does provide the dominant color to the present exercise but this is no melodramatic restatement, played for thrills.

"Sticks and Stones may break my bones, but words will never hurt me." The title of this first play is ironic. The Donnellys were hurt by one word, one epithet. The accusatory "Blackfoot!" was a label from the old Tipperary, where the feuds started which exploded in Biddulph Township. Its cross-reference to the Whiteboys, the Irish secret society, or klan, is first used as a most effective brand by Reaney when young Will is consoled by his mother early in the play.

This being the first of three plays, Reaney has time to let the legend breathe. He brings it here to the return of James Donnelly from prison for a barroom murder, an unjust sentence fought magnificently by his wife, and to his determination to stay on, even when his barn is burned, his life and land threatened.

But the tragic ending is not lost sight of. Strolling players are foreseen enacting a bastard version of the massacre, for Reaney is not bound by chronology, and in an epilogue the Donnelly daughter describes a recurrent dream of the deaths of her parents.

The many such poetic sequences in no way idealize the Donnellys. We feel we know them as other than roughnecks, and can admire both the parents, but they still belong in their environment, shaped by it as squatters battling for the land others are attempting to grab too. Their family doggedness we must applaud, yet the Donnellys behave like a small and quarrelsome nation.

It is the artistic triumph of Turnbull's production at Tarragon that we seem to know all the Donnellys and their many neighbors, the tavernkeeper Keefe, the priest, the notary, the ghosts and even the Lieutenant Governor and his lady quite intimately, yet this is achieved by a cast of only eight [sic], plus two cunning puppets.

Set in a black interior, scribbled with legend, the chameleon-actors slip from personality to personality in a sequence of vivid scenes, slow at first, to teach us the Reaney approach, then accelerating until we see a midnight encounter between James Donnelly and his proudest enemy as vividly as a scene from *Mon Oncle Antoine*.

Everybody plays everybody, but each actor makes some character particularly his or her own. Patricia Ludwick dominates as Mrs. Donnelly, a staunch matriarch still at child-bearing age, but only perhaps because Jerry Franken must withdraw behind bars for part of his story as James. David Ferry contributes the evening's two most vivid characterizations as young Will and as the friendly Keefe.

Playing two major antagonists, Don MacQuarrie epitomizes the sinister forces against the Protestant Donnellys in a Catholic community, just as Bob Aarron stands in solidly for the materialistic opponents. Tall Fletcher Williamson enlivens many a scene as priest, constable and showman, all well-defined.

And there are two more actresses. Miriam Greene brings power and malevolence to the community and tender Carol Lazare speaks the epilogue as the surviving daughter. She and Ferry are the only two children we know, though we are convinced by Turnbull's use of a clothesline that we know them all.

There are many such imaginative devices, and sounds, employed in this direction. A fly buzzing in a silent church stays in the mind's ear, the ritual burning of miniature barns, the women's disguise worn as it was in Tipperary, are other images, as are the rough road to London Mrs. Donnelly must climb, and James' lonely encounter with an enemy's horse and cart.

The production, built up through earlier workshops in Halifax, offers a great concentration of poetic and theatrical components which demands close attention. You may have to see it twice.

Herbert Whittaker, *Globe and Mail*, 26 November 1973*

• •

Sticks and Stones, the first part of James Reaney's trilogy about the Donnellys, is just plain overwhelming. Its première at the Tarragon Theatre Saturday night affirmed that theatre's status as the most important source of new plays in this country, just as it reaffirmed Reaney's position in the front ranks of all our imaginative writers.

This is fascinating history, fascinatingly told. Reaney takes the early stages of the Donnellys' epic narrative and shapes out of it a dramatic hand which tightens itself into a fist. Though we are given ominous flickerings of the final violent massacre which terminates the family's history (without finishing it), the thrust is upon the forces, internal and external, which galvanize the Donnellys into defiance. It's a play about looking fate in the eye and outstaring it.

The world is of mid 19th century Biddulph township in western Ontario, where the furious urgency of getting land, as well as the cruel labor of keeping it, is linked with prejudice and fear. No matter how young a country is, it seems that outsiders must still be excluded, and if necessary, invented. The bigotry against the Donnellys doesn't arise simply from their Catholicism, but from secret societies—the whole Blackfoot-Whitefoot mystery—transplanted from the old world to the new. The Donnellys, with their seven sons (including one who is both lame and a fiddler, and thus a devil-figure out of folk-lore), are kept in isolation and then tormented for that isolation.

James Reaney tells this extraordinary tale in a form which is often as complex as a cat's cradle (an image he uses), but just as easily resolvable. It's a complicated series of events, but they unravel themselves with beautiful clarity and hypnotic momentum. (Only the murder of an Englishman, in the first act, is a little vague as to its relation to the whole.) And though the evening is a long one, it moves by exhilaratingly; one wouldn't wish a single detail displaced.

The 11 performers, always present, using beautiful props which are always on view, work through choric chanting, songs, children's games, soliloquies, plays-within-plays, indirect narration, mime and even marionettes to express Reaney's collage of history. The play has an exceptionally simple and evocative range of symbols and imagery; like the props, they are chosen from a common experience. The seven sons are represented by seven white shirts hanging on a line; horizontal country roads are seen as vertical ladders; the lieutenant-governor and his lady are dolls; a greedy fat woman is her "darling little laundry stove;" the Donnellys themselves are the solid stones, while their enemies are the dry, crackling sticks.

The visual is connected with the verbal with often unforgettable effects. The play is filled with the horrible recurrence of miniature burning houses and shadowy whispered hatred. A husband and wife, reunited after seven years, simply, movingly recite one another's names. Donnelly brings his wife a handful of earth, first hopeful, then stained with blood. Two men, disguised as old women, dance a frenzied jig with an ancient herself.

Sticks and Stones is a poetic drama, but like the poetic drama of the Elizabethans, it is also an unquestionably popular drama. Thus, while the shape of the play uncovers Reaney's thematic obsession with the daytime-night-time division in experience, its physical reality is strong, funny, concrete. We are reminded of the beauty of choric speech and are shown, at a time when we might have forgotten, how really thrilling the manifestation of courageous pride can be. What is staggering, too, is Reaney's imaginative invention; near the end, for instance, we may think that nothing could follow the Donnelly credo ("I am proud to be a Donnelly against all the contempt of the world"), but Reaney produces a haunting final dream sequence in which the elastic sense of time chills the blood.

Keith Turnbull's production is pretty overwhelming as well, even on the Tarragon's limited spaces. (If the Stratford Festival ever loses its fear of putting Canadian plays onto the open stage, *Sticks and Stones*, maybe the whole trilogy, must certainly head the list.) The actors, clearly in love with the work, are wonderful, and a few of them—Patricia Ludwick and Jerry Franken, fabulous as the senior Donnellys, David Ferry and Carol Lazare, their children—are magnificent.

I can't help feeling that it was a landmark evening.

Urjo Kareda, *Toronto Star*, 26 November 1973*

• •

Sticks and Stones, Part I of James Reaney's trilogy, *The Donnellys*, is not just another Canadian play. Quite frankly, it is a milestone in Canadian drama and I defy anyone, anywhere, to say that there is no such thing as good Canadian drama.

Being a reviewer is often frustrating because one so often hears of new Canadian plays being produced in Toronto and most people realize that there is little opportunity to experience that facet which is missing in Winnipeg. Well,the NDWT Company, a spin-off of Tarragon Theatre, the originator of *The Donnellys*, is on a national tour and Winnipeggers have the rare opportunity to see all of Reaney's trilogy.

This production may well be the theatre event of the season.

Reaney has spent the better part of 10 years sifting through the Donnelly legend of western Ontario, deciphering the facts from the legend. He has told the story of the feisty Irish immigrants with the authority of an historian and the artistry of a dramatist.

Sticks and Stones is on the scale of a massive, episodic novel, interweaving the lives of no less than 185 characters. The work is as intricate as the overlapping silken threads of a willowy spider's web, but director Keith Turnbull has miraculously maintained a crystal-like clarity. *Sticks and Stones* is quite simply a stunning piece of theatre, with the author and director operating in perfect harmony.

The Donnellys fled Ireland and came to Canada envisioning the new land as one of hope and opportunity. But the political and religious hatreds of their home followed them and flared with a greater impact than they ever dreamed possible.

Although all 14 actors are called upon to fill a multitude of roles and characters, only Patricia Ludwick remains in the dominant role of the wife, and thus makes it easy to single her from the remaining cast; a move which is perhaps unfair.

She sparkles as the staunch strongminded matriarch just as Jerry Franken does as the robust head of the clan.

Don MacQuarrie is outstanding as the malevolent forces bent on removing the Protestant family from the Catholic community, goading them into violent retaliation. Mr. MacQuarrie was nicely supported by Miriam Greene.

Sticks and Stones is a long play—almost three hours. There was some grumbling during the intermission between Acts Two and Three, but once the lights dimmed on the final act, time was totally irrelevant.

Sticks and Stones is a play people should get excited about.

Lee Rolfe, *Winnipeg Tribune*, 8 October 1975

• •

. . . *Sticks and Stones* shows Reaney's basic method at work. He accumulates the hard, particular facts of the real world—names, statistics, objects—and spins them together in theatrical games and rituals until they acquire a special resonance. As Judith Donnelly trudges through the countryside collecting signatures to save her husband from hanging, we are given the facts and figures on the construction of the gallows. The objects that clutter our pioneer museums—barrels, horseshoes, farm implements—become charged with danger. The lists of place and family names become through repetition as evocative as epic catalogues; even the straight lines on a map acquire drama. The actors play multiple roles, impersonate animals, and make up scenery; but they are never allowed to dwindle to puppets or abstractions, and their efforts become a celebration of the theatrical imagination at work. The method is familiar from *Colours in the Dark* and the children's plays that preceded it; the material is closer to the splendid Gothic horrors of *Listen to the Wind*. It is a dark, violent life that is depicted here—the ancient feuds imported from Ireland to what was supposed to be a new country, the bitter quarrels over land, the drunken brawls, the recurring terror of night. But Reaney also gives his characters vigour and dignity, so that while they are not sentimentalized their violence is seen as part of a life as intense as it is narrow. The Donnelly world, in its combination of violence and ceremony (the rough ceremonies of pioneer life as well as the dignified ceremonies of the church), is as multi-layered as the world of Elizabethan drama.

The main business of this particular play is to mark the Donnellys as special. It opens with a catechism: "Baptism, Confirmation, and Holy Orders can be received only once because they imprint on the soul—a spiritual mark, called a character, which lasts forever." One of the first characters we become aware of is Will Donnelly, whose lameness, he is told, is "God's marking you for His own." A chorus sequence towards the end of the play elaborates the theme: "once, before you were born . . . you chose to be a Donnelly and laughed at what it would mean, the proud woman put to milking cows, the genius trotting around

150

with a stallion, the old sword rusted into a turnip knife. You laughed and lay down with your fate like a bride, even the miserable fire of it. So that I am proud to be a Donnelly against all the contempt of the world." The Donnellys are stubbornly independent, they have a special dignity that cows their enemies, and they are associated, chiefly through the recurring "Barley Corn Ballad," with the organic life of the crops—an association that will be elaborated in the last play, *Handcuffs*. James Donnelly is proud of his large family and taunts one of his enemies: "I ask you what children have you? What have you got between your legs, Cassleigh—a knife?" Their chief enemies in the struggle for land, alone among the major characters, do not even have names of their own, but are referred to only as the Fat Woman and Mr. Fat. We are told "they have a certain on the ground quality which materializes everything, while with the Donnellys there is just the opposite feeling." It is not that the Donnellys are immaterial: they are associated with growing, living things (while the Fat Woman is obsessed with her "darling little laundry stove"); they have names, and their names matter to them; and when they die they have ghosts. In their final, tragic decision not to leave Biddulph there is heroic pride as well as brute stubbornness. The basic source of their appeal as figures of myth is that they are, in their own way, poets in a hostile community. Whether this has anything to do with the historical reality of the Donnellys is not at issue; what matters is that Reaney has shaped this material in a way that carries conviction to the imagination.

Alexander Leggatt, "Letters in Canada: Drama,"
UTQ, 45 (1975-76), 355-56

• •

The story of the Donnellys is familiar to many Canadians. It is the story of an Irish family with seven sons and one daughter who lived and struggled and died in and around the largely Irish township of Biddulph in the nineteenth century. The climax of the story is the massacre by a vigilante group made up of some thirty men of four members of that family—the father and mother and two sons, John and Thomas—as well as a niece, Bridget, shortly after midnight on February 4, 1880. In the two trials that followed no one was convicted of the murders, though six people were charged. To this day no one has been brought to justice for these brutal crimes. The story is included as no. VII—"The Biddulph Tragedy"—in a series of Famous Canadian Trials in *The Canadian Magazine* of August, 1915. It is perhaps the most famous unsolved murder in the history of Canadian law.

In his dramatization of their life and death Reaney sees the Donnellys as a family who would not submit to the pressures and prejudices of their society. Of the three plays into which he divides his story, Part One shows us the family establishing themselves in the community of Biddulph, after the migration of their parents to Canada in 1844, up to the year 1867; Part Two focuses on the stage-coach company run by the Donnelly boys and their rivalry with other stages, and brings us into the year 1879; Part Three concludes the saga with events immediately preceding and following the massacre of 1880, the trials, and the vindication of the Donnellys as perceived by Reaney.

The murder of the five Donnellys on February 4, 1880, was the subject of sensational newspaper articles in Canada and elsewhere for months after that fateful night. What was then called simply *The Globe*, in its edition of Thursday, February 5, 1880, featured on its front page a story "from our own reporter", which had no less than seven headlines, as follows:

> *Horrible Tragedy at Lucan*
> *Five Persons Murdered by Masked Men*
> *An Entire Household Sacrificed*
> *The House Fired and the Remains Consumed*
> *Result of a Family Feud*
> *The Story as Told by a Child Witness of the Crime*
> *20 Masked Men Engaged in the Bloody Work*

The story then began:

> *Lucan, Feb. 4—Lucan awoke this morning to shock the country with intelligence of the blackest crime ever committed in the Dominion. The crime consisted of the murder, or rather, butchery, of a family of five—father, mother, two sons and a girl. The victims were named Donnelly, a family that has lived in the neighbourhood for upwards of thirty years. They resided on lot 18, 6th concession of Biddulph. The farm consists of fifty acres. They bore the unenviable reputation of being*

THE TERRORS OF THE TOWNSHIP

The above sub-headline (all in capital letters) and much of the newspaper story, with its reliance on hearsay from those who were enemies of the Donnellys, are good examples of the biased attitudes that have permeated so much of the written and spoken accounts of the Donnellys right up to the present day.

After talk of the tragedy had subsided in the early part of this century, the book which revived widespread interest in the Donnellys was significantly called *The Black Donnellys*, by Thomas P. Kelley. It was subtitled "The true story of Canada's most barbaric feud." This immensely popular book, first published in

1954, has gone through over twenty reprintings, and is still prominent on news-stands. Its cover shows a picture of the original Donnelly gravestone with the word "Murdered" under the names of the five victims. Kelley's book is a sensational, melodramatic account of the lives of the Donnellys and goes out of its way to paint them as black as possible. In 1962 Kelley wrote an even more fictionalized sequel entitled *Vengeance of the Black Donnellys*, which purports to give an account of the terrible retribution meted out by the ghosts of the Donnellys on those involved in the massacre.

Unfortunately most people today have gained their knowledge of the Donnellys from Kelley's books. Part of James Reaney's intention in his trilogy is to correct the false impressions created by Kelley. He was able to use the more carefully researched and documented book by Orlo Miller, *The Donnellys Must Die*, which was published in 1962 with the stated intention of contradicting Kelley's view of the Donnellys. Reaney has also done much research on his own. . . .

One of Reaney's methods in discounting Kelley's books is derision. Kelley's *The Black Donnellys* becomes the model of the travelling medicine show in *Sticks and Stones* and is the source of much humour and satire in the play. Showman Murphy is clearly the writer Kelley; the performance by his Shamrock Concert Company is called "The Black Donnellys", which Reaney describes in an aside in the play as a "viciously biased melodrama, also the title of the book everyone reads about the Donnellys." . . .

Reaney goes to great pains in the play to emphasize the inaccuracies in Kelley's books. He uses the date of the logging bee at which Donnelly killed Patrick Farrell in 1857 as an example. The showman announces that it took place on June 29th; the "real" Mr. Donnelly corrects him by insisting it was June 25th. In the play the "real" Mr. Donnelly demands that the showman "Show me the scene where I kill Farl," and then corrects him again by saying that the killing was done "not with an iron bar, but with a wooden handspike." This incident is an indication of the extent of Reaney's own research on the Donnellys, for here he contradicts both the Kelley and the Miller books. Kelley says Donnelly struck Farrell with an iron bar; Miller says he struck him with an iron, not a wooden, handspike; Miller, also inaccurately, gives the date of the fatal fight as June 27th.

In this scene, as so often in the play, precise historical fact becomes the occasion of moving drama. There is a striking contrast between the huckster Murphy and Mr. Donnelly, who, with great dignity and disdain, forces "the living [to] obey the dead." A further indication of Reaney's art is the way he is able to make these scenes deriding Kelley into some of the funniest in the play and to use them both to dispel some of the misconceptions passed on by Kelley and to create sympathy for the "real Donnellys". It is worth recalling here that in the *Dictionary of Canadian Biography*, volume X (1972), the article on "James Donnelly, farmer" was written by James Reaney.

Although Reaney has immersed himself in the history of the Donnellys and their times, he has done much more in *Sticks and Stones* than simply write a documentary drama. He has created a vision in dramatic terms of a family who would not bow to the pressures and threats of the local community. Even if some of the historical details are altered, even if he does not give us a complete picture of the "real" Donnellys, we must remember that the play's importance lies in its dramatic, not in its historical qualities. The greatest achievement of *Sticks and Stones* is what Reaney as a poet-dramatist has made out of the bare bones of history that he has dug up, as he says, "from the attics of the local courthouses" and elsewhere. . . .

Reaney's technique in *Sticks and Stones* is something quite unique in Canadian drama and perhaps any drama. It is a combination of many things: poetry and prose, realistic action and mime, song and dance, games and ritual, fantasy and dream, past, present, and future. The work has been compared to that of such diverse playwrights as Aeschylus, Shakespeare, Brecht, and the Victorian melodramatists. Time and place frequently dissolve so that the spectator finds himself in 1884 at one moment and 1974 at another, in Tipperary, London, Lucan, or Goderich, in a farmhouse, a barnyard, a church, or a court, on a country road, a wagon, or a train. All these changes are evoked with the help of the simplest of props—ladders, sticks, stones, clotheslines, shirts, wheels, hayforks, barrels, chairs, noisemakers, maps, candles, lanterns. As in his other plays, Reaney's structural approach is to juxtapose many, many sequences of different times, settings and moods. In *Sticks and Stones* he has perfected this method over anything he has ever done before so that one sequence flows easily into another without the separation and numbering of scenes that occurred in his earlier plays such as *Colours in the Dark* and *Listen to the Wind*. He sometimes refers to the sequences in his stage directions as, for example, "the going-to-Goderich sequence", "a mass menace sequence", or "the Donnelly house sequence". He is always concerned about how one sequence blends into the next, as when he directs, "The Angelus should bridge between chase's ending and the vesper scene."

Yet all the sequences in the play are tied to a simple story line. Act One takes us from James Donnelly's settling in Biddulph to his killing of Farrell at the logging bee; Act Two shows the struggles faced by Mrs. Donnelly and her seven children before and after his sentencing until his return from prison seven years later; Act Three features the attempts of neighbours to drive the Donnellys from the township and their final decision never to leave Biddulph. The result of all this complexity in simplicity is an experience that leaves the spectator or reader immeasurably enriched though aware there is much he has not absorbed and much to be gained from further viewings and readings of the play. Reaney once said there are a hundred plays in the Donnelly story. He originally wrote one long play about it, and then expanded it into the present three. Of the first of the three, he wrote in the program notes:

The complete story of the Donnelly tragedy is too large for one evening. This play takes you as far as one of those moments after which things will never be the same again. When "persons unknown" burnt down his barn in 1867 James Donnelly defied this invitation to get out of the neighbourhood. He swore then that he would stay in Biddulph township forever. He is still there. It was at this time that the Donnellys decided to be Donnellys.

Reaney's exciting recreation of how the Donnellys came to be Donnellys is what awaits the reader in *Sticks and Stones*. More than a knowledge of history, what is required is careful attention to the play's poetry and free rein for the visual imagination to "see" the action on stage as directed by the author within the text. Given these qualities, the reader has an experience awaiting him comparable to that of the reviewers and audience on that landmark evening of November 24, 1973.

James Noonan, Foreword to *Sticks and Stones*
(Erin: Press Porcépic, 1976)

• •

RICK SALUTIN
&
THEATRE PASSE MURAILLE

1837: The Farmers' Revolt

First produced by Theatre Passe Muraille for a tour
of southwestern Ontario, opening 7 June 1974†

Directed by Paul Thompson
Designed by Paul Williams

Cast
(Multiple roles for each performer)

Eric Peterson
Janet Amos
David Fox
Miles Potter
Terry Tweed

†(An earlier version of *1837: The Farmers' Revolt* was produced at Theatre Passe Muraille
in January 1973)

Paul Thompson's Theatre Passe Muraille productions stand out from so much other current theatrical work because of a peculiar combination of distinguishing features—a cool, matter-of-fact geometric form, the inevitable choice of a social situation rather than a character as protagonist, a passion for local history and an uncompromised belief in the balance between individual rights and public good.

Yet, what happens to the characters in Thompson's plays is less important, dramatically speaking, than what the enacted events imply for the community as a whole. . . .

In choosing to look for drama in circumstances rather than personalities, Theatre Passe Muraille becomes subscriber to the view that the theatre's prime function is to present publicly and in dramatic terms, those conditions which most affect social well-being and stability. Such a premise would make Passe Muraille a political theatre in the most basic sense of the word, that is, the sense which derives from the notion that government is an activity and a responsibility rather than an institution. The intention of this kind of theatre is to awaken the slumbering social conscience through artistic means: art and politics being seen, in this context, to intersect at the point where men are moved to act for social change. The methods which such a theatre needs to employ are deliberately demonstrational and the attention of its drama is fixed on the effects of ethical, political and economic issues rather than on behavioral causes. A character's rise or demise, then, does not occur to elicit a flow of fellow-feeling from the audience; it serves to elucidate the point which the dramatist is making. Thus, dramatic efficacy resides in clarity not sympathy. Also, in the manner of acting which is appropriate to this kind of dramaturgy, the players do not concern themselves with assuming the emotional dimensions of the characters, but instead they (the words are Brecht's but they could be Diderot's) "take part in the intellectual decisions of the play."

The theatrical format described in the foregoing terms may help [us] to understand better the particular approach which Theatre Passe Muraille takes under Thompson's direction; and it may also be the key to an assessment of both the social and artistic gains which Passe Muraille is making. For this latter purpose, one of the more useful examples of the company's work—it must not be forgotten than the plays are produced collectively—is *1837*, written by Rick Salutin last year and recently restaged and remounted for a tour of Southwestern Ontario. *1837* mixes playing and subject matter rather deftly and to remarkably good effect. It helps, too, that the subject, the loss of fundamental social rights and the journey from activism to revolt, is so overtly a political one. The play might actually be said to have the form of a dramatic manifesto from the disenfranchised of Upper Canada who, in 1837, comprised nearly ninety percent of the colonial population. But *1837* is not just pointedly the reminder of a neglected past; it is consciously full of present ironies; and it is, as every theatrical event should be, an entertainment.

However, an entertainment with a socially didactic intent does not constitute potent theatre. . . .Passe Muraille's strength lies in its ability to make social necessity into art while maintaining the appropriate proportions of compassion and idealism. Take, for example, the character of William Lyon Mackenzie. As he appears in *1837*, Mackenzie is very much one who "takes part in the intellectual decisions of the play." He is also the personification of the reform movement; he is a man of action in both the political (that is, historical) and dramatic (central to the play) definition; and he is a character built to human scale. But his *function* in the play is more important and more interesting than the particular set of psychological attributes which have made him a revolutionary. Mackenzie is a vehicle for presenting the case for overthrowing the despotic, illegal and avaricious colonial government. Thompson and his collaborators make skillful use of this character in several ways, all of which are solidly non-illusionistic. Furthermore, as a figure from the actual past, Mackenzie appears within an aura of conveniently familiar factualism which gives the moral issues greater emphasis. Throughout this dramatizing process, history is preserved while the myth is specifically redefined.

Mackenzie is, on the one hand, made to approach the spectators, directly addressing them with the masterly political rhetoric of his newspaper, *The Colonial Advocate*. This is the technique of the public speech; its appeal is obvious. Mackenzie is also made to take part in a selected number of events reconstructed on stage to depict the development of the revolt; these scenes show the story of what took place. Finally, Mackenzie steps down front (more now as actor than character) to let the audience in on a few of the secrets of his act—tricks like how to turn the hoodlums of the Family Compact into a government and playful diversions such as John Bull, the Imperial Ventriloquist. In this third aspect of the role, the actor (a faultless performance by Eric Peterson) became completely removed from any identification with Mackenzie the man. The offering was purely a theatrical game. Yet, in spite of—because of—this theatrical obviousness, the play's stand on the subject of oppression was inescapably and pleasantly clear.

There are other factors which contribute to Passe Muraille's presentational strength. A strong sense of place has always been synonymous with its plays. History is, naturally, rooted in places. The present touches hands with the historical past in various ways and the place where it all happened is surely one of them. Instead of searching for riches in foreign fields, Passe Muraille has had a habit of uncovering mythology right under the noses of its audience. It was neither co-incidental nor theatrically immaterial that those who saw the Toronto version of *1837* found themselves sitting only a few hundred yards from the spot on which Samuel Lount and Peter Matthews were hanged for the part they played in the revolution. Similar instances of the immediacy of locale can be drawn from other Passe Muraille productions.

Concomitant with a strong sense of place is a preference for selecting history carefully—the theatre, remember, addresses the present. Present needs, therefore, are its life's blood. Moreover, by assuming the position of loyal and indispensable opposition, Passe Muraille chooses to stand for a minority constituency. The issues which revolve around Matthews and Lount are, then, naturally attractive. As representatives of a rightfully-held belief in and desire for self-determination, they were victims of political repression. But, in keeping with the attitude it espouses with regard to the function of character, *1837* does not champion Matthews and Lount for sympathetic effect. Its concern for this minority position is used only to infer the presence of oppressors and exploiters whose actions bespeak social decline. Social decline can mean trouble, perhaps even death, for those at the end of the line—Matthews and Lount, or you and me. In 1974, history, histrionics and artistic purpose are forged together to demonstrate a lesson learned in *1837*.

Brian Boru, *That's Show Business*, 3 (14 August 1974), 4, 7*

• •

After a year of fretful wandering caused by the sad demolition of its Trinity Square home, Theatre Passe Muraille has found by far its best substitute yet in the historic Enoch Turner Schoolhouse, on King St. just east of Parliament [in Toronto].

There, it is performing *1837: The Farmers' Revolt*, a revision of a show first produced two years ago, and now built again through the collective efforts of Paul Thompson the director, Rick Salutin the writer, and Janet Amos, David Fox, Eric Peterson, Miles Potter and Terry Tweed the actors. Two years ago, this was already a very fine show. Now, it is a stunner.

The outline of the narrative remains the same, a partisan, passionate account of the events that led to Toronto's 1837 rebellion and a grim, impressionistic depiction of that abortive confrontation itself. But Thompson, Salutin and the actors have shifted the emphasis even further toward the rebel farmers, exploring in even greater depth their grievances and casting an even more stricken eye at their failure.

Thus, while some of the tremendous anti-establishment set pieces remain—the giant performing visage of Sir Francis Bond Head, the extensive self-multiplication of the Family Compact—the overall performance leans toward humanizing and individualizing those who fought and fell. William Lyon Mackenzie himself emerges with much more force in this version, vividly impersonated by Eric Peterson.

This is emphatic and supple theatre, strikingly well-crafted. Indeed, so well performed is it that there is some danger of tossing the adjective ''marvellous'' toward the whole cast, and losing the merited attention to their individual contributions.

Mackenzie is only one of perhaps a dozen sharply detailed, versatile characterizations provided by the fantastic Eric Peterson. There are also two further historical figures compellingly re-created: Anthony Von Egmond, the rebels' military leader, enacted with a mad, fearful dignity by David Fox, and Tiger Dunlop, given edge and anxiety by Miles Potter.

Terry Tweed, in two scenes with Potter, creates a relationship between a farmer and his wife with fascinating emotional depth and dramatic economy. Janet Amos is able to repeat her wonderfully comic, satirically telling account of a London farmer who attempts to move to Detroit but finds himself simultaneously overwhelmed and chastened by the manifestations of prosperity.

Urjo Kareda, Toronto Star, 13 September 1974

• •

. . . Theatre Passe Muraille's production of *1837* has flaws in abundance, and a rampant spirit that throws these flaws aside: it's history as anarchy without anachronism. Fine moments in the theatre leap out at you, reminding you that you will never see an exact replica again; the frenzy of the pace seems to belong to the anarchy.

1837 is not distinguished by political complexity. It relates, rather curiously, the story of the revolt in Upper Canada led by William Lyon Mackenzie. Writer Salutin shrewdly recognizes that if you mix techniques of dramaturgy it is possible to build a subtle, effective momentum. He does this by introducing the farmers in vignettes, some serious and some hilarious, so that when the revolt comes you can recognize his people. In the second act you are with them because you have memories of them from the beginning to fall back upon.

By interspersing the heated outcry of Mackenzie with sketches of the people who follow him, the play coils and is ready to spring after intermission. Paul Thompson, the director, knows how to use sound expressively, like the sound of an axe hitting a stump, later counterpointed by a hammer hitting an anvil. Mackenzie's beautiful voice, sublime in rhetoric, sensitizes the audience for the later revolutionary outcry.

It is true that political matters are reduced to basics but it doesn't matter. The actors' sweat and swirling movement of pitchforks and muskets seem more important, especially when those who carry them have been shown to be human. Who would have thought all this was behind Montgomery's Tavern in the unsoiled pages of history texts?

History in *1837* is presented panoramically by revue sketch and it's alive. Caricature is pitted against caricature; social stratum against social stratum, and the acting becomes twice removed and intriguing when the farmer-actors act out the corrupt. It is a fine chance to display dramatic ability, and the five actors in this production who pull off the Parnassian job of playing many roles, are exceptional.

Eric Peterson does a brilliant parody of Edith Evans and is able to show Mackenzie's sweep and charisma. Miles Potter has great control over all his roles, and David Fox is believably corrupt as a magistrate. Janet English [sic: Amos] has sunken expressive eyes and uses them a lot. Terry Tweed knows how to wrench emotion from her gut.

Watching these actors play is like looking at a chameleon for two hours. They can be muggy and hammy, just like the play can start to get on your nerves, when it drags out a sequence, which it often does. The epilogue runs on much too long, like that senseless ten-minute walk at the beginning, and is too stretched out to be an epiphany. The ending speech, a variation of the no-we've-really-won-even-if-we-lost routine, is cut short when the two speakers are hung. The imagined snap of the neck tells all.

Lawrence O'Toole, *Globe and Mail*, 13 September 1974

• •

This book [*1837: William Lyon Mackenzie and the Canadian Revolution* (Toronto: James Lorimer, 1977)] contains three important parts. It begins with a long historical essay on the rebellion of 1837 in Upper Canada, then describes the creation (or group improvisation) of a play based upon these events, and concludes with the play itself. Rick Salutin wrote the history, and the play evolved through a number of performances by Toronto's Theatre Passe Muraille. The work is radical in intent; it seeks to challenge the traditional interpretations of Mackenzie and the "Canadian Revolution" to the point where both audience and reader can achieve a critical awareness of the true significance of 1837 and therefore of the independence issue at the present time.

The conjunction of history, drama, and radicalism is not new in Canadian history, but it does make the book very intriguing. It raises a number of questions that relate to historical scholarship—both method and interpretation—and the relationship between the past, an art form, and revolution (or at least a change of consciousness). Unfortunately, when the book is evaluated at these different levels, it is decidedly uneven. The drama itself is engaging, especially the description of how the drama was created; but the history is mediocre and the radical content of the work is curiously naive and even old-fashioned.

The organization of the book, for example, is genuinely misleading. By beginning with a history and concluding with a drama, it implies that the creative process moved from objective historical scholarship to a play that recreates the past in a dramatic form. The text itself shows that the process was quite different and a good deal more interesting. It began with a frustration that is often at the root of historical revision. The disjunction between the implications of the historical and mythical versions of the past and the demands of the present for a more relevant account leads almost inevitably to the articulation of a new past. In this case drama was the vehicle to carry this group from their own frustration with the present back to a new past. Drama led to history, history did not lead to drama.

The method that they used to create this new past is fascinating. Rick Salutin brought before the company a number of artifacts such as pictures, clothes, and newspaper clippings. The company would then respond to these documents in order to recapture the character of the period. Much in the manner of those professional historians who seek to have the "times" speak for themselves without the aid of interpretive metaphors, the company believed that the present could be transcended by having direct contact with documents. Gestalt techniques and group therapy intensified this process by ensuring that when the artifacts spoke, they would speak in dramatic terms.

The play sustains this ensemble quality. In its published form it contains two acts with several short scenes in each. It uses minimal settings, the actors often exchange parts, and whole scenes change according to mood and circumstance. When the play toured the rural communities of Western Ontario, for example, the company reworked the drama in order to tone down the revolutionary rhetoric that Toronto audiences would accept. Somewhat ironically the play is subtitled "The Farmers' Revolt." Nevertheless, the play is coherent, well paced, and engaging.

In fact, the play is quite able to stand on its own without the aid of the long essay on Mackenzie and the revolution that precedes it—which seems to be written to give the play an independent historical foundation. The interpretation that this history offers is very straightforward. The rebellion was a significant episode in Canadian history. There were major battles (even campaigns and theatres of war), and the repression and violence that followed the conflict attest to the genuine support that Mackenzie had earned. The man himself was neither unbalanced nor incompetent. His enemies were real and his attacks on them were rational and consistent.

These assertions do help to rescue Mackenzie and 1837 from those who have tried to tiptoe around the rebellion and to commit the man to an historical Bedlam. But the underpinnings of Salutin's analysis unfortunately tend to prohibit Mackenzie from enjoying a genuine resurrection. According to this account the primary division in 1837 saw the merchants, the family compact, the British (in sum, the colonially minded) face the farmers, the workers, and the aspiring industrialists. He defines the economic conflict by the merchant *versus* industrialist distinction. . . .

. . . It is important, nevertheless, to point out that when this distinction is carried back to the 1830s it serves to reinforce traditional interpretations of the rebellion rather than lead to either new or radical perspectives. It does acknowledge the reality of the confrontation, but the confrontation is still treated as a two-sided battle between reform and reaction, although some new groups are placed on each side of the line. . . .

The book is . . . somewhat less than revolutionary in the way it treats the relationship between history and drama on the one hand and the articulation of a social or revolutionary consciousness on the other. The story that the play tells seems to lead to a revolutionary conclusion, but the form of this story and many of the techniques in the play are traditional and conservative. In spite of the success of the play in dramatic terms, its revolutionary impact is superficial.

In order to use history to create a new past and break clear of a stagnant present, it is not enough to reinterpret past events. It is also necessary to attack the form of the story in which these events have been told and the social attitudes that are implicit in these forms. For example, the works of Roch Carrier and Michel Tremblay not only challenge the myths of Quebec's past, they also launch a violent attack upon the forms and the sensibilities that are a part of these myths. The world of Maria Chapdelaine becomes a funereal nightmare; Quebec becomes a transvestite working its way towards homosexual release.

1837: The Farmers' Revolt hardly touches this dimension. While the drama is reasonably new, the story it tells simply reworks the story of Canadian history in its traditional form. In Canada, Victorian art forms have enjoyed an incredible longevity. In history the narrative has usually been built around a single noble cause that is described in romantic and inspirational terms. Characters are divided into heroes and villains. In this play the noble cause is Canadian independence; the good guys are the farmers, workers, and frustrated industrialists, the bad guys are the compact and the merchants. The emotional power of the play relies often upon melodrama of the most traditional sort. A farmer who only met his immigrant bride at the start of the play must leave her at the homestead while he answers the call for independence. They fought the good fight and the glory of their cause lives on.

This is the same story that brought us the struggle for responsible government and made the railroad builders into our national saints. It now seeks to elevate a strange alliance of revolutionaries and industrialists. One must have serious doubts about the ability of a reworked form of Victorian hero-worship to sustain a change to a radical consciousness. The play is entertaining, but the work is neither good history nor powerful revolution.

William Westfall, *CHR*, 59 (March 1978), 71-75

• •

1837: William Lyon Mackenzie and the Canadian Revolution, by Rick Salutin and Theatre Passe Muraille, is presented as ''a history'' and ''a play.'' It's also a process. The bulk of the book, 182 pages, is Salutin's revisionist account of the 1837 uprising, significantly called a ''revolution.'' Here, and in the play, he dismisses the ''myth'' of a band of pitch-fork-carrying yokels, led by the fiery but incompetent Mackenzie, in comic flight from the equally comic Bond Head, the whole incident forming a Monty Pythonesque curtain raiser which ''made possible responsible government . . . the goal that was not achieved by force was then achieved peacefully.'' Rather, he says, ''Independence is the goal in the play, and the overthrow of political control. The play ends tragically, with a hanging, and the implication that the goal of the revolt—independence—has still to be won, in our own time.''

Salutin's view of the uprisings as a movement by the common people, the farmers, to throw off economic inferiority imposed by their colonial position, and his continual connections to contemporary economic and political issues, set him off from ''traditional'' historians. His version of history is always highly partisan (he's notably weak on the failure of the rebellion), often simplistic, generalized, and poorly documented (was Robert Gourlay really exiled, as Salutin implies, *just* because he documented farmers' grievances?).

But Salutin isn't writing for historians. He's writing for ordinary Canadians, and this means ''starting very far back: other countries may have to relive or reinterpret their past, but they know they *have* a past. In Quebec they may hate it, but it's sure as hell there. English Canadians . . . must be convinced there *is* a past that is their own.''

Even while disagreeing with Salutin, I found his opening chapter, on the economic/social conditions which produced the uprisings, far more clear and useful than my constitution-and-politics-oriented history texts. His oversimplifications made me go to more ''scholarly'' sources to find another version of ''what really happened.'' This is one of Salutin's successes: making Canadian history important enough that you will want to seek out more information. Moreover, the focus on social conditions, documented by plenty of effective quotations from contemporary sources, and packaged with lots of illustrations, accomplishes two important things. It makes the essay interesting; and it gives the reader not facts to memorize, but a sense of shared human experience. *1837*'s real revisionist view of Canadian history is not political but emotional: a new view of that history as *ours*, vital to our lives today. Thus the process begins.

Salutin's historical research on the 1837 uprisings became the basis for a unique theatrical project, in collaboration with Theatre Passe Muraille, an experimental group attempting to give documentary form to aspects of Canadian life. Salutin presents an informal diary of his work with the cast members to enter the spirit of 1837, to live out their rebellion, whether they were walking down Yonge Street in a snowstorm and realizing in their toes that ''December was a hell of a time to make a revolution here,'' or lashing out against the colonialism of contemporary Canadian theatre.

As the actors felt their way into 1837, so their improvised expressions of its reality became *1837*. The play itself opened in Toronto in January 1973; it was reworked for an Ontario tour in 1974, and the printed version was ''assembled'' after that tour. The collective creation is a collection of sketches: Act I depicts the economic and social frustrations of the farmers, Act II the rebellion and its aftermath, concluding with the execution of two leaders. . . .As a production, *1837* depends heavily on the effects created by blocking, pacing, blackouts, mime, the sheer energy of the Passe Muraille players, and, of course, audience response. As a production, I found it extremely effective. As a script, it stands up, is more cohesive and powerful than I expected (especially the Edward and Mary scenes); I can hear real people talking. The process that carries essay into production into printed play is flawed, of course; but ultimately, I think it has its desired effect. Taken as a whole, it provides a good start at making our history our own shared experience.

Susan Wood, *Canadian Literature*, 81 (Summer 1979), 111-12

• •

Zimmerman I'd like to switch to *1837* and the process of collective creation. What are the gains and losses of the process?

Salutin I think the real strength in collectives is the immediate involvement and commitment of the actors. They're saying their own words and I think that accounts for the immediacy and impact that collectives have. Unfortunately what can happen is that they can become formularized. They can become predictable so that after a while you just don't want to see any more. They all seem to be doing the same thing, with the same kind of earnestness, and you begin to suspect the earnestness. They lack the intricacy. It's hard to know where collectives can go. I would say that in the last few years there haven't been many serious attempts to develop the form, to do something more mature with it.

Zimmerman What do you think is the lesson to be learned from *1837*?

Salutin The idea was that the main problem with Canada today is the fact that it's not independent. It's still dominated by the structures of modern, American imperialism. I thought the one place in Canadian history that the Canadian people actually addressed that problem head-on was in 1837. That was the one time we had a mass movement for independence. Although they failed, at least they

165

saw the problem and they tried to do something about it. For us to do anything about this today, it's going to require first of all getting some agreement on what the problem is.

Zimmerman And that there is a problem.

Salutin Yeah, and that there is a problem. In other words, you have to go back to where they were in 1837, and then you have to do it successfully instead of unsuccessfully.

Zimmerman History books call it the rebellion of 1837 and calling it that is a way of diminishing its significance. The ending of *1837*—that we just haven't won yet—is optimistic as is the ending of *Les Canadiens*. Are these optimistic endings deliberate?

Salutin One of the main problems of writing for me has been the ending because any dramatic situation that you snatch out of the Canadian past, or the Canadian present, is basically an account of despair. Of course you lose every battle until you win. The problem is that if you describe the thing in doleful terms, it just discourages people and then what's the point of describing it at all? But you can't put in a dishonest, sugary ending either because then you've failed in your task as a writer, which is to be truthful, and you've also misled people. It's a struggle to find something hopeful in seemingly hopeless situations. . . .

Interview with Rick Salutin, by Cynthia Zimmerman, *The Work*, p. 257

• •

JAMES REANEY

The St Nicholas Hotel:
The Donnellys, Part Two

First produced at Tarragon Theatre,
Toronto, 16 November 1974

Directed by Keith Turnbull
Set Design by Rosalyn Mina
Lighting Design by Vladimir Svetlovsky

Cast
(Multiple roles for each performer)

Ken Anderson
Nancy Beatty
Jay Bowen
Tom Carew
Peter Elliott
David Ferry
Jerry Franken
Rick Gorrie
Miriam Greene
Michael Hogan
Patricia Ludwick
Don MacQuarrie
Keith McNair
Gord Stobbe
Suzanne Turnbull

One of the many joys of *The St Nicholas Hotel*, at the Tarragon Theatre, something that makes it pleasurable to experience and doubly so to recollect, is the confidence of a writer who has found his own voice.

James Reaney's way of putting a play together is both sophisticated, devilishly complicated, and yet so simple that a child could grasp it, and would probably indeed grasp it faster than most adults. Playful, sombre, giddy, moving, cartoonish, heroic, the Reaney voice isn't obviously for everyone but for those who are hooked on it—and I must declare myself among them—it is filled with delights. It is wholly original. There is nothing else quite like it.

This new play is Part 2 of *The Donnellys* trilogy, which began so overwhelmingly last autumn with *Sticks and Stones*. It is lighter-textured, more rambunctious, dealing with the stagecoach rivalry between the Donnellys (whose company bore the splendid name The Opposition Stage) and Pat Finnegan.

There is a whirl about this play, a motion reflected in its recurring images of tops and streamers, a rolling movement which also enfolds races, chases and wedding dances. The circular motion is also present in the play's time sequence, which rolls first forward and then back again, picking up in its recurring arc details which we didn't fully understand on their first appearance but which lock into place on the second rotation.

Yet the spirited roll of *The St Nicholas Hotel* doesn't exclude a continual darkening. Reaney won't get to the final Donnelly massacre until Part 3, but it is always looming. Two Donnelly sons die here, one of illness, the other by murder, and the play keeps an eye on a community waiting for the death of a family it fears, finally willing that death themselves.

Reaney's craftsmanship is breathtaking, particularly in the way he interlocks events—the number of marriages and courtships both mocking and melancholy, the two unhappy haunted sons, Tom Ryan (whom the Donnellys take in) and James Carroll (who organizes their destruction). There are some memorable incidents, like the one in which Carroll and Will Donnelly dance out their signatures, or the beautiful simplicity of Maggie Donovan's death, or the chilly planning of Mike Donnelly's murder. There is also a final moment involving a spinning top (its most haunting use since Chekhov's *Three Sisters*) which is as hair-raising as the incomparable final seconds of *Sticks and Stones*.

A very large cast (15 actors) works with unhesitating imagination in Keith Turnbull's immensely exciting and suggestive production. Collectively, they are a vigorous, impressive company, as earthy and yet resonant as every detail of Roslyn Mina's beautifully assembled designs (dazzlingly well lighted by Vladimir Svetlovsky). But even above the ensemble triumph, there are individual achievements: Patricia Ludwick brings the power of ancient tragedy to Mrs. Donnelly. Jerry Franken and David Ferry are dangerously irresistible as the Donnelly brothers, Nancy Beatty is unforgettably touching as Maggie Donovan.

The opposing forces are similarly creative, given Miriam Greene's comic yet alarming malice, Michael Hogan's comic-book detective, Peter Elliott's blandly unscrupulous businessman, and Don MacQuarrie's brilliant James Carroll, in whom the fires of hell seem already flickering.

The St Nicholas Hotel proceeds with such flair and gusto that we are left frustrated at the end only by the months we shall have to wait until Reaney's *The Donnellys*, Part 3. And one already dreams of the day that we shall be able— perhaps under the banner of the Stratford Festival?—to see all three together.

Urjo Kareda, *Toronto Star*, 18 November 1974*

• •

Emerging from the blizzard of poetic images summoned by James Reaney, as author, and Keith Turnbull, as his director, in *The St Nicholas Hotel*, Part Two of The Donnellys, comes the suspicion that poet Reaney has fallen in love with the notorious family from Lucan. Perhaps Turnbull has, too, for the actors at the Tarragon Theatre have brought a great deal of charm to these unruly lives.

St Nicholas Hotel refers to the hostelry from which the Donnellys launch their career as stagecoach proprietors, but the name they give their enterprise might have made a better title. The Opposition Line was what they called it, and whatever they come to represent in Canadian history, the Donnellys were certainly the Opposition in Biddulph County.

In Reaney's first play of the trilogy, *Sticks and Bones* [sic], we recognized that the antagonism of their neighbours was legitimately vented against a quarrelsome family of Irish squatters. Now we see it as less honestly motivated. They are rivals of the bad-tempered Finnegan, running the established line. The Donnelly boys are high-spirited, true, but now we favor them against a lying, conniving, highly political faction.

St Nicholas Hotel may appear simple, being concentrated on the stagecoach venture, but Reaney is not sending his Donnellys along any simple narrative line. They must pick up a great deal of documentation en route.

For Reaney is consciously creating an epic of southwestern Ontario, and he is highly successful. With a few more like-minded poets, Canada could catch up on the legends that feed and enrich older civilizations.

His documentation is always fascinating. The legend of the girl who did not marry one Donnelly, the ghost of another that haunts the barroom where he was assassinated, are woven, as are the plots their enemies hatch, including the hiring of a heroic detective.

But before such overlay deflects us, we are allowed to enjoy the hectic rivalry of stagecoach days. We are treated to a whole panorama of travel, of the tricks to win custom, of the customers who travelled, and of Ontario itself, in those untidy, exuberant days.

Turnbull's talent for inventive stage business matches his author's word-image. The 15 Tarragon actors double and re-double to keep two lines in business. Sometimes, it is true, we become the guessing team in a game of charades, but if you are on your mettle all evening you will inherit many more riches than slip past you.

The same is true of individual performances. Sometimes you may wonder which actor is playing what character, for The Reaney-Turnbull Method demands much nimbleness in doubling.

You won't need to be told that the admirable Patricia Ludwick is again the heroic Donnelly matriarch, but you might like to be reminded that she is also Mercilla Maguire; that burning Jerry Franken is both husband James and son William to her, and that David Ferry is now smiling wickedly as Mike Donnelly.

Also, that Nancy Beatty has joined the company as that Maggie Donovan who loved Will Donnelly, that it is the vivid Miriam Greene who is the other vigorous Donovan, clamoring for her cow, and that Jay Bowen is responsible for poor Tom Ryan, and gives a new meaning to stage-struck.

The venom of the Donnelly foes is concentrated in one figure, for Don Mac-Quarrie is the embittered Finnegan and also sour John Carroll. The dashing hawk-shaw is flexed out by Michael Hogan, and Peter Elliott brings alive that ambitious storekeeper, Stubbs.

When the Reaney Trilogy, which we are so lucky as to be sharing at Tarragon, becomes schoolbook material in the future, there will be no need to sort out the dramatis personae. By then they will be part of everybody's history. And by the end of the third play to come, the Donnellys may well emerge as a nation's heroes.

Herbert Whittaker, *Globe and Mail*, 18 November 1974*

• •

The Donnellys, a trilogy by James Reaney reviewing the events that led to a massacre of an Ontario family by their neighbours in the 19th century, has been universally acclaimed in Canada as the country's most significant contribution to 20th century drama. Tuesday night, Calgary residents had their first opportunity to see if the hoopla was justified when the NDWT Co. of Toronto presented the second section of the trilogy, *The St Nicholas Hotel*, at the University of Calgary.

And what those attending saw was that while the play qua play may not be a great work, the production itself—the mesh between directing and script—was extraordinary, inventive almost to a fault and a reminder that there are things theatre can do that no other medium can.

The Donnelly saga is too well known to bear repeating here, and the saga is not, except in the most superficial sense, the subject of Reaney's play—the real subject is prejudice, bias, bigotry, the roots of war (if we want to get pretentious about it): it is an intellectually exciting play and under Keith Turnbull's direction, a sensual extravaganza as well, that hammers home a point that in the theatre of the '70s, when soft headedness is the rule, it must be considered breath-taking: the persecuted and the persecutors co-operate with each other, fueling the other's fire until the inevitable holocaust burns both sides.

As Reaney reconstructs the story, a township in Ontario lives a normal life until the arrival of the Donnelly clan, a strange group of people who refuse to co-operate with the demands of society as symbolized by their neighbours.

The neighbours make them scapegoats. The Donnellys respond by acting like scapegoats. The circle tightens as neither side compromises and nooses are felt around many throats.

The play is saying that the Donnellys made it easy for the killers to rationalize murder (in much the way blacks rioting in Watts did) but that the Donnellys, ostracized and deprived of their dignity, had no choice but to act as they did. This is a dark play with a determinist vision of the human condition, offering analysis in place of hope.

It's a great subject, seldom explored in theatre, and the Donnellys are an ideal vehicle for that exploration, carrying with them—at this late date—none of the emotional freight that could get in the way of the ideas were the scapegoats to be blacks, French-Canadians, homosexuals, women or any other group for which the Donnellys can and should be taken as representatives.

It's also a primal subject, scapegoating, existing in almost all cultures, and Reaney has not missed the universality—he wrote the play in tandem with his director and the entire show has been staged in a mythic-epic manner that fractures time and place (à la avant-garde cinema) and calls attention to its own intentions (à la Brecht).

Toronto reviewers have tended to treat the play's stage-style as though it sprang full blown from Reaney's forehead, a theatrical Minerva. In fact, the treatment is highly derivative and owes an incalculable debt to the work of Tom O'Horgan, director of *Hair*, *Futz*, *Tom Paine*, etc.

Reaney was in Calgary for the Tuesday evening presentation and I asked him about O'Horgan and Brecht; he agreed, and added Thornton Wilder and Carl Orff as influences. (Reaney, by the way, is a diffident, slight man beyond middle years—artists rarely look like their work.)

But O'Horgan has been Canadianized by Reaney and Turnbull. Gone are the effects splashed stagewide for their own effect, the obligatory but alienating nudity, the unmotivated crudity—the aspects of O'Horgan's directorial hallucinations that have kept audiences at a distance, enthralled by the unending fertility of the theatrical manipulations but depressed by the meretriciousness of their use.

Reaney and Turnbull can vaudevillize their characters and then, in a second, knock the audience on its back with a jolt of real empathy for the suffering, something O'Horgan has never been able, or has never cared, to do.

The NDWT Co. actors are young and energetic; would that some of them were more competent, but individuals are not supremely important here and acting that would, in other plays, be fatally mediocre or worse, is tolerable in *The St Nicholas Hotel*. The play was written with specific members of the company in mind, Reaney said, and the care is evident.

I have one reservation about the trilogy and that is whether it can be performed by anyone else. It is unique theatre because the direction and the script are of a piece, but short of writing every move in the script, I wonder if another director unknown to Reaney could keep the vision intact; I wonder whether the vision is not totally inseparable from one specific style—I doubt that it, in contrast to Shakespeare or Chekhov, is open to free interpretation.

As long as the NDWT Co. has de facto control of the work, it doesn't matter, but this incestuous type of creation may severely hamper longevity, particularly when O'Horgan flashiness seems dated, as it will some day. For a play to be termed great, there must be an indication that it will survive theatrical fashion and I can't see that indication in *The St Nicholas Hotel*.

But for now, it is viable, virile, vigorous theatre. . . .

Scott Beaven, *Calgary Albertan*, 30 October 1975

• •

Merrill Denison once remarked that, lacking a national cultural capital, Canada was unlikely ever to have a national drama. Of the major literary forms, drama is traditionally the one most dependent on a particular, well-defined community; and a nation as large and diverse as Canada does not constitute a community of that kind. But it contains many such communities within it; and what has happened, as our drama has flourished in defiance of Denison's prediction, is that our dramatists have turned to local communities. not the nation as a whole, for their material—and the best of them, by telling us about one particular group, have made the rest of the country listen.

James Reaney has turned to the history of his own corner of southwestern Ontario for *The Donnellys*. The second part of the trilogy, *The St Nicholas Hotel, Wm Donnelly, Prop.* . . . shows, like the trilogy as a whole, a fascination with documentary details—place names, letters, advertisements. The title itself is deliberately contrived to look like a hotel sign. But this is also the most romantic play in the trilogy. The hotel of the title is not part of the Donnelly story proper; it is the hotel kept by Will ("Cripple") Donnelly and his wife Norah after the massacre of the other Donnellys, a vantage point from which we can look back into the past. More explicitly than the others this is a memory play: an early chorus speech evokes "Words blown away by the wind, dust & words in the stream of time we all lie dreaming in . . . " And if the main business of the first play, *Sticks and Stones*, was to identify the Donnellys and set them apart, the main business of this play is to create, through the operations of memory, a special affection for them. Throughout the play, the Donnelly household is a centre of love. In the first act, we have the secret, doomed courtship of Will Donnelly and Maggie Donovan, passing notes back and forth between the floorboards of the church, proposing and accepting by letter, living largely in the imagination. Maggie declares, "At night I am your wife; and in the daytime I drudge for a woman who does not know whether she wants to be married or no." The woman in question is Miss Maguire, whose cynical courtship with George Stub (a leading enemy of the Donnellys) is set in ironic contrast with the romance of Will and Maggie: "I needn't get married. So— make it worth my while." She specifies, among other things, that Stub should become a senator. Similarly, Maggie's brother Bill wistfully compares his sister's romance to his own wedding: "Your mother and my father put us together like a pair of cattle." Later in the play, we are introduced to Tom Ryan, who recites a sentimental monologue, "Waiting for Pa," then explains that his own home life is not quite like that: his father is a crazy sadist who locks food and fuel away from his family. Trapped in a loveless home, Tom is reduced to asking his mother "if it was true I had been born." He flees to the Donnellys, declaring "there's love there." The link is made between Tom and Maggie when his mother asks, "Would you live with people whose sons tried to carry a poor girl off, Tom?" and he replies, "Yes, because she wanted to be carried off from a house that was worse than this." The final crisis of the play is the murder of Mike Donnelly; his wife Nellie broke off her engagement with Sid Skinner to marry Mike, and while the murder is part of the larger pattern of persecution of the family, Sid is the actual killer. A pattern is set up whereby outsiders go to the Donnellys for love, and their own connections—Tom's father, Maggie's family, Nellie's rejected fiancé—become through jealousy and resentment part of the conspiracy against the family. When Will is arrested at his own wedding, or John at a wedding dance, the reliable melodramatic effect also carries a weight of commentary—the Donnellys are associated with love, their enemies with its denial. The point is reinforced by the emphasis of the play on the sons and their various love affairs, and by the recurring song "Buffalo Gals," a song of courtship.

The courtship motif is linked with the play's other controlling image, the competition between the Donnelly and Finnegan coach lines. Will wins a customer from the rival line by declaring "We'll take you for a kiss and a penny. Michael, take the fare." There is a competition over the delivery of a wedding cake, and the Donnellys win. Mike's wedding is jokingly related to his occupation: "Mike didn't show up for a week after that, too tired, still abed at two in the afternoon his brothers said, stagedrivers make good husbands, all that jouncing up and down . . . " Reaney's introductory note identifies the play as "a race between the Donnelly boys and their enemies" in which "Their . . . enemies build stronger & stronger barriers until, at last, Michael is suddenly & brutally murdered." The killing of Mike, coach driver and lover, is the play's ultimate warning of the tragedy to come. The courtship of Will and Maggie also hits barriers: "There was always something between us that summer—a fence, a veil, a muzzle on him, a wall about me, a floor between us." Finally, her family imprisons her in the Convent of the Sacred Heart, which early in the play was just one more stop on the coach line; but Maggie dies there, and the Donnelly stage slows down as it passes the convent, because Will is the driver. Maggie in her last days laments, "I scrub the stones of the convent yard and as close to the gate as I can, but it is no use—the gate is locked." After her death the nuns debate whether to bury her in the grounds or by Will; in the end they bury her in the yard, close to the gate.

The Donnellys' enemies become increasingly formidable as the play develops, going from a comic pulp-fiction detective, master of disguise and winner of "over a thousand gold medals," to the genuinely frightening Jim Carroll, leader of the final massacre, who is—appropriately, given the scheme of the play—the product of a broken, loveless home. But the Donnellys' resistance is also formidable. A mob sets upon Will, singing a song of St. Patrick and imagining themselves to be driving out vermin as the saint did; but Will becomes St. Patrick himself, driving them off with the fiddle which his mother gave him long ago, and which is associated with him throughout the play. In a central episode, Will, answering the taunt that he is a cripple, compares the grace of his signature with the ugliness of Carroll's, and challenges him, "Dance the handwriting that comes out of your arm. Show us what you're like. Very well, I'll dance mine." The cripple dances gracefully, Carroll falls down in a fit. And finally there is the curious permanence of the Donnellys. A dying rival prophesies of Mike, "They'll never finish scrubbing up his blood." Uttered as a curse, the line predicts the play's ending in which a chambermaid, years later, tries unsuccessfully to clean the floor of the hotel bar where Mike was murdered, while his ghost watches her. This final image suggests that the Donnellys have won the race as well as lost it. In the long run they are indestructible, able to "look straight ahead past this stupid life and death they've fastened on you." And the scrambling of time and memory throughout the play is Reaney's way of lifting the Donnellys out of the world of history and circumstance, and making them figures of legend. In performance this is the warmest and most lyrical of the Donnelly plays; it is also the centre of Reaney's strategy of transforming local history into poetry.

Alexander Leggatt, UTQ, 46 (1976-77), 383-85

• •

JM When you talk about working with Jamie [Reaney], and having him around as a writer, how much of what happens visually is you and how much is him? Is that something you can separate?

KT It's really hard to separate.

JM I suppose you've learned a lot from each other over the years.

KT Yes. It depends a lot on the play. In something like *The Donnellys*, for instance, a lot of the initial ideas, of the lines, of things spinning, really come directly from Jamie. Whereas a lot of the execution of them or the refinement of them or the expansion of them would come from me, and some would come from the cast too.

JM Is it a democracy?

KT No. It's not a democracy. There's a lot of consultation and a lot of dialogue. I enjoy dialogue. But it's in preparation to making the decision, and I have to make the decision. There's no question there. That's why it's not really a collective, either, although we do have a collectivity sometimes in our work. But no, it's a fairly formal structure, and the director is theoretically the boss. Sometimes the puppets form an uprising, though.

JM I was thinking about the ladders that are in *Sticks and Stones* that keep reappearing again in the other plays. Are you conscious about that sort of thing?

KT Oh yes, oh golly, yes.

JM Because it's so rich. I sometimes wonder how much of it is just because you have lively minds, and how much of it you're doing on purpose.

KT Doin' it on purpose. I'm very aware. Sometimes I'll go back to Jamie and say "I don't understand this image here, because if we put it here we've got to develop it somewhere else, or we've got to prepare our imaginations for it." If he agrees, then we look to putting the image in somewhere else, so the audience isn't just suddenly hit with it.

JM I've had arguments with people who aren't for instance, Donnelly fans, who say that it's just a hubbub. And I defend the position that it's shaped intentionally.

KT No, no, no. Yes, down to subliminal sounds. We set audiences up for the fall constantly. We had to work on *The Donnellys* to see if we could make the tiniest tiniest *tiniest* sound, I think it was in Part II at the Shivaree. There's a whole series of night sounds that are all displaced. We were just focusing the audience's ears down, down, down, and then I think we finally did the sound of wet on the end of the tongue [does it]—that. So their ears were absolutely focused down. In the Tarragon here, they have those risers? We took the great big two-by-fours and

175

banged them up under the risers, and physically put the audience about two inches up. So we just set them up for terror. It was wonderful. Those risers physically moved.

No, it's all very intentional and the structures of stage action are very very intentional. Sometimes you just have to get the right image for yourself. I went in and did a very angular blocking for Part II. And I realized, after two weeks of rehearsal, "My god, I've been doing this ALL WRONG." The play is based on straight lines meeting spinning. And I had based everything on the geometrical patterns, like Part I, on the lines without the spin. Well, the rhythm of the language didn't work properly. The lines are punctuated in a different way and unless you're aware, unless the stage action is moving properly, it doesn't mean what it's written to mean. Things like that are very very conscious. I would love to be able to simply throw it on the stage and have it all just work, you know. But no, it's all worked with much debate and care.

JM *The Donnellys* trilogy made the NDWT's method of working obvious to the people who got interested in it . . .

KT . . . *The St Nicholas Hotel*, the second part of *The Donnellys*, is still my very favourite of all. I had quite a bit of difficulty with Part III. We got through it, but it just seemed to me we weren't matching the size of poetry and images. I loved the lyricism, and I loved the pale yellow colour instead of the rich—funnily enough it's the actors who had the most trouble with Part II. They thought it was just terrible, some of them, during rehearsals. But then Part III they just loved. I found it just a tiny bit obvious, but, you know, you had to kill 'em (laugh). Jamie'd done fifteen years writing it: he had to finally end them off.

JM John Fraser remarked in a review that some people said that within this three there is perhaps the bare bones of one play. You don't think it's too big?

KT No. I guess there are the bare bones of one play if that's what you want.

JM But why bother?

KT Yes. The richness of the vision. Doing it when we did it here [Tarragon], all three in one day, it was just a wonderful experience. The reverberations in Part III of a moment in Part I, and variations, and reflections. All those things just took off. Exhausting, but just wonderful experience.

JM That would be exciting for Jamie.

KT Well, it was a chronicle for Jamie. He'd been working on it I guess ten or fifteen years then, and I'd been working on it about five years. It was a bit like a retrospective, too. Part I is difficult for me to even relate to now, it has such spit-and-vinegar young fuck-the-world energy in it, you know? Like, stick my chin out DARE you to hit it. Which is very much what we felt when we were doing it. We'd just left the establishment theatres, most of us, and had kind of gone "Well, let's go!" Expected to absolutely be killed in Toronto. We thought we were going to close in two days and head our asses back to Halifax.

JM The whole sense that I got, watching some rehearsals and then some of the plays was that the actors were not *being* themselves, but they put more *of* themselves into the production than you sometimes see in traditional theatre. And having them sit along the sides, and then mix into the action when they have to is blurring the edges of—

KT Reality, yes.

JM And the plays starting with singing or top-spinning, moves you in slowly so that you don't know, as an audience, when the "play" begins. You tend to think when you're brushing your teeth before you come to theatre that you're part of it too, there's that very strong—

KT Community. The whole design of them, too, which also looked very happenstance, but which was carefully developed so that one really had the distinct feeling of being in a room. So that you and the audience were in the same room, you decided to take *this* end because it was more convenient, and they took *that* end, and you got together to put on a play. It was very important for the dynamic of the internal workings of the play that you really commit the audience to it. The whole thing is like purgatory; we all have to make our decisions and choices.

JM It's not speaking down to the audience from a position of higher knowledge.

JM No, no. With the hidden fact that Jamie's prejudices were very strong (laugh). You know, he was pro-Donnelly. There's no question about that. . . .

Interview with Keith Turnbull, by Jean McKay,
ECW, 24/25 (1982-83), 152-155.

• •

JAMES REANEY

Handcuffs: The Donnellys, Part Three

First produced at Tarragon Theatre,
Toronto, 29 March 1975

Directed by Keith Turnbull
Set Design by Rosalyn Mina
Lighting Design by John Stammers

Cast
(Multiple roles for each performer)

Jay Bowen
Tom Carew
Caryne Chapman
Peter Elliott
David Ferry
Jerry Franken
Rick Gorrie
Miriam Greene
Patricia Ludwick
Don MacQuarrie
Keith McNair
Jill Orenstein
Gord Stobbe
Suzanne Turnbull

. . . *Handcuffs*, a title not to be taken literally, brings the unruly Irish clan to the night of their massacre by the townsfolk of Lucan on February 3, 1880. But it does not seek to make this act of conspicuous unneighborliness the finale, or even the climax. The fate of the murderers at the hands of the dead is set forth before the final vision of The Donnellys, waiting in the heavens as "in a fiery furnace."

It may come as a shock that Reaney has allowed the massacre to become something of an anti-climax, diffused by his poetic concern with this subsoil of Ontario legend. But we had been warned in *St Nicholas Hotel*, the second play, that the poet-dramatist was falling under the spell of the family.

Sometimes we suspect we are being asked to admire the Donnellys because there were 10 of them—one splendid matriarch, one late daughter and the rest of them rowing, vital, unpredictable squatters—in a new land, fighting for their new rights.

Church and politics attempt to impose upon them. Reaney details the attitude of McSweeney, Bishop of London, towards this particular family. The priest dispatched to quell them is distracted. Although they are devout Catholics, they are not Conservative. The bishop frowns from his heights, the priest thunders from a lesser height. At last, church and politics join hands to stamp out their influence, and indeed their lives.

That the Donnellys still ride the local farmer's horses at night, refuse to allow another's wheatcrop to be harvested and run in drunken riotousness through Lucan fades before the meanness of the persecuted [persecutors?]. The Donnellys are snubbed, ostracized and plotted against. We do not now ask if Reaney has twisted his research to their favor, for we have been persuaded to join the Donnellys against their false witnesses.

Take the case of young Feeney. He is bribed and trucked into betraying the family who befriended him, for now we see the Donnellys' better side as they mellow. His sworn relationship with young Tom Donnelly is unexpectedly moving.

Then there's Theresa O'Connor, who runs an illegal shabeen and swears by the Donnellys. And the young Irish cousin they take in. And Dr. O'Halloran who meets his true love in Mrs. O'Connor's bedroom and unites with her in double suicide. The Donnellys' supporters are persecuted cruelly, in preface to the massacre.

When the black night comes we glimpse the event through different eyes in classic tradition. Scorched by the fire that followed murder, James Carroll is elated. Mrs. Marksey has turned a blind eye. None of the vigilantes are punished when the truth emerges, not even Magistrate Carroll, so the Donnellys must rise up from the graveyard to avenge themselves and haunt St. Patrick's graveyard forevermore.

Has Reaney contributed an Ontario classic to Canada's dramatic literature? We are persuaded to make the hasty judgment, yet we are responding to Keith

Turnbull's direction as much as to Reaney's folk-tragedy. Generally enmeshed, sometimes they seem unexpectedly at odds.

Where Reaney is refusing to supply anything that might be mistaken for another melodramatic reconstruction of the massacre, Turnbull tends to dramatize the material more theatrically. To supplement the burning model barns or the spinning wheels of the first two segments, Turnbull employs a pair of white curtains.

Introduced to conceal Mrs. O'Connor's bar (and used to good comic effect when the priest comes) they flow in and out of the action from that point forward, concealing and revealing. They become useful as shadow screens in revealing action which moves closer towards ritual, with music and dance.

Although it is leading up to massacre, *Handcuffs* is the happiest play of the three, starting off with a delightful parlor singsong. Mrs. Donnelly herself reveals terpsichorean tendencies that are endearing and everybody sings in church and at funerals, no matter how many times repeated. A square-dance actually brought forth happy applause on opening night.

The collaboration of Reaney's imagery, born of his fascination with all things pertaining to the Donnellys, and the invention evoked from it by Turnbull's versatile and devoted actors perhaps adds to the diffusion of the work. It certainly extends the playing time.

The third Tarragon production is filled with recognizable devices from the earlier ones: window-frames, horse impersonation, the comic impersonation of a threshing-machine and even a touch of transvestism.

And the Tarragon actors are asked to be as nimble as ever, taking on about four times their number in characters. Jay Bowen, first on the list, is responsible for at least six, including tragic Dr. O'Halloran. When you get a strong personality like Miriam Greene, you may suspect Mrs. O'Connor is switching allegiance, instead of jumping into the skin of Mrs. Marksey.

It is amazing how few hurdles are insurmountable for the wide awake member of the audience, however, for Turnbull has given them instant identities in most cases. Only when Jerry Franken, a quiet, staunch and upright citizen as Mr. Donnelly, quickly dons the role of his oldest son, Will, are you likely to have to backtrack at massacre-time.

Patricia Ludwick stands unmistakably heroic as Mrs. Donnelly, the actress rising to the admiration of the dramatist until the matriarch is pure legend. We may lose sight of her on the fatal night, but she is welcome back as an active ghost later.

It is impossible to keep count of Donnelly sons with all this doubling and redoubling of cast but David Ferry again stands out as the ideal representative junior Donnelly, his curling lip establishing the balance between Irish deviltry and pioneer generosity.

Then on the other side, Don MacQuarrie makes a doubly strong impression as both the insidious James Carroll and the lofty Bishop McSweeney, hand-in-glove with himself in mischief to bring the proud Donnellys down. Of the others,

Keith McNair strikes a pure note of rural ignorance as Jim Feeney, one of the several secondary characterizations which enrich the Tarragon production, as in their own way Rosalyn Mina's setting and John Stammers' lighting do.

They are a group happy in their accomplishment. Reaney must be so, too.

Herbert Whittaker, *Globe and Mail*, 31 March 1975*

• •

Now it is finished, *Handcuffs*, which opened at the Tarragon Theatre Saturday night, concludes James Reaney's trilogy, *The Donnellys*, with no lapse in power or vision from the stature of its predecessors, first *Sticks and Stones* and then *The St Nicholas Hotel*.

The whole cycle is not just beautiful, but also dangerously exciting, a work of such controversial originality and demanding complexity that it will genuinely arouse audiences, emboldening its partisans and infuriating its detractors.

It will attract and frustrate imitators, and it will leave its mark forever on the people who helped create it.

In *Handcuffs*, Reaney moves at last to what has been lying watchful and waiting throughout the other two plays, the final massacre of the Donnellys on February 3, 1880.

The uneasy community of Biddulph, which had used legal and social pressures against the defiant Donnellys, which had attempted—in Reaney's striking phrase— "teaching them not to be so different," now finally moves to the mass violence implicit in their fantasies for so long, the fire required to obliterate fire.

Because we've known all along that this would be the conclusion, Reaney is able to shift from the thrusting, exploratory rhythms of the first two plays to a pattern of re-assembling and unifying. Thus, *Handcuffs* is as autonomous as its predecessors, but its greatest pleasure may be for those who can unite it to *Sticks and Stones* and *The St Nicholas Hotel*.

The many-textured experience is now complete, the fragments have locked together, and we can hold a hypnotic and credible myth within our hands.

But *Handcuffs*, which is as long and densely-packed as the other two, is not merely a melancholy postlude. Parts of it, particularly Mrs. Donnelly's scenes in Act 2, are as passionately turbulent as anything in the trilogy, and Reaney's extraordinary range of symbols and images is even further extended here.

Priests appear literally in wolf's-clothing. Curtains divide and conceal. Much is made of shadows and ghosts. Scenes with seeds and grain now define the community's neurotic, self-imagined sterility.

All these are added to earlier echoes. The dry sticks and solid stones recur, as do the wheels and ladders. Illicit love relationships beyond community sanction again end tragically. Songs from the earlier plays are re-sung, and their lyricism—*Handcuffs* in fact begins as a homemade, family entertainment, all beaming choristers—challenges the brutality.

Promises are kept and revenges of all sorts taken. The cycle revolves to a close, taking the lives of the Donnellys with it, leaving only their spiritual power and our ambiguous, unresolvable responses to it.

Keith Turnbull's contribution as Reaney's collaborator and director is surely revolutionary, creating a performing style as extraordinary and original as the text to be performed. His most stunning skill is in assembling textures, linking words and objects (superlative help here from Rosalyn Mina's designs and John Stammers' lighting), sounds and silences, the keen professionalism of some of his actors with the eloquent, untrained simplicity of others.

In this context, Jerry Franken and the incredible Patricia Ludwick as the senior Donnellys, David Ferry as various sons and Don MacQuarrie as certain anti-Donnellys have all built and sustained characters with magnificent imagination and authority.

Rick Gorrie has grown from an amiable bystander to a memorable participant, as the eyewitness to the murders. Miriam Greene, more a force than an actress, has only to utter the fragment "Stole my cow" to send a ripple of recall through the audience.

Caryne Chapman's Jenny Donnelly is much less haunting than either Carole Lazare in part 1 or Nancy Beatty in part 2, but Jill Orenstein, as the niece Bridget is wonderfully believable.

The others, Suzanne Turnbull, Gord Stobbe, Keith McNair, Tom Carew, Peter Elliott and Jay Bowen too are distinctively committed.

Long live the Donnellys. They will, too.

Urjo Kareda, *Toronto Star*, 31 March 1975*

• •

Handcuffs was the last play in James Reaney's thrice-told tale of the Black Donnellys of Biddulph Township, Ont., as presented Thursday by the NDWT Company of Toronto at Simon Fraser University Theatre.

As I have not seen the first two segments of the trilogy, my understanding of Reaney's work cannot help but be limited. Even though each part has been advanced as complete in itself, the very fact of the form implies the presence of a texture and continuity surely vital to the fullest appreciation.

Handcuffs, in which the Donnelly clan, who refused to be taught "not to be so different," is finally extinguished by an intractable tide of civic hatred, is reported to be quite different from the more exploratory, event-chronicling parts of one and two.

Handcuffs seems to unify themes, attribute the blame, examine character, expose the pathetically credible dynamics of persecution and dare to offer the proposal that the roistering, hot-headed Donnellys were murdered on that February day in 1880 because the inhabitants of that hostile community were human.

Handcuffs is heavy with a tragic minor-key tonality, the more powerful in that lyricism and mellowness are suddenly granted entrance to what is the crux of the trilogy. Again, as in the two previous parts, Reaney lets us know fully in advance the bloody end of the Donnellys. The course of this ironic play bears us ceaselessly into the past, and how the Donnellys meet their fate is presented in a sort of re-weaving of events.

Just as we see the coffins borne in to a choral requiem, or see the four stones marking the corners of the razed house, the yarn is pulled apart and the needles are set clicking obsessively at another variation on the same pattern—a new twist that yields a different insight into a character and a new fact to the total inevitability until a horrible, sad whole stands revealed.

Time, for Reaney, is taken as a completely manipulative tool in a work that deals in fragments and a rhythmic pattern of constant crescendos and diminutions. Everything about it has the virtuosity of daring, yet the play is not soured by a consciousness of its own virtuosity.

In the use of a Brecht-like distance effect, Reaney, or more likely the play's gifted director, Keith Turnbull, defies our forming sympathies via one actor or another by suddenly re-casting him or her in the role of a character completely opposed to his former one—Donnellys becoming anti-Donnellys, etc.

Reaney's imagery evokes a powerful redolence of human clay aspiring to more than dust. Kate [sic] Donnelly, the daughter, holds a salvaged slender bone from the arm of her mother. These arms are described in remembrance as bird-like, as when the matriarch would swoop her children up into the air in play.

The production rings, rattles and drones with a strange sort of musical counterpoint: the relentless clack of the sewing machine treadle in Theresa O'Connor's house accompanying the news of the Donnellys' massacre; the fond antic songs sung by a choir; the fiddling jigs; the Greek choric chants that mark off the approach of the awful day; the sound of dry sticks and wheat falling on sterile ground—all these reverberate in sympathy with the poetic text of Reaney, whose search is for the myth in the common man.

The 14 actors are an extremely fluid ensemble, as they must be for a play in which transitions are sharp and segues turn hair-pin corners. In fact, if there is any one overriding impression of the merits of the production, it is that one discipline has been answered by the other—poetic, visual, dramatic, scenic—in such a way that you cannot imagine an alternative.

Lloyd Dykk, *Vancouver Sun*, 17 October 1975

• •

. . . We can now see the shape of the trilogy as a whole. *Sticks and Stones* was concerned with naming and defining the Donnellys, setting them apart as characters marked with a special integrity. *St Nicholas Hotel* put them into direct conflict with their enemies, a conflict exemplified by stagecoach races; it also added to our view of their identity a romantic and lyrical quality. *Handcuffs* gives us not only the final massacre of the Donnellys, but a sense of their whole past circling back on them. It is full of echoes of the previous plays, old songs sung again and familiar lines and images recurring. . . .

The title of the play gives us its dominant image: there are literal handcuffs, which are put on Mrs. Donnelly when she is arrested and on Tom Donnelly before he is murdered; there is also a general sense throughout the play of closing up a circle. The play's own structure is more obviously circular than those of the other two. The massacre and funeral of the Donnellys take place early in the play, and we keep coming back to them. At the same time, there is a resistance to the image of handcuffs in Mrs. Donnelly's recurring gesture of raising her arms above her head. (We are told early in the play that she had "arms like wings"; and her daughter keeps an arm-bone as a relic of her.)

Appropriately, the tone of this play is darker than that of the other two. Besides the image of handcuffs, there are recurring images of fire, sickness, and death, and of men reduced to animals: "The Donnellys are like lions attacked in the desolate wilderness by a pack of wild dogs." Mary Donovan, a figure of fun in *St Nicholas Hotel*, where she made a comic fuss over her missing cow, becomes cold and savage as she watches her enemies' home burn: "I won't stop watching, Bill Donovan, till there's nothing more to watch." There is a story of star-crossed lovers, parallel to that of Will and Maggie in *St Nicholas Hotel*; but the story of Dr. O'Halloran and Katie Johnson is tough and brutal where the earlier story was gentle and romantic. They make love in a brisk, bawdy scene early in the play; in the end they drink poison. The new hardness of manner is reflected in a greater concentration on the Donnellys' enemies. In particular, the Church, a source of ceremony in *Sticks and Stones*, becomes in *Handcuffs* a cynical political organization, out to bring the Donnellys to heel; the parish priest literally wears wolf's clothing. There is also a slightly darker view of the Donnellys themselves. Where *St Nicholas Hotel* focused on the more attractive older brothers Will and Mike, this play pays more attention to the younger brothers Tom and John. Their adventures are coarser and more violent; they are closer than the rest of their family to being simply louts. And there is a darker side to the recurring theme of the Donnellys' immortality. The ghosts of Mr. and Mrs. Donnelly are menacing figures, terrorizing a group of modern teenagers who have come to their graveyard looking for a cheap thrill, and causing the deaths of two of their enemies by holding their horses in the path of a train.

There is, in short, a toughness in this third play that prevents Reaney's ultimately romantic view of the Donnellys from being too soft-centered. But it is a romantic view for all that. Throughout the trilogy the Donnellys are associated with the assertion of life, with the finding of true identity, with human love and with the life of the land itself. In theatrical terms they are given a special authority, stepping out of the action to take a broad view of their own lives and deaths. Their immortality is confirmed by their existence as dramatic characters; as Mr. Donnelly says, in *Sticks and Stones*, "I'm not in Hell for I'm in a play." In *Handcuffs* the bodies of the murdered family are represented throughout the funeral sequences by four stones and a candle, as though they have finally been reduced to something merely physical. But five living actors accompany the props; the characters are still alive. This convention allows Jenny to have one last dance with her mother, a living woman dancing with a dead one, before the coffins are taken away for burial. In the end, a great wheat field (represented in the first production by hand movements from the actors) grows around the ruin of their home; as Reaney remarks in his prefatory note, "It's hard to handcuff wheat."

Alexander Leggatt, *UTQ*, 47 (1977-78), 375-77

• •

. . . Two facts from the Donnelly case provide the basis for the play's elaborately wrought and opposing image patterns. The first fact is that the Donnellys made their living growing wheat. The second detail is that the men who led the attack on the Donnellys carried handcuffs with them. . . .In Reaney's play, a tension is developed between images of wheat and images of handcuffs.

Growing wheat is an activity which is in keeping with the natural cycle of the seasons. It is Biblically sanctioned, and requires family and community harmony to be successful, for sowing and harvesting are tasks which cannot be carried out single-handedly. In *Handcuffs*, the Donnellys are identified with this wholly good activity but are shown as being thwarted in their efforts to pursue it. "What's the use of sowing wheat in a township that hates us?" Mrs. Donnelly asks, and her question is well-founded for wheat is being left to rot because of the rift between the Donnellys and their neighbours. The waste of life-sustaining wheat reflects the consequences of human discord. The speeches of the Donnellys are laced with references to their wheat, and a threshing machine often accompanies their words. It serves as a rhythmic complement to their identification with the natural cycle. Even in death, the Donnellys remain identified with their wheat, for at the wake the Chorus implores us to mourn "their sheaves of time."

In contrast to the image of God-given, growing, and golden wheat is the image of the handcuffs: man-made, inanimate, and grey. The Donnellys' enemies are continually associated with these freedom-denying agents: "Handcuffs must be forged and plans must be made," cries Jim Carroll. Shadows of a hand and handcuffs are projected on a screen and loom ominously over the stage as a warrant is issued for Mrs. Donnelly's arrest. Yet Mrs. Donnelly recognizes that those who seek to deny her family its freedom are themselves "handcuffed and tethered by one fear or another," and her perception is in keeping with the play's theme that evil cannot arrest good. This view is best summarized in the play's epigraph:

> Like slowly closing handcuffs *people* (priests, constables, farmers, tavern keepers, traitors, threshers, among others) openly and secretly, legally and illegally fasten the disturbing Donnelly family still so that it can murder them. . . .Where the Donnelly house once stood the remaining family place four stones; it's hard to handcuff wheat.

Consistent with the wheat/handcuffs imagery and its implication that the Donnellys can overcome the forces which oppress them is another series of images in the play. The Donnellys are repeatedly associated with flight. Playing a game with her grandchildren, Mrs. Donnelly vows that she will "fly through the air with the right answer." When she is handcuffed, we are informed that "her wings have now been clipped." Foreshadowing the eventual moral victory of the Donnellys is a scene in Act Two in which a bird is rescued from the ashes of a chimney, and flies away triumphant and free. The allusion is surely to the phoenix who rises from the ashes. Indeed, in the final act of *Handcuffs* the Donnellys rise from their ashes in St. Patrick's Churchyard in 1974, on the anniversary of their death. Having refused to surrender to the forces which sought to persecute and banish them, the Donnellys have achieved immortality and freedom: "Look we are everywhere / In the clouds, in the treebranch, in the puddle, / There. Here. In your fork. In your minds."

Reaney's achievement in *Handcuffs*, and in the trilogy in general, is based on his ability to sustain the drama's image patterns throughout the many facets of the work. Drawn from the facts of the case, images of handcuffs and wheat, bondage and freedom, manifest themselves in the plot, the characters' speeches, the props, dances, and overhead projections of the drama. The Donnellys have finally been given their due: their side of the case is presented by Reaney in a finely crafted work of art which towers above all other treatments of the legend and draws universal insights from the Biddulph massacre . . .

George Wicken, *ECW*, 11 (Summer 1978), 262-63

• •

MICHAEL COOK

Jacob's Wake

First produced at Festival Lennoxville, 11 July 1975

Directed by William Davis
Set and Costume Design by Michael Eagan
Lighting Design by Douglas Buchanan
Sound Design by William Skolnik

Cast

Mary	Rita Howell
Rosie	Candy Kane
Skipper	Griffith Brewer
Brad	R. H. Thomson
Alonzo	David Calderisi
Winston	Roland Hewgill
Wayne	August Schellenberg

Compared to his latest two-and-a-half hour, lavender-tinted melodrama, *Jacob's Wake*, which on Friday officially opened Festival Lennoxville's fourth summer season, Michael Cook's earlier works, *Colour the Flesh the Colour of Dust*, and *The Head, Guts and Soundbone Dance*, appear to have been little more than a couple of theatrical warm-up exercises.

Family life in the outport communities of Newfoundland, as he presents it this time around, is filled with unmitigated hatred, masochism and unconscious longings for death. In reference to the latter, one character, halfway through the piece, states: "There are some who work for it and some who wait for it."

In *Jacob's Wake*, the people working and waiting for death, in one form or another, are all too familiar to the average Canadian theatregoer.

Members of the Blackburn family, they include two, instead of the regulation one, tyrannical fathers; three, instead of the regulation one, recalcitrant sons; and the standard work-horse mother and embittered spinster aunt. All have their moments of black humor.

Skipper, who is both father and grandfather, is a legless old man, ruling the roost from his deathbed located above the regulation kitchen. He has never recovered emotionally from the shock of sending his son Jacob out on the ice floes where he froze to death, and insists upon regarding his remaining son, Winston, as the dead Jacob.

Below stairs, Winston drinks beer, torments his unmarried sister and threatens to maim, if not kill, his three grown-up, bachelor sons, an unsavory bunch to say the least. Alonzo is a conniver, dealing in prostitution, illegal booze and questionable motels. Wayne is a member of Parliament who reluctantly turns contracts Alonzo's way and siphons off his expenses to keep his family in beer. Brad is a recently defrocked minister in danger of becoming seriously unhinged. As a younger man he had impregnated a girl who, some time later, was found during a spring thaw by Winston, having frozen to death with her infant during the winter.

The action takes place over a Maundy Thursday and Good Friday, during which Brad and Wayne have returned home for their annual family scourging.

Aunt Mary urges Wayne to have the old man upstairs put away in an institution. Bribing Alonzo with the promise of new contracts, Wayne persuades his brother to forge Winston's signature to a document which would have Skipper committed within the week.

Winston discovers the forgery and attempts to kill them all with a shotgun, but unfortunately misses because of a sudden power failure.

Brad rushes out into a blinding blizzard insufficiently clad, and is heard of no more. Wayne turns on his Aunt Mary and shows himself up as the rotter he is . . . and by this time author Cook finds himself backed into a corner by all the overcharged "realistic" melodrama which obviously has gotten completely out of hand.

Copping out, he baffles his audience by turning the last few minutes of the play into an hysterical, non-realistic fantasy.

At the height of the storm ominous footsteps are heard on the back stoop. Is it Brad come back to pick up a warm coat? No, it's Skipper, rejuvenated and wearing both legs.

Insisting the house is a ship, cut adrift in a turbulent sea, he orders Winston to man an imaginary wheel and, as the wind howls and lightning flashes, fires off orders to his family, who have now become the ship's crew. In less time than it takes it say Festival Lennoxville, the whole kit and kaboodle are swooshed into oblivion.

We know they're gone because the lights come up to prove there's nobody left. The moral seems to be the goblins will get you if you don't watch out.

Cook's persistent attempts to present Newfoundland as inhabited exclusively by hideously venal, self-serving mini-monsters, seems to indicate a deep and abiding contempt for the province he has chosen to call home. In none of his plays does he give any indication of the Newfoundlander's legendary warmth, hospitality, indomitable spirit and capacity for enjoying life in a cold and brutal climate. He hacks his characters out of cold stone without compassion.

In spite of the script's antiquated dramatic paraphernalia and lack of perception, it has been given a highly professional surface production under the skilled direction of William Davis, who obviously believes it should be taken seriously.

In the first-rate cast, David Calderisi is outstanding as Alonzo, and excellent performances are turned in by Rita Howell as the aunt, Roland Hewgill as Winston, Candy Kane as the mother, and Griffith Brewer as Skipper.

Michael Eagan's costume designs are eminently suitable and the intricacy of his set design makes us curious to see the blueprint for the entire house, of which the three visible rooms, the upper hall and interior stairway are but a part. Douglas Buchanan's subtle lighting lures our attention to the appropriate areas where the action takes place, and William Skolnik's sound effects are entirely realistic.

Myron Galloway, *Montreal Star*, 14 July 1975*

• •

Playwright Michael Cook once said, in an interview with the *Canadian Theatre Review*, "I'd rather, if a play is too bloody awful to go on as it is, go away and write another, hopefully a better, play."

Jacob's Wake, currently being staged at Festival Lennoxville, seems to qualify admirably for the re-write treatment.

The strange thing is that Mr. Cook has managed to create some relatively interesting characters, and then apparently doesn't know what to do with them dramatically.

Take a house in an isolated outport community on the coast of Newfoundland. People it with the following—a half-mad, legless, dying old man who has lain in his bed for the past 30 years reliving the days of the great seal hunts and the death on the ice of his son Jacob; the old man's surviving son, a coarse, drunken good-for-nothing; his warm, placid, simple wife; their three sons—a fallen priest, a pimp and a crooked politician—and a fairly standard maiden-aunt schoolteacher.

You'd think something would happen, with all that ranting and raving, all those recriminations, all that crudeness and ugliness. Especially since the action takes place on Maundy Thursday and Good Friday with a howling blizzard and, inexplicably, the sound of creaking timbers for incessant sound effects.

What actually happens must surely be one of the most ludicrous cop-outs in the annals of Canadian theatre. After all the purple melodrama, cheap sentiment, ringing phrases and dragging of skeletons out of cupboards, the playwright finally extricates himself from his play by having the legless Skipper come striding downstairs (on two perfectly good legs, of course) announcing that it's time for action.

"There comes a time," intones the Skipper, "when ye must steer into the storm and face up to what ye are."

So *that's* what it was all about. That, presumably, explains why the house suddenly becomes a ship and sails away into the storm and, supposedly, the Great Beyond.

But not before we've been acquainted with all the seamy details of this remarkable family. Like how the fallen priest fathered Millicent Tobin's illegitimate child, and how she was thrown out in the snow and found in the spring by the priest's father with her hour-old babe frozen to her breast. Or how the Skipper bitterly reproaches himself, not only for having caused Jacob's death but for having had the bad taste to father a girl. Or how Winston goes into a black depression whenever he gets drunk, at the thought of his infant daughter who died, leaving him only with three good-for-nothing sons and no grandchildren.

In the face of all this, the Lennoxville cast and director deserve special credit for having tried so hard to take *Jacob's Wake* seriously.

Direction by William Davis endeavors to give some meaning to the unrelated events, and Mr. Davis has drawn some remarkably fine performances from his cast.

Most memorable of all is Candy Kane as Rosie. She gives the character of the mother a real feeling of solidarity and is the one sane and comforting note in this cacophony of misfits.

Roland Hewgill shows unexpected depth in the role of Winston, the Skipper's despised son who never went to sea. It's a big change for the normally suave and sensitive Hewgill, and it's interesting.

Griffith Brewer does his best as the crazy old Skipper, faced as he is with lines like, "The frozen breath of fallen men tinkling over their dead hands like spoons in teacups.'' Do Newfoundland fishermen really talk like that, I wonder?

David Calderisi and August Schellenberg do well as two of Winston's sons; R. H. Thomson struggles manfully with the implausible role of the priest, but it's a losing battle. And Rita Howell gives the maiden aunt more depth of character than you would think possible from the lines she is given.

Michael Eagan has successfully overcome the horrendous task of designing a set where people have to appear in the living room, kitchen, upstairs landing and two bedrooms of the same house, all at the same time. And William Skolnik is the indefatigable producer of the sound effects.

If, after *Colour the Flesh the Colour of Dust*, *Head, Guts and Soundbone Dance* and now *Jacob's Wake*, Michael Cook still insists on being a playwright, we can only hope for better things from his next foray into dramatic territory.

Audrey M. Ashley, *Ottawa Citizen*, 28 July 1975*

• •

. . . *Jacob's Wake* is difficult for me to talk about. It's still very close. I only finished the last rewrite some six weeks before Festival Lennoxville produced it in the summer of '75. I threw just about everything into that, including an apocalyptic end-of-the-world scene, with the Old Skipper upstairs coming down as a ghost to lead the broken family into death. The family in this case, I suppose, being a little more than a family. The Old Sealing Skipper upstairs, his son, Winston, living on welfare, a man of critical sensibility and conscience trying to drown his despair in drink and sardonic wit; his three sons, a politician, a bar-owner, and a religious maniac, and his wife, Rosie, the real power, dominant, yet rarely forceful, secure, without confusion, mother-image constant in the face of disaster, relying upon instinct not intellect . . . to hold her family together. And Aunt Mary, Winston's sister, prim, old-maidish, a schoolteacher, struggling to preserve her dignity in a disruptive house. Outside, the storm becomes a living thing, which threatens and finally engulfs them all.

I suppose one of the germane ideas for the play comes from E. J. Pratt, whose evolutionary vision informs most of his major poems about Newfoundland, or the sea. There is a point at which man's cupidity or greed, or simple desertion of the instinctive laws of nature that bind each to each, will result in disaster. ''The Titanic,'' for instance. As Pratt writes it, the iceberg had been born thousands of years before, a neolithic monster waiting for a time of challenge, when it became the avenger, and the teacher. And again, in the ice floes, he creates a powerful image as the men, agents of man's greed, his stupidity in ignoring all the warning signals, becomes caught in a terrible storm and one, in death, is bonded in brotherhood with his victim, the seal. He is found with ''his teeth fleshed in its frozen heart.''

191

My ending then is deliberate. It's not for me to say whether it works theatrically. I like to use the theatre. I like to risk and challenge an audience in all the ancient ways. What's wrong with a ghost? What's wrong with enraged nature? Are we so secure and smug that we believe neither is possible? And in any event, what's wrong with the sheer enjoyment of the theatricality of the thing? I like lots of things happening on stage too. I enjoy what I do. And I enjoy movement and vitality and surging on the stage which are the only things which give point to silence, to the moments of contemplation at which time we share the crisis and the catharsis which makes the tears flow, which brings the release.

Jacob's Wake is also close to me because, of all the plays I've written, it's the one that is most clearly based upon people I know. . . .

Stage Voices, pp. 226-28

• •

. . . The realism of these family relationships (which have more than a whiff of O'Neill about them) is deepened by religious symbolism. Placing the action on Maundy Thursday and Good Friday not only provides a realistic excuse for the family's reunion but is also meant to relate to Elijah's sacrifice of Jacob on an April 5th many years before. Thus the mourning for Christ is also Jacob's Wake, and their parallelism is driven home by the crucifixion image, borrowed from David Blackwood's striking series of Newfoundland etchings "The Lost Party," in which the Skipper recalls his last sight of his son: "The way dey was, so far away, dey seemed to form a t'in black cross on the ice. Den the ground drift swallowed dem up. . . ." This image is recapitulated later as a premonition of disaster: "'Tis the shape of death, boy. I kin see'n jest like that first time, rising out of the drift, moving across the ice widout a sound, a man like a cross growing up into the sky."

The key names are also significant. The Old Testament Jacob was, of course, the favoured son who wrestled with the angel and who, by fathering twelve sons, established the tribes of Israel; thus Jacob's death is clearly the loss of Elijah's hopes for the future. Similarly, Elijah himself was the Old Testament prophet of doom to Ahab's false gods, and his ascent to heaven in a chariot of fire is probably meant to relate to the Skipper's curious apotheosis at the end of the play. A level of religious awareness is also maintained by the Eastern hymns coming over the radio, which the Blackburns occasionally join in. Not only do these incorporate Cook's usual device of song realistically into the play, their sentimental rendering makes a point about the religious shallowness of contemporary society, while the particular relevance of several of them to the sea—"Eternal Father," for example, and John Newton's "Amazing Grace"—deepens the symbolic significance of the action, though that significance is far from being Christian.

As usual in Cook, there is also an attempt to use the set to suggest several levels of response. Wayne's type of society is represented by the blandness of the radio's music and its stilted weather forecasts, which gradually give place to the real thing as the storm increases in violence, screaming round the house and finally overwhelming the radio and the lights. Within the house itself a distinction is established between the ground floor and the bedrooms. On the ground floor the ordinary aspects of outport life are converted by realistic conversation and methodical processes of quilting, cooking, drying firewood, playing cards, and even preparing drinks—"a traditional part of the family ritual." The bedroom level, by contrast, is appropriately the realm of vision—Brad's nightmares of the last judgement and the Skipper's reliving of his son's death and premonitions that the house is a ship drifting to disaster.

At the end these levels are suddenly reversed. While the apparent corpse of the skipper is visible on his bed above, his "ghost" enters below to take charge of the house like a ship, impressing his son and grandsons as part of the crew, and heading, he says, defiantly into the truth of the storm: "Comes a time. . . .When ye has to steer into the storm and face up to what ye are." There is also the sound of seals, and Elijah exults, "The swales is back. Newfoundland is alive and well and roaring down the ice-pack. . . ."

But then the play ends with nature triumphing in "a blackout and the sound of a cosmic disaster . . . the final release of the insensate fury of nature that has been building throughout the play." When the lights go up, the fragile house is empty save for the death mask of Elijah, and "All fades into the lone quiet crying of a bitter wind."

This conclusion is certainly not "one of the most ludicrous cop-outs in the annals of Canadian theatre," as one reviewer complained [*Ottawa Citizen*, 28 July 1975]. Its significance is clear in the context of Cook's other work; he has mingled realism and symbolism in all his plays; and *Jacob's Wake* itself has a persistent symbolic level, with the identification of house and ship repeated many times before the transformation. Nevertheless, the experiment fails: the reversal of levels is too extreme, and the significance of the end remains unclear. Cook himself tacitly admits this when he suggests that, instead of a realistic set, an "acceptable alternative" night be

> a stark skeletonized set . . . as white as bone, stripped of formality, the house equivalent of a stranded hulk of a schooner, only the ribs poking towards an empty sky . . .

thus freeing the director for "an existential interpretation of the play."

The failure is an instructive one, however, because of its very boldness. The dilemma Cook faces as a playwright is that the experience he wishes to convey arises from an only too actual reality—the awesome environment of Newfoundland—which he cannot present on stage. He is forced to convey its significance poetically, through heightened language and stage symbolism, but this has an allegorical effect, removing the experience from the actuality that is its very essence. Only in *The Head, Guts and Soundbone Dance* has he found a form to fuse these levels, and even there it is at some cost to the realism. *Jacob's Wake* switches between the levels too abruptly; while the "epic" looseness of *Colour the Flesh* allows realism and symbolism to coexist without a proper fusion. Perhaps the problem is insoluble in stage terms; but unless it is solved, Michael Cook's imagination itself remains "on the edge," its undeniable power denied an adequate dramatic form.

Brian Parker, "On the Edge: Michael Cook's Newfoundland Trilogy,"
Canadian Literature, 85 (Summer 1980), 39-40

• •

JOHN MURRELL

Waiting for the Parade

First produced by Alberta Theatre Projects,
Calgary, 4 February 1977

Directed by Douglas Riske
Set Design by George Dexter
Costume Design by Jane Grose
Lighting Design by Peter Van Johnson

Cast

Catherine	Sheila Junor-Moore
Janet	Marie Baron
Margaret	Joan Boyd
Eve	Patricia Connor
Marta	Merrilyn Gann

If you enjoyed Barry Broadfoot's book, *Six War Years*, you will love *Waiting for the Parade*, John Murrell's new musical play about wartime Calgary.

It's that kind of play; a photo album of staged nostalgia guaranteed to make people start exchanging Second World War stories at intermission.

However, if the legend "Texaco news flashes" means absolutely nothing to you and if you have no idea who recorded Elmer's Tune (it was Glenn Miller for RCA), chances are you might find the current offering from Alberta Theatre Projects a little dated.

Like *A Great Noise, A Great Light*—Murrell's play about Depression-era Alberta which started off the ATP season in November—*Waiting for the Parade* is primarily of sociological and historical value; the only feature its subject matter has in common with 1977 is that the Wartime Prices and Trade Board instituted Canada's first round of wage and price controls in 1941.

The play deals with five women whose menfolk have varying involvements with the war. We never see these men, but during the course of the play we learn a lot about them; in fact, it's fair to say that most of the action in this play takes place off stage.

The story unfolds in an episodic series of vignettes, linked with music, song, sketches and monologues. The play is so bereft of physical business that if read over the air, it would say as much (or as little) as it says from the bare boards of the Canmore Opera House. It's the kind of closet drama that would probably make for a good radio play; it is more theatre for the mind than theatre for the senses.

The characters are potentially interesting because they have biographies that suggest the possibility of climactic futures: Catherine (Sheila Junor-Moore) has a husband overseas and a putative husband at the plant; Eve (Patricia Connor) has a detested older husband and a set of guns in her home that she has learned how to use; Janet (Marie Baron) has a husband who avoided the war by working as a radio announcer and avoided her by working on the emotions of another woman; Marta (Merrilyn Gann) has an immigrant father who believes she is a Canadian spy; and Margaret (Joan Boyd) is a widow trying to recapture some of her lost youth.

But the fragmented nature of the play is such (most of it is pure exposition) that the characters are never really given an opportunity to develop beyond the introductory stage. There are no real conflicts or sustained impetus leading to climax. The play is as unstructured as a raw egg spilled on a kitchen floor and the finale, after about two and one-half hours, is an anti-climactic cop-out.

Add to that the disappointing fact that this new play from a Canadian-based playwright is nothing more than mere historical reconstruction; well done, mind you, with authentic hairstyles, costumes and songs of the period, but without contemporary relevance. It has nothing to say to a person under 30 living in Canada today.

The actresses do as competent a job as one might expect, given the undemanding nature of their roles. Miss Baron seems a bit young to be the dried-out figure of self-importance played in the script, and Miss Gann's German accent seems unnecessary considering she is supposed to have lived in Canada since she was four. But they sing and act adequately, giving as much to their performances as required. The other players are similarly proficient.

Brian Brennan, *Calgary Herald*, 5 February 1977*

• •

. . . This play—subtitled *Faces of Women in War*—focuses on five Calgary women and how they confront the realities of the Second World War. One is a widow with a son in the conflict. One has a husband overseas and finds herself turning to other men in her loneliness. One is a community busybody with a husband who has managed to avoid enlisting by claiming he has a crucial job. One is a young woman with a much older husband whom she loathes. And finally there is a German immigrant's daughter whom many consider to be a spy.

It's a deliberately fragmented play, semi-documentary in flavor—an amalgam of vignettes, monologues, and vintage song interludes. It's part sociology, part history—an attempt, à la Barry Broadfoot, to show what it was really like for those who stayed at home. And if the references to Leslie Howard and Glenn Miller's recording of "Elmer's Tune" and the hoarding of rations will touch off nostalgia in many viewers, it is nevertheless nostalgia with an edge.

The ATP production, sensitively staged by Douglas Riske and featuring a quintette of fine performances dominated by Sheila Junor-Moore's work as the wife with the roving eye and Joan Boyd as the war mother, revealed a play which deserves productions in other parts of Canada.

And if it revealed Murrell's solid qualities as a playwright, it also at times revealed his main failing, which is a tendency to be too manipulative in some of his plotting.

Yet there can be no denying his strengths. He can move and absorb audiences in a very special way. And if he sometimes resorts too much to the easy cliché device to make a point—the long-suffering but infinitely good-hearted fraulein in *Waiting for the Parade* is simply too good to be true—he compensates for this by an overriding compassion and honesty in intent.

Jamie Portman, *Edmonton Journal*, 18 March 1977*

• •

Bill Glassco, director of the Tarragon Theatre, offers artistic and commercial successes so consistently that a flop, or even a mediocrity, would occasion astonishment among the cognoscenti. Those theatregoers who attended the first night of Glassco's latest presentation, *Waiting for the Parade*, by John Murrell of Calgary, were not surprised to see yet another hit. *Parade* is a sweet, warm, tender study of five Alberta women caught up in the social and emotional whirlwind of the Home Front in the Second World War.

The craftsmanship of the play's construction, the graphic quality of the character studies and the sensitive nature of the many different scenes bear the stamp of the man who wrote that brilliant new translation of Chekhov's *Uncle Vanya* that we saw at Stratford last season.

The director, Eric Steiner, and the designer, Shawn Kerwin, divide the stage into five tiny settings, all of which are on view throughout the action and each of which, in the choice of a sewing machine, an upright piano, a sofa or a chest of drawers vividly suggests, symbolically, the life style of the five disparate women.

Frequently one of the women, sitting alone in her home, addresses the audience directly. Yet her lines are so expertly written that the dramatic illusion remains intact. At intervals we see the women in twos or threes, and sometimes all together on stage.

Instead of a conventional plot, the author provides an endless series of vignettes or cameos, an episodic string of tiny dramas, each creating a vivid image of women trying valiantly to be of help at home to the war effort. Brilliant sound and light effects by Robert Thompson evoke visions of troop trains passing through Canadian cities, battalions marching up and down the streets behind brass bands, fighter pilots training overhead, canteen dances for troops hosted by local women and of great battles overseas.

The sound effects of D-Day, against a scene of women listening to the progress of the landings on the radio, provide the audience with a form of double vision, a sense of being in two places at the same time and an overwhelming awareness of the full splendor, squalor, nobility and outrage of war.

Fiona Reid plays Catherine, an attractive young woman whose beloved husband is overseas for so long that she forgets what he looks like. Her tipsy scene when she hears her husband is missing at Dieppe is shattering. And the heart-rending uncertainty with which she enters into an affair with an older man as a panacea for a demoralizing degree of sexual starvation makes her infidelity instantly forgivable.

Susan Hogan plays Eve, a young pretty woman whose husband, too old for combat, is a tiresome firebrand. She sublimates the shame and irritation she feels about her husband's exclusion from the war by hero-worshipping the movie star Leslie Howard.

Kay Hawtrey plays Margaret, a plump, middle-aged woman driven between pride in one son sailing on dangerous Atlantic convoy duties with the RCN and humiliation by a second son who is arrested for distributing seditious Communist pamphlets.

Nonnie Griffin plays Janet, the bossy matron who organizes all the others in the rolling of bandages, serving of canteen snacks, waving at troop trains, and exercising in air raid defence routines. Janet is overzealous at war work because she is secretly ashamed of her husband, who is fit enough for combat but ducks action in the reserved occupation of a radio announcer.

Clare Coulter plays Marta, a middle-aged German woman who has been in Canada since she was 10. She is ostracized because her slightly potty 75-year-old father, a pro-Nazi, is interned. Ms. Coulter's study of a woman standing up with dignity to humiliations she has done nothing to deserve is magnificent. When her father dies a few days after the war is over, Marta stands over his grave, torn between love for him, and love for Canada. Few women actors are so powerful as Ms. Coulter in the mute expression of violently mixed feelings.

It seems certain that once again the Tarragon Theatre, with its 250 seats, will be packed to capacity throughout the run of *Waiting for the Parade*. If this quality of production is maintained a larger building will become essential.

McKenzie Porter, *Toronto Sun*, 8 January 1979

• •

John Murrell's play *Waiting for the Parade* sneaks up on the audience at the Tarragon Theatre. Occasionally funny, sometimes poignant, but often rambling into shapelessness, the play seldom lights up the stage. But slowly and quietly it makes itself at home in the imagination of the viewer.

The play and its effect are defined by the title: It's about the paralysis of ordinary life in wartime, even for five women at home in Calgary, far removed from the action of World War II. An historian might call it a play about what *didn't* happen. And so it often seems annoyingly domestic and vague. But to write movingly about the triviality of life is one test of a writer.

Murrell doesn't give much clear-cut dramatic shape to either play or characters, leaving much to the actors and director. At Tarragon, the women are made whole by five remarkable performers, but Eric Steiner's direction seems slack and unresponsive.

The play is a series of vignettes, and Steiner allows them to bleed into one another so that some stretches are as ill-defined as 6 feet of wartime sausage. This may be true to life, but not to art.

It's not until the second act that he begins to mark them off with blackouts bridged with sound. Until then, the climax of one scene is often lost in the distracting entries for the next. There's little sense of pace, and the layered perspective of Shawn Kerwin's intriguing set (with imaginative lighting to match by Robert Thompson) is barely exploited.

The action begins rather tentatively. Fiona Reid, for instance, establishes a strong presence and then undermines her own lines by running one into another. But eventually Miss Reid comes into her own, etching a portrait of frailty that captures unreserved sympathy. It's a versatile, detailed and winning performance.

Perhaps it's because they play so many scenes together that Miss Reid and Susan Hogan dominate the production. It's not because the other women let them walk away with it.

Miss Hogan . . . demonstrates impressive versatility. This time out, she's a milquetoast high school teacher hiding a spark of personality that slowly takes fire.

Clare Coulter is effective in a difficult role, that of a young German-Canadian woman minding the store for her aged father who's been interned by Canadian authorities suspicious of his nostalgic nationalism.

This is a topic barely touched by Canadian writing, but Murrell doesn't treat it sensationally. He traces the degeneration of the old man's mind, estranged behind barbed wire from new culture and old, through the daughter's under-stated narrative of alienation.

Miss Coulter . . . fits her new part like a glove. Her ironic detachment underlines the defiant independence of the lonely girl, and survives to keep her on an even keel as she's gradually accepted by the other women and rejected by her father.

Kay Hawtrey is cast less sympathetically as an aging pessimist bewailing one son in the navy and another in prison for sedition. She's also stuck with Murrell's brief indulgence in melodrama when she has to die onstage. But she's convincing, as is Nonnie Griffin in the play's other unappealing role: a female sergeant-major regimenting the war effort of the ladies' aid. Did you know that there's enough explosive power in one cup of fat to launch 49 anti-aircraft shells? Miss Griffin would like you to feel guilty for every scrap you waste.

Waiting for the Parade is no theatrical bombshell, but like the moment it makes you wait for, it ends a winner.

Art Cuthbert, Toronto Star, 8 January 1979

• •

. . . it is easy to see why this gentle pastoral look at five Canadian women's lives during World War II has become such a favorite of artistic directors around the country: it's charming, nostalgic, and offers the chance to bring in Canadian leading ladies, like Fiona Reid, to star in the play. Yet it's really the weakest of these three scripts [Linda Griffiths' *Maggie and Pierre*, David Fennario's *Balconville*, and *Waiting for the Parade*].

The period John Murrell has chosen to set the play is certainly a rich one, and by focussing on various women he manages to touch on a broad spectrum of issues and attitudes. There is the fatalistic Margaret ("Death runs in my family") who endlessly broods over the fact that her son may be killed in the war; the pacifist schoolteacher who angrily watches her underage students enlist; the strident patriot who organizes excavation drills (determined to single-handedly prevent the invasion of Calgary!); the lonesome soldier's wife who finds solace in the arms of another man; the German-Canadian seamstress whose aged father is suspected of being a Nazi sympathizer and incarcerated in a labour camp in Alberta.

While the experiences and characters Murrell deals with may well be historically true-to-life, he fails to give them much depth or dimension, with the result that they rarely rise above the stereotypic. Murrell's perceptions on the wartime situation seem equally limited. The play is basically a nostalgia piece about a bygone generation, and Murrell never manages to plumb the depths of these women's lives. For that reason, he cannot relate their experiences to a larger segment of the population.

The other serious flaw in *Waiting for the Parade* is its lack of conflict. The enemy—the war in Europe—is distant and unseen. There is talk among the women of personal struggles on the home front, but again the antagonists—the schoolteacher's warmongering husband, say, or the racists who paint swastikas on the German woman's shop window—are never seen on stage, and the telling of the conflict through monologues is far from dramatic. Without a more immediate, insistent conflict to thrust the action forward, the various scenes remain passionless and unfocussed, and the structure arbitrary. The characters are resigned to waiting for the parade; unfortunately readers must be resigned to waiting for the ending.

Thérèse Beaupré, *CTR*, 32 (Fall 1981), 115-16

• •

AVIVA RAVEL

Dispossessed

First produced at the Saidye Bronfman Centre,
Montreal, 18 June 1977

Directed by Sean Mulcahy
Set Design by Muriel Gold
Costume Design by Claude Pelletier
Lighting Design by Claude-André Roy

Cast

Roochel	Sylvia Lennick
Seymour	Paul Kligman
Benjie	Richard M. Davidson

Hopelessness and despair; selfishness and futility; self-pity, loneliness and death; these are the exclusive ingredients Montreal playwright Aviva Ravel uses to present a relentlessly grim view of life in her new play *Dispossessed* which opened Saturday night at the Saidye Bronfman Centre.

When the curtain falls on the final act, in a manner of speaking, all we are left with is an immediate impulse to run into the street and hurl ourselves in front of the first fast moving bus that comes along. But hold it!

Mrs. Ravel deals from a loaded deck.

Life is not entirely as she would have us believe—black on black. There really are such things as honest relationships possible between human beings and life has as many small joys as it has overwhelming miseries.

There are, Mrs. Ravel notwithstanding, occasional shafts of light to illuminate the darkness and help us find our way out of the lower depths, if we are interested in raising our heads from time to time. And there is also laughter as well as self awareness. And love is not always as bitter as gall.

Dispossessed, however, contains no evidence that any of these exist and therein lies its greatest weakness. . . .

Before arriving at [the] dismal finale the playwright takes swipes at stereotype Jewish mothers, Jewish mothers-in-law, Jewish ladies who collect hats, ruthless Jewish factory owners and a cruel and merciless God.

Mrs. Ravel's play is unredeemed by any sign of warmth, compassion, perspective or humor.

Under the skillful direction of Sean Mulcahy three fine performances are turned in by Paul Kligman, Richard M. Davidson and Sylvia Lennick.

Using material reminiscent of 19th century melodrama, Mrs. Ravel offers us a view of life as being nothing more than a can of worms. In parlous times like these we could do with a somewhat more affirmative message.

Myron Galloway, *Montreal Star*, 20 June 1977*

• •

A note in the program of Aviva Ravel's play *Dispossessed* says that play takes place in the present.

But though it may have been meant to take place in the present, the play's emotional time-slot is back 30 years or more, around the time its main character Roochel stopped really living.

Dispossessed, which opened at Saidye Bronfman Centre this week, is a weak play in many ways. It is repetitive and needs to be severely edited; it loses power by saying, and saying again, things that would have greater impact if they were only implied.

If these changes were made, however, it probably would not be the play Ravel had in mind when she wrote it last year. . . .

While the play is a subjective slice of Jewish life, it is a very narrow slice indeed that Ravel presents us with—leaving out the schmaltz (sentiment), the chutzpah (charm) and overdosing us only with kvetch (nagging or complaining).

It is humorless, and one cannot accept that even a miserable life can be so totally barren of the odd joke or a frivolous gesture.

While the play has a realism that comes from elements of autobiography—emotional if not factual—along with details supplied by the lives of acquaintances and neighbors, it leaves so much out and focuses so heavily on one aspect only that it feels like the work of a beginner. . . .

The play's strength is in creating an absolutely terrifying revulsion in us that a situation like this actually exists, or that we might be stuck in the flytrap of memory, as Roochel is.

But it is a play about losers, who talk at us, talk at each other and kvetch endlessly.

Directed by Sean Mulcahy, Paul Kligman (Seymour), Richard M. Davidson (Benjie), and Sylvia Lennick (Roochel) were surprisingly convincing in what are probably the dreariest parts they will ever have to live with.

Julia Maskoulis, *Montreal Gazette*, 21 June 1977*

• •

"What difference does it make?" a character asks despairingly at the very end of Aviva Ravel's new play, *Dispossessed*. Intended as a lamentation on the futility of existence, this question might well be applied to the play itself.

Dispossessed is strictly a long night's journey into dramatic oblivion.

Aviva Ravel is a compassionate playwright. She cares about human loneliness. She quite properly sees personal relationships as being the most important subject one can write about. Nevertheless, *Dispossessed* simply will not do.

Its recent premiere at the enterprising Saidye Bronfman Centre Theatre in Montreal generated an unusual amount of interest, not only because of this theatre's past success in spotting worthwhile new Canadian drama but because the play itself was a 1976 winner of the Women Write for Theatre Competition, sponsored by the Playwrights Co-op in Toronto.

But what has regrettably emerged is contrived and maudlin melodrama in which naturalism veers into grotesque and in which legitimate human emotions are cheapened. . . .

The trouble is that [the] characters reveal themselves to us not by doing but by telling. And as they inform us of their past, present and future to an interminable degree, they kill off whatever remaining dramatic momentum the play possesses.

In attempting to win the audience's attention through the hazardous process of the searing revelation, the play merely shows up the murkiness of its psychology and a woeful lack of theatrical values.

As a result, *Dispossessed* becomes unhinged—moving from dialogue to monologue, and from monologue to recitation, while the drama concurrently recedes.

The play is not helped by Sean Mulcahy's direction which tends to be so static that it flattens whatever dramatic potential may still cling to the work. Paul Kligman achieves occasional moments of truthful dignity as the 75-year old Seymour, but is hampered by the fact that he appears to be about the same age as Richard M. Davidson who portrays the unlovable Benjie.

Davidson's Benjie comes across like a Dead End Kid gone to seed, and Sylvia Lennick's Roochel is not so much indomitable as indefensible, reminiscent of the character of Momma in Neil Simon's *Come Blow Your Horn*.

Jamie Portman, Edmonton Journal, 7 July 1977*

• •

. . . Aviva Ravel could be described as a Jewish Absurdist playwright. These two concepts may, at first, seem incompatible but Ravel has managed to balance them successfully. She establishes a Jewish sensibility in this play not only through the careful creation of Jewish language and characterization but also through the celebration of a determination that, in the face of all obstacles, continues to espouse hope in the future and defiance of present problems, an attitude that could be described as an integral part of the Jewish tradition. The absurdist overtones of the drama are fairly obvious.

As the title of her play indicates, her characters are much more than financially dispossessed. They live a life over which they have little control. Their shabby apartment, buried in the basement and darkened by the heavy frost that covers the windows, seems cut off from the rest of the world. There, the characters live in predictable tedium. More acted upon than acting, it is outside forces that determine their lives, extending from the landlord upstairs who neglects to turn up the heat, to Joseph Feldman who still exerts a strong control over them from beyond the grave. Their world is monitored by an apathetic God who likes to play "lousy jokes" on his characters. Seymour, the most overtly religious of the three, proclaims "everything counts for nothing. You don't count. I don't count. Money doesn't count. The snow doesn't count . . . " The God of his conception is more concerned with the affairs of His angels than the affairs of mankind. "To him we are all horses, dolphins, chickens. No better, no worse."

Ravel's play, however, does not consist of unrelieved pessimism. Despite the hopelessness of their situation, the characters do reveal a genuine affection for one another. Roochel delights in pampering her son. Seymour rocks and sings Benjie to sleep. Benjie dreams of buying a fur coat for his mother. Ravel allows each of her characters to reflect on their past. These memories make them more sympathetic and believable for the audience. We catch a brief glimpse of the youthful Feldman. We understand why Benjie never defended himself in fights at school and why he was so desperate to discover the identity of his father. We see a younger but still pragmatic Seymour caught between two families for forty years.

Perhaps the most moving and revealing moment of the play occurs in Scene Four when the characters dream of the possibility of inheriting Feldman's fortune. Seymour imagines himself building a luxurious synagogue and finally winning the respect of the rest of his congregation. Roochel wants to be "the finest example of a Jewish mother," antagonizing daughters-in-law, doting on grandchildren, attending Hadassah meetings and wearing outrageous hats. Benjie, ignoring his own desires, dreams of providing a life of luxury for his mother. But the opportunity for all three to right the wrongs of their lives is ironically dashed when Feldman, who is convinced that money brings unhappiness and longs to return to the honesty of his early relationship with Roochel, entrusts her with his sentimental collection of leaves and desk diaries, but no cash.

In *Dispossessed*, Aviva Ravel successfully turns commonplace lower-class people and events into a vision of universal validity. She accurately reproduces the inflections and rhythms of Jewish speech and her use of metrical, unrhymed verse reinforces the poetic power of her language. Throughout her play, she sustains a balance of the tragic and the hilarious, a subtle comment on the absurdity of life. But when the play concludes, as it began, with Seymour's cursing of the landlord, the effect on the audience is not necessarily hopeless. The [Playwrights Co-op] competition judges concluded that "there is an authentic despair developed in this play which renders it engrossing . . . a stunning portrayal of betrayal and impotency." But it can be argued that Seymour's last words reflect a defiant determination to carry on in the face of Roochel's death and Benjie's desertion. Pointing his finger at God and then banging on the roof for his landlord's attention, Seymour refuses to be silenced. Although, in his eyes, Roochel, Benjie, Feldman, God, his landlord, in fact, the whole world, may be playing dirty tricks on him, Seymour continues to demand his rights as a human being. In this character, Aviva Ravel has created a portrait of hope deceived and deferred but never extinguished, existing in the midst of life's absurdity.

Margaret Pappert Martinello, ECW, 9 (1977-78), 113-14

• •

GEORGE WALKER

Zastrozzi

First produced at Toronto Free Theatre, 2 November 1977

Directed by William Lane
Set Design by Doug Robinson
Sound Design by Wes Wraggett
Lighting Design by Gerry Brown

Cast

Zastrozzi	Stephen Markle
Bernardo	George Buza
Verezzi	Geoffrey Bowes
Victor	David Bolt
Matilda	Diane D'Aquila
Julia	Valerie Warburton

As swift and clean as a rapier through the guts—and just about as lethal. That's *Zastrozzi*, George F. Walker's new play upstairs at the Toronto Free Theatre. And the way the current theatre season is shambling along, *Zastrozzi* blew in last night like a cool breeze on the Sahara.

Subtitled *The Master of Discipline*, the play is a sort of Gothic tragedy with a gift for farce. And with Stephen Markle starring as Zastrozzi, the murderous, mystical master criminal, it absolutely oozes darkness. Markle stands at the beginning in black leather and sword, and simply announces that he is the world's deadliest man, totally without weakness. By the end of the evening, we're ready to believe him.

It's a superb performance, the steely confidence and mad sanity seeming to pour from somewhere deep inside the villain. Zastrozzi is an impossible character, a mythical devil who destroys whole cities, ravages their women, kills mediocre artists "just to prove that even artists must answer to someone." But between Markle and director William Lane, he becomes entirely believable . . . and a little something more, as well.

You hesitate to use a word like joy in describing a play whose inevitable climax is a bloodbath which kills off everyone except the hero-devil. But unless I'm a closet sadist, I don't know how else to explain the exhilaration the play gives.

That kind of praise makes it sound like a masterpiece. But, for all its good points, *Zastrozzi* is hardly that. For one thing, none of its other five characters is anywhere near the hero's class—and one or two are badly flawed, in fact. And though Walker has seeded his play with a number of sharp, insouciant quips, the Free Theatre cast had a heck of a time delivering them.

The play—which Walker based on a capsule description of the Shelley novel, *Zastrozzi*—centres on the master criminal's search for revenge on Verezzi (Geoffrey Bowes), who apparently committed some atrocity on Zastrozzi's mother years ago. The way Walker sees him, Verezzi has become a raving religious lunatic in the meantime, full of messianic delusions. And the way Bowes plays him, as a whining, silly weakling, he's about the last man in the world with whom an audience can identify.

The effect, naturally, is to take away any conflict there might have been. Zastrozzi is a fascinating, extraordinary evil dynamo. His intended victim is a little fop we'd just as soon see dead. Who cares, therefore, about the deadly bond between them?

That weakens the play greatly. But, fortunately, there's a cast of vastly more interesting side characters for Zastrozzi to deal with. There's Matilda, for one, who plays master seductress to his master criminal. Diane D'Aquila makes her a hard, wild temptress who's in love with Zastrozzi but falls just short, fatally short, of being a match for him. David Bolt is also good as the brains behind Verezzi, an ex-priest who rises to challenge the villain's sword.

Then there's the huge George Buza, a near-cartoon as the henchman who "strives hard to be Zastrozzi's shadow," and Julia, also a caricature of the young, blond virgin who is trampled by the unstoppable evil.

Walker has, as I say, given them all a sort of dramatic-comic duality. When the temptress Matilda tells Julia she hates her, for example, because "women like you make me feel like a tart," the virgin replies innocently, "Nonsense. It's the way you dress."

And though there are lots of funny lines like that, director Lane hasn't been able to integrate them properly. No matter who's saying them, the delivery is inevitably deliberate and obvious. The actors are painfully aware of the quips, and handle them like grenades, dropping them as if afraid they will blow up in their faces.

That's more than a tiny quibble, but it's not nearly enough to defeat *Zastrozzi*. Markle takes hold of the play early, draws his sword, and cuts a straight line with a vigor and a power that are damn near irresistible.

Bryan Johnson, *Globe and Mail*, 3 November 1977*

• •

If whips, chants, women in bondage, brutal sex and nudity turn you on, Toronto's the place to be these days. These ingredients are all in evidence in most of the new plays written by Toronto playwrights and currently being presented by the city's network of subsidized alternate theatres.

They're certainly all present in George F. Walker's curiously enigmatic melodrama, *Zastrozzi, The Master of Discipline* now in its third week at the Toronto Free Theatre and headed for a holdover. . . .

Having said that, however, let me hasten to add that *Zastrozzi* was the best piece of theatre I saw in a week of theatregoing in Toronto. It has a literate, well-constructed and theatrically effective script by a playwright who obviously knows what he's doing.

It has been given an outstanding production under the direction of William Lane and it features a handpicked cast of first rate performers each of whom makes an invaluable contribution to its success.

Walker lets Shelley off the hook in a program note by pointing out the play is not an adaptation of the poet's novel (written when he was a student at Eton). He does admit however that a brief description of the novel he once read in a biography of Shelley did serve as the source of his inspiration.

In Walker's play, Zastrozzi is the master criminal of Europe at a time referred to as being 1893. Evil, ruthless and bent on murder, he is devoting his time exclusively to the pursuit of a young man by the name of Verezzi whom he holds responsible for the death of his mother.

Verezzi, a golden-haired simpleton, is being protected by Victor, a friend of Verezzi's father who has promised to look after the boy.

For years Victor has been able to keep Verezzi one or two jumps ahead of the pursuing Zastrozzi and throughout those years Verezzi—who may or may not be as simple-minded as he appears to be—has assumed various personae. He has been a man of God, a painter, a dramatist, a self-styled visionary and of late passes himself off as the Messiah.

But it is not Verezzi we are interested in, it is the magnificent Zastrozzi himself and his continual battle with the wily Victor whose wits are a match for Zastrozzi's muscles any day until the final moment of reckoning when he is put to the sword.

That moment comes near the end of the play when the stage is littered with corpses; the dead bodies of Zastrozzi's would-be mistress, Matilda, a beautiful virgin, Julia, whom Verezzi imagines himself in love with, and Bernardo, Zastrozzi's giant henchman.

Face to face with Verezzi at last, Zastrozzi allows him to escape, by giving him a day in which to hide so that he may continue to seek him out with the eventual intention of killing him. It is the pursuit which gives his life its only meaning . . . the never ending pursuit of good by evil.

This epic melodrama moves along with a kind of classic grandeur without ever taking itself too seriously. It is the sort of play which must stand or fall on the strength of its individual performers and in Lane's production they are a little short of superb.

The undisputed star of the piece is Stephen Markle in the title role. Markle's spectacular physique, clothed and unclothed, resembles the sort of idealized body sketched by the creators of such comic strip characters as Buck Rogers, Captain Marvel and Superman. The difference being of course that Markle is for real.

Add to this his ability to convey sensitivity as well as pitilessness in his interpretation through subtle facial expressions and admirable control of a magnificent vocal instrument and one has a performance which surely must stand out as one of the highlights in a decade of Canadian theatre.

Next in importance is the brilliantly executed performance of David Bolt as Victor, full of unexpected psychological nooks and crannies which keep the audience in a constant state of surprise. The beautiful Diane D'Aquila gives a memorably gutsy performance as Matilda notable also for her vocal as well as physical beauty.

And while these three stand out like beacons in this stunning production, full marks must also be given to Geoffrey Bowes as Verezzi, Valerie Warburton as Julia and George Buza as Bernardo, all individually splendid.

The black environmental setting by Doug Robinson is most impressive as is the dramatic lighting design of Gerry Brown. And special mention must also be made of Wes Wraggett's sound design as well as the choreography of Patrick Crean's fight scenes.

Walker's *Zastrozzi* may easily be classified as a unique theatrical triumph.

Myron Galloway, *Montreal Star*, 28 November 1977*

• •

Zastrozzi: The Master of Discipline is the work largely responsible for Walker's growing international reputation, and it is easy to understand why. This is a revenge play, not quite in the tradition of *The Spanish Tragedy* or *The White Devil*, but nevertheless sharing with them the virtue of a firmly developed plot. For the first time in his career as a playwright Walker has a story to tell.

It is the story of an extraordinary man, a master criminal with an unblemished record, a charismatic person of unrivalled mental power and physical skill. Still, it is a story of failure. Zastrozzi begins by announcing his desire to kill his last remaining enemy—the man who has killed his mother. The intended victim is a gentle and self-deluded Italian amateur, Verezzi, identified in the *dramatis personae* as "an artist, a dreamer." In the final scene Zastrozzi has his prey at his mercy. He stands over the drowsy figure of Verezzi, draws a knife, interrogates and threatens the victim, only to dismiss him at last: "I am giving you a day and I am coming after you. And do you know why I am coming after you? . . . Because it will keep me preoccupied. Now leave. And hide well. I wish to be preoccupied for a long time."

In fact, Zastrozzi and Verezzi are both artists, or, to alter the terms slightly, they are opposing forces within the same artistic temperament. Verezzi is the artist as divine fool; Zastrozzi the artist as demonic artificer. Verezzi can calmly paint a German landscape without leaving the Italian countryside because, as he explains, "art has nothing to do with truth." Zastrozzi can describe himself without boasting as "lucid, calm, organized and energetic." His is a creative power that includes destruction: "I hate amateurs. Death to all of them. Remember that." The two artist figures are complementary opposites in the sense that neither would have a purpose without the antagonism aroused by his opponent.

The sexual dimensions of the play are defined in ways that precisely parallel the artistic outline. The two actresses required by the cast play not two women but two female archetypes: goddess and whore. Julia is a fair-haired temptress with a gypsy background and a high masochism threshold. She explains her infatuation with Zastrozzi in terms that bring the archetypes perhaps too close to the surface: "The whore sleeps with the devil so she can feel like a virgin." Eventually the two female forms confront each other in verbal and physical combat. Innocence accidentally kills experience, only to die a few minutes later at the hands of a would-be rapist.

211

And if this isn't schematic enough, the two remaining characters are again complementary opposites. Both are loyal servants to their artist-masters; both play Horatio to their respective Hamlets. Bernardo is the lifelong associate of Zastrozzi, ready to act even when he fails to understand. By his own admission he is "a more simple man than Zastrozzi," though simplicity in this context can be expressed as brutality. Victor is Verezzi's bodyguard, and a remarkably successful one, for he has managed to help his blundering fool of a master to escape Zastrozzi for three years. Victor is the only character who can defend himself with any success against the swordsmanship of Zastrozzi. During the climactic duel Victor explains the source of his strength: "Sir. The point is that I *am* an ordinary man." Ordinary mortality can challenge but not win in the struggle against evil. Zastrozzi kills both Bernardo and Victor; at the end of the play only the two artist figures are still alive.

In choosing to dramatize the conflict between good and evil, Walker has committed himself to a dangerous path indeed. And he must be aware of the hazards, to judge by the disarmingly frank description, "a melodrama," on the cover of the published play. The jarring absolutes in the world of *Zastrozzi* are a serious limitation, but no doubt they will also be a source of popular success. To move beyond these hateful contraries will require a maturity that Walker may before long achieve.

I hope I have said enough to indicate that George F. Walker deserves respect as a playwright of considerable talent and even greater promise. His imagination is intense and his craftsmanship is rapidly improving. Indeed, the ability to write crisp dialogue is what saves (and sells) *Zastrozzi*. I can't help but admire a writer who allows a "good" character to ask: "In effect, doesn't it make sense that a good man should also be a cunning man?" And I am impressed when the henchman Bernardo says of Zastrozzi: "He is the sanest man I have ever met. He is also the most perverse. The combination makes him very dangerous." These are not the glib paradoxes of television serial drama, nor are they the richly revealing ambiguities of Marlowe's *Doctor Faustus*. But they are something between the extremes, and that means they are worth having.

Ronald Huebert, "Letters in Canada: Drama," *UTQ*, 48
(Summer 1979), 368-70

• •

. . . On the simplest level, *Zastrozzi* is an outrageous melodrama. It seems to be borrowed from an exhilarating variety of likely and unlikely sources. And the first response may be the laughter of recognition, the pleasure of a detail precisely observed. But there's something more deadly urgent here. And it's that something which makes the play linger in the mind's eye, long after the final incidents have passed.

Zastrozzi stakes out its own exact place in the history of Western Europe. Towards the end of the nineteenth century, the modern era is already struggling to be born. Impressionism is beginning to change the course of art. Liberal notions of universal progress and enlightenment are finally beginning to turn the heads of the more popular thinkers, and new social and political ideologies are finally emerging. *Zastrozzi* is already a figure out of his time. He comes on like some mediaeval nightmare, wielding his sword and dagger as though they were still the most lethal weapons on earth. Revenge is already permanently out of fashion in the more progressive salons of Paris and Vienna. But Zastrozzi makes it his sole obsession. And if the old code of honour dies hard, this man will make certain that more than half of all Europe goes with it. At the end of the play, it is the end of the nineteenth century, and the killing is over. But the spirit of this man will be alive in our collective imagination for as far in the future as any human being can foresee.

Zastrozzi's attitude is mercilessly aristocratic. His foe is the new middle class with its shiny new liberal education and its fancy for art. In short, his foe is Victor. And at first glance, the play's moral statement appears to be focused in this remarkable character. Like every middle-class hero, Victor comes from behind. It's a long time before he appears to be a true contender. In a world that still neatly divides itself into masters and servants, Victor is a self-made man, a servant who comes to rule his own master. Zastrozzi is out for revenge on Verezzi, a feeble-minded impressionist painter, and he won't accept substitutes. But it is Victor who has dragged his student Verezzi from pillar to post, always keeping him just one or two steps ahead of his nemesis. And as Verezzi's mind turns to jelly, Victor's resolve to defend him becomes progressively stronger. So, it is Victor who speaks for the audience, giving voice to our inevitable sense of wrong about Zastrozzi's implacable mission. What's more, he is the only character with a moral dilemma. By his own account, he couldn't care less about Verezzi,but an ancient promise made to the younger man's father has committed him to a course of action which he has no desire to take.

Victor isn't cut out for a hero. So, his heroism is totally pragmatic. He makes it up as he goes along. He shares with Zastrozzi an ability to see the world as it really is, in the most immediate and practical way, and it is this common ground which makes them fitting antagonists. There is one crucial difference. Appearances can be deceiving, but one might also think that Victor had a heart. Such a man must be reckoned with.

But the sympathetic character with the moral crisis is not necessarily the moral focus of a play, any more than the character who weeps is the focus of sadness. The real moral centre of the play is Zastrozzi himself—the very one who never has a moral crisis. In fact, Zastrozzi is out to annihilate the whole of culture and morality itself:

> It is my responsibility to spread out like a disease and purge. And by destroying everything make everything safe . . . Alive. Untouched by expectation. Free of history. Free of everything.

His revenge on Verezzi is immaculately reasoned, with the reason of a man who sits at zero latitude on any philosophical scale:

> Life is a series of totally arbitrary and often meaningless events and the only way to make sense of life is to forget that you know this. In other words, occupy yourselves.

This man lives totally outside the moral system. Many of his actions are beyond normal comprehension. His true love for Matilda is all the more unusual because "we haven't made love in over a year." And his infatuation with Julia is based on a kind of psychic possession which bluntly transcends good and evil.

But Zastrozzi is still an appalling creature, and his domination is all the more disturbing because it runs entirely counter to all the accepted notions of Canadian culture. The main thing about Zastrozzi is that he always wins. His pride is never punished, by god or man. And in a culture whose preoccupation with losers is well out in the open, that's bound to make for a subversive statement. What's more, at a time when true Canadians are insisting that we're habitually too hard on ourselves and on our culture, this man comes along to tell us the opposite. Mediocrity must be punished—and Zastrozzi is there, to do it with style. And to add insult to injury, he resurrects that unfashionable virtue called "discipline" to explain his power to make us answerable.

So, in fact, the moral issues are shoved right out of the play. What's in question is our own perception of the action. On the right, there's the master of evil—calm, collected, and very deadly. And over there, on the left, are the good and the innocent—sensitive, sympathetic, and utterly misguided. Every good and decent impulse tells us to go left. But sheer theatricality is bound to win. And more likely than not, we suddenly find we've been rooting for the one on the right.

Of course, it's probably true that villains are always more dramatically persuasive than heroes. But Zastrozzi is such an extraordinary creation that he makes us share his fascination with the sheer mechanics of his triumph. He makes a very gracious host. And in the end, it's this very fascination with the inmost workings of evil which fires the play. Sure, there's a moral statement here. And the play assaults a whole area of popular assumption. But in the end, the important part of Zastrozzi is the part which passes understanding. There is something untouchable about this man who never sleeps, and whose waking nightmares "would petrify the devil." This man who is too "preoccupied" to save the lives of either one of the women he loves. Whose revenge is too long to be wreaked in anything more hasty than his own nightmare slow motion.

Zastrozzi is always a work of genuine imagination. Walker's razor-sharp sense of irony pushes the moral statement over the top, and we're left with a bundle of imagery that burns a hole in the brain. Sometimes, it looks outrageous. You can laugh. But sooner or later, you have to stop. And the peril hasn't passed. Then, perhaps, you find you want to stop and think. It's hard to do better than that, in the theatre.

William Lane, introduction to *Zastrozzi*
(Toronto: Playwrights Co-Op, 1979), pp. 4-6

• •

"An idea is the product of an ordinary mind," says the title character of *Zastrozzi*, George F. Walker's new play at the Public Theatre [New York]. By this line of reasoning, Mr. Walker must want us to conclude that he has an extraordinary mind, because he surely hasn't produced any new ideas in *Zastrozzi*. This trying 90-minute fable is a precious repackaging of other writers' thoughts— starting with those of Molière's *Don Juan* and plodding onward through Camus and 1950s absurdist theatre.

The play is set in the 1890s—in "Europe, probably Italy," according to a program note that captures the cute tone of the script. The antiheroic protagonist (Jan Triska) is the Continent's "master criminal," a self-proclaimed "force of darkness" who has killed more than 200 men. Zastrozzi is also a razor-tongued philosopher, who likes to rail against his civilized, bourgeois society—the poor fools who delude themselves into believing that life is given meaning by such concepts as "God," "art," "morality" and "history." For Zastrozzi, life is pointless—"a series of arbitrary and meaningless events"—and murder is an existential act. "The world is in need of action," he explains, "and the most decisive action is always violent."

So what else is new? It might have helped if Mr. Walker had trotted out his familiar conceits with zest, but *Zastrozzi* refuses to rise above pedantry. The cast wears black costumes and inhabits a rubble-strewn, smoky, apocalyptic void that's been routinely designed by Manuel Lutgenhorst. (The clever lighting is by Jennifer Tipton.) The plot is that of a revenge melodrama, with all the fun, if not the killings, removed for the sake of pretentious stylization. Each character speaks in the same flat, windy voice—presumably the playwright's. "It's 1893 and language, like everything else, has become pleasantly vague," says Zastrozzi. Vague, yes; pleasant, no.

215

Most of the talk reminds us that no one can judge who is good or evil, moral or immoral, sane or insane. For laughs, there are several grotesque sex scenes, in which two hideously caricatured women—a virgin (Frances Conroy) and a seductress (Judith Roberts)—are the butts of the jokes. ''He's going to rape me and murder me, not necessarily in that order,'' says one of the heroines in a typical punch line. Mr. Walker also tries to amuse us with that increasingly tired gimmick of having his characters step out of the play to call attention to the fact that we are, after all, watching a play. In the case of *Zastrozzi*, we're left unconvinced even so.

Andrei Serban, the director, has asked the cast to perform at a shrill, frenetic pitch that never adds up to comic style; Mr. Triska and Miss Conroy, at least, deserve better. By the end, the actors must struggle not only with their lines, but also with a carpet of dirt that's been poured across the stage. As they kick clouds of dust into the audience, *Zastrozzi* ceases to settle for assaulting one's sensibilities and goes to work on the sinuses as well.

Frank Rich, NYT, 18 January 1982

• •

JOHN GRAY WITH ERIC PETERSON

Billy Bishop Goes to War

First produced at the Vancouver East Cultural Centre
(in association with Tamahnous Theatre),
3 November 1978

Directed by John Gray
Set and Lighting Design by Paul Williams

Cast

Billy Bishop   Eric Peterson
Musician/Narrator   John Gray

Billy Bishop Goes to War is made-in-Vancouver entertainment that's going to be a national knockout.

It's a virtuoso piece of theatrical acrobatics, done in classic seat-of-the-pants style.

Actor Eric Peterson is the sole and brilliant star—breathing life and action not only into the character of First World War flying ace Bishop himself, but 17 other characters as well, ranging from officers and generals to nightclub singer Elene, Bishop's eccentric benefactor Lady St. Helier, and King George V.

As anyone who saw him in the original *Herringbone* (or in Theatre Passe Muraille's *Farm Show*) will know, Peterson's talents for convincing characterization are phenomenal. His laconic conversational delivery, his command of accents and his uncanny insight into the human psyche—come together to create a stunning reality.

Billy Bishop never wanted to go to war, as this mischievously funny musical proves. But go to war he did—as a member of the Mississauga Horse, making the ocean crossing in the "good ship Caledonia, Latrine of the Atlantic."

Eventually, he escaped the cavalry and made his way into the Royal Flying Corps—and, as history records, became Canada's most successful aerial combatist, with 72 "kills" to his official credit.

Billy Bishop Goes to War gets at the man behind the myth—an engaging, devil-may-care scoundrel from Owen Sound who found his vocation shooting enemy airmen from the sky.

Composer-writer-director John Gray has taken a kind of fictionalized-documentary approach to his subject. He has fashioned a script and musical score (14 songs in all) that provides a remarkably vivid portrait of the man and his time.

The production is impregnated with an odd and lasting charm—a blend of honesty and humanity. And there is a strong sense of the pathos of lost innocence.

Gray and Peterson touch some delicate depths in their treatment of the war—no simple pacifism, this, but an intriguing look at the conflicting emotions and motivations in the mind of every fighting man (in the process they also skewer forever the concept of "colonialism" as a second-class affair—from both sides of the fences).

Paul Williams's daring set design attempts to capture the effect of being aloft in open sky, chiefly by using suspended cotton clouds, and a roller-screen backdrop. It doesn't quite come off—the visuals are the show's only weak spot—but Peterson and his material are so strong it hardly matters. . . .

Max Wyman, *Vancouver Express*, 6 November 1978*

• •

There is a wing of Canadian theatre—especially Canadian little theatre—that is hungry for heroes. In the same tradition as Pierre Berton's lonely rehabilitation of scruffy Canadian rascals, it exhumes barely remembered characters, puffs life into them and sets them striding across the stage. At worst, these efforts have been dreary polemics, a waste of an evening and a disservice to their subjects. At best, in such productions as James Reaney's sprawling Donnelly trilogy or Rick Salutin's muscular *Les Canadiens*, they are splendid. The most recent entry in the tradition of luminous myth-mongering is the Vancouver East Cultural Centre's production of *Billy Bishop Goes to War*, a musical two-hander written, scored and directed by John Gray and starring Eric Peterson as the Canadian World War I flying ace who overcame colonial guilelessness and a tendency toward accidents to shoot down 72 German planes, gain the Victoria Cross and stay alive.

Peterson, a small, boney Saskatchewan native with a trim moustache and grown-out brush cut, brings a seamless blend of insouciance and street smarts to the character of Bishop. A judge's son from Owen Sound, Ontario, Bishop flunked out of Royal Military College and ended up in the cavalry at the beginning of the war. He spent months mired in French mud before seeing a biplane and its dry, spotless pilot land on the battlefield "like a dragonfly on a rock" and deciding the Royal Flying Corps was for him. Peterson's deft and lively portrait has the colonial innocent mired anew in the cheerful Colonel Blimp absurdities of a crumbling Europe. Bishop tells of his meeting with the doomed half-mad British ace Albert Ball (Peterson plays Bishop, Ball and 15 other characters, wearing a British accent like a mackintosh), of travelling the rough North Atlantic on "the good ship Caledonia, soon called the good ship Vomit." He tells of building his kill total with vicious inevitability, clearly, surely, coming to enjoy it. In a climactic scene that could be called the Blooding of Billy Bishop, Peterson buzzes Gray's piano (virtually the only prop on stage) with a plywood biplane, miming a cathartic, utterly unnecessary solo attack on a German aerodrome. It is the high and low point of his flying career.

Peterson's Bishop is a triumph—unfaltering and reminiscent of a thousand savvy underachievers one has known. War for him is not a moral question: it is a bitter fluke that tests him until the winning makes him love it. *Billy Bishop* falters only in the last half, when Gray allows a malingering anti-war message to creep in. He would have done better to leave Billy alone and blinking into the stage lights. We know about war. It's hell. Increasingly, what we don't know about is warriors.

The idea for *Billy Bishop Goes to War* came after Gray and Peterson, both bored one week during the run of a play in Ottawa, read Bishop's autobiography, *Winged Warfare*, written at the tender age of 26. Using seed cash from Toronto's Theatre Passe Muraille, they travelled to the war archives above Ogilvy's Furniture Store in Ottawa and rooted through cabinets for Bishop's correspondence and papers. "Bishop was a hawk, a survivor, a hero and a killer. His is a side of Canadians that doesn't get shown very often," says Gray, who has written only one other play, *18 Wheels*, a trucking musical performed last year and which opened last week at the Tarragon Theatre in Toronto. "I think people are getting tired of the old loser image." After several workshop run-throughs, Gray had three full hours of play ready last May, which Chris Wootten, the director of the Vancouver East Cultural Centre, agreed to produce—sight unseen—in a scaled-down version. . . .

Thomas Hopkins, *Maclean's*, 91 (4 December 1978), 70-71

• •

Though a perky, grinning, apparently reckless young fellow named Billy Bishop rather quickly became Canada's most celebrated aviator of World War I—and indeed, one of the world's most celebrated, with at least 72 enemy planes tumbling away from him to destruction—he would seem to have arrived at this destiny in a most peculiar fashion.

As the new two-man, one-plane evening at the Morosco informs us during its cheeky, amusing and genuinely persuasive beginnings, the unlikely hero of *Billy Bishop Goes to War* got where he did by failing to cheat his way through the Royal Military College ("Well," he acknowledges boyishly, "I handed in the crib notes with the exam papers"), by never, never, never becoming a particularly good flyer (the Morosco's program remarks a bit primly that "he was often very careless about His Majesty's aircraft"), and by just happening to be mired deeply in mud on one messy, but historic, day.

The mud is important, as things go during the partly spoken, partly sung saga that John Gray has written and composed for Canadian star Eric Peterson (Mr. Gray also accompanies Mr. Peterson on the piano, boomingly). Mr. Peterson, alias Bishop in this instance, has got himself into the cavalry of 1915 and is, at the moment, having a terrible time with a steed that keeps sinking into bogs. To help free his mount, the rider—who is doing precious little riding—must descend into one such bog with him. It is from there that he sees his first single-motor plane.

It is rising, miraculously, over the crest of a hill. There is nothing to impede it, not a thing to hold it down. No sand, no mud, no filthy, earthly resistance. Staring upward, Mr. Peterson sees what amounts to a revelation. He is looking at something "warm and dry—and free!"

You believe on the instant in his revelation and its logical consequences. As Mr. Gray has written the passage (simply) and as Mr. Peterson acts it out (sans horse, sans mire, but with the moral certitude of Joan of Arc), it becomes one of the most tactile arguments for the existence of aircraft I've ever felt tugging me skyward. If we must be lured into believing in Mr. Peterson's sudden determination to turn pilot (or even observer, the chap in the second seat who takes pictures and things like that), this is the way to do it. Sold.

The evening, which originated north of the border and has been brought to Broadway by Mike Nichols and Lewis Allen, has some less exalted moments to record once our aviator is learning, however haphazardly, to be an ace. On his first solo flight, for instance, an ace really oughtn't to make three false stabs at a landing and then flop down into a horrendous pancake, practically at his superior officer's feet. Wrong splash. Wrong spot.

What is right about this funny and semisuspenseful sequence is how actor and director have managed it. It's done with a toy airplane, dipping and banking and approaching solid earth at unthinkable angles. Mr. Peterson manipulates it, providing the narrative as well as the sound of the aircraft's motor, Mr. Gray adds risk and comic overtones on the keyboard, the whole wild flight is brought off with a minimum of mechanical equipment.

Contrast this with a second-act passage in which the rear doors of the stage, pleated to resemble a hangar's, are thrown open to show us what must be a full-scale reproduction of a 1917 fighter, while before it a portion of the floor rises to carry Mr. Peterson upward, cloud-smoke swirling at his heels. Guess which passage is the more effective of the two?

Back to what our ace is gradually learning. He's gone off to battle happily enough, impersonating 15 or 16 other people—in brightly varied vignettes—along the way. In fact, he's first joined his composer-companion in one of the songs they so briskly interpolate: "We were out to find the Hun/It looked like a lot of fun/Somehow it didn't seem like war at all, at all, at all." And he still finds it fun to watch a foe's plane explode in midair, spiral downward. But he knows now that explosions are mere lucky shots; you can't hit a gas tank that often. The only way to win every time is to "go for the man." There's something blood-curdlingly complacent in his "I always go for the man."

In fact, it's along about this point that we begin to wonder about our hero, to grow neutral about him. It's clear that he is not an unfeeling man: watching two opponents whose chutes have never opened hit the ground in a free fall, he is sickened, briefly. Yet when he resists being relieved of fighting, he gives his reason plainly: "I like it." At evening's end, he is recruiting, in very conventional rhetoric, for World War II.

Does he have any rationale for himself, for heroism, for killing, for war itself—something to tie his varied responses together? About as close as we get is in a snatch of song: "Remember, war is not a place for deep emotions/And maybe you'll come out alive." In short, the ace who lives longest is the man who's taught himself not to feel. Kill cool, as it were. Not that the evening ever says that. But by the time we have attended to the first experiments with bombers that tend to behave like "crippled ducks" and the one-man raids on enemy airdromes that lead our hero into philosophizing, we discover we've grown a bit cool—a bit detached—about Billy Bishop himself.

He's not firmly defined, though he does a dozen interesting things before he comes home from war. Some of the interesting things have been done just too often before: a one-man raid that catches the enemy squadron on the ground, for instance. Of course, there's always the honest sense of flight to help us past the repetition. When Billy Bishop realizes that, so long as he is in the ground forces, he is "a casualty in training, and the only way out is up," you understand him and you're with him. It would be a saving grace to understand the Billy Bishop who came down as well.

Walter Kerr, *NYT*, 30 May 1980

• •

. . . My colleagues have complained, accurately enough, that the Canadian two-man show, *Billy Bishop Goes to War*, contains no ringing condemnation of war and does not show Billy Bishop degenerating into a militaristic, fascist pig, but rather mellowing into a Jimmy Stewart folk hero: ergo, it must be a weak and superficial play, unwilling to grasp the prickly realities of our time. Those whose idea of entertainment is to hear someone explaining why eating people is wrong may well agree with them; but what *Billy Bishop* does express is a colonial bemusement at being drawn, by scarcely visible ancestral ties, into wars which are none of Canada's making and perhaps none of its concern.

Hence, the "Empire Soirée," a danse macabre in honour of squabbling, snobbish European nations, comes as a startling climax to a play which makes a virtue of amiability. We are not expecting anything quite so powerful. Billy Bishop is, of course, the Canadian ace fighter pilot of the First World War, and his musical biography, written by John Gray, who shares the stage with Eric Peterson, is likely to be as charged with patriotism as one of Douglas Bader would be for us. Peterson, with a breathtaking command of accents, physical mannerisms, and sound effects through a mike, plays Bishop, other characters in his life (including an imposing aunt, a butler, the King and the War Office) and several squadrons of fighters, with machine guns and various bombs. It is a *tour de force*, but what impressed me more was the quality of the writing, a polished use of that distinctive Canadian style—reportage charged with a delicate, quiet irony in the Leacock vein; so that when, as it were, all the casualness is thrown away, and we are left with the bare bones (and how bare they are, how sepulchred, on a dim stage, with a distant, tinkling piano) of an innocent hell-raiser accepting the invitation to dance with the phantoms of the imperial opera, the shock is multiplied by the gentleness of our approach to it. Billy Bishop cops out of nothing: he really does go to war.

John Elsom, *The Listener*, 18 June 1981

• •

After countless missions in foreign countries, John Gray's *Billy Bishop Goes to War* finally landed at the Royal Alexandra Theatre Tuesday night—a place which is not unlike a foreign country in itself.

Never having seen the original show, I will not bore you with predictable and meaningless comparisons. As an investigation of the life of a First World War pilot, a poor colonial from Owen Sound whose glorious exploits in the sky earned him more medals than he could play with, the show is now as legendary as Billy Bishop himself. And Peterson, who has played the role for more than three years, deserves his medals for his brilliant and quicksilver characterizations—18 of them to be precise, including the transformation of Bishop himself from accident-prone loser to the confident and cheeky hero who shot down more than 72 enemy aircraft.

"War," as one of Gray's songs has it, "is not a place for deep emotions." It is only on that score that Gray's script can be faulted. According to Gray's version of Billy Bishop, to survive one must be as "calm as the ocean," and get into the game of it, hunting Huns like pheasants, getting a thirst for the kill and an appetite for the practical details of the maiming.

While the script and songs don't delve into the full consequences of shutting off pieces of oneself to fight inane wars for inane empires, much can be inferred from it. Peterson, who collaborated with Gray on the script, is now so at east with his character that a fundamental sadness and sense of futility is evoked in spite of Bishop's ingenuousness, an ingenuousness fed by enforced shallowness.

It is, of course, the context of the war which provides the source of Peterson's tour de force. In the course of the evening we see Bishop confronting not only his fears, his stated enemies, but all of the armaments of the British class system, who were only too glad to use the colonials as expendable cannon fodder. Peterson's humorous characterizations are so skilful they keep you chuckling with recognition.

Sir Hugh Cecil, for instance, who first dissuades Bishop from pursuing a career in the Royal Flying Corps (Bishop was originally a cavalry officer; he quickly realized that being mired in mud was not a particularly attractive way to die) is your typical ineffectual upper-class stiff whose idiocy is couched in bonhommie. His prim, poetic Lady St. Helier, who tutors our poor colonial in the ways of the ossified world, is a delightful companion as Bishop rises to fame and the tedious dinner parties which accompany it.

The whole tone of the show is so quiet, so understated, that its effects never peak; nothing builds but our understanding. That is risky since Peterson must carry the weight of imperceptibly changing before our eyes. The quiet approach is effective—it brings you in—and yet there is not enough energy sometimes to carry you through. (His miming of his first solo flight with a toy airplane is, incidentally, pure theatrical magic.) This understated quality is further emphasized by the simplicity of the set and the lighting. Although this simplicity is effective, the starkness becomes unnerving; the pretty effects seldom cross over into the dazzling.

This Billy Bishop flies all right—it even soars at times—and it's about time that it takes off, eh, here at the old colonial dowager.

Carole Corbeil, *Globe and Mail*, 14 January 1982

• •

Wallace   What contributions did Eric Peterson make to *Billy Bishop Goes to War?*

Gray   He has an enthusiasm for history and historical detail that I don't. His interest in the particularities of the machines and the men, the times and the places added a lot to the play.

Wallace   How closely does the script follow Bishop's memoir, *Winged Warfare?*

Gray   Very closely. *Winged Warfare* is the basis for the show in a sense. It covers the same period in his life.

Wallace   Although Bishop is a winner, he's also a killer. It seems to me that you're concerned to set up that contradiction in the show, that behind the hero there's a real scoundrel. What attitude do you want the audience to have to that contradiction?

Gray   I call it a paradox. Bishop was doing the finest thing that a man could do at that time: he was fighting for his country, and everyone who meant anything to anybody was encouraging him to do so. Now you can't except a nineteen-year-old not to do that, right? So you can't knock it. You also can't knock him if he gets to like it. You see, what I did with the show was approach it as being not about Bishop but about someone that I know in Truro, a type of person that is useless in peacetime but whose destructive urge is really useful in war if channelled right.

Wallace   So in that sense the play is very contemporary, particularly to Vietnam veterans.

Gray   Oh absolutely. It's also contemporary in that it approaches war in a new way. It doesn't suggest that war is either good or bad. It's not involved in that question. *Billy Bishop*'s main value lies in its pointing out that war is exactly like life, only faster. If you survive, you'll get to see your friends die. . . .

224

Wallace Why do you think *Billy Bishop* struck such a chord in the Canadian psyche?

Gray Because there has been a conspiracy of silence since the Second World War. Men, tremendously touched by the war, came back to people who didn't want to talk about it. Men, Second World War people, come to the play and say, yeah, that's exactly what I went through. You feel this wave of recognition from them.

Wallace Do you think there is something particular about the play, say its ironic tone, that doesn't play well in the United States?

Gray No. *Billy Bishop* was tremendously successful in Seattle. And it was a big hit at the Mark Taper Forum in Los Angeles.

Wallace But it wasn't in New York.

Gray No, but that was a different matter. Going to plays in New York is a form of souvenir-hunting. It's very much like going to a rock concert. If you go to see the Eagles play, you won't hear their music as well as you would on a record. But you can say you saw the Eagles. We opened *Billy Bishop* across the street from *Barnum*, and *A Day in Hollywood, A Night in the Ukraine*, and we were next door to a magic show with a disappearing elephant. Now if you're gonna go souvenir-hunting, are you going to want to tell the neighbours that you saw a couple of unknown Canadians perform a show about a World War One hero? I doubt it very much.

Wallace So you think a subjective analysis of the differences between American and Canadian audiences is irrelevant?

Gray Absolutely. Look, Americans aren't particularly interested in anyone but themselves. They're a big, imperial country. The primary characteristic of imperial countries is that they think the world revolves around them. They don't like countries next door to them behaving like foreign countries. So here they're watching people from another country perform a play about someone who shot down more people than Rickenbacker in a war they didn't win. They don't want to see it.

It's so fast in New York. We opened in New York at night, we got rave reviews the next day. The producers listened to see how many phone calls were coming in and by noon they were talking about closing the show. I mean, that's how fast it happens. We're talking about a situation where the investors are best served by a big loss or a big win. The only way they don't make money is in a break-even situation. If a show's not gonna win big, they want to make sure that it loses big. You're dealing with something very, very peculiar there.

Wallace In an interview with Judy Steed [*Toronto Life* (May 1981)] you discussed your experience in New York as a process of demystification.

Gray Oh yes. I understand the particularities of how the business works in both New York and London in a way that I never did before. Before, no matter how much somebody told me it worked that way, there would always have been a part of myself that believed it wasn't true. It is.

Wallace In *Billy Bishop Goes to War*, Billy Bishop recites a Robert Service-style poem about Albert Ball, in which he says, "the British like their heroes/Cold and dead." You're suggesting a British attitude towards heroism. Is there a Canadian one?

Gray One of the themes of that play is that a decadent culture worships death. At that time, if somebody went up north and disappeared, then came back alive six months later, a Canadian would consider him a hero. A Brit would prefer that he had died—that would make him a hero. Scott, for example, wasn't the first or the best of the Antarctic explorers but he was the one that died, therefore he was the hero. For Canada, at that time, survival was an issue. It still is, because of the cold. In Britain, survival isn't a question so death has a value. Dying for something is a value. In Canada, living for something is a value. It's an essential difference between a colonial and imperial country.

Wallace And yet you maintain this difference doesn't translate into audience reaction?

Gray Well, okay, the imperialists aren't going to like a play like *Billy Bishop*. The Brits didn't, in the sense that they didn't recognize, for example, the whole question of motivation. We received a lot of criticism in England because I didn't explain why Billy Bishop had killed so many people as though it should have been because his mother didn't like him or something. They couldn't accept the notion that because he was a colonial he tried harder. They couldn't accept that the political position of a colonial really defines what he does and therefore serves as motivation. Imperialists don't like that.

Wallace You're talking about imperialism here as the British?

Gray British and American. . . .

Robert Wallace, interview with John Gray, *The Work*, pp. 50-53

• •

DAVID FENNARIO

Balconville

First produced at the Centaur Theatre,
Montreal, 2 January 1979

Directed by Guy Sprung
Set and Costume Design by Barbra Matis
Lighting Design by Steven Hawkins
Sound Design by Peter Smith

Cast

Claude Paquette	Marc Gélinas
Cécile Paquette	Cécile St-Denis
Diane Paquette	Manon Bourgeois
Muriel Williams	Terry Tweed
Tom Williams	Robert Parson
Johnny Regan	Peter MacNeill
Irene Regan	Lynne Deragon
Thibault	Jean Archambault
Gaetan Bolduc	Gilles Tordjman

David Fennario is a closet humanist.

The times aren't safe for humanists, and many have to parade around disguised as Socialists. But for all Fennario's rose-tinted propagandizing—his politely avowed leftist philosophy—his fourth play, *Balconville*, which opened at the Centaur Thursday night, has more heart than party line, more blessed doubt than dogma, and more humanism than a political platform could ever contain.

It's a loveable, funny play. A delicious exercise in observation and understanding, its only easy answer is that we had better start recognizing each other as human beings, or, to put it even more in the spirit of the play itself, as brothers . . . and sisters.

In *Balconville* unions come under fire, but not unity. Union is a battle cry, unity a word of peace. Fennario's politics in this play might be just as easily defined as non-violent anarchy as socialism.

No politician comes out smelling like a rose in this work. Yes, the rich exploit the poor, but the escape route is sketched more as a matter of self re-evaluation and personal change than as something that can be achieved through political channels.

Is it socialism to say we must look into our own heart and mind to find the answers to our problems?

Fennario's claim that there are three sets of conflicts in *Balconville* is a more accurate description of the play than his statement than it is an expression of political philosophy. The exchanges spoken by his eight Pointe St. Charles characters are often pure confrontation: young against old, male against female, French against English.

Fennario has an incredibly fine ear for the way people talk and there aren't more than two lines that don't ring perfectly true. I doubt that there is anyone writing in North America today with as fine a sense of verbal realism. Whatever they do, Fennario's characters talk like real people, people with slightly impoverished vocabularies and a penchant for expletives, but unquestionably genuine, complete characters.

Without wishing to slight Fennario's talent, the raw material lends itself to theatre the way the Third World has always been a photographer's gold mine. No sarcasm intended, the underdog is the poet's meat and potatoes.

People living virtually in each other's pocket, who collide on back balconies because their homes are cramped cubicles and they can't afford vacations, are truly more colorful, more explosive, more interesting in the dramatic sense than people separated by carpeted hallways, dens, garages, lawns and tree-lined driveways. The very density and nakedness of a slum is theatrical.

For all its literal destitution and ugliness, Barbra Matis' brick backyard has a poetry to it, a brutal and painful accuracy that always reinforces our sympathy for the plight of its inhabitants. No one in his right mind would want to live there, but it sure is an exciting place to visit.

One couldn't ask for more entertainment than to spend a few hours with the Paquettes, the Regans, the Williamses and a kind of latter-day Shakespearean fool, Thibault, even if their collective story is little more than an account of subtle spiritual awakening. . . .

The tensions smolder steadily hotter until a fire breaks out down the street. Somehow, in the circus act of emptying each other's apartments to save what few worldly goods they can, these people come to realize they are a family. And it's all wonderfully funny and deeply moving.

The cast is brilliant, every performance a bulls-eye. Marc Gélinas as Claude makes us want to reach out to cradle him like a baby when, on the brink of tears, he tells his wife he has lost his job. Peter MacNeill, sounding very much like Fennario's alter-ego as Johnny, makes us flush with hope when he reassures his wife that he doesn't melt in the rain, that he is a survivor.

Lynne Deragon as Irene is perfectly balanced as a woman on the brink of a new identity. Her awareness grows as gently and naturally as the plants on the balcony, and her warmth and strength are in sublime harmony.

Terry Tweed is the tense, tight, frustrated and frightened Muriel, and Cécile St-Denis plays Cécile, Muriel's serene counter-balance whose every gesture is a caress, whose quiet voice is a lullaby. Robert Parson is the bashful Tom and Manon Bourgeois the bewildered Diane. Jean Archambault is the slow but deadly wit on the bicycle. We're torn between a laugh and a shiver as he thumbs the skin magazines.

Guy Sprung directed with a fine eye for character and a gift for restraint, although he lets the first few minutes of the play seem like a string of 45-second vignettes.

It's a wonderful evening of theatre, not to be missed.

Maureen Peterson, Montreal Gazette, 6 January 1979*

• •

The title of David Fennario's *Balconville* comes from the punchline of a grim joke popular in the slums of Montreal. "Where are you going for the summer holidays?" is the question. And the answer, from those who cannot afford trips to the Laurentians or resorts with elegant French names, is "Balconville." By which is meant those rickety verandahs, with their peeling paint, on tenement buildings in the ghettos. This is the setting for Fennario's latest play, produced at Montreal's English-language theatre, the Centaur, and now in the process of touring Canada.

Even while we're waiting for the play to begin, we're introduced to the decor of Balconville, highlighted by crates of empty beer bottles and clotheslines filled with tattered underwear. Like earlier Fennario works, this is an autobiographical chronicle of his life in the anglo working-class ghetto of Pointe St. Charles, southwest of downtown Montreal. Fennario's plays seem to be gradually moving from the public to the private: *On the Job* took place in a factory, and *Nothing to Lose* was set in a tavern. With *Balconville* he moves as close to home as everybody's front porch. And that's not the play's only distinction.

Balconville is billed as Canada's first bilingual play. Half the characters are francophones, and though they switch to English when they're talking to the anglophone characters, they speak French to each other. Roughly a third of the text in the Montreal production was spoken in French, though it is always clear to those in the audience who don't speak French approximately what is happening. Since it was assumed that audiences outside of Montreal might be less attuned to hearing French dialogue, some of the lines were translated for the tour. . . .

Balconville is the most commercial play Fennario has written, and I don't mean that as a put-down. He has an ear for sharp dialogue, and even if it were no more than light entertainment, *Balconville* would compare favourably with such successful examples of the most-lovable-eccentrics-from-my-colorful-neighbourhood genre as the Broadway hit *Gemini*. But Fennario aims higher than that, and Balconville catches a peculiar aspect of Montreal's underside; as a sociocultural record, it ranks alongside Michel Tremblay's *Les Belles Soeurs*.

Fennario introduces us to three households peering at each other through the cracks in the walls, as it were. The only French family in the complex has trouble getting along with its anglo neighbours, who feel squeezed by the rise of French nationalism and make bitter jokes about separatism and the language laws, such as "The hydro bill is all in French now . . . Tell them we'll pay in English." Cécile, the francophone matron, doesn't have much to do, except wander around in her housecoat feeding the birds (known to the neighbours as her air force). Her husband, Claude, feels superior to his anglo neighbours because he's the only male in the building with a good steady job, but he's crushed by the news that (as his wife puts it) "the company is moving to Taiwan, and they don't want to take Claude with them." Meanwhile, downstairs, Muriel complains about the husband who deserted her and nags her son Tom to get a job, but Tom doesn't want to work for the minimum wage and get up at five a.m.

The cock of the walk is Johnny (perhaps a stand-in for Fennario), an engaging ex-teen rebel who lounges around slurping up beer while making devastatingly witty remarks about the faults of a system that makes him wait ten weeks for his unemployment insurance cheques. As played with show-stopping flair by Peter MacNeill, Johnny is by far the most attractive character on the stage. His wife, Irene, supports him by working as a waitress, but when she gets a dose of women's lib and threatens to leave, she merely demonstrates how she's becoming just like the other women in the neighbourhood. "Don't count on me to be here to wipe up your puke," she tells Johnny. In Fennario's world, women aren't any more effective at solving the problems of poverty than the men; they just nag and complain more. And here, unconsciously, in his portrait of women, Fennario reveals the limitations of his working-class male point of view. His women are all either mousy nonentities or whining shrews who know how to spoil a guy's good times.

Poverty and misery do not sound like promising subjects for a high-spirited entertainment, but Fennario demonstrates that there are compensations in shared deprivation. He has a kind of loyalty to these people, as if he wanted us to feel we could have a better time in their company than at any fancy party in Westmount. The camaraderie of the dispossessed builds to a kind of mock aria in a noisy outdoor party toward the end of the first act, and the exuberance of the singing, dancing, and mirth-making among people with little cause for mirth invites comparison with the celebrations in Brendan Behan's *The Hostage*. But for Fennario, the lively slang dialogue and the raunchy comic routines are only so much foreplay for the political wham-bang of his finale.

There's a grim comedy in the unifying hopelessness of these desperate lives. Language and culture may be great dividers, but in this world disaster is a great leveller. Fennario plays it for laughs when Johnny puts up a maple leaf flag and Claude counters by raising Quebec's *fleur-de-lys* flag, but the antagonism vanishes when, in the ultimate gesture of conciliation, Johnny tells Claude *in French* that he's sorry he lost his job. The black joke is that whereas in the old Quebec working WASPs had an advantage over working French Canadians, in the new Quebec they're all equal: nobody has a chance. Fennario's cynicism about political solutions is indicated by his use of a candidate running for elected office who appears in the play mainly as a voice over a PA system. That voice, calling for law and order, is last heard just as Balconville itself is going up in flames and Fennario's people are scurrying out like frightened rats, carrying their most precious possessions—cases of beer, old TV sets, pieces of chrome furniture. They leave us with an unanswered question: "What's to become of us? What are we going to do?"

Emotionally and theatrically, Fennario's finale works because it has the ring of personal conviction. But Fennario is far less impressive as a political thinker than he is as a dramatist. For him, the answer is always a Marxist uprising of the exploited against their oppressors. To Fennario the villains are landlords, bureaucrats, obscenely prosperous Westmount doctors, and double-talking politicians. But there is nothing in *Balconville* to suggest that these desperadoes of the urban slums are capable of doing anything to improve their lives. For all their talk of breaking out, they cling to their role as victims. Is it possible that Fennario, who did break out, feels guilty for doing so? If he hadn't taken a creative writing course, published a journal, and been invited to write for the Centaur, maybe Fennario (whose real family name was Wiper, until he took a new one inspired by a Bob Dylan song) would have wound up like Johnny. And what is *he* going to do now?

Martin Knelman, *Saturday Night*, 94 (November 1979), 101-104

• •

The setting for *Balconville* is the upper and lower balconies of a tenement house, not far, one assumes, from the tavern which enclosed *Nothing to Lose* or the dress factory which served as the habitat for *On the Job*. The people who converse, complain, drink and quarrel on this double balcony are ordinary in the attractive sense of the word. Claude Paquette—fat, forty-ish, and French—has lost his ideals, his faith in the future, and the respect of his teenage daughter. Cécile, his wife, emerges from every domestic crisis with the firm conviction that the best thing she can do is to water her plants. Muriel Williams, still hoping vaguely that her husband will return to her section of the balcony, spends most of her energies trying to supervise the life of her teenage son. Johnny and Irene Regan, in their mid-thirties, are mournfully aware that life is no longer what it used to be. In his youth Johnny played lead guitar for ''J.R. and the Falling Stars''; now he is resentfully dependent on what Irene can earn as a waitress and what he can get from the UIC. Irene explains her predicament to Muriel with a shrug: ''Oh, well, ya know how it is? Ya marry a prince and he turns into a frog.'' This pattern of disappointment is the one experience which makes Fennario's collection of characters more than an assortment: which defines them, in fact, as a community.

Balconville is by far the best of Fennario's plays to date. His ability to create atmosphere by using simple touches of setting or dialogue is rapidly improving. In support of this claim one could cite the broken step on the stairway which connects the two balconies, or Thibault's position on bilingualism: ''Oui, and me too. I don't speak the English since last week. Maybe a few times, but that's all.''

Still, *Balconville* is a static play because the characters do nothing beyond creating the atmosphere. The only events are imposed by external forces. Paquette, after grumbling for years about his mechanical job, is crestfallen when he loses it because the company is moving its plant to Taiwan. Everyone shares Paquette's dejection, except his daughter Diane. ''Je vais m'en trouver une job, moi,'' she announces. ''C'est facile. Ils ont toujours besoin de waitress cute.'' The final event is a fire which rages out of control, offstage, while the *Balconville* community unites in order to salvage the goods and chattels which have arranged themselves in the few private corners of their disappointed lives. Even the title of the play signifies the embittered passivity of its characters. Ask any of them where they are going this summer and the reply will be, ''Moi? Balconville.'' In any language this is the fatalism of people who no longer believe that their world will change.

Ronald Huebert, ''Letters in Canada: Drama,''
UTQ, 50 (1980-81), 60-61

• •

As the tourist sees it, Montreal separatism is amusingly inscribed in the bilingual road signs and the affluent English and French communities each winding up their own side of the mountain. This is not the case in the working-class Pointe St. Charles area—the setting of David Fennario's play—where poverty drives the old enemies into sharing the same narrow territory and hanging the maple leaf and the fleur-de-lys on adjoining windows.

Guy Sprung's Centaur Theatre production arrives at the [Old] Vic, via Bath and Belfast, with the rare distinction of having overcome Québecois bigotries in its casting and Canadian audiences. (One of the company, I note, is Marc Gélinas, son of the intransigent founder of the Comédie Canadienne.) For all its Franco-English hostilities, separatism is not the play's theme. So far as fire hazards, extortionate landlords, and the 40 per cent unemployment rate are concerned, all the tenement dwellers are in the same boat. There will be time enough to restorm the Plains of Quebec when they have all moved into Westmount mansions.

The main action centres on three families, two English and one French, whose apartments overlook the corner of a grimy yard. Inter-connecting balconies are occupied by the Paquette family with its proudly employed male bread-winner, and the joblessly demoralized Johnny who goes drinking every night on his wife's earnings as a waitress. Down below lives Muriel, a permanently enraged grass widow whose main target is her unemployed teenage son. To the nationalist tensions are added those of physical congestion; and the general atmosphere is one of an uneasy truce, repeatedly exploding into open aggression, or surly retreat behind closed frontiers.

There are many touches that must surely have hit the Montreal public with a sense of recognition: such as the affronted Paquette père's refusals to pollute his lips with the English language; and the sight of the two men each sitting back to back watching the same ball game on two separate television sets. The periodic crises all derive truthfully from the environment; a drunk scene that wrecks a party, the destruction of poor Mme Paquette's cherished pot plants, and all the shouting and door slamming, spring from the no-hope frustrations of society, with no judgments against individual characters.

Women convincingly emerge as stronger than the men, politically as well as domestically. Johnny merely throws an egg at a visiting election candidate; but in the fire that ends the play with the collapse of the next building, it is the women who have the last line: "We're next!"

I cannot pretend that *Balconville* is much fun at the Vic. If you compare it, say, to O'Casey, you see what is missing. There is no theatrical projection of national character; and however authentic the performances of Susan Wright, Jean Archambault, and M. Gelinas, they appear as if through the wrong end of a telescope: a slice of life going on in the far distance. However clear the statement of the whole play, its moment-to-moment plotting is cumbersome, with events stitched together episodically so as to give each group a fair deal. And the production is cruelly under-lit. What it shows is another world; well worth seeing but hard on the eyes.

Irving Wardle, The Times, 3 April 1981

• •

. . . from beginning to end [*Balconville*] is loaded with conflict and dilemma. The English, landlords, punks, separatists, immigrants and Jews are all singled out at one time or another as being the cause of the characters' destitution. But the playwright rules out racial conflict as the basis of the problem in favour of class conflict. As one English character says to his French neighbour, "We're all equal. Nobody's got a chance." According to Fennario, it's only pride and stubbornness which keep the French and English tenants from joining forces against rich landlords. Fennario's a Marxist and this isn't the first play he's laced with his own special brand of facile politics. But it's the first play that such simplification has, for the most part, improved rather than detracted from the quality of the drama. This is a humane, rich and genuinely moving play about the dreams, quirks, fears, lusts and snafus of very real people who are struggling to stay afloat in a sea of ashes.

Unfortunately, the playwright's desire to write a political play betrays him in the end. The raging fire in the final scene is as contrived as the rest of the play is genuine. The final scene in which the characters turn to the audience and ask "What are we going to do?" is straight out of the most bareface agit-prop skit. Other political playwrights like Brecht or Dario Fo frequently ignore the fourth wall to confront the audience with life-like dilemmas, but this device is built into their dramas from the beginning. Fennario has tried to solder a cartoon ending onto a naturalistic play, and it is jarring and totally inappropriate. Still, *Balconville* is an important and exciting script; a deserving winner of the 1980 Chalmers Award for outstanding play.

Thérèse Beaupré, CTR, 32 (Fall 1981), 113-14

• •

Zimmerman   How do you feel about the different productions of *Balconville*?

Fennario   So far there's been three different Irenes, two Muriels, two Dianes, two Céciles. I preferred the first production for a number of reasons. One was the mood of the first production when the play was brand new and we didn't

234

know what the hell we had. A lot of heavy things happened to a number of people in the cast. In my case, my very good friend Jackie, the character that Johnny is based on, had died. The woman who was playing Irene broke up with her old man. Barbra Matis, she designed the set, her father had just died and the woman who played Diane was half-crazy at the time.

Zimmerman What happened to Jackie?

Fennario Jackie was working on the boats like a lot of guys from the Point. They went out drinking and he came back onto the wrong wharf. It was a government wharf. He got into a scrap with the security guards and they said he jumped in the ocean. And that was that. So the whole mood and feeling of the first production was just haunted. I still feel it from the set. Barbra's magic with that set still freaks me out. For those reasons and also because I think the cast was more together than the later ones, I prefer the first production.

Zimmerman There was a lot of comedy in the touring production.

Fennario I found that production getting dangerously close to situation comedy.

Zimmerman Did the importance of the incest incident vary from production to production?

Fennario Yes. I thought the actress was over-reacting in one production. I put the suggestion of incest in because it happens, a guy gets drunk at a party . . . I didn't consider it that serious whereas the actress tended to. And I felt, well, maybe she's right. It does create a tension. There's been a lot of discussion over that. I never had it in my mind that her father was really bothering her, or trying to rape her or anything like that.

Zimmerman In the ending of the first production the house is safe from the fire and they decide together to take political action against the landlord. Why did you change the ending later?

Fennario I and a lot of other people liked seeing the French and English sit down together for a change. But I felt, looking at it, that it was too much of a magic-wand number and that it was best to leave it as a question to the audience. So in the published version, as far as I remember, the roof is collapsing, the fire's heading their way, and then they hear Gaetan Bolduc's voice. It ends with Cécile saying, what are we going to do? I think maybe the other ending was more enjoyable but this one seems more true.

Zimmerman   How was *Balconville* received in Belfast? A number of the British reviewers thought it was about separatism.

Fennario   Well one thing touring Europe shows you is that Montreal, Quebec, is not a big deal to the world. If it wasn't for the FLQ they never would have heard of us. We got a collection of reviews and one of them calls it *Baconville*, another calls it *Balcony Man*. And they have a very vague idea of where the hell Quebec is, let alone Canada. On the tour we also played Bath. Bath was like playing Victoria B.C. It was really ultra-bourgeois. And they enjoyed it.

Zimmerman   Some critics have asked why you didn't explore more fully the French/English tension. I take it your statement is that the real barrier and the real problem isn't language.

Fennario   No. It's a class thing; that's one of the main things I wanted to show in *Balconville*.

Zimmerman   One of the issues in the play is work. Eventually Tom gets a job. He hates it but he's probably going to conform, though he may become another Johnny. Diane quits school and plans to look for work. But it's her father, Paquette, who seems the most compulsive about it. He has worked at a hateful job every day of his life. Is his hard work intended to serve as a reproach to the others?

Fennario   Paquette went through more changes script-wise than any other character and ended up the way he was because nothing else worked on him. I tried to make him a more impressive character but he ended up being a guy who would resign himself to that life, that pattern. Diane, I don't know about her.

Zimmerman   One of the comments a Toronto critic made about *Balconville* was that your villains are faceless, nameless and rich, yet the truth is that they are not to blame for the greatest cruelties. Those are inflicted by the downtrodden on each other.

Fennario   Well, I think that until they get revolutionary, the downtrodden will continue to take it out on each other rather than confront the faceless rich. It's not particularly the fault of the faceless rich but that's where the change has to come.

Zimmerman   So it isn't reasonable to expect that people will be kindly and good-natured when they are dealing with the stress of poverty and despair.

Fennario There is a myth about the happy poor. Forget it. One of the differences between the rich and poor is that while the rich may be as alienated as the poor, the poor are more bored because they've got less opportunity to do anything about it. I've met people who are well-off and still continue to believe the myth. Of course it helps their conscience if they can figure that the poor are happy.

Zimmerman Or believe that the poor are at fault to some degree, that if they had the guts they'd get out of their predicament.

Fennario Yeah, that's the more vulgar rich. A lot of the rich just assume that the poor are better off being poor. And there's a lingering myth that the poor have some kind of community. Even that's not true any more. The working-class communities have broken down over the last thirty years. There really isn't any community. Being poor is just more miserable and more boring than being rich. Maybe at one time you could say ignorance is bliss, but that's not true any more. Ignorance is just ignorance. The poor have been educated now so they know better. They just feel trapped so it's worse. You don't have any peasant poor here, everybody's got a fucking TV. They look at the TV. Hey, I don't have that. Hey, father knows best.

Zimmerman Do you feel that at the ending of *Balconville* . . . the characters are trapped? That the fire is coming and they can't do anything about it?

Fennario Well, maybe not about their house but something has already happened. They have been forced to work together and to organize to help themselves in that situation. That is a start. . . .

Cynthia Zimmerman, interview with David Fennario, *The Work*, pp. 298-301

• •

DAVID FRENCH

Jitters

First produced at Tarragon Theatre, Toronto, 16 February 1979

Directed by Bill Glassco
Set and Costume Design by David Moe
Lighting Design by Sarah Adler

Cast

Patrick Flanagan	David Calderisi
Jessica Logan	Charmion King
Philip Mastorakis	Les Carlson
George Ellsworth	Miles Potter
Robert Hall	Matt Walsh
Tom Kent	Jim Mezon
Nick	Morison Bock
Susi	Amanda Lewis
Peggy	Sheila Currie

There's a cliché which advises writers to stick to things they know, and David French has certainly obeyed that maxim in *Jitters*, his new comedy-of-the-stage. The play is crammed with the nightmares which haunt the theatre, and seems destined to break up visiting theatrical types on their nights off.

The question, though, is whether *Jitters*, which opened last night at the Tarragon, will do the same for civilians.

It is, after all, a play with no real plot or much discernible purpose. It is simply *about* a new play's opening and the myriad complications of "getting it on," theatrically speaking. And from that quite inventive springboard it plunges into a series of sight gags and one-liners.

French isn't exactly trying to do a Neil Simon (if you were thinking of Simon—the term "one-liner" summons him up like Banquo's ghost), but he's very definitely trying to whoosh us away in some frothy comedy. And at times he's marvellously successful.

There's that lovely moment when one of the play-within-a-play's stars (David Calderisi) exclaims, "I have no desire to leave this country—we have a unique situation here . . . " and the audience almost chokes on its own ironic laughter. And the Toronto insiders set up a knowing cackle when somebody cracked, "Maybe *now* there'll be some interest from the regional theatres!"

But *Jitters* has a long way to go to become the hilarious romp French seems to be seeking. The play-within-a-play is a superb idea, especially with the director (Miles Potter) screaming from among the real audience during the "rehearsals." But it also causes more problems than it can solve.

Being both "actors" and real people, all the actors need two separate acting styles so we can see them shifting in and out of character. Only one, Les Carlson, as a neurotic, line-forgetting loser, manages it consistently. The others are in the ridiculous position of moving on and off stage without so much as a shift in gears.

Beyond that, all that talk about acting and forgetting lines means their "offstage" scenes must create a kind of super-realism to be believable—a super headache for director Bill Glassco. And it's only achieved in bits and snatches here. Just when you make the credibility jump, one of them will stumble over a line for real, and the jig is up.

Then, too, there were some terrible opening-night problems with the timing—little comic bits would happen, a punch-line would be dropped and the audience would sit in bewildered silence (one of the nightmares French is playing on, but this time, ironically, for real).

In fairness, comedies are notoriously hard to get a handle on, and this cast is obviously still finding its way. So there's reason to hope the play will get funnier.

But Glassco may have dealt himself an insurmountable problem in the casting. There are many fine actors in *Jitters*, but astonishingly few accomplished comedians. Carlson has the sort of cartoon face which prompts TV commercials to cast him as a buffoon and Potter can turn on a sort of open-eyed astonishment at will.

The others, however, take their comedy far too seriously. Charmion King, for prime example, makes her barbed fencing with Calderisi a vicious (and unfunny) little knife game. Calderisi has a lot more of the comedian's flexibility, but poor timing cost him at least half his scripted laughs.

Bryan Johnson, *Globe and Mail*, 17 February 1979*

• •

The transfer of *Jitters* from the Tarragon to the Toronto Workshop Theatre, to give the play a longer run, was a felicitous move. This is one of the finest Canadian comedies ever written, possibly the best.

An important aspect of the work lies in its fresh treatment of a hackneyed theme: backstage life. And that life behind the scenes is unmistakably Canadian. Lying beneath every turn of the plot by David French is a constant theme—the struggle of Canadian theatre to free itself from the influences of New York and London and to establish a unique identity.

Another impressive distinction of *Jitters* lies in the ingenious craftsmanship French has applied to the construction of a play within a play. The complications usually associated with this well-worn theatrical artifice melt away in French's smooth, witty and sometimes side-splitting dialogue and in his nicely dovetailed situations.

The "play within" hardly matters. It serves solely as a hinge on which to hang funny rehearsal scenes in Act I, a hilariously disastrous first night scene in Act II and tragi-comical actors' private problems scenes in Act III.

We see a company of Canadian actors preparing for some such small stage as Toronto Workshop, The Tarragon, or the Toronto Free theatres a Canadian play. Its plot turns on the hostility of a 20 year old son to his middle-aged mother's younger lover. In the one brief scene that we see rehearsed several times there gleams a gentle satire on contemporary dramatic obsessions with sex.

Far more important is the relationship between the actors and their ever more critical interdependence on one another as the first night approaches.

The mutual dislike of the leading lady, a fading star with a Broadway background, and the leading man, an Irish-Canadian who has never played outside this country, yields much of the fun since in the "play within" they are supposed to be in love. The contrast between the on stage personality of a man playing the part of an Anglican vicar and his off-stage idiosyncrasies is another rich source of comedy. And a young actor who gets drunk a few hours before curtain time on the first night initiates a long, uproarious sequence based on the apprehensions of companies that cannot afford understudies when one member of the cast is late turning up.

The laughter is relieved by excellent dialogue on more serious matters, notably the dominance in English language theatre of New York and London; the need for Canadian actors to play New York or London before they can acquire star status; the sensitivity of some actors to critics' comments and the indifference of others; the struggle to find really comfortable and congenial small theatres; the bitter fights between actors, directors and dramatists over the changing of odd words and passages of stage business; and the vagaries of audience response. One of the most amusing lines springs out of memories of an "audience of academics all looking for a message."

Miles Potter, as a director, forms the fulcrum of the show, most of the situations depending upon reactions to his brilliant studies of authority, harassment, diplomacy, despair and triumph.

Charmion King's slightly haggard star, struggling to show adoration of a stud played by a man she hates, is a marvellously subtle display of a double emotional ambivalence. David Calderisi's on-stage stud and off-stage cynic is equally impressive even if the Irishman he is supposed to be sometimes appears to be more Italian in his volatility. Les Carlson creates a vivid comical image of the on-stage Anglican priest and the off-stage middle-aged child, still dominated by his mother. Jim Mezon, on stage and off, is a good silly ass kid. As a stage member and stage hands Morison Bock and two beauties named Amanda Lewis and Sheila Currie offer strong support to a distinguished production. . . .

McKenzie Porter, Toronto Sun, 7 May 1979

• •

Off-stage, actors can blame incompetent playwrights, dogmatic directors, and unknowing critics, but when they are on stage, they are largely at the mercy of themselves and their fellow actors. Actors can be very vulnerable and very funny people, as demonstrated in David French's delightful new backstage comedy, *Jitters*, now playing at the Long Wharf Theater's intimate Stage II [New Haven]. This is an insider's affectionate tribute to the theater as a flawed way of life. . . .

This is Mr. French's first comedy—in 1974 I saw his naturalistic drama, *Leaving Home*—and if *Jitters* is typical of the author's humor, he may turn out to be the Canadian Alan Ayckbourn. In common, each of these playwrights writes not jokes but character comedy.

Very early in *Jitters*, Mr. French establishes his characters—their fears, habits, vanities and failings. After that, anything they do in character becomes identifiable and humorous. We even begin to look forward to the repetition of certain crotchets—and because we come to know the characters so well, at moments they are also touching.

For example, there is a character actor with a terrible memory. He begs for a prompter. On stage, he is a bundle of exposed anxieties, changing lines at whim, confusing cues and walking off in the middle of a scene. In the dressing room, at a crucial point of the plot, he is asked to remember someone's name. Looking at the blank face of the dumbfounded actor (George Sperdakos), we laugh out loud. Can he even remember his own name? Naturally, when the play opens, this actor steals the notices, the critics misinterpreting his fumbling for a character's tentativeness.

Then there is the blustering Irishman, a star in the provinces who is afraid to tempt his fate on Broadway and covers up his own insecurity with rude remarks to his leading lady. The fearful playwright wants to sit out front on opening night and when he is reminded of his disastrous behavior at his last opening, he says, "Anyone can faint." Anyone can faint, get drunk, arrive late, or get locked in the offstage bathroom, and Feldman may never get to the theater, but the curtain will rise, if the stage manager has anything to say about it.

This stage manager is rigid, guarding his call board as jealously as Captain Queeg tended his strawberries. Desperately trying to massage all egos and to whip the show into shape, is the eager young director, a master of the classic theatrical plot, the severely qualified compliment. "The last scene was stupendous," he exclaims, adding without a pause, "It still needs toning down."

Unlike most backstage comedies, *Jitters* is not a frenetic farce, although there are several bits of physical humor that are certain to dissolve an audience into laughter. The play is easygoing and low key. Under Bill Glassco's confident, restrained direction, the actors stress the reality of their situation, a reality that is abetted by Eldon Elder's tasteful onstage and backstage settings. We believe that the play is about to open, and we begin to take a rooting interest in the actors; if only they can get past the critics.

The performers strike exactly the right balance between satire and sentiment, and when called for, they convincingly pretend to be awkward actors on stage. There are collaborative performances from the entire cast—from the feuding stars, Roland Hewgill and Charmion King, down to Sarah Chodoff as an all-purpose errand person. Special mention should be made of Jim Jansen's director, a man who is edging toward exasperation; Josh Clark's nervous author; William Carden's assertive stage manager; and Mr. Sperdakos's forgetful actor.

After the opening of "The Care and Treatment of Roses," a review is read aloud to the company and it is a dead-on spoof of an attitudinizing critic. He calls the play "a seamless fabric of passion and redeemed hope." The author wonders why the critic hedged at all. Why didn't he come right out and say that the play was perfect?

With that review in mind, I will hedge a little. *Jitters* is an almost perfect comedy of its kind. The play finishes with a letdown rather than a lift-off. Mr. French should reconsider his ending. Any day there will be a real-life Feldman in the house.

Mel Gussow, *NYT*, 6 November 1979

• •

The job of a reviewer, says Broadway composer Lehman Engel, is to direct people to whatever kind of theatre they may enjoy.

The possible combinations of taste and revulsion are endless, says Engel. Therefore it's the reviewer's duty to concentrate on those qualities in a show that may find a sympathetic audience response. Otherwise he is guilty of depriving a segment of the public of something they may enjoy and of plundering the theatre.

Playwright David French says much the same sort of thing in *Jitters*, except in a more subtle, almost persuasive way.

That's why I'm wondering at the moment whether I should go along with all the critics who have hailed this play as a witty, affectionate tribute to the theatre as a flawed way of life, or go along with my own responses which tell me that *Jitters* is a bitchy, whiny melodrama about Canadian theatre people who threaten to quit unless they get more respect from critics—who write nasty things about them they know to be true but don't want to see in print.

A Theatre Calgary ad in yesterday's *Herald* tells us that *Jitters* is Broadway bound and it quotes the *New York Times* to the effect that the play is "an almost perfect comedy."

There's a tremendous irony there because *Jitters* is, in fact, about a Toronto theatre company trying to make it to Broadway with a new play.

If the *Medicine Hat News*, or even the *Vancouver Sun* had said *Jitters* was "an almost perfect comedy"(an out-of-context quote, by the way, which is severely qualified in the original *New York Times* review), the effect wouldn't be quite the same.

The whole thrust of Canadian theatre recently has been to find acclaim in New York (there were 14 Canadian scripts optioned by American producers, at last count) and *Jitters* shows how ludicrous and sad that situation is.

A play shouldn't need a Good Housekeeping Seal of Approval from the *New York Times* to find its proper place in the hearts of Canadian theatregoers. If it's a good play, it should survive on its merits and gain acceptance, regardless of what they say in New York.

But of course nobody in Canadian theatre really believes that. Hence the mad rush toward New York of *Billy Bishop*s, *Artichoke*s, *Automatic Pilot*s, *Hey Marilyn*s, *Memoir*s and *Bistro Car*s.

Like lambs to the slaughter they go, abandoning the velvet coffins of Canadian regional theatre for the sake of a review (favorable, they hope) from Clive Barnes or Frank Rich. And the majority end up devastated, their hopes for success dashed by condescending, lukewarm notices from critics who know very little about Canadian theatre. David French, for example, was described by the *New York Times* as the "Canadian Alan Ayckbourn" which doesn't do justice to the talents of either playwright. But still the march on Broadway continues.

Jitters, as it transpires, is not "an almost perfect comedy." *As You Like It* is an almost perfect comedy. *Jitters* is flawed and esoteric, dependent for its success on audience familiarity with certain theatrical figures and conventions.

Nobody laughed at the references to *Macbeth* during last night's opening, because obviously not many were familiar with the traditional superstitions surrounding this play. Nor did they laugh at references to Pinter or Mike Nichols. That's what happens when you do this play for people who don't spend their lives thinking about theatre.

The play is too long. It runs for almost two hours and 45 minutes, with two intermissions. It droops at the middle under the weight of such stock situations as the washroom door that won't open and the actor who shows up drunk on opening night. And the closing bit about an actor who gets his stomach pumped is contrived. It's fairly obvious the playwright ran out of steam after having his dig at the critics, because the ending is anti-climactic.

The Theatre Calgary production is marred by jerky acting, swallowed lines, peculiar lighting design (are those spotlights on the audience really necessary?) and uneven pacing.

Rita Howell, who plays the leading lady, seems to be intimidated by all the references in the script to an actress who performs like an opera singer. Her performance is too under-stated.

Peter Jobin plays the leading man with two different accents (one for the play within a play and one for our play) and neither does anything for his characterizations. Paul Jolicoeur, as the stage manager, also has difficulty nailing down a vocal style amounting to more than a distraction.

David Francis overplays his nervousness as the jittery director. Guy Bannerman is appropriately inarticulate as the playwright who doesn't want to sacrifice any of his deathless prose.

And the best performance (a case of art following art) is turned in by Les Carlson as the blundering actor who forgets his lines on opening night and steals all the notices.

He mugs and indicates shamelessly, but somehow, in the midst of the low-key playing, that seems to be just the right size for the role.

Brian Brennan, *Calgary Herald*, 19 September 1980

• •

Jitters is bitchy fun, once. In this harshly drawn cartoon of a theatre company in rehearsal, David French confirms all of one's worst suspicions: actors are spoiled, catty manic-depressives, playwrights are paranoiac cranks, and critics are naive, humourless pedants who write badly. In the first act, a scene is rehearsed several times while the actors complain about their wigs, lines, blocking, and one another. The wit is sharp, but shallow and repetitious, and although the rehearsals are cleverly engineered with subtle variations each time, there is no dramatic progress, either for the rehearsed play or for the frame play. Once the prickly, hysterical atmosphere is established, nothing happens. French has assembled his characters to tell us a few smart truths about Canadian theatre—"Where else can you be a top-notch actor all your life and still die broke and anonymous?"—but the actors remain caricatures, and the irrepressible wisecracking does not flower into comedy.

The second act takes place backstage just before opening. The actors are still squabbling about their shoes, wigs, and one another while coping (in that histrionic "show must go on" bravura style that is the essence of theatre and this play) with a sequence of truly awful disasters thrown brilliantly together by French. In the third act, the company must come to terms with the critics' responses— mixed, of course. The star of the show is panned in a clever, parodic review; what rankles is not the critic's judgement—the actress knows she went over the top—but the damnation in print, in heavy, adjectival prose flung like a wet fishing net over her tender ego. French also pulls malicious humour from the fact that the production's flaws are perceived by the critics as strengths; thus the actor who regularly forgets his lines is described enthusiastically by the critic as "vulnerable in an almost painfully childlike manner, fumbling for words that seem constantly to elude his grasp . . . " The critic mistakes ineptitude for craft, but the joke tacitly acknowledges something else: that intangible process whereby character and performer merge which, when it works, is the magic of theatre.

I am not sure about the extent to which French's piece works; it is a clever, well-crafted exercise, sometimes funny, but it is also peevish, slight, forgettable. I think I might leave the theatre with an odd sense of having yet to see a play.

Marian Fraser (the original text of a review published
in *Canadian Literature*, 91 [Winter 1981], 139-40)

• •

ERIKA RITTER

Automatic Pilot

First produced by the New Theatre, Adelaide Court,
Toronto, 17 January 1980

Directed by William Lane
Designed by Roderick Hillier

Cast

Charlie	Fiona Reid
Gene	Geoffrey Bowes
Nick	John Evans
Alan	Patrick Young

A lady stand-up comedian named Charlie does the stupidest things. She marries a man who turns out to be gay. She gets plastered and wakes up in a strange bed trying desperately to convince her pickup's brother (whom she takes for the pickup) that she had great sex with him. She falls in love with the brother until she realizes he's really as decent as he seems, and promptly dumps him. So much a seventies denizen is she that her lip-shaped lapel clasp seems as superfluous as a red star on Brezhnev's coat.

Automatic Pilot (at the Adelaide Court) is an up-to-date comedy by a very funny playwright—Erika Ritter. Although not a farce, it has inspired farcical scenes (a producer laments that his director is running off to Spain with a faggot, not noticing that the guy he's just been introduced to is searching for his passport). In fact, Miss Ritter's script spills over with humor to the point where her scenes often dissolve into miniature comic crescendoes with the actors at a loss during the quiet parts. Occasionally they look as if they have forgotten their lines.

Structural faults aside, the play is outstanding entertainment. To Miss Ritter, comedy is not an end but a tool for caring about the characters she creates. Charlie, far from being pathetic, uses superb humor as a weapon to attack anyone who starts sniffing around her neuroses. Alan, the "late husband" turned faggot, needs his ex-wife as a touchstone to his past self. Even Nick, the producer who abandons her with a form letter, is not the standard chauvinist punching-bag. Gene, the younger brother who loves her, proves both their points by being the only one to get hurt. But, on an upbeat-note, he is the only one who matters.

Stand-up comedy, in a clever scene where Fiona Reid as Charlie segues in mid-sentence from the stage act to a bedroom where she's (later) listening to the same act on a tape recorder, is seen as a whole world view. In a society where making one person durably happy no longer seems possible, why not make a roomful happy instead? Reid's excellence is not only that she makes Charlie's offstage fractious and chameleon moods believable, but that she can perform the difference between a successful stage act and one that's bombing.

The same satisfying authority comes from John Evans, whose Nick is towering and energetic enough to ward off the pettiness another actor might bring to the role. Geoffrey Bowes as Gene was alert and often affecting, as the kid who inherits both the sixties and seventies at a blow and *still* believes that for straight males there is peace without dishonor. I didn't like Patrick Young's approach to Alan's sexual identity crisis, which was too much lower lip a-tremble and quaking voice—the one problem characterization.

The jerkiness of pace may be only partly due to Ritter's writing. Director Bill Lane has left numerous pauses sitting around that don't do anybody any good, especially considering that they must be added to the pauses between scenes while Roderick Hillier's awkward sets are changed. I also wonder if it's necessary for everybody to be either smoking or drinking continually. It is nerve-wracking to sit through the sledgehammering of Western sexual mores, but surely somebody relaxes sometime.

Ray Conlogue, Globe and Mail, 18 January 1980*

• •

Automatic Pilot indeed! Erika Ritter's new play, which opened last night at the smaller of the two theatres in Adelaide Court, should really be retitled *Fear of Flying*—with all the sexual connotations of the phrase underlined.

And I should add, Erika Ritter has nothing to learn from Erika Jong, the author of a racy novel of that name, in the matter of one-liners.

Ritter is, I would say, a compulsive wisecracker. Every time she plucks up the courage to write herself into a situation which requires emotional depth, she succumbs to her evil genius—wit.

On the surface, Ritter's wit would seem to be her saving grace; I would rank her as one of the most stringent writers of dialogue among contemporary Canadian playwrights. But in fact, as *Automatic Pilot* proceeds, it emerges again and again as her downfall.

Mind you, Ritter's downfall is great deal more absorbing than a lot of other playwrights' downfalls. *Automatic Pilot* is bursting with vitality and with unfulfilled possibilities and Ritter has a refreshingly bold and dramatic instinct. The idea for her last play, *Winter 1671*, which was about a straying mail order bride from France who got lost in her emotions and the New World, was promising. The premise of *Automatic Pilot* is even more so; a female stand-up comic who can only be funny when she's unhappy.

But Charlie isn't unhappy the way many thirtyish women trying to survive the singles bar scene are unhappy. And here is the first of Ritter's misdirections. Charlie has a problem so complicated that it ultimately overtakes the play and knocks its major strength, Charlie's stand-up routines, right out of the picture.

After 8 years of marriage, her husband Alan stepped out of the closet and acknowledged he was a homosexual. Meat for the comedy routine right enough. I haven't yet seen a play in which a woman attacks homosexuals with quite such relish as Charlie on the rampage. Not that too much should be made of that. The insults flung are after all pretty much the same as those flung by anyone suffering defeat in a skirmish between the sexes.

For Alan's rejection of Charlie has triggered all her neuroses, it turns out. By day, she is a soap-opera hack churning out sudsy story lines; by night she schlepps down to the only too appropriately named Canada Goose and gets her excitement with one-liners honed by the feelings that are tearing her apart, pushing her to act out her anguish verbally, or in a series of strange beds. Clearly, Charlie's course is set for crash.

If you pick over the wreckage of *Automatic Pilot*, a pattern emerges. It is a familiar one that any Joan Crawford fan will recognize. Melodrama is the style, and doom is written in every line. Charlie is clearly a masochist. She cannot allow herself to be happy and when happiness threatens, she falls to pieces worse than when she's beaten to the ground.

Now, amid the mishmash of psychological insight and despite the hetero-homosexual hostility which tends to overcomplicate the plot, there is a strong play struggling to be written in *Automatic Pilot*. The medium is there for it. Charlie's routine is a device through which she could reveal herself totally without having to realise what she's doing. But Ritter is like Charlie, she'll talk herself out of anything good. And sure enough, when Charlie has reached the point when she has to face her own self-destructiveness, Ritter lets her off the hook. Instead of writing Charlie a routine which strips away all her pretences, and tells the truth, what is surely the appalling truth, because in Charlie there must be stored up a terrifying paranoia about men, and the society that conditioned her to please them, Ritter backs off. She just lets Charlie retreat into the safety of failure with a few sad jokes about the last man she's lost.

The entire production, which is the first New Theatre production this season, follows this tactic of evasion. There's a lot of talk, but little genuine emotion; the characters are so busy explaining themselves to each other, or indeed to themselves, that they rarely seem to listen to anyone else. What *Automatic Pilot* needs above all is a mensch as director, someone who has a warm human touch.

William Lane's strengths veer toward the bizarre and the sinister, and he directs the play in a curiously disconnected way, as if he were unplugging the characters at the end of scenes.

Automatic Pilot also needs a great many laughs to keep it rolling along; and indeed to keep Fiona Reid rolling along as well. But the production's style is stifling her particular qualities.

I don't think she's by any means ideally cast as Charlie, her insouciant, ding-bat comic style quite at odds with the hard-drinking, hard-swearing stand-up comic who spits out jokes as if they were nails. And her stand-up style is anything but raw; Reid's much too polite; she can't help charming the audience when she should be hitting them over the head. When she curses, she sounds like a little girl who'd overheard the words but doesn't know what they mean. This interpretation has its comic moments but it unbalances the play and makes Charlie's relationships with men unbelievable.

Under the circumstances, even the most unregenerate Amazon would pity the actors struggling to make Charlie's men credible. As it is, John Evans does well as a breezy philanderer and Geoffrey Bowes displays a singular sweetness and a welcome light touch as the gentle Gene. Patrick Young is valiant as Alan; an ambiguous character who is completely scuppered by the fact that this Charlie is no termagent but a rather pathetic youngster. All of them are hampered by Roderick Hillier's sprawling set which appears to allow them so little leg room.

However, this production is obviously in a workshop space, and must be regarded simply as a try-out for a play that I hope will be reworked and produced again when its short run at Adelaide Court is over.

Gina Mallet, *Toronto Star*, 18 January 1980*

• •

Erika Ritter's *Automatic Pilot* is beyond a doubt the finest piece of homegrown writing to grace a Toronto stage this season. Ritter's ability to write comedy was evident in last year's production of *The Splits*, but what makes this piece of writing so powerful is its extremely personal, emotional turmoil. One can't help wondering how much of *Automatic Pilot* is autobiographical.

A simple recitation of the plot is enough to make anyone moan in despair; another lost woman trying to find herself; another husband discovering his homosexuality after years of marriage; another chauvinist boyfriend who thinks he's God's gift to the world; another nice guy who tries to save a woman from herself. Needless to say, in the hands of a less gifted writer, this could have been a disastrous script, loaded with clichés and hopelessly unappealing. What emerges instead is a painfully funny comedy, full of fresh insights on an old theme.

That is not to say that *Automatic Pilot* is a perfect script. The characters are still a bit too stereotyped and Ritter's attempt to have us identify instantly with them suffers as a result. It is obvious that her interest lies with Charlie, the female stand-up comedienne who provides the pivotal struggle within the play, and in concentrating on Charlie's development as a woman who needs pain in the way some of us need cigarettes, Ritter has sacrificed equal development in her male characters. The base for each of them is there, but the flesh is still missing from the bones. The actors are forced to rely on witty one-liners to add necessary dimensions to their performances which creates a strain in otherwise flowing performances.

John Evans as Nick, in particular, seems bound by the limitations of the script and he becomes the least believable character of the play. Evans struggles valiantly within the confines of a part that demands he be ''the Male Chauvinist Pig'' of the evening. Complete with anti-''fag'' jokes, Nick comes across as repulsive as anyone could be. But when Ritter demands that he suddenly develop sensitivity and understanding, the trouble begins. At the very end of the play, Nick, who previously couldn't relate to any woman in anything other than sexual terms, is able to ''understand'' and explain Charlie's psychological turmoils to his younger brother. That Ritter should ask this of Nick is a good move, but since no clue to this softer element in his nature is provided earlier, the audience is directed to take too great a leap of faith. Gene, the "nice" brother, is the counterbalance to Nick, and these black and white characterizations cause the play to lose some of the emotional punch it could deliver.

On the other hand, Ritter's creation of Alan, the homosexual husband, shows just what this playwright can deliver at her best. The scene in which he and Charlie finally say goodbye is truly moving and avoids all the usual clichés of such partings. Patrick Young as Alan must also be credited with making this scene so touching. Young succeeds in blending comedy with a three-dimensional agony, and his finest moments by far come out of the pain he so beautifully portrays. What choppiness exists in his performance is largely due to production faults, in particular the endless blackouts between scenes. The set seemed to be designed without proper thought for scene changes and each change demands a complete redressing of the stage. The audience is left in total darkness at least a dozen times, and each time the pace of the production falters.

The final accolade must go to Fiona Reid, as Charlie, who turns in a memorable performance. Reid has quickly established herself as a leading Toronto actress, and *Automatic Pilot* can't help but focus the spotlight even more solidly on her. Best known for her portrayal of Al Waxman's dittsy wife on *King of Kensington*, Reid is exceptional in her ability to play parts against type. Not only does she play them, but she plays them successfully.

Even with its minor flaws, *Automatic Pilot* emerges as a fine play, a potentially even better play, and certainly a very worthwhile evening of theatre.

Mira Friedlander, *Scene Changes*, 8 (March 1980), 35-36*

• •

The Bastion Theatre Company [Victoria], which is currently celebrating its 10th anniversary as a fully professional group, launched its second production of the new season over the weekend.

The play chosen by Bastion artistic director Edwin Stephenson is Erika Ritter's *Automatic Pilot*, a stage work that created something of a sensation when it was first seen earlier this year at Toronto's New Theatre.

Productions of the play have also been planned for Ottawa, Winnipeg, Montreal and Vancouver and the author, who was in Victoria for Friday night's opening, has had the pleasure of hearing herself hailed as a new "hot property" in Canadian theatre.

The play, which grew out of a Ritter short story called "You're a Taker," is a dark and at times ruthless comedy about life and what passes for love on the extreme edge of the Toronto showbusiness community and, while the Toronto emphasis is particularly sharp, the universal implications of the piece carry it far beyond its actual setting.

The "automatic pilot" of the title has nothing to do with the flying of aircraft, but refers, rather, to the singular ability of the leading character—a female soap opera writer and stand-up comic called Charlie—to make a mental adjustment that allows her to avoid responsibility for portions of her hectic emotional life.

The action of the play concerns Charlie's relationship with three of the men in her life: her estranged husband, a homosexual who has recently emerged from the closet; a hard-boiled and down-to-earth "lady's man"; and a sensitive youth, almost a boy, who offers her a species of conventional "happiness" that she is unable, in the end, to accept.

Ritter examines these relationships and Charlie's inability to cope with them with a considerable degree of wisdom and insight. Her writing is tartly amusing and she displays an admirable ability to expose the various facets of the dramatic situations under examination. *Automatic Pilot* is, at times, almost painfully funny and, at times, shatteringly moving.

Erika Ritter's great strength as a writer for the stage lies in her ability to create strong situations, richly detailed characters and vivid dialogue that seems to be written in italics.

Less successful, however, is her use of the stage itself. *Automatic Pilot* sits rather awkwardly on the stage. The frequent changes of scene are cumbersome and suggest that Ritter's mind is more closely attuned to film or television.

In this production she has not been helped out of her difficulties by designer Terry Gunvordahl who has provided stage decor that simply serves to draw attention to Ritter's dilemma.

Director Edwin Stephenson might also have done more than he has done to help the novice playwright out of the difficulties of staging that her script presents, but he has, in other regards, served her well. The piece is well orchestrated, nicely balanced and the performances all do much to enhance the proceedings.

Tudi Wiggins is especially effective as the troubled Charlie, and she gets sound support from Ron Halder, David Brown and Bruce Gray as the various men in her life.

Automatic Pilot is a sharp, reverberating and effective piece of dramatic writing that hits hard. It was too potent for some members of Friday night's audience and there were a number of walkouts at the interval. For those who stuck it out, however, it provided a generally pleasing and deeply moving theatrical experience. Erika Ritter is clearly a writer to watch.

Christopher Dafoe, *Vancouver Sun*, 12 November 1980

• •

Automatic Pilot is entertaining, in a frenetic, self-conscious, ingratiating kind of way.

It's contemporary, trendy and very Toronto. It's fine amusement as long as it's content to be witty and clever.

But it also asks to be taken seriously and it's here I have problems with the play. It's hard to warm to characters who seem to come equipped with their own gag writers and who persist in delivering one-liners when they might be revealing glimpses of their souls. They may be the hit of every party but nobody wants them around for breakfast on a Sunday morning.

The play is about a neurotic, hard-drinking stand-up comedienne named Charlie (Sharon Corder) who uses her off-stage life as material for her act. She performs twice weekly at a comedy club, except when her domestic life is tranquil. Then she writes dialogue for a television soap opera. (Does anybody in Calgary know people like this?)

Charlie's ex-husband (Stephen Hair) deserted her for another man. But he's still around to keep a platonic eye on her. Homosexuality is trendy nowadays, we are told. Even the straights are dressing better so they don't disgrace themselves.

Charlie's male pickup at the start of the show (Jack Ackroyd) is a part-time hustler, restaurant owner and movie investor. When he splits, she takes up with his younger brother (Michael Bianchin), a law school drop-out, part-time department store clerk and would-be novelist. Like Charlie, he too draws his material from the soap opera of his life.

Director Martin Fishman has opted for a realistic approach to the script, which works up to a point. It's obvious he wants us to look beyond the funny lines and to see how human, warm and vulnerable these characters really are.

But he is defeated to some extent by the material, which still calls for laughs in almost every scene.

There is one scene, however, that doesn't owe anything to Neil Simon or Woody Allen.

It occurs at the end of Act One, when the younger brother tells Charlie he cares for her. She asks him whether he wants to sleep with her. He hesitates for a second and replies: ''It's crossed my mind. From time to time . . . to time.''

It's a beautifully touching moment, nicely handled by actors Bianchin and Corder. And it doesn't need a punch line to work. But such moments of truth are rare in this break-em-up play.

The acting is fine.

Sharon Corder seems too self-possessed and disciplined, somehow, to be a neurotic, semi-alcoholic, stand-up comic. She is also a bit young-looking for somebody who is supposed to be seven years older than the younger brother.

But there's nothing wrong with her performance as a comedienne. The brand-name jokes work, even if the unrehearsed Theatre Calgary audience doesn't behave like a club crowd.

Jack Ackroyd is a macho, arrogant stud in this production, and convincing. You want to believe him even when the lines suggest he has been programmed by somebody who never listened closely to male conversation. But his clothes need to be refitted.

Stephen Hair, tackling one of the more difficult assignments of his career because his character doesn't allow him to do any shtick, is persuasively effective as the confused, bisexual actor who used to be Charlie's husband. His scene in the bar with her is not very good because the dialogue is a jumble of platitudes, but his first farewell scene works beautifully.

The other actor in the show, Michael Bianchin, has a good sense of comic timing but I had great difficulty understanding him because of the ornate speech patterns he adopts. He also needs to remember that a naturalistic delivery doesn't carry to the back of the room in that theatre.

The set is a real confusion.

Rather than go with a revolve or one of those vaguely undefined impressionist affairs, Fishman has settled for a solid, multi-purpose set that functions simultaneously as a nightclub, Charlie's apartment and the apartment of the two brothers. It's obvious that direct lighting is supposed to isolate these different playing areas, but it just doesn't work. When the show opens, it looks as if Charlie is doing her stand-up routine at a garage sale.

Brian Brennan, *Calgary Herald*, 28 November 1980

• •

Zimmerman   The *Calgary Herald* described *Automatic Pilot* as contemporary, trendy and very Toronto. The reviewer suggested that that voice, those problems, those one-liners, were just "too Toronto." Do you agree?

Ritter   No. I think I know Calgary better than that critic does. I'm from western Canada and he's from Ireland. I think that's one of the big problems with Canadian theatre, we have critics who have been brought from other places who don't understand the audience yet make pronouncements about what that audience likes. He is a nice guy but he is radically misinformed about Canadian theatre. He didn't even know how the Canada Council worked which I thought was appalling for a theatre critic. So I wasn't surprised that he found the play too Toronto. In fact the audiences in Calgary were riotous. They really got into the stand-up thing even more than Torontonians; they were really playing the part of the club audience. Anyway, in any part of this country you can always get a laugh on jokes about Toronto. I had been a little worried that the show business aspect would be an impediment. That if people believe show business is glamorous they cannot take seriously the problems of somebody in the business who, while not starving to death, is having career problems. But that didn't seem to constitute a problem either. I think people have always seen show business as a kind of metaphor for life itself, life as a play and people as players and so on. Show business just happens to be an occupational thing and they get right into it.

Zimmerman Martin Fishman, the director of the Theatre Calgary production, said he wanted to keep the Toronto references partly because Calgary's urban problems are so different from Toronto's.

Ritter Well he would have to keep the Toronto references because that's the script they bought. I mean there's that practical fact too. I don't like people altering plays. It's a condescending attitude to your own locality to think that it won't understand unless you change the street names, for Christ sake. I mean these people watch *Dallas* every week. They know that there are other towns out there. It's a looney concept. I think that the more something is particularized the better possibility it has for being universal. I don't know what this critic's other criticisms are like but I can't imagine him saying that *Romeo and Juliet* is too Verona or that Neil Simon is too Manhattan. In fact a lot of it probably has to do with a sort of east/west enmity which I find personally interesting because I'm a westerner originally. I live in the east and I get it in the neck both ways. Most Calgarians come from somewhere else anyway. . . .

Zimmerman It's unusual in Canadian drama to have a woman as the central character. Your women are in transition. They are also beleaguered, troubled, and anxious.

Ritter I'm not sure how beleaguered these people are. I'm also not sure how unusual this kind of depiction of women is. But in terms of their oppression and their beleaguerment, this is where I have my wildest differences with feminists. My women don't go over terrifically well with a lot of feminists. My contention in the plays is that their beleaguerment and their oppression is largely a product of their own mentality and their attitude about themselves. In actual fact they are independent and achieving people. It's not what people are doing to them; it's what they're doing to themselves. My women tend to betray their neurosis by drinking a lot, like Charlie, and they tend to be women who find their sense of self in terms of men. In fact, the subject matter of my plays is sexual. I think that's what life is like. I have been criticized for portraying a negative picture of women. I don't think it's negative. I think it's fairly accurate. It's like those awful stories in *Ms. Magazine* for free children. How about stories for real children? How about stuff that doesn't necessarily have a proselytizing message? I tend to feel, both about myself and about other women that I know, that one's attitude to oneself is the basic determination of what happens. It should be a good life. The fact that it's not very often, that it's sometimes a lonely, confusing and troubled life, has more to do with oneself than almost anything else. I don't think of these people as oppressed. And these people are incidentally female as far as I'm concerned. . . .

Zimmerman   One of the critics from the Toronto *Star* felt that the play was essentially evasive, that Charlie should have had to confront herself.

Ritter   I remember that criticism. If I were going to write a play about somebody who knows himself at the end and confronts himself I would say that was a valid criticism. It's like saying this play fails to be a play about a horse because there isn't a horse in it. Gina Mallet wanted the horse, not me. I wish Charlie did know herself, I guess, but I don't think she does. In the end I want the audience point-of-view to be Gene's. The whole second act of the play is an attempt to change focus. He takes over her role in the play: she started the first act, he starts the second act; she was discovered in bed, he's discovered in bed in the second act. At the end the audience sees her from a distance, hopefully, and sees him close-up.

Zimmerman   Most of the things that she talks about in her act we don't, as audience, experience directly. But their relationships we do. To experience that directly and then to see what she does with it at the end was very striking.

Ritter   It should be an affront. It's been hard on the actress because it's hard for somebody playing a comic not to get laughs. Normally an audience would never have seen the reality of that relationship. But in the theatre they have a certain loyalty because they've seen the relationship and they like Gene.

Zimmerman   It is also clarifying to see this character's creative process, how she creates her material.

Ritter   And her need. In those monologues at the end she is the victim of the monologue. In one there is this younger man who wants to move in and the whole thing is ludicrous beyond belief. The monologues are an interesting view of history. It's like the way literary critics look at an author's biography and then look at the transmutation as it appears in the work. One sees the imputed characters who are clearly, let us say, the father or the lover or something like that. It is most revealing. And it's true of Charlie. The audience is given a chance to see the creative process at work. It's not very nice.

Zimmerman   Have there been different interpretations of the character of Charlie by different actresses?

Ritter   They're all different. Actresses, if they're smart, will play their own strengths and mold the character to fit themselves. In fact, I rewrote some of the stand-up material for all the different actresses to conform with their physical type so that Charlie's jokes were accurate for the Charlie that it was.

Zimmerman   There has been a real clamour among actresses across the country to play the part of Charlie. Did you expect that to be the case?

Ritter   I didn't feel very good about the play when I first wrote it. I thought it was bitter and badly organized and stupid, but I guess it had the germ of something in it. So I didn't have any expectations about the part or about anything else. By the time we opened the show I knew that it was going to be successful to some extent because I had seen the preview audiences. But now I can certainly see why there would be a lot of interest among actresses in that part. Even though the lot of women in the theatre is probably improving, there still aren't that many good female roles. Charlie is the big enchilada in that play; it's her career, it's her life, it's her loves, it's her sex life, it's her drinking problem. She's got very male problems in that play. She's taken as seriously as a man would be in a play and she has a lot of colours in her life, a lot of different moods. The really big thing is that she gets to do stand-up. As well as act in a fourth-wall convention where the audience is ignored, she also gets to play with the audience. I can see why actresses would want to play it. I think there should be a lot more parts like that for women.

Zimmerman   When *Automatic Pilot* was transferred to the Bayview Playhouse in Toronto and became a bigger commercial number, what kinds of changes did that mean?

Ritter   Really all it meant was that the profits from the play were going in to repaying the people who had invested money in mounting it. In a standard commercial situation, for example a Broadway situation, the rights that the producing body gets go on in perpetuity and the producer is really a heavy element. This was the remount of an already existing play and the terms, from my point of view, didn't change very much for me. In terms of the actors, gradually I think the commercial run changed them. The Bayview was a different house. It was bigger. Their performances got broader as indeed they had to, but they also got deeper. I thought that everybody got better as the play went on. Those actors played over a hundred performances of those parts. So they had a lot of opportunities to develop the characters, to go stale and then go fresh again and all the things that happen in New York theatre where people play the same part for maybe a year. The only alteration I made at the Bayview was I cut Gene's final monologue. I did think it was right that he ended the play, but for some reason in that theatre it wasn't working. Somehow the statement had already been made. I've seen other productions since where the monologue is back in again and I like it back in, but I know why I cut it. I had a difference of opinion with the director over that. It's unusual when it's the writer who's clammering to cut and the director who's clammering to keep it. But in the end we both thought it was a good move, that it gave the play a more decisive ending to end with her. And somehow the spectacle of her standing up there and saying all this stuff was sufficiently tragic that you didn't need Gene's commentary. . . .

Cynthia Zimmerman, interview with Erika Ritter, *The Work*, pp. 283-290

• •

SHARON POLLOCK

Blood Relations

First produced at Theatre 3, Edmonton, 12 March 1980

Directed by Keith Digby
Set Design by J. Fraser Hiltz
Costume Design by Kathryn Burns
Lighting Design by Luciano Iogna

Cast

Miss Lizzie	Janet Daverne
Actress	Judith Mabey
Emma	Barbara Reese
Doctor/Defence	Wendell Smith
Harry	Brian Atkins
Mrs. Borden	Paddy English
Mr. Borden	Charles Kerr

The Borden murders, which occurred at Fall River, Mass. in the summer of 1892, still rank high in the annals of American crime. . . .

Blood Relations by Calgary playwright Sharon Pollock is the latest in a long line of fictionalized accounts of the Borden case. The story has already been enshrined in American folklore and told in drama, ballet and opera. But Pollock's play, which opened Wednesday night at Theatre 3, succeeds in opening up whole new fields for conjecture. . . .

Blood Relations offers an intriguing, albeit unashamedly *theatrical* version of the events surrounding the brutal murders of Andrew J. Borden and his second wife, Abby, on that hot August morning in 1892. The story is told as a post-trial game of charades, with an actress friend of Lizzie retracing her movements on the day of the crime, while Lizzie adopts the role of an Irish maid-of-all-work who lived in the Borden home and was once suspected in the case though never charged.

Pollock has taken some liberties with the historical facts for the sake of heightened dramatic impact. For example, she suggests a symbiotic relationship between Lizzie and the maid, which doesn't appear to have any basis in reality. She substitutes a relative named Harry for Uncle Vinnicum Morse and, in accordance with post-Freudian convention, she gives the spinsterish Lizzie a romantic involvement with a married physician who doesn't appear in any of the books on the case.

But these theatrical devices hardly impair the essential integrity of Pollock's treatment. This is a balanced account that should provoke renewed discussion among playgoers on the question of Lizzie's guilt or innocence.

Pollock seems to believe in Lizzie's guilt, although she never really spells it out in her play. Did Lizzie actually kill her parents? Pollock is marvellously ambiguous, although we can see that Lizzie probably was guilty. The playwright simply lets her characters behave as they might have done on that fatal day, and prompts us to make up our own minds.

Although the principal characters in the scenario—Lizzie and the maid, Bridget—are supposed to be involved in a game of let's pretend, they emerge with more genuine human failings than any of the polemizing mouthpieces in Pollock's *One Tiger To A Hill* or the *Komagata Maru Incident*. The playwright, for a change, has given us a play about real people instead of bombarding us with propaganda in her efforts to dramatize a pet theme.

Pollock shows us that Lizzie had motive and opportunity to commit the crime, while various circumstances made it almost impossible for an outsider to be involved. Lizzie wanted freedom and happiness, and for a 33-year-old spinster in 1892, these could only be bought with money.

She couldn't take a job, no gentlewoman of her day could, and because her father planned to will his money away from his children, she stood to lose the only compensation available for a woman without a husband in 19th century New England. If her father had left a will, Lizzie would have been in the absolute power of whoever in her family (probably her stepmother) inherited the money, and Lizzie absolutely detested her family.

Lizzie killed her parents and got away with it because a 19th century all-male jury couldn't bring themselves to accept her—a "Christian woman, the equal of your wife and mine," as one defence lawyer put it—as an agent of brutal murder. Her story is still of concern to us and Pollock's play is significant because it goes beyond mere study of an individual pathology to show us why the women's movement of the 20th century was inevitable.

The Theatre 3 production has a few blocking and lighting problems, and the show could be improved by cutting about 15 minutes worth of talk out of the second act. The role switching between Lizzie and Bridget in the early part of the first act takes some getting used to, while the mysterious smile and angular moves of Janet Daverne, the actress playing the "real" Lizzie, are somewhat stylized and untruthful.

However, Judith Mabey is constantly convincing as the actress who recreates Lizzie's movements on the day of the murders. She displays a wide emotional range and establishes easily identifiable relationships with each of the characters in Lizzie's story. The other actors are solid in supporting roles.

Director Keith Digby has wisely avoided any attempt to dramatize the actual murders and the staging strikes a nice balance between the realistic and the ritualistic. There's an austere, empty, uninviting ambience about the set, appropriate for a house where the wretched inhabitants hardly ever spoke a civil word to one another. . . .

Brian Brennan, *Calgary Herald*, 14 March 1980*

• •

. . . Sharon Pollock is interested in violence . . . but her concern is with violence to the heart and mind. Her wonderful new play, *Blood Relations*, may be inspired by the Lizzie Borden case, but she has absolutely no interest in going the Grand Guignol route and leaving the stage knee-deep in blood.

Her real concern—and it's a concern reflected in virtually all her writing—is with the spiritually maimed. . . .

Blood Relations is something special. It's indicative of Sharon Pollock's immense gifts as a playwright that she has been able to take a gruesome 19th century murder and use it as the basis for an exquisitely beautiful evening of pure theatre.

This play, which received a splendid premiere last week at Edmonton's Theatre 3, is presumably Pollock's answer to those who believe she has no poetry in her soul. Furthermore, in response to those who have accused her on occasion of sacrificing character to polemic, she has woven a psychological study so subtle and penetrating that it sets off endless reverberations in performance.

Did Lizzie or didn't she? The question is posed at the beginning. It lingers, wraith-like, at the end. The play teases and ultimately haunts, shifting and shimmering like a kaleidoscope.

To examine the Lizzie Borden legend, Pollock employs an unusual and sophisticated variation on the old device of the play within a play. The real time is 1902, which is ten years after the murders. We meet the older, acquitted Lizzie and an actress friend. There are hints that they are more than just friends—intriguing hints—but there are also signs of a void sustained by the uncertainty as to what really happened that terrible August day in 1892.

Gently, and hypnotically, past and present start to merge as the two become participants in a reenactment of a 10-year-old scenario, with the actress assuming the identity of Lizzie while the real-life Lizzie becomes a household maid named Bridget.

Gradually, the tableau of household life starts to unfold. The household is bound by fear and hostility, with an uncomprehending father preparing to will away his fortune to an avaricious stepmother and her grasping brother, condemning Lizzie and her sister to perpetual dependence and servitude.

There's no doubt that Pollock, the socially concerned dramatist, is creating a microcosm for a wider North American society of the day. Lizzie Borden is unmarried and likely to remain so. The times do not allow her to go into the world and seek her fortune. She yearns for the happiness and independence which should be the natural claim of anyone, but she sees her options dissolving and her life constricting.

However, Pollock's play goes far beyond glib rhetoric. In this Edmonton production, staged with delicate perception by Theatre 3 artistic director Keith Digby, *Blood Relations* casts a hypnotic spell, achieving a curious dreamlike dimension—Pollock uses the expression "dream thesis" in her script—which hovers tantalizingly between basic realism and elusive fantasy.

The purpose seems not so much to set down the specific as to evoke feeling, texture, the emotional climate, the undercurrent of pain. Members of the Theatre 3 cast rise to the challenge remarkably well—in particular a stunning actress named Judith Mabey, who gives a powerful utterance to Lizzie Borden's conflicts, tracing with infinite care the terrible dilemma of a spinster daughter whose horizons are limited, whose destiny is determined by chauvinistic strictures of the day, whose intelligence can recognize yet not easily define those strictures.

Mabey receives fine support from other members of the cast—Janet Daverne, Barbara Reese, Paddy English, Charles Kerr, Brian Atkins and Wendell Smith—but her real debt is to the play itself for offering such a magnificent challenge. . . .

Jamie Portman, *Calgary Herald*, 20 March 1980*

• •

. . . Blood Relations . . . shows inventiveness and a good deal of subtlety, and if the play does not quite work in the way the playwright tries to make it work, it remains forceful and impressive in reading and in the theatre. Her central character is the infamous Lizzie Borden, and one of the questions the play opens is that which preys on the mind of Emma, her elder sister: did she or didn't she? Lizzie, despite the children's rhyme, was acquitted at her trial. The play toys with ambiguity on this score, but leaves us without much doubt that indeed she did; we are led to understand how the murder comes to be a necessary act, a release, for Lizzie and the people around her. The issue of motives is complicated by the dramatization, within the frame of the play, of the story of Lizzie and her parents: her life is impersonated by an actress, schooled by Lizzie herself, ten years after the time of the murders. The reality of the events we see on stage is therefore always subject to our sense that they are doubly a fiction—inventions, rationalizations, wishes, nightmares. This is hardly an original technical trick, of course, and its danger, which Pollock largely avoids, is that its cleverness obtrudes itself and simply parades, which is boring. The only place where the play becomes somewhat pretentious on this score is, unfortunately, at the end, as if the playwright could not quite trust the suggestions the action has made, and wants the characters to say everything once more: the text seems about two pages too long.

Lizzie, in either manifestation of herself, is attractive because she is an ironist, involved in the action and yet outside it, with a mocking analytical awareness of the limits imposed on her by sex, money, and social class, against which she struggles, and which arouse her passionate disgust. She interests us as a character first; her trap is in some way meant to be representative of the traps of dependence in general, but she is not that weary thing, a typical figure. When her speech approaches thematic generalization, it is safely grounded in her own force and intelligence; she is not often made to say things that we cannot believe arise from her own characteristics, so that she is importantly speaking from herself when she says of her father: "I thought you could talk to him, really talk to him, make him understand that we're people. *Individual people*, and we live separate lives, and his will should make it possible for us to do that." Here, stated as clearly as we could wish, is "the problem of the family"; it is to Sharon Pollock's credit that in context the speech does not sound like a slogan.

The play is also a kind of confession that the problem is largely over and done with, at least socially and legally, and probably to some extent psychologically too. The family, if not dead, is not what it once was. The play is set in 1892 and 1902, and the production photographs remind us that the costumes and settings are those of the interiors of Chekhov, and of those formidable axe-men Ibsen and Strindberg. Lizzie's situation is of her time: today she would be gone. Ghosts of the older dramatists haunt the play, whether or not Pollock was making conscious reference to them; *Miss Julie* in particular seems to lie somewhere behind certain parts of it, though the peculiar sexual pathology of the earlier play has no place here. If Lizzie found herself in Julie's place, she'd finish Jean off with the razor, and good for her. Both women insist that they are not cowards, but Lizzie Borden is a survivor.

John H. Astington, *UTQ*, 51 (1981-82), 374-75

• •

Pollock   I find newspaper reviews very strange. Did you read any of the male reviewers on *Blood Relations*? Well, they go to some trouble to state that this play has nothing to do with feminism. Some of them see it as a mystery play. Others see it as *maybe* a sociological or psychological study of a woman. It's only women who see it making a statement about women today. *Of course* it says something about women today. It says something about me today, things that I've felt. It's just another example of the review revealing either the poverty of imagination or the lack of sensitivity of the man who's reviewing it.

Wallace   Why, in *Blood Relations*, did you choose to use the flashback structure in which Lizzy and the Actress change parts? You're obviously wanting the audience to consider more than Lizzy Borden's history.

Pollock   I'm saying that all of us are capable of murder given the right situation. The structure is a way of maintaining the ambiguity. You see, I don't say that Lizzy did it. The defence says she's not guilty. The Actress says she's guilty.

Wallace   You mean because the Actress plays Lizzy revealing the facts of what happened, everything is suspect?

Pollock   That's right. One of the things I am trying to do is to somehow make 1902 as important as 1892. This will preserve the ambiguity, and make us remember that it is always the Actress who's feeling her way through Lizzy's story.
   One of the original questions that I asked myself was, why does Lizzy play the game? In the original Theatre Three production, the reason Lizzy played the game was that there was something that could not be said. There was no right answer for her to give the Actress when the Actress asks, did you do it? I want that to be clear from the Actress's line: "If you say yes, I'd be horrified; if you say no, I'd be disappointed." In fact, if Lizzy actually said, yes I did do it, I'm sure the Actress would say to her, no, no, tell me, you can tell me, I mean, *really* tell me. Lizzy *can't* say yes. If she said no, then the Actress would say the same thing: you can tell me, tell me, *really* tell me. Lizzy knows she cannot answer

the question. The whole play was an effort on Miss Lizzy's part to bring the Actress closer to her. It made her draw away once she had that information. Now the way it was done at the National Arts Centre, with very little change in the lines, Miss Lizzy played the game not out of an effort to bring the Actress closer, but out of impatience—you know, you keep asking me that and asking me that; all right, you want to know what it's like, I'll show you what it's like. Here. You live it. You feel what it was like to live in this God damned house. Maybe then you'll stop asking me that fucking question. It was much more of an angry reaction, even malicious. I found that more interesting than the way we had done it first time around.

Wallace How based in fact is the relationship between Lizzy and the Actress?

Pollock In anything I've ever read, she did have an ongoing relationship with an actress called Nance O'Neill who worked out of Boston. Anything I've ever read has also gone to great pains to deny it had even the slightest hint of homosexuality about it, which, given the edition date [of] the books I read and the background of the people who have written them, is a perfectly natural response.

Robert Wallace, interview with Sharon Pollock, *The Work*, pp. 123-24

• •

It isn't easy to write an absolutely bloodless drama about the Lizzie Borden case, but that's what Sharon Pollock has done in *Blood Relations*, her new play at the Hudson Guild. Not only does Miss Pollock shroud her story's murderous payoff in a blackout, but she also precedes it with two hours of exceedingly anemic and repetitive talk. A blue pencil wouldn't be enough to edit this script—it's a job that cries out for an ax.

Miss Pollock is a prize-winning playwright in her native Canada—a fact that may say more about Canadian theater than the quality of her work. Her last play seen in New York, *One Tiger to a Hill* (at the Manhattan Theater Club two seasons ago), was a clumsy prison-hostage melodrama in which platitudinous polemics and cardboard characters managed to muffle any gunfire. *Blood Relations* is in the same vein. Looking back at the Borden case, Miss Pollock has come up with the thesis that Lizzie was a feminist before her time—a strong-minded, justice-seeking rebel at war against the stultifying Victorian society of Fall River, Mass. The author hammers this point home with relentless preaching that is conveyed by colorless language and primitive agitprop tableaux.

The overriding message isn't new in any case: Agnes de Mille, for one, postulated a similar view of Lizzie in both print and dance four decades ago. Yet Miss

Pollock does have an additional twist. Noting that her heroine became a close friend of a Boston stock company actress in the years following her acquittal, the playwright has decided to decree that Lizzie was a lesbian as well as a feminist. The thematic or dramatic value of this bombshell, however, is far from clear. No sooner is the heroine's homosexuality announced in the first scene than it is shoved into a closet for the rest of the evening.

That first scene reveals Lizzie (Jennifer Sternberg) and the actress (Marti Maraden) at the height of their presumed liaison in 1902. But most of *Blood Relations* is a play within a play, in which the two women and the supporting cast journey back a decade for a slow-motion re-enactment of the fateful events leading to the murders. For these flashback sequences, the actress plays Lizzie, and Lizzie, inexplicably, plays the Bordens' Irish maid. It's a precious theatrical gimmick that adds little beyond confusion. As the playwright cross cuts between 1902 and 1892—with a few cryptic stopovers at the 1893 trial—Miss Sternberg's "real" Lizzie must frequently hover awkwardly in the shadows of the Borden parlor while Miss Maraden's actress impersonates her center stage.

The other participants in the 1892 segments include Lizzie's various family members, most of whom are one-note melodramatic villains. The heroine chews them all out regularly, and no wonder. Her father (Maurice Copeland) is given to such pronouncements as "a woman is like a horse" and is fond of decapitating birds. Her stepmother (Sloane Shelton) is a "fat cow" who combines the worst personality traits of Aunt Pittypat and the Wicked Witch of the West.

Under the less-than-fluid direction of David Kerry Heefner, the cast does a competent job, with Miss Shelton even managing to extract a few laughs from the evil Mrs. Borden. Miss Maraden and Miss Sternberg both work hard, trying to pump life into the heroine by playing her as if she were Hedda Gabler at full tilt. While we never learn for sure whether Lizzie hacked her parents to death, there's no question that these talented actresses are done in by a playwright practicing some lethal hackwork of her own.

Frank Rich, *NYT*, 16 February 1983

• •

Every country has its playwrights of conscience, artists whose work is more notable for its moral and political themes than for its aesthetics. In English theatre the leading playwright of conscience is still John Osborne whose *Look Back in Anger* and *The Entertainer* have proven to be works of enduring value beyond their initial shock as sociological studies. In American theatre, it is Arthur Miller who has most frequently written (sometimes well, more often ploddingly) with the mind of a moralist. In Canadian theatre, there have been few plays produced dealing with human rights and social issues: about one such play every five years seems to be the average judging by David Freeman's *Creeps* (1971) and John Herbert's *Fortune and Men's Eyes* (1967). It is hardly surprising, therefore, in a country where social criticism is regarded as a sign of radicalism, that Sharon Pollock has managed to become Canada's pre-eminent playwright of conscience—for the author of *Walsh*, *The Komagata Maru Incident*, *One Tiger to a Hill*, and *Blood Relations* (which recently received its American premiere in a handsome production by the Hudson Theatre Guild in New York) is determined to make audiences think more about the issues she raises in her plays than about the plays themselves. . . .

Blood Relations is Pollock's slickest and most commercially successful play, having brought the author earnings of around $50,000 to date. Yet apart from suggesting a feminist interpretation of the famous Lizzie Borden murder trial (that is, that Lizzie was a 20th-century woman—and a lesbian—trapped inside the 19th-century lifestyle of Fall River, Mass.), the play appears to have no moral concerns or ideas. One could easily go away with the impression that it's understandable for a woman to be absolutely ruthless—to the point of killing her father and stepmother—in order to protect her property rights and secure an inheritance. . . .

Blood Relations is the second Pollock play to reach New York in the last year (preceded by a Manhattan Theatre Club production of *One Tiger to a Hill*). Critical reaction was lukewarm ("Miss Pollock is a prize-winning playwright in her native Canada—a fact that may say more about Canadian theatre than the quality of her work," said the *New York Times*), but public response gave the play a good run in the 142-seat theatre. Hudson Theatre Guild is an off-Broadway company with high production standards: the set design by Ron Placzek was of Broadway calibre; the performances of Marti Maraden as Lizzie Borden and Sloane Shelton as Abigail Borden were of definitive perfection. . . .

It would be a mistake to attribute *Blood Relations*' appeal to American audiences to its Massachusetts setting and its roots in criminal legend. The play has no distinctive geographical or sociological feel to it. . . .If anything, it is the *feminist* stance of *Blood Relations* that makes it popular wherever it plays and that allows it to cross cultural borders with ease. The audience I saw at the Hudson Theatre Guild production was composed almost entirely of middle-aged women, many of whom could identify with the sympathetic character that Pollock has created in her Lizzie Borden and go away mulling over the play's chief contention: "Lizzie did what thousands of women dream of doing . . . either you kill that which oppresses you or else consent to letting it kill you. A woman's life leads either to murder or to suicide—real or symbolic."

Anyone familiar with Pollock's family background—the alcoholism and eventual suicide of her mother, the rigid masculine code of her wealthy and socially prominent father (described in Dalton Camp's political memoir, *Gentlemen,*

Players and Politicians, as always looking "like Clark Gable about to meet Carole Lombard at the Ritz, as though the world were his oyster and he could win at anyone's game") will find many instances in *Blood Relations* where she has drawn on real-life saga, though with quite a different end. It is as if the playwright were revenging her mother's death and, in the process, exposing the patriarchal world that makes such a desperate choice—murder or suicide—the *only* one for some women. Almost all of Pollock's work can be seen as a lifelong dramatic dialogue with her "establishment" father, and *Blood Relations* is her most revealing in this regard, though it is too imbalanced to be considered her best play. . . .

John Hofsess, *Books in Canada*, 12 (April 1983), 3-4

• •

. . . Lizzie's character and her relationship with her father are beautifully drawn. She is a spirited spinster who does not fit into the social role approved for women, and her loving relationship with her father is blighted by his sense of obligation to make her conform to the social ideal. Lizzie and her stepmother despise each other. Her sister Emma, a colorless good girl who brought Lizzie up after their mother's death, mediates between Lizzie and the older Bordens. On the day of the murders, the stepmother and her brother have persuaded Lizzie's father to alter his financial affairs to keep Lizzie and Emma financially dependent even after his death. The day is as stifling as Lizzie's life, and Emma withdraws from the heat and the conflict into the country. Lizzie's murders of the stepmother she hates and the father she loves are both convincingly motivated.

Drawn into a persuasive portrayal of a murderess, we are then jolted back into the recognition that this is the actress's creation, and the question "Did she or didn't she?" remains technically unanswered, though the play unambiguously suggests that she did. The device of the actress taking Lizzie's part while Lizzie looks on in a neutral role is illuminated in the closing sequence when Lizzie reminds Emma, "It was you brought me up. . . .Did you ever stop and think that I was like a puppet, your puppet . . . me saying all the things you felt like saying, me doing all the things you felt like doing. . . ." The actress taking Lizzie's place is a metaphor for Lizzie taking Emma's, which adds depth to the psychological, social, and artistic implications of the play, as well as distancing us from the horror of the deed enough to permit an objective view of Lizzie's character. The strength of the play's appeal has been proved by numerous productions and its merits acknowledged by the first Governor General's Award for drama.

Susan Stone-Blackburn, *Canadian Literature*, 96 (Spring 1983), 131

• •

SHARON POLLOCK

Generations

First produced by Alberta Theatre Projects
at the Canmore Opera House, 28 October 1980

Directed by Mark Schoenberg
Set and Costume Design by Richard Roberts

Cast

Charlie Running Dog	Stephen Walsh
Old Eddy Nurlin	Stephen Hair
David Nurlin	Brian Paul
Margaret Nurlin	Doris Chillcott
Alfred Nurlin	Bob Aaron
Young Eddy Nurlin	Ric Reid
Bonnie	Marlane O'Brien

Generations is Sharon Pollock's first attempt at dramatizing the special relationship that exists between man and the land on the Prairies.

Like many plays of its kind, it's a disappointment. The experience of the empty land, as many CanLit students are fond of pointing out, is something that theatre—because of its very nature—finds it difficult to deal with.

Generations, which was adapted from a radio play, might work as a motion picture or made-for-television drama. It might even work as a short story or novel. But it doesn't work very well as theatre—especially not in the Canmore Opera House, where Pollock's sweeping landscape has been reduced to the Munchkin Land proportions of the province she describes so wittily in the play.

Wit, by the way, is something I don't recall associating with Pollock's playwriting in the past. Usually, she has a serious purpose when she writes a play—whether it be to show how inefficient the prison system is, or how poorly we treat our non-Caucasian neighbours—and there is little room in her theatrical heart for levity.

But there's plenty of it in this show. The anti-Trudeau jokes seem so timely, one would have sworn Pollock sat down to write the play after watching Lougheed on television the other night.

It's a weak production. Designer Richard Roberts, who usually achieves miraculous results working in severely confining spaces, has failed in his attempt to give a striking visual dimension to the great symbols that express a relationship between man and his environment in this play.

If you sat at the back of the hall and squinted your eyes, you might believe the designer's blue back-drop as a depiction of the Prairie sky. But not while it is picking up shadows from other parts of the set. Even in the land of make-believe, we expect a certain amount of consistency. . . .

The other main problem with the production is the casting. One youthful actor, Stephen Walsh, has been heavily made up and saddled with a funny accent to do an Old Indian role that might have been written for Chief Dan George.

Also heavily made up, to look like a 77-year old man, is Calgary actor Stephen Hair. He isn't very convincing, either.

Hair, as many local theatregoers will know, is a talented and versatile character actor, with a special gift for playing stylized and caricature roles. Naturalistic playing is not his forte.

He is wrong for the part, even if it does give him an opportunity to stretch. Only an older and more experienced actor could handle this difficult role.

The central figure in the play is David Nurlin (played by Brian Paul), a third generation farmer in southern Alberta, whose older brother has left home to become a lawyer. The stay-at-home brother has inherited the farm, and the play deals with his coming to terms with whatever destiny made him become a farmer rather than a lawyer or a politician.

The young farmer is more articulate than his lawyer brother, and that strikes a dissonant note in the play. He claims to be stupid, but it's hard to believe him. He would be more credible as a writer or as a student.

That's what happens when a playwright uses a certain character to express ideological exhortations and moral judgments. One can almost hear the playwright in the background, prompting and giving cues.

Actor Paul does what's required of him, I expect. He acts suitably artless and lovable when discoursing on such mundane concerns as beer drinking and replacing gasoline filters, then explodes abruptly on cue when the playwright calls for him to sermonize self-righteously. He can hardly do otherwise. He is ruled by the script.

The mother, played rather stridently by Doris Chillcott, also expounds on cue. We have to believe she chose rural deprivation and a husband over urban living and loneliness. The script says so.

The father, played by Bob Aarron, the lawyer, played by Ric Reid, and the young farmer's fiancée, played by Marlane O'Brien, seem more authentic somehow. They possess a momentum of their own, and don't sound as if they're speaking in clichés or rhetoric imposed on them by somebody with ideas.

They dramatize the conflict between traditional and contemporary values, between urban and rural priorities, in resonant tones. Their problems are universal and they supply a solid core for what could be a stimulating work of creation.

But Pollock's play is not that creation. Not the way it's been staged, at any rate.

Brian Brennan, *Calgary Herald*, 1 November 1980*

• •

"I feel a power out there," says young farmer David Nurlin in *Generations*, which opened last night at Tarragon Theatre. He is talking about the prairie land, not oil. Alberta farmers, as depicted by playwright Sharon Pollock, continue to feel a connection to mother earth, a connection so strong that it makes their hard work and never-ending penury worthwhile. This may very well be true, but there is something awfully familiar about the way the three generations of farming Nurlins interact on the subject of hanging in, or selling out.

Generations is one of those slight plays which, while hampered by clichés and by stock characterizations, has some true moments that dignify ordinary lives. It should not be faulted for being small; it has to hum along like the power lines of the set, occasionally crackling and illuminating deeper conflicts, to work at all. When it does succeed unequivocally, however, it is due to the performances rather than the writing. The first half of the play seems to be over in 10 minutes. It is mostly concerned with exposition; the structure of *Generations* consequently feels unbalanced.

Old Eddy, played with humor and grit by Ed McNamara, built up his farm in the early 1900s, passing it on to his only surviving son, Alfred. Alfred (Colin Fox), whose ambitions resided elsewhere, nevertheless carried on the work. One of *his* sons, Eddy (Matt Walsh), has left the farm to become a city lawyer, and on this particular weekend, comes home to ask for money. He wants to start his own firm, and therefore conspires to convince his brother David (Stephen Ouimette) that farming is a waste of time. He thinks that he could get Old Eddy and Alfred to sell a section of the land if he could show that David was not prepared to carry on the work.

David's girl friend, Bonnie (Jacquie Presly) seems to be on Eddy's side. A schoolteacher armed with her own set of platitudes—"you have *choices* David"—Bonnie has "identity problems." According to grandpa, she lacks the backbone to be a farmer's wife; she also seems to lack courage, to be a spoiler by nature. One of the best scenes of the play, apart from every scene with Ed McNamara, who shines in his role, has David's mother (Charmion King) talking to the young Bonnie. Miss King is completely believable as the hard-working, cheerful woman who has made peace with the conditions of her existence, and she makes the self-righteous young Bonnie, with her fashionable questions, her hard-hearted dismissals, look superficial. The young people in this play, with the exception of David, whose contact with the soil somewhat roots him, are all lightweights. Ouimette has some good duelling moments with Miss Presly, but the two have a hard time with some of their more artificial lines.

On top of these family conflicts, there is an underdeveloped plot concerned with the Indians' ownership of water rights. Charlie Running Dog (Jack Van Evera), an 81-year-old, represents his people. Again, there are moments here between Old Eddy and Charlie Running Dog that are heart-warming and funny. As directed by Cecil O'Neal, the staging of *Generations* is imaginative; it makes use of the space in an unconventional way, including as it does the stairs and the entrance ramp. The set, by Pat Flood, is refreshingly bright. We may be stuck once again in a farm kitchen, but this is a cared-for kitchen. And the lighting is evocative of the landscape.

The artificiality of some of the performances is mostly due to the script, which errs on the side of preaching, and the lack of theatrical sparkle has to do with the small viewpoint of the author. *Generations*, consisting as it does of evocative vignettes, would seem more suited to television than to the stage. It lets you in slowly, doesn't let you down, but it doesn't exactly take you away either.

Carole Corbeil, *Globe and Mail*, 3 April 1981

• •

Tarragon Theatre's *Generations*, by the Calgary-based playwright Sharon Pollock, is fat with plots and sub-plots.

1) The Prairie family itself. Grandpa (Ed McNamara), Mom (Charmion King) and Dad (Colin Fox), and young David (Stephen Ouimette). They have farmed the land since 1908 . . . and the men share a visceral attachment to their rolling acres of corn. But now there is a drought and trouble with the Indians and the feds—I can't tell you exactly what kind of trouble because it is never explained. David simply goes off to create some aggro with a neighbor and break up a meeting, while Grandpa goes to the hills to consult with an aged Indian sage.

2) Sibling rivalry. David's brother Eddie (Matt Walsh) is a lawyer who got off the land and likes it that way. Bonnie (Jacquie Presly) is David's fiancée and she's mad at Eddie because she thinks he has left his brother to rot on the land. Eddie wants Dad to sell some of his precious acres to stake his new law firm.

3) Women's lib. Bonnie looks at Mom slaving away in 90-degree heat over an even hotter stove and says "no way". She's a teacher and she wants her own life. But she also wants David, who will expect her to be Mom.

Now, these elements are not original in terms of ideas, but if they were organized skilfully, they might be very revealing of the characters involved, not to mention the character of the region. But organization is Pollock's weakest point as a playwright. Her play, *Blood Relations*, which is now playing at Ottawa's National Arts Centre, seems almost entirely superficial up to the last scene, when at last an intriguing and plausible idea about the murder is offered. In *Generations*, she is equally vague about construction, failing to provide the necessary overarching theme, the most important and wide-ranging conflict that will make all the different parts of her play come together and make dramatic sense.

As it is in *Generations*, Pollock just presents her ideas and then leaves them where they were. But in dramatic terms, it isn't enough to just suggest things. The audience wants to know where the suggestion leads, or what action it prompts or thwarts, or why it was made. The drought? Give us the details of what it threatens immediately. What is the Indians' role? What are the feds up to? Why doesn't she let Dad sell a few acres for Eddie; in other words, make Dad care enough for Eddie that he will betray his own father and his other son David?

Why is Mom so secure in her role as doormat? Wouldn't it be more interesting if Mom had an inner life rather than just a stove life? Why not make Grandpa so desperate about his land that the mere thought some of it could be sold under him leads him to murder?

I'm almost tempted to call *Generations* a lazy play because so much is started and so little finished. But that would be unfair. It is probably more accurate to call it a muddled play. Pollock needs help. She has to get committed to the people in her plays before she gets committed to the plots. What is missing from *Generations*, and from *Blood Relations*, is surprise and spontaneity, the risky sense of human life.

Cecil O'Neal's production, which I saw in a preview at Tarragon Theatre, often seems to emphasize the play's flaws. Pat Flood has designed the small theatre as a prairie environment, the walls covered with canvas painted as blue sky with fleecy clouds, the playing space stretching up the auditorium's steps to the entrance of the theatre.

If the idea was to evoke the sense of infinite space, forget it. Watching a couple of actors crouched on the stairs, surrounded by the audience, does not give the impression of a vast prairie but of a conversation on a crowded city fire escape.

Gina Mallet, *Toronto Star*, 3 April 1981

• •

Wallace Do you feel pigeon-holed as a "social" playwright?

Pollock Yes, I feel pigeon-holed. When *Generations* was produced in Calgary, for example, the reviewer for the *Herald* said something about Pollock attempting to amuse and we aren't used to her doing this. I believe there are lots of funny things in my plays. This reviewer seemed to resent the fact that he had never noticed them before. He was saying, don't surprise me, please. With *Blood Relations* people who don't like social comment plays seem to think that I've "moved" considerably and I'm finally beginning to concentrate on character, that I've learned a few character traits and maybe they can expect some "better" work from me. I get a little nervous. I don't want to be pigeon-holed, but I don't want to be patted on the back as if I've finally moved on to become a real playwright because I'm writing about real people as opposed to the issues that I used to deal with, either.

Wallace I read that you started writing plays about historical subjects because you were interested in expanding your own consciousness about particular historical events. You also said that you hoped to expand the audience's consciousness about them as well. Is this still true with plays like *Generations* that deal with fictional characters?

Pollock Yes. If I stopped wanting to do that I don't know what I'd be writing for. With *Generations* I'm still dealing with something that concerns me. I don't know, for example, whose side I'm on in that play. Part of me relates to Margaret and part of me is with Bonnie. I don't know whether there's worse things than being lonely or not. I have a real interest in people who are willing sacrifices. On the other hand, it can't be a sacrifice to the person who does it. That's what I'm trying to deal with in that play: when a society no longer has those kinds of people who realize what it is they're doing and still do it willingly, that society is doomed.

Wallace Hitherto, your plays have dealt more with polarities, with blacks and whites. In *Generations* we've got a number of people who suffer ambiguities. I think this is particularly true of Bonnie. Are you ambivalent about what Bonnie is saying?

Pollock I don't know if I'm ambivalent. I've always had trouble writing women. Bonnie is always starting things and never finishing them. She probably has more dot, dot, dots after her speeches than anybody I've ever written; she can't finish what she starts to say. At the end of the play, David asks her, who are you? And she says, I don't know who I am. I believe she's a person in the process of change.

Wallace Margo Dunn suggests that the progress of your plays reveals a growing feminism. Certainly in *Blood Relations* there is a greater focus on the oppression of women. Do *Generations* and *Blood Relations* represent a growing feminist attitude?

Pollock If I took two steps backwards and looked at the plays I would have to agree with Margo. On the other hand, I don't write them with that in mind. I mean, I've read how my early plays represent a rebellion against authority figures and my ambivalent feelings towards my father. I always thought I was extremely close to him! I do think I'm gradually moving into myself, however. Certainly I feel stronger and more able to write plays involving women, or to write from the point of view of women, or with a woman as a major character. I never for a moment thought of writing *Generations* from the woman's point of view because, after all, Margaret is a willing sacrifice. There's something bigger worth being a part of, which is what David says too. . . .

Wallace One of the things I've consistently appreciated in your work is the way in which you place naturalistic scenes within a highly imaginative structure. *Generations*, being more straightforwardly naturalistic, is the exception here.

Pollock I had a lot of problems with *Generations*. We went through that whole thing where you paint rooms, you build the set, you take it down. If I had had my druthers, if I could have found a way to do it, the play would not have happened in the house. There would be no kitchen because once you're in the kitchen, you've got all the stinking things you've got to do in the kitchen, like cook the food. If I could have placed the characters into space, into that field with the prairie going on forever, I think I could have created a more interesting piece. It's a play that could have been much better if during the early stages I had had a designer who was interested in the kind of work I do. You can't put the Prairies on the stage so you have to find another way of doing the outside scenes. Yet you've got the highly naturalistic inside scenes. I don't want to mime it all because then we get into the NDWT style which I don't like, or the Passe Muraille technique: now you're the tractor; I don't want that. It was such a problem for me that I gave up. I simply did it, eh? Maybe someday there'll be a director who'll come up with an idea of how to do it in that kitchen and not feel bound by Naturalism. . . .

Robert Wallace, interview with Sharon Pollock, *The Work*, pp. 117-20

• •

Generations is a naturalistic treatment of a day in the life of three generations of an Alberta farm family. "THE LAND," Pollock directs, "is a character revealed by the light and shadow it throws on the Nurlins' lives." The play depicts the characters' attitudes toward the land and the conflicts among them, activated by three different plot devices. Despite the interest of its character relationships, the play lacks structure and satisfying resolution. Any urgency in the plot derives from the pressing need to solve the problem of lack of water on the farm, yet no solution is provided except the temporary one of rainfall. The relationship between Old Eddy and an ancient Indian is absorbing but irrelevant to the outcome. The same is true of the relationship between Old Eddy and his son, and one grandson's interest in the other's fiancée. Such resolution as the play offers comes in the younger grandson, David's, affirmation of devotion to the land, a devotion that is tested by all three plot devices. Scene by scene, the play is a convincing and entertaining portrayal of farm life, but as a total work, it is weakened by David's lack of weight: his affirmation is not enough to pull together all the play's various strands of interest.

Susan Stone-Blackburn, *Canadian Literature*, 96 (Spring 1983), 130

• •

MARGARET HOLLINGSWORTH

Ever Loving

First produced at the Belfry Theatre,
Victoria, 13 November 1980

Directed by James Roy
Set and Costume Design by William Heslup
Lighting Design by Bryan Francis

Cast

James Michael O'Sullivan	William Dunlop
Luce Maria Marini	Angela Fusco
Ruth Watson	Alison MacLeod
Chuck Malecarne	Blaine Parker
Paul Tomachuk	Robert Seale
Diana Manning	Donna Carroll White

Margaret Hollingsworth has been called a "playwright of potential" for the last six years, ever since the New Play Centre presented a one-act play of hers (*Operators*) as part of its du Maurier Festival.

That potential has now matured, and as a result, Victoria's Belfry Theatre has a significant show on its hands. The play is called *Ever Loving*, a Hollingsworth script that gives us two decades in the life of three war brides.

Hollingsworth has achieved something quite remarkable—a play about romance and sentimentality that does not indulge in romantic, sentimental clichés. The result is a profoundly moving evening.

We meet Diana, a no-nonsense British girl married to Paul, son of a Ukrainian farmer from Saskatchewan; Ruth, a simple Scottish girl married to James, a Hamilton millworker; and Luce, an upper-crust Italian girl married to Chuck, an aspiring musician from Halifax.

The play begins in a piano bar where Chuck and Luce are providing the music while Paul, James, Diana and Ruth enjoy a reunion get-together. Through a series of flashbacks, Hollingsworth traces the events—the first meetings, the courtships, the emigration and the subsequent traumas—that have shaped their lives. Skilful use of music spanning the 20 years provides a consistently effective backdrop to the story.

Hollingsworth has woven a richly-textured tapestry. She shows us the contrast between the fantasies the three couples had and the realities of their lives.

Without ever resorting to preaching, she also touches on such sensitive issues as national identity and male-female role-playing within the marital structure.

Although the flashback technique creates some initial difficulty in establishing the thrust of the play, the problem is overcome quickly. By the end of the evening, one is profoundly moved by the rich, three-dimensional scope Hollingsworth has brought to her characters and by her sensitivity to their situations.

For that, much credit must also go to new Belfry artistic director James Roy for the extraordinary production he has assembled. Hollingsworth's script is a gem. Roy's production provides the ideal setting. . . .

Bob Allen, *Vancouver Province*, 23 November 1980*

• •

It is said that virtue is its own reward.

Unfortunately the same cannot be said for virtuosity.

Six talented performers—two of them exceptionally so—poured their considerable talent down the drain this week at the Centaur Theatre in *Ever Loving*.

The problem is that author Margaret Hollingsworth never finished *Ever Loving*.

As it stands, it's hardly more than a set of rhythmically repetitive improvisations.

The fact that they are good improvisations makes the show seem like fake Theatre Passe Muraille.

The players are cast as three Canadian soldiers and their European war brides and the play takes place between 1938 and 1979.

The time references are muddy, however. The action shifts backward and forward, presumably to challenge our attention.

Like a vanity mirror, *Ever Loving* breaks a single image into three, but without enough variation to stimulate for two and a half hours.

There are no real frictions between the country and its immigrants, partly because there are no Canadians (other than the husbands) to be contended with. It would also appear that no French Canadians fought in Europe, which is a more serious oversight.

What references there are to in-laws and neighbours seems artificial—like personal details in a Xeroxed letter.

Because the writer failed to bring the specific conflicts faced by war brides into focus (the presumed reason for creating such a play) what is left is the story of three couples with marital difficulties.

If Centaur subscribers get a *déja-vu* sensation, it may be because Miro Kinch's set is reminiscent of the one seen in *Waiting for the Parade*—another war saga.

Still, the lustrous performances make the evening tolerable, even though the dialogue—with rare exceptions—is flat as a plate.

Maja Ardal as the Scottish Ruth Watson evolves from an apple-cheeked, star-struck cannery worker to a drawn and grey brood mare, lumpy from the wear and tear of raising six children. It is an irresistible performance.

Ardal created the role (under the direction of Pam Brighton) when the play was originally workshopped in Toronto, so it is no wonder that she is master of the situation.

Linda Sorgini—who has done stunning work in French theatre here and is making her Montreal debut in English—is adorable (and adorably irritating) as the somewhat snobbish Luce Maria Marini, who thought her ticket to Canada was a ticket to stardom.

Her clowning rendition of *I'll Never Smile Again* and a vignette that finds her a broadcaster on ethnic radio are unforgettable.

Michael Rudder does some fine work as Chuck (read: Chump) Malecarne although the role is pitifully narrow. His hotel night-spot singer routines are right on target.

Louise Martin and Morris Panych did honest work throughout and rose to brilliance in the play's re-union dinner finale.

There was no lack of nuance in Lee J. Campbell's work either, although he had a crude stereotype to work with. Jane Heyman directed.

Maureen Peterson, Montreal Gazette, 18 April 1981

• •

That much hackneyed and abused term Canadian content takes on a fresh and fundamental meaning in Margaret Hollingsworth's absorbing and intricate play, *Ever Loving*, which opened last night at the Neptune Theatre in Halifax.

This play is all about being Canadian. And if you think that it must, therefore, be a bit of a bore, you would be quite wrong.

Perhaps it takes an author who became a Canadian by choice, rather than by an accident of birth and geography, to examine the realities of Canadian-ness within the frame of interesting and eventful theatre.

Margaret Hollingsworth was not, herself, a war bride; she is too young for that experience. But her English background and subsequent post-emigrant experience of Canada and Canadiana has armed her with the knowledge of how three of these most vulnerable of all this country's mid-20th century immigrants, the war brides from Britain and a few other European countries who had married Canadian servicemen overseas, must have thought and felt on seeing this new, huge, strange, rather frightening and, in some cases no doubt, disappointing land.

The playwright—and this is her first major theatrical drama, although she has written numerous works for radio—uses six characters to instruct us in the nature of Canadian-ness, of dreams that never become reality, and of love (the sort that becomes, eventually, ever loving) which can be represented as the triumph of hope over experience . . .

Ever Loving follows the fortunes of these three couples; indeed, through Miss Hollingsworth's remarkable system of flashbacks and flash-flashbacks, we are whisked from Niagara Falls in Expo year to Halifax in 1945, then back to the war years in Britain and Italy, then half-forward to a train taking Ruth and Diana to Hamilton and Lethbridge respectively, and subsequently onwards to show how the three marriages are faring.

Under the skilled direction of Tom Kerr and with the expertise of the Neptune's technical staff, who must have been taxed to their utmost with the many intricate scene changes and the split-screen-like montage, *Ever Loving* is accomplished, or consummated, triumphantly.

Alison MacLeod gives an outstandingly fine portrayal of Ruth Watson, who runs the gamut from bright Scottish Land Army girl to anxious war bride who thinks Canada's fir trees house bears, to drab and unhappy, alcoholic and ever pregnant and home-sick wife, with a glamorous flash of Rita Hayworth thrown in. Her disintegration, abetted by her sullen, bitter husband (played excellently by Kim Coates), is moving.

Jill Frappier's Diana, always the contained Englishwoman who becomes a proud Canadian and learns to love the flat nothingness that is her Alberta home—and to cherish, despite his failings, her stodgy and erratic husband, played by Bill Carr—is a nicely paced and well-drawn performance.

Nicola Lipman, who seems to make a habit of playing spirited Italian women, gives the discontented Luce Maria—discontented with her lethargic Halifax husband and her Halifax home—suitable Italianate vivacity and anger as well as charm.

And Rick Fox gives the part of Chuck Malecarne, perhaps the least satisfactory of Miss Hollingsworth's characters, as much depth as he can; and provides, on the piano, the many tunes that serve to authenticate, musically, the periods through which the play passes.

Ever Loving's many costumes, also reflecting varied times and places, were designed by Maxine Graham and the effective lighting by Ted Roberts.

Basil Deakin, *Halifax Chronicle-Herald*, 27 February 1982

• •

. . . If anyone wants to see just how good theatre can be in Toronto, they must step right along to *Ever Loving*. Margaret Hollingsworth's play, which is the first production of Phoenix Theatre's new season, is a very simple account of three war brides' adjustment to post World War II Canada.

The story is familiar. But just when you think you have heard it all before, the disillusionment, the culture shock, the despair, you suddenly get a catch in your throat. Hollingsworth's voice is thin, but it's clear, and the emotions it evokes are profound because the actors invest them with a truth that is palpable.

These are people you know up there on stage. The charming and cool upper-class Diana married Paul, a stolid Ukrainian from Saskatchewan, thinking he was going into politics. When she steps off the train she is met by a farmer and led to the Alberta plains to live in a one-room shack with an outhouse. At least, however, Paul is rational. Bubbly Ruth Watson, all baby curls, upturned nose and lilting Dundee accent, thought she was marrying a Canadian Tristan when she fell for Dave O'Sullivan. In Hamilton she discovers he is a loser. They live in one room in mom's house and she has six kids in quick succession.

And then there are Luce and Chuck. Theirs, it must be said, is the most intriguing but the least fulfilled relationship in this production. Luce (Nancy Barclay) is a rich Milanese who marries Chuck (Michael Fawkes) to get to New York. She only gets as far as one room in Halifax and is spat upon by the local Neapolitans as a fascist. I have a suspicion that, handled differently, Luce and Chuck could be the smoldering heart of this play. They are on the cutting edge of culture shock. And interestingly enough, Luce is the one who goes the farthest from her roots. She goes into show business and makes it on her own.

The play flows along in short, swift scenes, set against Michael Eagan's abstraction of a set. Three large black screens are set at an angle to each other, the screens changing color to reflect different moods. The set's spareness sets off the predicament of the war brides, as if they were pitting themselves against something incalculable. As indeed they have. Wars change people fast. The men and women took chances that they would not have taken in peace time. The men rushed into marriage as a mascot against death. The women acquiesced. In the cold gray dawn of peace, the men found themselves alive, back home and regretting the whole damn thing. Meanwhile, their wives had embarked on an epic journey, halfway across the world.

Ever Loving does not tell us anything new about this experience. But Graham Harley's precise and unsentimental production tells us how heroic such a venture was. The acting, for the most part, is top notch, from [Domini] Blythe's tough-spirited Diana to Alison MacLeod's enchanting Ruth, Brendan McKane's unwavering Paul and David Ferry's weakling Dave. Michael Fawkes is a tad superficial as Chuck, but Nancy Barclay's Luce is as enigmatic as Alida Valli.

Gina Mallet, *Toronto Star*, 15 April 1983

• •

ALLAN STRATTON

Rexy!

First produced at Phoenix Theatre,
Toronto, 17 February 1981

Directed by Brian Rintoul
Set and Costume Design by Paul Weeks
Lighting Design by Sholem Dolgoy
Sound Design by Brian Aitken

Cast

William Lyon Mackenzie King	Larry Reynolds
Joan Patteson/Mrs. Mackenzie/ Enid Simpson	Jill Frappier
William Lyon Mackenzie/ Lord Riverdale/Voice of Winston Churchill	John Gilbert
Ralston/Lester B. Pearson	Allen Doremus
Franklin D. Roosevelt/ General McNaughton	James Hobson

"High up in the courts of heaven, a little dog angel waits," chants William Lyon Mackenzie King's spectral mother, and Canada's crazy Prime Minister marches into theatrical history.

Not that Allan Stratton's *Rexy!*, which opened at the Phoenix last night, is immortal theatre. Far from it. But it's an amusing, occasionally deft play about a man whose major quality was evasiveness, and whose use of the English language would make a truck driver weep. And that's not easy . . .

Stratton's scenes are short and snappily written, and never cease to be entertaining. But an occasional speechiness reminds us that this is supposed to be a serious play. Too often Stratton's gift for a comic turn tempts him away, until the audience loses the little man with tragically big dreams, and begins to enjoy a buffoon. Only at the moment of death does a sudden stark self-examination ("I turned history into the shape of my mind") remind us of the play's loftier aims.

Larry Reynolds is a supple character actor whose King has immediate density and texture. His facial skin is like stretched parchment, his eyes alive and eager with both ambition and the mean-spirited fearfulness that always does it. He relishes the pungent lines ("It's hard to leap on a horse and wield a sword," he says to his rebel grandfather's ghost, "when you *have* power") and even when mired in the implausible scenes with Roosevelt, he acquits himself well, albeit with moments of thinness.

Both Pearson (Allen Doremus) and Roosevelt (James Hobson) are mimicked rather than played; it's a bad decision, because the audience tends to be dazzled by the imitated mannerisms and to overlook the essence the actor is trying to evoke. Doremus wasn't too bad in this respect—in fact, his one-note Pearson had considerable charm. But Hobson's Roosevelt was a horrible caricature, something out of a Soviet cartoon magazine. It struck a false note in the play.

Both actors play two roles. Hobson is also the incompetent General McNaughton, and he is a good enough martinet. But Doremus really shines in his dual role as Ralston, the defence minister sacked by King for making him face the death and misery that his dithering on conscription was bringing to the front-line troops.

Jill Frappier was excellent as all the women—Mrs. Patteson, King's mother, and the chewy vignette in which she appears as cantankerous prostitute Enid Simpson. John Gilbert, with his stiff upper lip and great authority, played the British delegate whom King tortured with his querulous nationalism.

A leaning too hard into the comic side of the play may be partly due to Brian Rintoul's direction; but given the play's lack of other dimension, it was a smart decision. He has encouraged his actors to scale their performances to a modest space and a script whose strengths are more in its details than in its sweep.

Ray Conlogue, Globe and Mail, 18 February 1981*

• •

"Let us not tarnish the good name of the Liberal Party with broken promises. If we Liberals have anything, Ralston, it is honor."

Not surprisingly, these lines received a big laugh last night at the opening of *Rexy!* This is a new play . . . by Allan Stratton, who is the happiest surprise of this Toronto season, a playwright with true comic flair and, if he goes on writing such tight, funny dialogue, a limitless future.

Rexy! is not only as topical as the debate on the constitution, but it is a good deal wittier. Here is Canadian history rendered with tongue tucked firmly in cheek, without, however, demeaning King himself.

King is so obviously a gift to a playwright, a cunning, indeed superb politician, as well as a rare and fascinating eccentric, that it seems amazing no play about him has been written before. The grandson of the rebel William Lyon Mackenzie, he was in thrall to history. He was also a spiritualist who conducted seances in his Ottawa home, and a lifelong bachelor who bought sex from prostitutes.

And as Stratton makes clear, and Larry Reynolds in a gloriously devious and twinkling performance makes outrageously engaging, he was also vain as a turkeycock, a little man fretting to strut on the world stage denied him by his Quebec constituency.

As the play opens, war is about to start, and King is teetering on the brink of world history, juggling British demands with his own political needs. Roosevelt wants to make King the go-between for neutral America and embattled Britain. The role becomes window-dressing. While the diplomats snicker, King insures that he is in every photograph, that Canada, while dragging its feet over conscription, is still seen in the forefront of Allied consultations.

Stratton has set up such double-edged situations as much for their inherent pathos as for their obvious humor. He has not quite fully exploited this duality to its full potential. King could be made into an allegorical figure, embodying even more clearly and powerfully the internal Canadian conflict.

On the other hand, Stratton shows such a welcome light touch with Canadian history that asking him to go deeper may be a serious error. Canadians having a sense of humor about other Canadians is a rare sight on stage, and curiously enough, the last show with this kind of cool, jokey affection was *Billy Bishop Goes To War*. Perhaps it is the confrontation with either the British or the Americans, or both, that forces Canadians to realize that they can only be themselves.

The trap in historical plays lies in creating a famous person convincingly. Yet King is completely credible both as a politician and a man. His manipulations of his ministers are as much fun as a board game played psychologically; concern for power is marvelously mingled with concern for self. The day after Westminster was bombed, King is telephoning Lester Pearson in London asking him to pop around and see if he can't find a couple of ruined arches for King's country house.

The cast do just fine, some rich, even inexhaustible characters. Larry Reynolds' face has the pinched wintriness that lights up with a manic glee reminiscent of the late Alastair Sim. Allen Doremus makes Pearson delightfully wry and smooth, and he is a most intimidating Ralston, the defence minister. James Hobson is a cut-up as Roosevelt, and suitably menacing as Canada's own backfiring bazooka, General McNaughton. John Gilbert's range goes from William Lyon Mackenzie to Winston Churchill to Lord Riverdale, who may be described as the most persistent thorn in Mackenzie's side. Jill Frappier is a cheeky blackmailer of a prostitute as well as Mackenzie's mother and an old, platonic friend.

The doubling up of roles is part of this production's special charm. It must be emphasized that this is a small scale production, and while it is tempting to think that *Rexy!* may deserve to be transferred to a larger stage, many of its effects might be diminished on a larger scale.

On the other hand, historical subjects almost beg for distance from the audience, and several medals must go to the director Brian Rintoul for keeping history and the audience at arm's length from each other in the Phoenix Theatre's cramped quarters: a feat helped by Paul Weeks' economical sketch of a set.

Gina Mallet, *Toronto Star*, 18 February 1981*

• •

. . . The former prime minister's diaries have provided copious material for Stratton's portrait of this vain, repressed, lonely politician and Larry Reynolds conveys these qualities perfectly, pomposity and despair alternately strobing across his dry, sinewy features. King's soul-searching over conscription reflects a central truth about Canadian politics: because Quebec votes Liberal en masse, Grit prime ministers must nail the common good to the ideological cross of national unity. Since *Rexy!* focuses on this illuminating paradigm of the national condition, it doesn't seem to matter that the play lacks the scope one might normally expect from an historical drama. The cast is excellent and director Brian Rintoul conjures out of thin air a sense of momentous events. However, the play is stuffed with unfulfilled dramatic promise. In King's seances with his occult soul mate Joan Patteson (Jill Frappier), the voices of his dead mother and grandfather, the rebel William Lyon Mackenzie, rouse King to evangelistic fervor. However, this manic trinity only serves as ironic commentary on King's impotence at all endeavors except cockfighting in the political arena.

Rintoul presents an effective pastiche of directing styles. Black absurdity has its moment with James Hobson's jovial yet menacing caricature of Roosevelt (''What's history between friends?'' he asks King), and the surreal is well-represented by King's ancestral ghosts. For the most part though, it's the straight dramatic goods as King and his pro-conscription Defence Minister Ralston, incisively played by Allen Doremus, face off over dead bodies overseas in passages that amply display Stratton's scene-building skills and vibrant dialogue. Some tedious expository speeches early on suggest that perhaps the playwright was right not to attempt a sweeping historical panorama at this time, but these do not dim the highlights of an evocative and surprisingly relevant cameo.

Mark Czarnecki, *Maclean's*, 94 (16 March 1981), 60*

• •

. . . King emerges as a cunning little operator ruled by a few obsessions; we almost grow fond of him, but no one would mistake him for a great man. The public crisis around which the drama revolves is the question of conscription. What the doubletalk—"Conscription if necessary but not necessarily conscription"—amounts to is this: when King finally bows to the pressure of world events and his own increasingly rebellious advisors, he is perceived by both sides as a hero. The anglophone, pro-conscription side is delighted that he has finally come round; the francophone, anti-conscription side applauds him for having waited so long that the war is almost over. In Stratton's final vision of him, Rexy sees himself in childishly heroic terms: "When they write me down, they'll treat me like a Vancouver winter; I'll be so much drizzle and mist they won't even see the mountains . . . But I will be remembered . . . My grandfather was a rebel. And I was a prime minister! Once upon a time."

Stratton's power as a myth-maker is that he manages to keep his eye on both the mountain and the drizzle at the same time. And he does what historians and biographers have been reluctant to do: he tries to make the logical, and psychological, connections between the two sides of King's decidedly split personality. The Canadian public has been for the most part bewildered by the two different Kings. First there was the public leader, clinging to power longer than anyone else in our history, seemingly sober and colourless in the familiar Upper Canadian way. Then there was the amazing private Rexy, revealed in his own secret diaries and tantalizingly described in C. P. Stacey's *A Very Double Life*—the repressed Victorian who couldn't stay away from prostitutes, the devoted spiritualist who used seances to stay in touch not only with his mother and his maternal grandfather, the renowned rebel hero of English-Canadian history, but also with his beloved dog, Pat.

In Stratton's play, even while we see King running the country and taking stands on the war, we also see him seeking advice from ghosts—and the ghosts become characters, as if this were not a historical pageant we were watching, but rather, say, Noel Coward's *Blithe Spirit*. Our attitude to King's dotty side, we discover, is deeply ambivalent. We may be appalled that this country was controlled for so long and crucial a period by a peculiar man whose true nature was completely unknown to those who elected him—as unknown, certainly, as the Germans would claim Hitler was to them. Yet we're also secretly thrilled and relieved to discover our leaders are not as boring as we assumed. Until recently no one would have thought Canadian prime ministers to be promising subjects for high drama or high comedy. Now, within a year, we've had *Maggie & Pierre* and *Rexy!* . . .

Martin Knelman, *Saturday Night*, 96 (July 1981), 59-60

• •

. . . There's not much sympathy for Canada's 10th prime minister in Allan Stratton's irreverent comedy which opened Friday at the Arts Club, Granville Island. His professional accomplishments are set aside for the most part in favor of a more personal look at the PM—his fascination with spiritualism, his obsession with glory, his fear of death.

The way Stratton draws him, he's such a self-serving, duplicitous, namby pamby little bungler, it's a miracle Canada survived the Second World War, let alone helped win it. (It's a blessing for the playwright that there are no laws against libelling the dead.)

But bruised family feeling aside, *Rexy!* is an eminently approachable bit of Canadiana with some clever, if not altogether belly-shaking, laughs tossed in as a bonus.

It's easy to give in to a temptation to emphasize the comedy of King at the expense of his humaneness. And while Colin Miller's is certainly a theatrical first minister, it's to director Bill Millerd's credit that King's vulnerability and loneliness are respected as well.

As a respite from an otherwise perpetually pompous King, we also get a glimpse of the fragile side of the man in a brief, but poignant scene in which King suffers the death of his beloved dog, Pat. Cradling the dying animal in his arms, he rocks it back and forth, singing hymns and invoking prayers for a more permanent future together "on the other side."

Miller, as mentioned, occasionally risks a burlesque of King, but manages ultimately to shy away from any real danger.

Dermot Hennelly's send-up of the archetypal stuffed-shirt Brit, Lord Riverdale, is a comic pleasure as is Stephen Ouimette's lisping Lester Pearson.

The biggest problem is the set. While each end of the stage has been freighted with a junk shop of clutter, a gaping hole has been left at stage centre to facilitate a display of distracting, unnecessary historical slides. They're images better left to an audience's imagination.

Nicholas Reed, *Vancouver Sun*, 27 March 1982

• •

. . . The play is essentially one of characterization, examining the personality of Mackenzie King as a serious (and highly adroit) politician, ineffectual Prime Minister and lonely spiritualist. The action moves abruptly by means of lighting changes in a simultaneous set while it progresses chronologically through the war years and the events of King's fight over the conscription issue. The play situates itself in historical detail and personal episodes revealed by King's recently published diaries. The character Joan reminisces about King in the voice of a surviving friend and the figure of Lester Pearson comments on the decisions of the former P.M., but the majority of the action is in the present and the documents used are not presented as artifacts as they are in much contemporary Canadian drama. The result is an emphasis on the man, not the history, an emphasis which sustains investigation because of the schizophrenic contradictions of King's public and private *personae*. Stratton maintains the tension between these two faces of the man, showing King as vain and star-struck, obsessed and guilt-ridden, shrewd and opportunistic. He shows King's skill in destroying his political enemy and buying time for Quebec and, therefore, the Liberal Party but he pictures King's death as a final retreat into his Oedipal dream world, as a final failure to leave a monument, and as the end of a life sustained as fiction: ''And I was a Prime Minister! Once upon a time.'' Ironically, the diaries which Mrs. King's ghost assures her son replace the unwritten memoirs underscore the fairy tale quality of his public role; the memories he leaves are those of an actor, filling in time until he can rejoin his mother and the ''dog angel who waits . . . along at the gates . . . '' of heaven. They also provide Stratton with the stuff of the play's dream interludes which are often highly effective moments of theatre . . .

S. R. Gilbert, *CD*, 8 (1982), 107-108

• •

GWEN PHARIS RINGWOOD

Garage Sale

First produced by the New Play Centre,
Vancouver, 14 April 1981

Directed by Jace van der Veen
Lighting Design by John Beatty
Sound Design by Michael McLaughlin

Cast

Reuben   Peter Jaenicke
Rachel   Dorothy Davies

. . . [*Garage Sale*] is an adult, literate, comic, and often lovely little portrait of an elderly couple (touchingly played by Peter Jaenicke and Dorothy Davies) who are moved to reminiscences of their own life and times by the apparent break-up of their young neighbours, who are disposing of their goods by holding a garage sale.

The play still has some structural flaws, including an unconvincing scene where the hero abruptly rushes off to "buy" the neighbors' baby.

But it's affectionately directed by Jace van der Veen, who will no doubt tighten some nuts and bolts as performances continue. . . .

Wayne Edmonstone, *Vancouver Sun*, 15 April 1981*

• •

Garage Sale was written only three years before Ringwood's death. In some respects it represents the logical culmination of her career, the triumphant conclusion to a lifetime spent perfecting the playwright's craft. In other respects, however, it stands somewhat apart from the main body of her work. *Garage Sale* shows a markedly different dramatic technique from that found in such works as *Dark Harvest* and *Pasque Flower*, the plays by which she is perhaps best known. These dramas, set in her native prairies, attempt to do justice to the larger-than-life figures of the pioneers who built the Canadian West in the early years of this century. The stories are broadly drawn; the characters are towering and the passions raging in these epic struggles of human beings pitted against a hostile and frequently deadly environment. In *Garage Sale*, Ringwood moves to the more personal, and perhaps more poignant, drama of individuals pitted only against the limits of self-knowledge.

Garage Sale recounts a morning in the life of a retired couple, Reuben and Rachel, who spin out their time quarrelling and reminiscing until an interruption in their daily rituals forces them to re-evaluate the nature of their existence. The one-act comedy is focussed entirely on the couple, and the setting is confined to a back-yard verandah with two chairs. Perhaps alone among Ringwood's dramas, *Garage Sale* could be satisfactorily performed as a radio play with little or no adjustment. What Ringwood has captured here are the eccentric, quarrelsome, but sympathetic characters of Rachel and Reuben. In their conversation they reveal a lifetime of loving, hurting, arguing, and caring; their constant teasing exposes two vital and warm personalities, under the thick crust of idiosyncracy that has slowly grown up around, and frequently hides, them. While Ringwood's canon certainly is rich in humour, ranging from musical comedy to farce, only in the much longer and wider ranging *Widger's Way* does she achieve such comic success.

Coupled with the spareness of the setting is the simplicity of the play's physical action. Reuben and Rachel spend most of the play talking on the verandah, interrupting themselves only for the occasional exit into the offstage house. As the title suggests, their conversation centres around a garage sale: at first, the one being organized by their neighbours, and then theirs, were they to have one.

Ringwood uses the motif of the garage sale deftly. The simple and commonplace occurrence not only helps define the two characters, but also introduces the major crisis points in the couple's lives. Thinking the sale heralds the end of their neighbours' marriage, Reuben and Rachel relive their own trials: the death of a child, the time Rachel left with the children, and a lifetime of imperfect communication. Reuben is easily recognized as a romantic figure with a strongly idealistic streak, while Rachel shows herself as essentially practical, but with a tendency towards pessimism.

The next step follows logically as the couple plan, on Reuben's insistence, their own garage sale. An impasse results, as each creates a list of things to go that the other automatically rejects. The differences in their characters, clarified by their two lists, are summed up by their respective dreams. Reuben's is a fantasy of beautiful, far-away places; Rachel's is of a missed appointment.

Ringwood carefully balances the two garage sales, the real and the proposed one, to reveal the gnawing loneliness of the two characters. As the neighbours' gets underway, the isolation of Reuben and Rachel is given dramatic expression by a phone call that brings news of a daughter's visit postponed indefinitely. Simultaneously they are misled, and mislead themselves, into thinking that the couple next door are planning to sell their baby. In their loneliness they determine to buy it, touchingly but mistakenly believing that it will complete and satisfy their empty lives. Ringwood successfully balances the tragic against the comic when Reuben returns humiliated. Rachel's loving support and Reuben's good intentions make a moment that is potentially either farcical or pathetic deeply poignant, and Ringwood builds on the emotion of the scene by having the two, faced with the evidence of their own unhappiness, attempt to come to terms with their real selves. The satisfactory conclusion finds the two enthusiastically planning their own sale as the prelude to a fuller life.

In the summer of 1984 *Garage Sale* was produced by the Graduate Centre for the Study of Drama at the University of Toronto and the Department of Drama, University of Guelph, directed by Denyse Lynde. Following two performances in Toronto, it ran for a week in Massey Hall, University of Guelph; the success of the production established conclusively the stageworthiness, effectiveness, and appeal of the piece. Only the verandah was used; Rachel's opening monologue was easily handled using a bird-feeder placed just off the verandah within easy reach. The house was suggested by a centre, workable door. Within this simple setting it was easy to suggest the larger scene evoked by Ringwood, since much of the conversation springs from the neighbours' preparations for their sale, which

Reuben graphically describes with the aid of his binoculars.

Leigha Lee Browne and John W. Browne performed the roles of Rachel and Reuben. Care was taken to establish the moments of Rachel's pain, as in the conversation about her dream and the references to her flight to Minneapolis, to balance Reuben's crestfallen return from the absurd baby-buying expedition. This potentially awkward scene was on the whole successfully handled by the actor's characteristic ruefulness complemented by his partner's deep-rooted concern and shared embarrassment. The relative absence of physical action was in the end found to be unimportant; it was more than compensated for by the dynamics of the relationship developing and unfolding on the stage.

Denyse Lynde, Memorial University of Newfoundland

• •

GWEN PHARIS RINGWOOD

Drum Song

First produced at the Phoenix Theatre,
University of Victoria, 22 June 1982

Directed by Carl Hare
Set Design by Bill West
Lighting Design by Giles W. Hogya
Costume Design by Nicola M. Williams

Cast

Part One: Maya

Josephina	Jennifer Langley
Martha	Jeanette Hazelden
Mrs. Roland	Fiona Matthews
Maya	Sandra Ferens
Gilbert	Boyd Norman
Ellen	M. Joan MacLean
Allan	David Dossor
Harmonica Player	Arlin McFarlane

Part Two: The Stranger

Alphonse	Robert Lloyd Mitchell
Seraphina	Arlin McFarlane
William	Jean-Marc Morin
Jason	Boyd Norman
Jana	Jeanette Hazelden
Women of the Tribe	Terri Andrews
	Jacqueline Cecil
	Roberta Conklin
	M. Joan MacLean
Larry	David Dosser
Johnny	Denis Johnston
Andrew	Kaz Piesowocki
Lucy	Felesidade Rego

Part Three: The Furies

Martha	Fiona Matthews
Celestine	Sandra Ferens
Selina	Jacqueline Cecil
Anne Marie	Jennifer Langley
Ellen	Roberta Conklin
Josephine	Terri Andrews
Rose	M. Joan MacLean
Young Selina	Felesidade Rego

. . . The three plays are tragedies, linked by a single theme—betrayal of a kind frequently experienced by women of all races.

The language is poetic, and Ringwood uses a chorus as a frame for each panel of the tryptich. They are highly atmospheric and potentially emotionally evocative.

Each of the first two plays—*Maya* and *The Stranger*—written 10 years apart, has been produced previously and published. The third, *The Furies*, is still in manuscript. However, the three presented as a trilogy take on a definite form and balance, having a crescendo in the middle *Medea*-like deadly rage of the foresaken woman, and ending in the subliminal sisterhood sacrifice of *The Furies*.

The latter was based on an actual incident at Dog Creek.

Ringwood herself has worked with Indian casts in the first two plays, from which experience she has undoubtedly derived much of the tone and color that is implicit.

The Dan George is essentially an intimate theatre, but on this occasion audience closeness to the playing area did not make it easy to hear the low-level utterance of some of the actors much of the time.

There was little feeling for pace, pauses lacked the essential gap-bridging electricity, and tempo, except for brief intervals, was monotonous and close to lethargic.

The strongest performances came from Sandra Ferens as Maya, Jeanette Hazelden as the vengeful Jana in *The Stranger*, and the ensemble in *The Furies*. . . .

Ringwood had come to Victoria for the event and felt that the plays stood up well in their relationship with one another. Although 10 years separated the writing of all three, she says she had visualised them as a trilogy. . . .

Audrey Johnson, *Victoria Times-Colonist*, 24 June 1982*

• •

GEORGE WALKER

The Art of War

First produced at Toronto Workshop Productions,
23 February 1983†

Directed by George Walker
Set Design by James Plaxton

Cast

Tyrone M. Power	David Bolt
Jamie McLean	Jim Henshaw
John Hackman	David Fox
Brownie Brown	Dean Hawes
Karla Mendez	Diane D'Aquila
Heather Masterson	Susan Purdy

†The first fully professional production. The play was commissioned for, and performed at, a conference on Art and Reality, Simon Fraser University, 10 August 1982.

George F. Walker seems to be pioneering a new form of entertainment: the fascist two-step, or, play it again, Fritz.

That seems to be the only way to avoid concluding that *The Art of War*, which opened last night at Toronto Workshop Productions, is either part of a continuing investigation into the nature of evil (which is ponderous) or a playwright spinning his wheels (which is tempting, but unfair; the show is still entertaining).

Let's say it's a symmetrical three-on-three encounter on the edge of a provincial park. In this corner is a retired Canadian general, his psychopathic bodyguard, and the beautiful daughter of a third world dictator. They have the guns.

In the other corner is a drunken investigative journalist, a kid who hangs around with him, and the daughter (cute but not beautiful) of the local farm news publisher. They have the morals.

The show answers the question: What does a murderous commando with a steel plate in his brain do to "kill time" on guard duty? Answer: he sings "getting to know you, getting to feel free and easy." Or: What can you do to really upset a mad general who has just killed your best friend? Answer: transplant his roses so they get brown petals.

Nobody would deny that George Walker has a wickedly assured sense of humor. But there's an eleventh-hour quality about the humor in *Art of War*; the eleventh hour of a long evening in a bar, that magical moment when you've had enough to loosen the flow of wit but not yet enough to slur your words. That slaphappy moment when you know that whatever you believe in, if it wins, will for sure be corrupted. So you have that last drink, and you slur your words.

Walker was slurring when he had David Bolt, who plays the feckless humanist of a journalist, stand up at the general's table and blurt out: "Any idiot can make the trains run on time! The hard part is to have a society where people get on the train for any other reason than that they're terrified of whoever made them run on time!" Whew. Now that's earnest. It's the earnestness of the poor guy who believes that goodness is weak, and strength wouldn't be caught dead hanging around with it.

C. S. Lewis once dramatized the banality of evil by showing his villain plucking feathers out of a living bird while reciting a nonsense verse. Walker does that, too. Unfortunately, his good guys recite nonsense verses too, even if they're only plucking feathers out of dead birds. Everybody is enervated.

But even when he is coasting, Walker demonstrates a certain assurance. The play, after all, is about a general who has been transferred from the Ministry of Defence to the Ministry of Culture ("his idea of a cultural event is bombing an opera house") where all kinds of timely swipes at arts cutbacks and the interviewing techniques of Barbara Frum can be giddily admixed with speculation on the nature of creation. The whole thing is so loosely assembled that the scenes sometimes feel like cabaret skits. You expect the cast to return swinging parasols in unison after a blackout. In fact, it actually ends with—but that would be telling.

Walker, who also directed, has assembled a cast of the stalwarts who make his plays a particular delight. David Bolt makes each production's nebbish endlessly fascinating and funny; Jim Henshaw's malleable and hyperventilating youth is a personal addiction of mine; and Diane D'Aquila (as the deadly dictator's duelling daughter) seems made for taffeta and medals, but only if she can wear them at the same time. She adds a new touch in tonight's incarnation, Karla Mendez, a grimace of disgust, as if she had swallowed a bug, which indicates that she is about ready to shoot somebody.

David Fox plays the general, who appears to be a satire of the mild-mannered Canadian military man who secretly hankers for a Casa Rosada in which to become a power freak. Dean Hawes is his sidekick, a deadly side of beef called Brownie Brown. Susan Purdy rounds out the cast as the half-bright good girl, Heather, perhaps the least convincingly written character in the play.

Ray Conlogue, *Globe and Mail*, 24 February 1983*

• •

"Give enough money to create five superficial spectacles and you will have culture," says the general, John Hackman, aka the minister of culture and former minister of defence. Yes, George F. Walker's new play *The Art of War* is all about Canadian culture. In the manner of a comic strip, it is brilliantly on target, a crude spoof of the pretensions of cultural policy, and of what Walker pinpoints as its innate hypocrisy. Art is supported as a distraction from darker political designs. Death is the prevailing image, and the gun is the greatest intellectual argument offered all evening.

The Art of War, it must be said right away, is very, very funny and very, very Toronto. It manages to be irreverent without being cynical. Its flaw, I suppose, is that it's about something (art) that too few people take seriously, which means that it can be dismissed as jokey fun. But, again, like a comic strip, the funnier the play is, the more accurate it seems to be.

The play is set in Nova Scotia where the general hunkers down of a summer, and James Plaxton has designed a fetching set of fir trees set on a spur of rocks overlooking a mylar-striped cottage. On the spur is Tyrone M. Power, played once again by David Bolt. Power, as anyone who saw *Gossip* and/or *Filthy Rich*, will know, is an entirely ineffectual journalist and private eye. He is also, here, made into a parody of a liberal. He comments on the situation rather than doing anything about it. He has fetched up on the general's doorstep with a sidekick. It is Walker's conceit that Power is sympathetic but idiotic. "Throw my tent," he orders a puzzled Jamie McLean (Jim Henshaw).

Grasp of camping lingo beyond him, Power strides off to investigate the sinister

Hackman who is clearly hiding militaristic designs behind his arts brief. "His idea of a cultural event is bombing an opera house," Power observes. David Fox, giving the funniest performance he has ever given, is a suavely ridiculous Hackman whose ruling passion is the keeping up of appearances and the keeping down of everyone else. He is aided by Karla Mendez, a sultry Diane D'Aquila, from a South American fascist state and Brownie (Dean Hawes) who gets a headache when emotion strikes.

Hackman grows suspicious of his new gardener, spy McLean, who insists on moving large rocks around in what is described as a "personal concept of gardening." And he is irked by Heather Masterson (Susan Purdy) who is head of the historical board and wants a grant. He has to be reminded, "You are not God, only the minister of culture." Why, precisely, these young people are ganging up against him bewilders Hackman. He knows that what he does has no meaning. "Art," Hackman declares, "is the leisurely reflection of a dying society." He proves it with a hilarious description of how the cultural bureaucracy works. And he does not have everything under his wing. There is a deputy minister in charge of song lyrics.

A showdown between Power and Hackman is eventually engineered. Power and Heather are drinking wine and Hackman and Mendez enter in full ceremonial pirouette that stuns their audience. It is like the opening night of the Stratford Festival: stuffed shirts strutting: the essential truth of government attitudes to art. Art is an occasion to dress up for, to be seen at, to express the *power* of government money and government presence. Hackman, dressed to kill, uses art as a camouflage for his lust to kill.

Power is so confused by such a show that he fails to understand his life is in danger. Thus he is disarmed. The end, as they say, is silence.

Walker's mastery of verbal collage has never seemed so sure, nor has his use of the perception that we do not live original lives but ones borrowed from TV and the movies. We are a regurgitated culture one way or another, and we speak in platitudes because that is all we hear. That is why there is no defence against the Hackmans of the land. We believe, as they believe, that power is what comes out of the barrel of a gun, not from imagination.

The acting is just fine throughout, and Walker shows, as he did with the larky *Theatre of the Film Noir*, that he is the wittiest director of his own work. He makes his points with a light but deadly sting, and he has also produced a play that in its laconic acceptance of the absurd projects an authentically Canadian sense of self-mockery.

Gina Mallet, *Toronto Star*, 24 February 1983*

• •

George Walker has admitted two things important to understanding his plays: "I don't have any wisdom" and "sometimes I replace what is a normal dramatic conflict with conflict between two obsessions." The first saves those of us who agree from the embarrassment of resorting to *ad hominem* arguments in reviews; the second gets to the heart of what is so disturbing about his work. . . .

The battle lines [in *The Art of War*] are obvious, even too familiar, to regular Walker watchers. They aren't, however, the two obsessions which replace the natural dramatic conflict Walker talks about. Those really belong to General Hackman and the playwright himself—the general's obsession is for the culture of order, the playwright's is with the knocking knees of the well-intentioned.

Fair enough. We do have something to fear from the ineffectual dithering of people of good will. But Walker's *idée fixe* makes for unwholesome and single-tracked drama. He so disarms his benevolent characters with indecisiveness, irrationality and softness that they are just unlikeable twits. I'd much rather spend an evening with Karla Mendez—as distasteful as her ideas are—than Power's friend Heather Masterson (Susan Purdy) because Mendez is at least passionate. (If Walker truly wants us to prefer the company of fascists in his plays, then his ideas are more dangerous than I thought.)

None of this troubles Walker's fans who love his unlikely wit. His comedy comes from the timeless pleasure of enjoying unavoidable human foibles. His special flair is for the SCTV sort of comedy—off-beat, contemporary cynicism that leaves middle class intellectual poseurs content in the knowledge that *they* would never stoop to being well-intentioned.

The author is also lucky to have found a group of artists who take so readily to his comic manner. Jim Henshaw, Susan Purdy and David Bolt were surely made to play Walker's screwy, irresolute characters. With her dark good looks and statuesque bearing, Diane D'Aquila should always be his strutting, gutsy fascist women. And David Fox and Dean Hawes are perfectly menacing as the military strong men. Only Jim Plaxton lets the side down this time with an uncharacteristically mediocre set of artificial trees and hills juxtaposed to a slatted house front of indeterminate purpose.

Boyd Neil, *Canadian Forum*, 63 (May 1983), 38*

• •

JAMES REANEY

The Canadian Brothers

First produced at the Reeve Theatre,
University of Calgary, 24 November 1983

Directed by Keith Turnbull
Set Design by Douglas McCullough
Costume Design by Gavin Semple
Lighting Design by J. James Andrews
Sound Design by Quenten Doolittle

Cast

Young Gerald Grantham/Captain Villiers/Sylvannus	Mark Bellay
Henry Grantham	Kevin Cork
Samuel	Tag Danforth
Matilda Montgomerie	Kelly Ann Donais
Phil Desborough	Kevin Farran
Major Montgomerie/General Hull/The Playwright	Bill Gemmill
Father André/Captain Raymond	Jeffrey Haggett
Ernest Forrester	Gerald Hertz
Young Matilda Montgomerie/Betsy Hull	Chantelle Jenkins
Tecumseh/Julia De Gaspé/Salome	Veda Kenda
Young Ernest Forrester/Commodore Barclay/Captain Forrester	Darren Kent
Jeremiah Desborough	Grant Linneberg
Gerald Grantham	Tim Mahoney
The Prophecy/Magistrate Grantham/Colonel De Gaspé/Captain Buckhorn	Gerald Matthews

302

General Brock/Major Killdeer/The Mayor of Frankfort/Bill	Darrell Moore
Young Henry Grantham/Lieutenant Cranstoun/Darnley/Steersman	Peter Morrow
Musician	Pat Osoko
Isabella Grantham/Madame De Gaspé/Higgs	Josephine Rose
The Prophecy/Mrs. Hull/Gertrude De Gaspé	Alison Brethour-Smith

My play tonight is set during the War of 1812 when our American cousins invaded us for the last time—unsuccessfully. They did, however, manage to kill one of their greatest enemies—the noble Indian leader, Tecumseh. He appears in my play tonight and is part of my reason for writing it because ever since I read about him in one of my readers at school I have been fascinated by his character and fate. My reader said that, after they had killed him, the Kentucky riflemen took off his skin and made it into souvenirs—razor straps, shoelaces and the like. With scenes like this, the War of 1812 should have twenty plays, two operas and a big cinemascope movie made about it. In order to make up this deficiency, I have adapted the only novel written about it—by Major John Richardson, our literary grandfather, an actual participant in the war during which he did some of the things (but not all!) you will see Gerald Grantham doing. I don't know why we've left out the flaying of Tecumseh, which I'm still appalled and fascinated by, but sometimes the real reason for an evening such as you're now going to experience must remain concealed. It cannot simply be a lack of courage on the part of my brave, young actors or of ingenuity on the part of my equally courageous director.

The point is that tonight you will see just about everything except the flaying of Tecumseh. If the historical background isn't enough, there is the foreground action with its story of two brothers haunted by a mysterious prophecy or curse which embroils them with another family south of the border. Into their lives comes a beautiful adventuress who is fearless with snakes and bent on vengeance for a gross insult she has suffered from a young officer in the regular American army. Her father, a tall smuggler who can't decide whether to live in Kentucky or Canada and so keeps shuffling back and forth between those places, also has the unfortunate habit of concealing his identity with a black mask. How will he avenge the scalping of his impossibly cocky and annoying son—early forerunner of some of Hollywood's spoilt brats? Reader, prepare yourself for some shocks and for an evening that is so devoted to story that it may often sound not so much like other plays you have seen as a dream, a nightmare, a phantasmagoria—not unlike such recent film triumphs as *Star Wars*, or *The Return of the Jedi*. It is my sincere hope that just as I, as a child, fell under the spell of Tecumseh's cruel fate and also the bizarre events of Major Richardson's old novel, you too will find something magic about tonight's scenes. . . .

Author's program note, 24 November 1983

• •

A plot revolving around passion and prophecy notwithstanding, James Reaney's latest work is unlikely to become a theatrical hit.

The premiere production of *The Canadian Brothers*, which opened last night at the University of Calgary, boasts a myriad of special effects—foggy battle scenes, dazzling lighting, realistic sound—and inventive staging making full use of the new, open-concept Reeve Theatre.

But the play's storyline, although full of romantic and wartime intrigue, is convoluted and confusing to viewers unfamiliar with the two 19th century novels on which it is based. Left in its present form, the play is doomed to become an obscure theatre piece set during the War of 1812.

John Richardson's novel *Wacousta* is a tale of treachery set in the early days of Fort Detroit. Its sequel, *The Canadian Brothers*, centres around a curse placed on two rival families in the earlier novel, and some knowledge of the family's tangled history is necessary in order to follow the scenes unfolding on the stage. Program notes are not enough and an explanatory prologue would make the first act more accessible to many viewers.

The faults of the production itself are niggling ones, mostly involving the limitations of young, student performers.

Reaney's decision to divide the role of the heroine, Matilda Montgomerie, among two actresses was an unfortunate one. Chantelle Jenkins portrays the young Matilda as a cute, kittenish girl, lacking the stature, the sense of determination which Kelly Ann Donais brings to the part. Donais should have been allowed sole possession of the role.

Other performers who added spark to the show are Gerald Hertz and Kevin Farran as the two American desperados, Josephine Rose in what may be one of the stage's most robust deathbed scenes and Tim Mahoney as one of the courteous Canadian brothers.

Rosemary McCracken, *Calgary Herald*, 25 November 1983*

• •

Playwright James Reaney and director Keith Turnbull have happily broken the recent rather disheartening lull in Canadian theatrical mythmaking. Their new collaboration, *The Canadian Brothers; or, The Prophecy Fulfilled*, premièred at the University of Calgary's new experimental space, the Reeve Theatre. The play is [a] sequel to the 1978 *Wacousta!*, both works drawn freely from the novels of colonial writer John Richardson.

In *The Canadian Brothers*, the Pontiac Wars of the 1760s are now of distant although ominous memory, the time setting having been advanced to the War of 1812 between the rebel Republic and British North America. Once more historical events provide the opportunities for gothic romance. The ancestral curses of Wacousta and Mad Ellen are refuelled in their descendants, stoked by new exigencies of war and new motives for revenge. Reaney's method, as usual, is through "play" in its double sense—this work for the stage is essentially a grown-up version of let's pretend, and is legendary in style as well as in matter.

The work opens and, three acts later, closes with the death of Gerald Grantham during the Battle of Queenston Heights, shot mistakenly for an American by his brother Henry, who failed to recognize him without his uniform. Almost everything that follows is a re-enactment of events leading to this unhappy occurrence, punctuated by Gerald's and occasionally Henry's narrative. These are the *Canadian* brothers, the last descendants of Col. de Haldimar, who was the initial object of Ellen's curse. (The Canadian origin is emphasized because there are few officers of their kind among their British military associates and a familiar colonial defensiveness occasionally pertains.)

Their contemporary enemies, the Wacousta-Ellen progeny, are one Jeremiah Desborough, a ne'er-do-well Yankee smuggler, and his ragged son Phil. Jeremiah also has a daughter Matilda whom he abandoned in Kentucky as a child; she lives there, initially innocent of her true family connections, with her adoptive uncle Major Montgomerie. Desborough's sinister plots against the Granthams, his renewed contact with his daughter, her subsequent rejection by her Kentucky suitor, plus the convenient and inconvenient exigencies of war all add up to heady melodrama.

Needless to say, the staging of the whole complicated tale takes all the theatrical ingenuity director Turnbull can muster; he well knows that mimicry of reality rather than its imitation is the hallmark of a Reaney text, especially since over the years he himself has collaborated in the development of the style.

For this production Turnbull carved an arena design out of the versatile Reeve Theatre to provide multiple playing areas, some fixed, others flexible, functioning vertically as well as horizontally. Such physical mobility allows cinematic shifts of time or place at an instant, continuity or contrast further highlighted by such devices as then-and-now character doublings and an occasional ghostly intrusion from an earlier age.

As the recent history of the war unfolds, military assaults on miniature forts are led by monumental effigies of their generals (E. G. Brock and Hull); a capture on the Detroit River is illustrated by model ships; one memorable improvisation suggests a stealthy canoe-crossing, mimed by actors moving waist-high through two strips of fluttering blue cloth. Events are further complemented by musical motifs (composed by Quenten Doolittle) and homemade stereophonic effects that mimic whippoorwills, rattle snakes, Niagara Falls, not to speak of maple sap flowing into settlers' pails.

The Calgary theatre students who primarily comprise the company have responded to this "playful" kind of production with enthusiasm and discipline. There is much multiple characterization, with 19 actors for 42 parts, only seven of which are single roles. In keeping with the melodramatic structures and presentational style, characterization itself if a form of let's pretend. Whether in single roles or several, the actors are tacitly enlisting audience collaboration in the creation of their storybook world of passionate contrivance and predestined doom.

The performance tone ranges from the almost quaint civility of the *Canadian* Grantham brothers (played with appealing starchiness by Tim Mahoney and Kevin Cork, respectively) to the surly contemptuousness of Jeremiah Desborough (Grant Linneberg). A comic streak emerges in Kevin Farran's spiky portrayal of Phil, sidekick and tool of his father's black arts, a cocky urchin worthy of Dickens.

Sister Matilda, the pivotal character in the play's complex machinations, the lady who, among other things, can charm rattle snakes and knows the secrets of henbane, is given clear delineation by Kelly Ann Donais in moods varying from offended virtue to passionate outrage to chilling calculation. Her self-inflicted death by poison also has its pathos; like her grandmother Ellen before her, she is never able to render her revenge directly on the person who most deeply harmed her. Ironically her ex-lover Ernest Forrester (Gerald Hertz) is the only principal character to survive, presumably to repent his carelessness with the heart of a young sorceress.

In most of his recent playmaking Reaney has shown himself much attracted to stories of a legendary flavour that reflect on the 19th century traditions of rural southwestern Ontario. The Black Donnelly tales he remembered hearing as a child provided the seeds of his well-known trilogy; poltergeist mysteries collected by his friend Marty Gervais led to collaboration in the play *Baldoon*. Reaney shows that legendary elements may be transmitted through literary as well as oral transmission in the case of the half-forgotten Richardson romances. Richardson himself (1793-1852) was an early romancer who drew on his own ties with the past: he learned stories of the Pontiac Wars, in particular the siege of Fort Detroit, at his grandmother's knee; the War of 1812-14 was his own first hand adventure, including capture by the Americans at Moraviantown where Tecumseh was killed and flayed. In taking on *The Canadian Brothers*, Reaney seeks to revitalize a once living link with both history and romance. In so doing he offers a model for play-making that Western Canadian dramatists might more fully explore.

Diane Bessai, *NeWest Review*, January 1984, 14*

• •

Index

311

319